Third Edition

Elements of Park and Recreation Administration

by

Charles E. Doell

Superintendent of Parks Emeritus
Minneapolis, Minnesota

Louis F. Twardzik

Michigan State University
East Lansing, Michigan

Burgess Publishing Company   •   Minneapolis, Minnesota

Copyright © 1963, 1968, 1973 by Burgess Publishing Company
Printed in the United States of America
Library of Congress Card Number 73-78963
SBN 8087-0425-7

3 4 5 6 7 8 9 0

Preface

The social developments of the past five years have affected the administration of parks and recreation sufficiently to justify some modification in this third edition.

The population growth rate has abated to some extent but the movement of people from rural areas and small towns to the cities and their suburbs has continued so that now three fourths of all Americans are living in metropolitan areas. The number of suburban cities has increased a great deal and each has rapidly grown to a size requiring a full-time park and recreation executive. Young and usually inadequately equipped to fulfill major administrative positions although with college and university degrees in some specialty, many of these executives may have difficulty growing in professional stature fast enough to keep pace with the population increase in their respective communities, much less becoming capable of accepting larger assignments elsewhere. In point of fact they are now experiencing their internship in the profession. Graduate study would now be most appropriate. To such this edition has new pertinence.

Some redirection is also necessary to more closely relate to a much more sophisticated student body. Improvement in quality and quantity of communication media as well as a spin-off of the ever-present increase in mobility, affluence, and leisure has broadened the outlook and the ambitions of the young. They have experienced protest against the Vietnam war, the established power structure, religious ethics, and almost all else that a previous generation believed in. Their influence has been felt, albeit the world still goes on. In the process they have learned much and have matured early enough to have been accorded adult status at age eighteen. In this edition the authors hope they have correctly interpreted the idealistic ambitions this new generation aspires to.

The past five years have witnessed mammoth increases in numbers and age variety of the users and the great assortment of recreation vehicles they come in. Increased numbers coupled with the social unrest of the times brought about some nasty confrontations between users and managers of all sorts of physical recreation resources from city parks to national parks and forests. Problems of management found common cause, parks to forests to other public recreation facilities. This realization of recreation as the common denominator of all services, local to national, prompted additional emphases in this edition.

The educational process as it affects park and recreation administration has tended to be fractionalized into combinations of vocational and professional techniques rather than to emphasize any central coordinated theme. A professional identity which would respond to the aspirations of organized practitioners has not been found in the academic community any more than it has, for example, in the National Recreation and Park Association. The diffusion of recreation responsibilities among many bureaus and departments of the states and the federal government (often headed by managers not well versed in recreation resources or philosophy) has only compounded the difficulty of identifying a park and recreation professional. Although this problem is much too complex for easy solution and could well be avoided in a textbook of elementals, the authors have deemed it fundamental enough to give more attention than previously to education and the professional problem.

The usual elementary treatment of a number of the administrative subjects has been repeated in this edition with added reference to current practices. The appendix is almost all new. The essays presented there are usually directed toward practical questions of the day.

In calling attention to the authors of this edition, it is interesting to note the difference in their backgrounds, training, and ages and yet, having worked together for several years at Michigan State University, they have had ample opportunity to exchange views in practices and philosophy based on their varied experiences as academicians and as practitioners, to come to a common understanding on all major issues.

April, 1973   C.F.D.
                            L.F.T.

Contents

Chapter One

Preliminary Considerations

INTRODUCTORY

Change—inexorable as time itself—is an essential part of the story of life. Those phenomena which are new and possibly superficial may sometimes appear to change more rapidly while the old, more familiar, and probably more prosaic things linger on. But that which survives, even though in a new guise, is the foundation upon which new growth with current meaning can flourish. It is the purpose of this book to identify the elements of park and recreation administration most likely to endure and then to clothe them with contemporary practices and philosophy for a useful introduction to professional practice.

In this first chapter fundamental elements are defined in basic terms only, with just enough description of them and of closely associated ideas to acquaint the student with their general nature. Extended discussion with more contemporary investigation, research, and theory will be found in succeeding chapters. This chapter identifies the core; later chapters provide the more complete nature of parks, recreation, and administration needed for present-day practice—and hopefully for the immediate future.

AUTHORITY FOR TAX SUPPORT

The discussion of park and recreation in this book centers principally on tax-supported rather than privately owned or supported services. This is not implying that privately owned services are not important, for they are becoming more so as time, mobility, and money become more available to more people. Even the heretofore well-established American work ethic and the presently accepted efficiency of the "division of labor," with its stultifying effect upon factory workers, are undergoing reappraisals which may well attach an even greater importance to both private and public recreation. Indeed, so pervasive are becoming the needs of recreation that in some instances government and private enterprise may enter into cooperative alliances, even partnerships, to provide adequate recreational fulfillment. Nevertheless, the most comprehensive systems of recreation service are tax supported and tax support holds the promise of the development of a national policy.

Initially, therefore, the question is raised, "where does the government obtain its authority to raise taxes and expend money for recreation services?" Answer—the welfare clauses of the federal Constitution.

Here it is in the preamble to the Constitution of the United States: "We the people of the United States, in order to form a more perfect Union . . . establish justice . . . *promote the general welfare*" etc. Then proceeding on to Section 8 of Article 1, we find, "The Congress shall have power to lay and collect taxes, duties, imports and excises, to pay the debts and provide for the common defense and *general welfare* of the United States" etc.

In the years since the adoption of the Constitution a multitude of public services has been adjudged "public welfare," including the establishment of parks and recreation services, all of which prompted President Harding in 1921 to comment: "Just government is merely the guarantee to the people of the right and opportunity to support themselves. The one outstanding danger of today is the tendency to turn to Washington for the things which are the tasks or the duties of the forty-eight commonwealths."

President Harding notwithstanding, the U.S. Supreme Court in sustaining the District of Columbia Redevelopment Act of 1945 unanimously agreed: "The concept of the public welfare is broad and inclusive. The values it represents are spiritual as well as physical, aesthetic as well as monetary. It is within the power of the legislature to determine that the community should be beautiful as well as healthy, spacious as well as carefully patrolled."

In the 1970s, the general welfare clause is so much taken for granted that the question of adequate authority for the multitudinous welfare function of government (including park and recreation services) is seldom given a thought. Taxing authority is, however, one of the fundamentals that need an occasional recall to be sure that a chosen path of action is a correct one. It is especially significant when a distinction between *special* welfare and *general* welfare is called for.

MANAGEMENT—AN ART

To manage (management), and to administer (administration) are terms used interchangeably in this book. In some situations, by general local acceptance there may be a distinction between the words, i.e., one may mean the direction of a broader spectrum of functions than the other, but acceptance of such difference in meaning in all situations does not seem to exist. So the least confusing thing to do is to use the words interchangeably.

Park and recreation administration is not an exact science—at least not yet. The practice does not rest upon well-established natural laws or on formulas derived therefrom, but upon policies emanating from tradition, experiences, popular demand, social evolution, and similar more or less emotional manifestations of the body politic.

Scientists are certainly needed in the total park and recreation service—scientists in the biological field, the social field, the fields of humanities and the natural sciences. Professionals, technicians, skilled tradesmen are also needed. These include engineers, lawyers, foresters, some doctors, accountants, recreation specialists, mechanics, gardeners, clerical help, and common laborers. The task of coordinating all these varied talents into a single unified team operating with efficiency to manipulate the resources of land, structures, and money to the satisfaction of people and their elected politicians may someday be reduced to formulas which with the aid of computing machines may produce some administrative decisions. But, for the time being, such is not the case. The administrative process cannot yet be termed anything like a science. It can be termed a profession only because some in the business call themselves professionals and then only so far as the public accepts that terminology. But art it is—art in the sense of creating beauty, and art in the sense of evolving a basis for action out of a nice evaluation of many social factors that relate to a recreation service.

Being an art rather than a science, management's decisions are to be accepted as being reached largely through the exercise of personal judgment and only sometimes through the application of natural laws. Hence, the decisions reached are mostly opinions. The dogmatic statement, even when made by a widely accepted authority, does not constitute an absolute and enduring verity. Minds must be kept open for new evidence; the attitude of practitioners and students alike must be one of constant inquiry even to the reexamination of previously accepted principles. Times change, environments change, cultures change, and conventions change. All of us need to keep abreast of these changes. In spite of this warning, the student will find in these pages principles of practice which have been widely accepted up to the present and the background reasoning that has won general acceptance, much of which is dealt with in succeeding chapters. From this sort of springboard one may proceed into the future with reasonable confidence if one heeds the warning given.

PLAY, RECREATION, LEISURE, AND THE GOOD LIFE

In America the concern for the play of children induced government, in all its levels—local, regional, state, and federal—to assume responsibility for what developed into a broad spectrum of recreation services. Since play and recreation occur in times of leisure an examination of the nature of leisure became general; this was followed by a concern for the "proper" use of leisure as part of the general welfare. "Proper" use of leisure implied goals, and hence the quality of life was searched for alternative objectives. The logical next step, and probably final step, points to the eternal quest for the purpose of life itself. Play, recreation, leisure, quality and purpose of life are all essential elements in the selection of the ultimate goal of any recreation service.

This entire matter is only very sparsely treated in this introductory chapter, leaving it to succeeding chapters (Chapter 2 and selected essays) to expound on current philosophical theories and contemporary professional attitudes.

In the many attempts to define recreation, a lot of hairsplitting has taken place and many words and paragraphs and pages have been written about it. Not all of that voluminous discussion is a mere exercise in semantics, for there are delicate shades of interpretation important to field practices. For the moment, and for us, it is sufficient to say that recreation is the *refreshment of mind or body or both through some means which is in itself pleasureful.* If one thinks about this a little, it will be noted that almost any activity or mental process may be recreation depending largely upon the attitude assumed in the approach to the process itself, and, perhaps, upon whether one is immersed in the process deeply enough to obtain re-creation.

In consequence, recreation may be a bodily exercise (which we may call active recreation) or a mental or contemplative exercise (which we might term passive recreation). A cultural flavor bordering on education is imparted when recreation is taken by employing cultural and handicraft arts such as music, drama, painting, sculpturing. Religious overtones are present when the spirit is moved by contemplation of inspiring environment. At the other extreme, if one is fiendishly inclined, recreation may be taken in any one of a number of degrading activities.

In this text, when we write about opportunities for recreation which are appropriate for the taxpayer to support, we reduce all recreation processes to those which are wholesome and socially acceptable by the general public. Anything that is degrading, off-color, or unconventional is left out. Otherwise acceptable forms of recreation may also be left out because of financial limitations. These include high-cost processes and those forms of recreation which appeal only to very small sectors of the population unless it can be shown that providing recreation for very small groups actually promotes the *general* welfare and not the *special* welfare of a few enthusiasts. Theoretically, the taxpayer supports only such recreation as has wide acceptance and relatively low net unit cost to the taxpayer.

The kind of recreation, therefore, that is suitable for government sponsorship changes with the changing times and may be different for different localities—a point which it is well to keep in mind. Note, too, that there is no scientific or factually based formula that can be depended upon in the selection of appropriate kinds of recreation for government to foster other than as stated above.

Words are used to express ideas. If the same word is used to convey different ideas in different situations, the message becomes confusing. Unfortunately, the word recreation is such a word. When used by the general public it probably has a more uniformly understood meaning than when used in the "trade"—that is, the language used by the people in recreation work who come from a widely varied background.

Recreation workers who reached maturity at the time of the clash between the so-called "recreation" people and "park" people (see Chapter 3) refer to each other just that way—"he is a recreation man," or "he is a park man." This meant that the one specialized in recreation leadership and his thinking was colored by that sort of background, whereas the other was trained in facility construction and maintenance and so thought that way. These men were usually engaged in municipal work, but that distinction carried over into the state and federal services.

In the latter services (national and state parks, forests, and wildlife) the term recreation connotes a service on the local or urban scene and seldom is associated with the state and federal services.

"Outdoor" recreation, while not a new or recent expression, has carried a special meaning since 1961. It was then used to distinguish the great unsupervised, unorganized recreation represented by hunting, fishing, traveling for pleasure, camping, etc., as distinguished from the organized, promoted, supervised, and often scheduled recreation conducted by the municipalities on the playgrounds and community playfields of the cities. The former was supposed to be outdoor recreation while the latter was simply recreation.

So, for the time being we have recreation as meaning, to various people in the business, (1) what Webster and this text say it is, (2) the restricted meaning of a municipal, supervised service, and (3) coupled with the prefix, "outdoor," all unorganized, free-time nonurban recreation offered fered primarily by various state and federal agencies.

In times past, recreation has been justified as being an aid to efficiency in work; it rejuvenated the mind and body for renewed labor with a renewal of interest and vigor. Recreation was a surcease from work and was practiced at such times as could be spared or made available after the hours spent in survival activities—work, sleep, eating, and the personal chores attendant to those necessities. These were the leisure hours and hence there arose a close association of recreation and leisure. While these have some attributes in common (e.g., the absence of compulsion) they are not identical. Leisure in particular needs more explanation.

Leisure time is free, unoccupied time during which most recreation takes place and, as we noted in the previous discussion of recreation, the latter may be almost any activity or mental process depending on the attitude one assumes in the approach to the process. It may even be some activity that is usually classified as work, but it is not work if it is done as recreation, that is, as a freely chosen project without any compulsion present. Some may call leisure a state of being free from the necessity of doing anything that a person does not want to do. An old American saying puts it in reverse but most succinctly: "Nothing is work unless you would rather be doing something else."

In our continually increasing affluence, leisure time is growing in amount to the point where it may equal work time. This observation causes some concern as to the ability of a future society to wisely choose those uses of leisure time (recreation) which will promote the general welfare in contrast to mere time-consuming experiences—or worse. More and more the philosophically minded are looking to the wise use of leisure time as a manifestation of a culturally great people.

But what *is* the proper use of leisure time? What is the standard by which "proper" is to be measured? Whose leisure and leisure time—those to whom leisure is a vocation? Those whose leisure is enforced, such as the retired, the unemployed, and the unemployable? Or leisure for all at times, as part of the good life?

As these questions are pondered there arises the notion of what the quality of life should be. It is not a single prescription concocted of a fixed recipe of ingredients; yet there are research organizations which are polling thousands of people in an attempt to identify those ingredients. There is no mistaking the idea that some advances in this direction are important to both present and future generations—for individual direction toward a more or less homogenous public good.

This also calls for some speculation as to objectives of both a personal and a national ethical standard. Preconceived philosophical, religious, and ethical codes need reexamination either to confirm old standards or to modify them.

Such meditation is intriguing, somewhat disturbing, and quite often humbling—humbling in the sense that solid facts, lasting verities, ultimate truths are quite elusive and very, very hard to come by. The administrator will be cautious about assuming a dictatorial posture or imposing his judgment without a fair hearing of the views of others. When he knows that right and wrong are not as recognizable as black and white he will learn to confine major attention to identifying alternatives and arrive at a selection after due consideration with others. The normal progression of ideas, from play on through recreation, leisure, the quality and purpose of life itself, is a road worth following to the end of the line.

THE "TOOLS" OF RECREATION

Various things are required to provide recreation opportunities for the public, even on the restricted basis heretofore outlined. We need land—land with many characteristics. We need the native land in abundance where recreation can be taken in solitude for the rediscovery of nature's processes and the rejuvenation of the human spirit. We need land that has been made suitable for games and outdoor exercise of various kinds. We need land that has been made beautiful by the hand of man—horticultural exhibits, beautiful lawns, gardens, buildings that are architecturally attractive; land that provides pleasant ways on which to travel leisurely (parkways); land that includes lakes and streams, both native and man-made.

On this land we sometimes need to build structures to provide various facilities such as courts for games, fencing to enclose certain activities, ball diamonds of one kind or another, wading pools, swimming pools, children's play areas, and a host of other facilities necessary in carrying out a well-rounded program. We have mentioned buildings for various purposes, for so-called community center work, for workshops, for the housing of equipment.

The land and structures all require servicing through the maintenance of grounds and buildings, a police organization to guide and discipline, an organization to promote activities, organize leagues, and supervise general use, and above all, an organization that finances and manages the whole recreation service.

There are, therefore, assets in land, assets in structures, assets in personnel; all have been assembled to produce a recreation service. The character and quality and quantity of that service are in harmony with policies evolved by the governing agencies. Those policies, in turn, are responsive to the will of the body politic in the same sense that laws reflect the attitude of people; in both policy and law determination both professional and lay guidance are required. The initial step in that guidance procedure is made by the administrator, if an orderly sequence and review is to result. The administrative function, then, is not only the management of the elemental assets that have been mentioned, but the proposal of broad policies as well.

PARKS AND PARK SYSTEMS

A park is a piece of land or water set aside for the recreation of the people. Improved land is that land which has been specially prepared for public use—ball diamonds, courts for games, playgrounds, picnic grounds, horticultural exhibits, etc. Unimproved land is native land. The latter should contain characteristics which in themselves induce and promote recreation such as hunting, fishing, hiking, winter sports. Native park land should also be of such a nature as to induce and promote recreation through contemplation, nature appreciation, history, geology, archeology, etc. Consequently, a park is both a tool for active supervised recreation and by itself, and standing alone, an instrument of recreation.

Lands called parks are not the only land masses that are used for recreation. Others include forests, river and other water impoundments and adjacent lands, the public domain in general and specifically large mountain and desert regions, historic sites and battlefields, and others of lesser significance. These areas are used only partially for recreation purposes and hence cannot properly be called parks. Nevertheless, some forest areas are more than reminiscent of the forest parks of antiquity which were the progenitors of today's parks.

Without going into the details of how a park and recreation system is made up, it is enough for the moment to know that a complete system for a municipality, for a metropolis with satellite towns, for a region, state or nation, includes various sizes of land parcels. These may be improved as well as native, each performing a distinct function and so fitted into the complementary function of other parks making up the system of parks for that particular agency as to result in a service of the scope intended by that agency. Consequently, there are municipal systems; metropolitan, regional or county systems; state systems; and national systems. Theoretically all such systems have a joint responsibility to adequately provide the complete spectrum of recreation opportunities.

That "joint" responsibility aspect has been long in evidencing tangible results, but great strides have been made in recent years. Through the Federal Bureau of Outdoor Recreation, federal aid for land acquisition is possible to the states on a matching basis. In turn many states make grants-in-aid to local governments. The Department of Housing and Urban Development makes grants-in-aid to local governments and, as a prerequisite, the plans of the local government must be based upon the planned services of an agency of greater geographical scope. These measures, together with the expressed goal of BOR, will ultimately result in a fully integrated and unified national recreation service.

CORRELATION

No park and recreation system, local, state, or federal in scope, is a completely independent entity existing in isolation separate and apart from all other public and private services on which the public depends for existence. The recreation need is only one of the myriad of services required for everyday living; any one of these needs may be paramount at some given time or situation. Such things as parks, highways, water reservoirs, sewer systems, transmission lines, power plants, businesses, and housing are often at loggerheads over finances, land, and the minds of men. All are engaged in the development of natural resources and are responsible in varying degrees for the polluting effect of their residual by-products on the air, the soil, the alteration of the landscape, and the ecology of nature. The weighing of conflicting values and the identification of alternatives are clearly called for. Conciliation, compromise, coordination of effort, and cooperation of operation may require unusual practices for the park and recreation administrator in order to conserve resources and minimize the unfavorable aspects of resource development.

The park and recreation services offered by government in all its levels need to be coordinated with those same kinds of services offered by other levels and other departments of government, with welfare and religious institutions in their local work as well as lake and mountain camp facilities, with private enterprise in development of new town sites, marinas, ski resorts, golf course-condominium developments, and the like.

Let us never overlook the fact that, like all our resources, those available for recreation are no longer unlimited, but, with our ever-increasing population, are definitely limited.

Chapter Two

The Nature
of Recreation

Regardless of the enthusiasm and vigor a person brings to his calling in life, whatever his profession—engineering, plumbing, or psychology—his ability to perform depends on his understanding of the nature of his field. So it is in parks and recreation. Skills in how to manipulate physical resources, land, water, and vegetation can be taught and applied by people trained in other fields. Forestry, fisheries and wildlife, physical education, and horticultural practices and procedures which involve keeping areas and facilities operational can similarly be mastered by others. And it is the same with those who are experienced in leadership and programming techniques as well as in planning and design.

If there is substance to the thought that others can equal the skills of the park and recreation professional, why is there a special profession of parks and recreation? Obviously, it is not because of the skills involved—they are not unique; rather it is the end product that is different from that of all other fields, and it is embodied in the professional practice of providing the public with adequate and proper recreation opportunities.

For a person to become as skilled in one or more of a variety of tasks usually associated with parks and recreation may merely mean that a repetitive task, regardless of the level of sophistication, has been mastered.

Quite often the skill positions are more effectively filled by people without formal training in parks and recreation.

The difference between a person who is equipped only with skills and one who knows why and how such skills are to be used is based on understanding a unique philosophy of serving people. This philosophy does not arrive prepackaged for immediate consumption. Instead, it is developed and refined according to the interests and intellectual capacities of each person. And as a primary prerequisite it is only when the nature of recreation is understood that a philosophy of parks and recreation as a public service can be developed and utilized by the aspiring park and recreation administrator.

The person equipped with skills and experience alone is generally incapable of formulating plans on how to cope with new and unexpected problems. Today, these problems are based on an increasingly complex mix of users and facilities, including the antisocial or deviant behavior of the users as well as the constantly changing demands for new recreation activities as exemplified by the increasing number of off-the-road recreation vehicles and indoor tennis centers. Lacking the ability to consider alternative measures to unexpected situations, he characteristically overreacts by calling for a "closing of the parks" or "we need more money." In the past these were safe reactions, but not today, because more money is often provided and these conditions may still persist.

This is not a field in which a superficial understanding of it will long be tolerated; it is too viable and important to individual development, society, and national policy. Any person charged with the administration of parks and recreation, at any level of public service or in private practice, must have a thorough understanding of its nature.

The term recreation, as used by the man in the street, is used to describe the kinds of recreation areas, facilities, and activities with which he is familiar. But recreation is also something more and in its most fundamental form it is essentially a human experience. It is this interpretation of the term that needs to be understood before a philosophy of recreation service can be formulated.

Once this basic interpretation is accepted, it quickly becomes apparent why many decision makers place undue emphasis on physical areas—parks, forests, rivers, beaches—to the exclusion of the actual human experience that takes place in these areas. It is understandable why such a limited view of recreation often leads to a feeling that parks and recreation involve only the maintenance areas and facilities instead of serving as a means toward achieving the human experience known as recreation.

This interpretation of recreation wherein the manipulation and maintenance of resources becomes the goal can be a comfortable concept. It suggests that a thorough knowledge of maintenance and operational fields, the biological sciences, and business administration is the sum and substance of parks and recreation as a field of study and practice. It also embraces the view that what is good for the resources is good for man and thereby identifies man as the intruder on the natural scene. This interpretation, with similar logic, lends itself well to solutions such as "limit man's activities or intrusions on nature and the crisis and the shortage of land will be resolved." It is also comfortable because except for man, nature is predictable. Under this arrangement recreation planning can proceed with minimal concern for the human experience and can be arranged largely through the natural laws that dictate how things grow, move, and change. It is becoming increasingly apparent that this is not enough. Areas and facilities are important only as they contribute to human needs, in this case, human enrichment and enjoyment. Man is an integral part of nature. It is not possible to separate him from it any more than it is to destroy matter. But he is unique in his relationships with all other forms of nature in that he is the only part of it capable of the creative acts of thought. This makes man special. His special needs have to be met within the framework of nature, as do all other forms of nature. It is this exceedingly complex and creative process of developing resources and programs from existing situations ranging from the purity of wild mountain ranges to the chaos of central city ghettos into recreational experiences that will fulfill his inherent needs for a quality life.

The idea of enriching and enjoyable experiences has been generally embodied in the terms play, recreation, and leisure. It is through the examination and study of these terms that the notion of recreation as a human experience begins to emerge. Understanding all three terms is critical because they are often used interchangeably to the point where they have become synonymous in public expressions. The result is that not only the users, but also the practitioners of parks and recreation are often confused.

QUALITATIVE AND QUANTITATIVE CONCEPTS OF LEISURE

There is a great and historic and growing body of literature on leisure. While becoming increasingly complex in theory, leisure in definition can generally be considered as being either qualitative or quantitative. Qualitative concepts of leisure embrace the writings of Aristotle, who effectively described it as the ultimate life style of the ancient Greeks, to contemporary authors such as Sebastian deGrazia, who holds similar views about the qualitative nature of leisure. To these purists, leisure is that part of life in which man has freedom to express the superior and spiritual activities of the mind and body. While Aristotle emphasized the need of freedom, generally from work, during which leisure activities may occur, without any

real restraints on kind of activity from contemplation to crafts, deGrazia represents a school of thought that refines this concept even further: "It is an ideal, a state of being, a condition of man, which few desire and which fewer achieve."[1] They view leisure as being more of a spiritual activity when man is free from constraints of work or any other human activity including the biological necessities of life, as well as, according to deGrazia, the time required to commute between office and home.

At present there are comparatively few students of leisure willing to follow the purists with their stout and strict adherence to leisure being not only limited to a "state of mind" but a state in which the mind is limited to the "superior" activities of contemplation and reflection. This euphoric and idealistic condition of man has traditionally been available only to those who were able to have other people do their work. It follows that they also were the more highly educated class. These constraints are not as applicable to the twentieth-century man, however, because mind-freeing drugs and alcohol can produce a similar state of mind and are rather easily available to any class of people.

Holding opposite views of leisure are those who consider it to be merely free time, but free time without any qualitative attributes, merely a block of time which can be filled with anything—thus, the quantitative nature of leisure. As discretionary or free time it is subject to measurement and analysis: hours and days and months of leisure.

As a quantitative term, leisure can be used for a large variety of purposes including those that are socially unacceptable as well as participation in family recreation activities. It becomes the prerogative of the individual to decide how he wants to use this free time called leisure.

The differences between the qualitative and quantitative interpretations of leisure are obvious. So are some of the implications. As deGrazia notes for the proponents of the qualitative view, not all people are capable of achieving a "leisure state." This is a patrician view upheld by the Greeks because the "unleisure" activities were the responsibilities of slaves.

There now emerges one of the chief characteristics of the qualitative interpretation of leisure and that is that its use is limited to a select group. Historically, they were either members of the nobility or merchants or had others, slaves or employees, to free them from responsibilities of work. This arrangement permitted them to engage in and develop that special leisure state of mind. They were eventually joined by a growing class of educated persons in contemporary society who became equipped through the educational process to appreciate the qualitative aspects of leisure. But they were

---

[1] Sebastian deGrazia, *Of Time, Work and Leisure* (New York: Doubleday-Anchor, 20th Century Fund, 1962), p. 5.

still a minority group. The masses of people today are just not equipped intellectually or financially to engage in the quietudes of contemplation and reflection and poetry, even though they have the time for such activities.

It is difficult for the man in the street to even comprehend why a person would rather back-pack in solitude through a wilderness area instead of camping in Yosemite Valley or in other congested public or private parks. Similarly, the performance of a string quartet has never competed with the attendance at the Circus Maximus or professional football. In essence these examples declare the differences between the qualitative interpretation of leisure—a life devoted to the superior and spiritual activities of mind and body—and the quantitative interpretation in which man is free to choose between the superior and the less than superior (including socially unacceptable and deviant) activities during his free time.

Judgments are not proposed in this work on what is specifically superior, and not so, in human activity. The authors, for purposes of this text, however, use the time-honored distinction that those activities which utilize a high degree of an individual's intellectual, spiritual, and physical capacities in combination are superior to those limited to any one of those capacities.

THE LEISURE CLASS

There is another facet of leisure that should be noted. It has its genesis in the vernacular that remains ageless—show-off. And it is not limited to the youthful expression. There seems to be an inherent need amongst some people to display their special talent, physical attributes, or extra material possessions. The idea of displaying artistic or physical talent seems always to have been acceptable social activity and has been developed and refined to a wide variety of artistic and cultural activities from painting to singing and ultimately to professional performances. Public display of these talents was obviously acceptable because of the satisfaction received by those who viewed or heard them even though the talents were greater than those possessed by the audiences. On the other hand, the display of extra material possessions has not always been accepted by society at large. Man and society have a long history of exhibiting envy over material possessions including objets d'art held in greater supply by others.

It required Veblen to articulate a rationale for such behavior in his classic, *The Theory of the Leisure Class.*[2] A leading American sociologist of the nineteenth century, Veblen depicted the ostentatious display of leisure as a function of social class. He referred to this display as conspicuous

---

[2]Thorstein Veblen, *The Theory of the Leisure Class* (New York, 1899).

consumption. In essence, Veblen attacked the basis for the Greeks' patrician qualitative concept of leisure—the minority upper class were free to pursue a leisure life style only because others of lesser status were forced to do their work. He condemned the aristocracy of history who not only exploited the masses to gain power and subsequent leisure but who also went to extraordinary lengths to display their leisure status through conspicuous consumption. They gave sumptuous feasts, became connoisseurs of culture and cuisine, displayed the accoutrements of expensive living from gentlemanly sports to lavish gardens and a multiplicity of residences, and became the patrons of the arts. These aristocratic activities, Veblen felt, were to remind and sharpen the distinction between the classes. In all the grotesque machinations to assure this distinction, possibly none exceeds the tradition of the ancient Chinese mandarins who grew fingernails to unbelievable lengths. A person with such embellishments obviously spent little time in a rice paddy.

Equally as obvious, and due to a properly programmed display of wealth, the nineteenth- and early twentieth-century millionaires did not need to work either. Tuxedo Park was an exclusive New York Club of that era, described by Cleveland Ammory[3] as being located in the Ramapo Hills overlooking Tuxedo Lake and forty miles northeast of New York City. The club was incorporated in 1886 originally as a hunting and fishing resort—"A short-season place between New York and Newport." To accommodate the members' needs, places such as "Duckhollow house" were constructed:

A beautiful white Georgian building, directly across the Lake from the Club, it consists, among other things, of 25 air-conditioned rooms, all mirrored master bedroom, a movie theatre, a swimming pool, a life-size granite Buddha, a boathouse, an electric motorboat (40 batteries), and $300,000 worth of shrubbery; the total cost was $2,250,000—in 1937. This charming cottage was presented to Mr. and Mrs. Angier Biddle Duke as a wedding present by her parents, the Duke and St. George families. . . .

Any Tuxedoite, merely by showing his gold oakleaf pin to the conductor, could have any Erie Railroad train stop at Tuxedo. Some of the residents, such as Mrs. Wm. Pierson Hamilton, daughter of the elder J.P. Morgan, and E. H. Harriman, had their own personal railroad stations in Tuxedo.

The belief of those who participated in this microcosm of the leisure society is described by Price Collier, who made his home in Tuxedo from 1898 until his death in 1915, when he said: "The best society of Europe is success enjoying an idle hour or so; the best society here is idleness enjoying

---

[3] Cleveland Ammory, "Tuxedo Park—Black Tie," in *Mass Leisure,* Larrabee and Meyersohn, Eds. (New York: The Free Press, 1958).

its success. . . . Society, to be permanently interesting, must be made up of idle professionals, not of professional idlers."[4]

A PLACE FOR THE LEISURE CLASS

Veblen voiced the deep frustrations of a civilization when he so clearly identified the "idle rich" as wastrels in developing his thesis of relative deprivation. As noted by Riesman, he first advanced these views in one of his earliest essays, "Some Neglected Points in the Theory of Socialism" (1891)[5]:

> The existing system does not make, and does not tend to make, the industrious poor poorer, as measured absolutely in terms of livelihood; but it does tend to make them relatively poorer, in their own eyes, as measured in terms of comparative economic importance, and, curious as it may seem at first sight, this is what seems to count.

Veblen's ideas about relative deprivation and a leisure class are dismissed today by many students of leisure because the "idle rich" are now not so idle and the leisure class, based on availability of discretionary time, is the working class. But Veblen should not be so lightly dismissed as one who merely proposed a theory applicable to the past. Riesman further states that:

> Veblen saw that the increase of well-being among industrial workers has led to their bourgeoisification through their leisure-time activities. He saw that the leisure class in modern Western societies extends almost to the very bottom, including all those who "keep up appearances." He argues, in his early work, that the motive of envy among working men may be strong enough to bring on a socialist transformation.

So, at least, in his early works, Veblen recognized that the leisure class is not limited to those of independent means, but in fact, all classes of people tend to exhibit similar tendencies of displaying wealth. Modern sociologists consistently use the example of the subsistence Tennessee mountain farmers who, after the Tennessee Valley Authority brought inexpensive electricity to the region, often displayed their new refrigerators on the front porch. Similarly, the first television owners in the early 1950s constructed extra high and fancy antennas on their houses to be sure they were noticed.

It is possible, however, that despite the motives of envy, ostentatious display, and relative deprivation, the old concept of conspicuous consumption by the aristocracy served some useful social purposes. Chief among these might be the function of patronage by which artists were subsidized and a demand created for their talent. A further brief can be made for those of the original leisure class who were not "idle" but instead studied—the law, justice,

---

[4] Ibid.

[5] "The Relevance of Thorstein Veblen," *Abundance for What? And Other Essays*, David Riesman (New York: Doubleday and Co., 1964).

medicine—including the Greeks who provided Western civilization with its first concepts of justice and scientific thought.

Today, it is generally conceded that the rich are no longer idle as a class—quite the opposite. Those who inherit vast wealth generally embark on useful careers in industry or social welfare, including politics. But the few contemporary idle rich, the jet-setters, continue to impact society, largely because of their high visibility and mobility. There is however, social drama in the difference of the impact on society. Historically, the leisure class served society in a variety of ways, many of them of questionable social value. Today, the jet-setters, though they are often ridiculed for their antics, may serve society to the extent that some people, without feeling envy or relative deprivation, get vicarious satisfaction from knowing that the system does provide for such activity.

PLAY

The term itself tends to mesmerize: flashes of childhood joy and nostalgia, and freedom, natural activities, and the anticipation of fun. It conveys a purity of emotion and joy not achieved by other symbols of universal communication.

To attempt a critical analysis of the term seems analogous to operating on a butterfly. But unlike the senseless destruction of the insect, one has to approach it like an entomologist, for the purpose of information.

Unfortunately, however, to carry the analogy further, it is not possible in this work to fulfill the demanding and detailed study required to completely dissect the play-butterfly. An overview of its appearance, from whence it comes, and some information about why it flies will have to do.

There is sound justification for this task. Play is often used synonymously with recreation and leisure. If there is a difference, it should be explored.

Kraus has compiled one of the better treatments of the terms recreation, leisure, and play.[6] It includes a comprehensive representation of the variety of psychologists, sociologists, and philosophers who through the ages have defined and defended the idea of play. And throughout, it quickly becomes apparent that play was used by the public as well as students of life to mean anything that was joyful and that is how it remains in common use.

The evolving theories seemed more attuned to the functions or benefits of play than to addressing the question, what is it? As a result during the nineteenth and twentieth centuries, there was a proliferation of theories about the importance of play, and always, as Kraus suggests, about

---

[6]Richard Kraus, *Recreation and Leisure in Modern Society* (New York: Appleton-Century-Crofts, 1971).

its positive aspects. It was never considered to be dysfunctional, dangerous to the participants, or breeding of antisocial behavior.

As noted by Meyer, Brightbill, and Sessoms, the various theories can be categorized in brief:[7]

Surplus Energy, proposed by Schiller and Spencer
That energy not needed by the playing animal to stay alive and perpetuate the species (excess energy) finds its outlet in play.

Preparation for Life, proposed by Gross et al.
That play is instinctive and is a part of the animal's educational experience. Through play the animal practices those things which he must follow later in life. It is, in a sense, preparation for living and a hereditary tract.

Recapitulation, proposed by Hall
That the animal repeats through play the activities his ancestors experienced (running, jumping and throwing, and the like); heredity is a large factor.

Instinct, proposed by McDougall et al.
That play is wholly instinctive and based on automatic impulses, a result of a drive, appetite, and inner urge; play instinct common among humans and perhaps other forms of animal life.

Relaxation, proposed by Patrick
That play is pleasurable and sought for its own sake; that it is a release from work, compulsion, and the struggle to live; that play results in its own satisfactions; play relieves stresses and strains of the individual. Note: The catharsis explanation of play—that play is an outlet for pent-up emotions—is closely related to the theory of relaxation.

Recreation, proposed by Kames
That play is the natural changeover from work and refreshes, replenishes, and restores energy. In this respect, it is quite as essential as rest.

Catharsis, proposed by Aristotle
That play is an outlet for confined emotions, a release for feelings which might otherwise remain suppressed and harmful.

Self-Expression, proposed by Mitchell
That play is the natural urge for action. Recognizes the nature and capacity of man, his anatomical and physiological structure, his psychological inclinations, and his desire for self-expression. Sees self-expression as man's supreme need.

Even a cursory analysis of the theories of play indicates a dominant theme of joy, child orientation, action and freedom, and instinctive behavior.

A few peripheral theories, however, attempt to ascribe some of the values usually associated with the qualitative concept of leisure and a generalized concept of recreation. For the purposes of this text, it will be understood that any activity undertaken by an animal or a person under the

[7]Meyer, Brightbill, and Sessoms, *Community Recreation: A Guide to its Organization,* 4th ed. (Englewood Cliffs, N.J.: Prentice-Hall, Inc., 1969).

age of reason, through instinctive behavior, at any time, place, or circumstance that results in a joyful experience is play.

Whether or not a particular play experience results in or contributes to a more effective or efficient organism, human or animal, is up to the physiologist to determine. Similarly, the kinds of individual or social behavioral traits that might result from the play experience will be evaluated by the psychologists and sociologists.

If this more limited view of the nature of play is acceptable, then the importance of engaging in an evaluation of theories becomes clearer. For instance, if it can be accepted that play is limited to activity of nonreasoning humans (usually children) and animals (all ages) then we can understand why the educators had mixed success in attempting to implement the brilliance of John Dewey, one of America's foremost educational philosophers of the early twentieth century.

Dewey expressed strong convictions about the importance of play to the totality of the educational experience:

> The idea that the need (for play) can be suppressed, is absolutely fallacious, and the Puritanic tradition which disallows the need has entailed an enormous crop of evils. If education does not afford opportunity for wholesome recreation and training, capacity for seeking and finding it, the suppressed instincts find all sorts of illicit outlets, sometimes overt, sometimes confined to indulgence of imagination. Education has no more serious responsibility than making adequate provision for enjoyment of recreative leisure; not only for the fact of immediate health but still more, if possible, for the fact of its lasting effect upon habits of mind.[8]

The terms used by Dewey are in themselves good reason to suggest that the examination of theory is not merely an academic indulgence. He reasonably refers to the "suppressed instincts" which are in the nature of play, but then equates them with "wholesome recreation" which is diametrically opposite in its nature because it calls for a rational response of a person as opposed to an instinctive response of a child or animal. Contemporary society will continue to have difficulty in following Dewey because he limited his charge to make "adequate provision for enjoyment of recreative leisure" to educators and the educational process. There is a growing social demand today for the attributes of what Dewey called play to be part of man's total life including during the work experience. More precisely, that experience is recreation.

RECREATION

There is little substantive theory on the nature of recreation. What is available has evolved from the practices and procedures used by those who

[8] John Dewey, *Democracy and Education* (New York: Macmillan, 1921).

have responsibility for recreation as a public service or private enterprise and is therefore based largely on their changing experiences during the past 100 years when recreation began to emerge as a public service. Quite naturally, in the absence of definitive theory, the practice of recreation is fragmented into wide-ranging differences in goals which often not only overlap but are in serious conflict in both use of physical or natural resources and in matters of policy.

The most obvious of such conflicts are of course at the state and national level where intensive recreation areas often detract from the emptiness and silence of surrounding wilderness areas. Similarly, the National Park Service and U.S. Forest Service collect admission fees to their areas whereas the U.S. Army Corps of Engineers, which attracts a greater number of recreation visits than any other public agency, strongly resists the policy. Or, admission fees are collected at federal and state recreation areas but not at local parks.

At the local levels of government, overlapping and conflicting responsibilities are most common in relationships with school boards in matters of developing areas and programming of activities.

But more serious in the lack of definitive theory on the nature of recreation is the confusion that exists about "What is recreation?" not only in the minds of the public but also among many of the professional people who are responsible for providing recreation opportunities at local, state, and federal levels.

While economic theory does embrace recreation as a productive function of society, it cannot be applied usefully without an acceptable base of what constitutes the recreation experience.

On the one hand there is a public and professional uneasiness about addressing the nature of recreation, and on the other recreation economists are being forced to measure the value of the recreation experience with a limited understanding of what they are measuring.

It is this state of the art that the development of playgrounds in the residual spaces under urban freeways is permitted and accepted and even considered good land-use planning. As long as recreation opportunities are not considered to be on a par with other land uses it can be assumed that the public's recreation needs are not being met. The reason is not mere costs, certainly not a lack of technology or even an absence of expressed interest from the public, but the fact that too few professional planners and practitioners are equipped to understand what they should be providing the public in the name of recreation.

Without an acceptable theoretical base, we are all limited to our personal experiences, likes and dislikes, which are ultimately foisted onto the public as an expression of their interests and needs.

DEFINITIONS

Historically, philosophers, psychologists, sociologists, anthropologists, and others have not addressed recreation in human terms, at least as we would today. They instead thought and wrote about leisure and play. Undoubtedly, precise meanings suffered in translation from the early Greek and Roman scholars and the terms became intermingled. The educational philosophers of this and the past century attempted to delineate those concepts and focused on play as a meaningful activity. And in order to give more conceptual substance they interjected the concept of recreation. While still not precise enough, at least the terms and concepts were being examined in modern languages—German, French, and English.

It required, however, the efforts of twentieth-century writers to begin the most definitive search for useful definitions of recreation—George Butler, Jay Nash, Meyer and Brightbill, and Neumeyer and Neumeyer. Except for Butler, who was on the staff of the former National Recreation Association, the others were university professors who began a move to interpret the emerging park and recreation movement in the U.S. as both a public service and a professional field. They articulated a logic for playgrounds and playground leaders, parks, and the importance of leisure. Their interests, and consequently those of their students, were largely urban oriented and their interpretation of recreation reflected this. The dominance of recreation in urban settings and especially the proposed human values related to social and physical recreation programs as reflected in their writings helped widen the schism between parks and recreation as a professional practice. Nevertheless, they made monumental contributions by undertaking a complicated and difficult task, which at best did not, at that time, have much status as a meaningful area of study in most universities.

The following is an attempt to develop a theory of recreation for the purpose of understanding the nature of the individual's recreation experience. This will, it is hoped, lead to a broader, and more precise, application of the term in its social, economic, and political context.

A THEORY OF RECREATION—A HUMAN EXPERIENCE

Any rational human activity that results in a pleasurable response, at any time or place or circumstances, with attendant enriching physical or intellectual or emotional benefits, within the constraints of individual morality and/or social acceptability, is recreation.

Any rational human activity enlarges on the concept of recreation. It can no longer be limited to the activities or experiences of the suppliers or manufacturers of recreation, or those which have been traditional for either the leisure class or the masses. It now embraces any rational activity that stimulates a response through any or all of the senses—seeing, hearing, tasting, touching, and smell. That the activity has to be made as a matter of rational choice and is enriching reinforces the positive nature of recreation as a human experience. It is this characteristic of the recreation experience that separates it from play, which otherwise incorporates all other features of recreation. Play then becomes relegated to an instinctive, unreasoned activity engaged in by humans, young and old, who cannot reason, and animals, neither having the powers necessary to make reasoned choices based on the consequences of their actions.

Each person determines for himself what is pleasurable or enjoyable. In essence, only each person can be the determiner of what is recreation. A playground is categorized as a place of recreation as is a national park, but certain persons, because of their experiences on a playground or national park, may have had traumatic experiences instead. Both types of areas were conceived, planned and developed and managed as places of recreation but not all users, for a great variety of reasons, gain a recreation experience from them.

AT ANY TIME OR PLACE

Activity. This is the most common use of the term recreation. While the particular activity is merely the vehicle for the experience, recreation is most often considered to mean enjoyable activities and they are variously classified as being sports, games, crafts, arts, and the performing arts, music, dramatics, nature study, travel, hobbies, and social activities.

Seldom do these classifications include activities other than those normally scheduled by public park and recreation department programmers; usually omitted is the vast array provided through commercial recreation enterprises.

Places. In tandem with activity, places of recreation are most easily understood but too often limited to parks, playgrounds, picnic areas, community recreation centers, marinas, etc.

Places of recreation are most often considered to be institutionalized places, areas, and facilities developed and provided and programmed by a government or volunteer agency. Although the entrepreneurial phenomenon of the various Disney enterprises, Disneyland and Disney World, forced a recognition that the public is interested in commercial recreation beyond professional sports, there is still lacking a general acceptance of the concept that recreation can take place anywhere, not only in public areas. The traditional practice of professionals in parks and recreation to limit their concern to those institutionalized places of recreation is not supported by historical fact or the contemporary public's interest in recreation. Today, more than ever, the home can be a place of recreation, and the same now for shopping centers.

Values-Experience. Without exception, recreation has been theorized, defined, and categorized as being a positive force. The recreation experience is expected to build character, citizenship, contribute to the safety of participants, lessen vandalism, develop aesthetic perception and appreciation and personal health; communities are better places to live because of their park systems and recreation programs. Obviously, individuals who participate in recreation activities may very well enrich and enhance their lives with these positive values, but this can only be determined through careful scrutiny and testing of the individual participants and communities that are supposed to be upgraded.

But it is fallacious to think that a man and his family and his community benefit if participation in a particular recreation activity exceeds common sense and family obligations or if a park system is developed for an elitist type of use while recreation needs of certain segments of the community—most notably today, the people of the inner city—remain unanswered.

The positive values of recreation are available to the user, but the actual experience of others who may be linked to the user and his experience may be negative.

Leisure. The concept that recreation must take place during leisure has been the most accepted criteria of the many theories of recreation—and the most damaging. This view effectively prohibits man from achieving his ultimate in personal fulfillment by isolating his attitudes and life style for joy and happiness to one segment of his life and continues to deepen the ancient schism between work and leisure.

Since a person's leisure represents his discretionary time, much of his planned recreation will take place then. If, on the other hand, recreation is also in part a matter of pleasurable response to any stimuli, then the individual who enjoys those activities normally known as work need not wait until his leisure to enjoy himself. Reality suggests, however, that because of the boring or physically demanding characteristics of many occupations, only a limited number of people are privileged to attain recreation experiences from their work.

Nevertheless, the omission of leisure as a prerequisite to recreation is an important conceptual approach to the dreams and aspirations of men everywhere for a quality life. Man cannot become the fulfilled man on a part-time, discretionary time, basis.

Since it is hereby claimed that man's recreation experience need not be limited to his discretionary time, neither then should the places wherein recreation takes place be limited to specially designated areas. One does not have to be in a park to experience recreation; it may, in fact, take place in a littered alley, or in an office building, or at home—it's where you find it. Therefore, all places and resources may be recreation resources.

ENRICHMENT OR POSITIVE BENEFITS TO THE INDIVIDUAL

The recreation experience that each person claims for himself is based in relativity. The sense of pleasure and enrichment that a person feels is by its nature greater than the experience, or set of experiences, that preceded it. The pleasure and enrichment derived from swimming exceed the feeling of not engaging in that activity. The same is true of reading or attending a concert—or there wouldn't be much sense in engaging in the activity. If the positive benefits of pleasure and enrichment do not occur, then the activity was not recreational.

It is important to note, however, that this relationship in relativity does not have to automatically deal in the extremes of a low psychological state of boredom or frustration to a high of pleasure as is the traditional interpretation of "re-creation." Instead it can also mean that a healthy and fulfilled person who goes swimming will also gain a recreation experience—the key here is that it is a different degree of fulfillment. To follow this interpretation of recreation means that man can aspire to a quality life based on a variety of quality experiences. He no longer need be categorized as an organism that is obliged to spend a specified portion of his life in unsatisfactory activities with occasional pleasurable activities to re-create him. Instead, he can aspire for a life that includes a kind of labor that provides a measure of pleasure and fulfillment such as teaching and at the end of that compulsory time he can engage in a different set of experiences, but also pleasurable and enriching ones, such as swimming, reading, or drag racing. So he can move laterally in his quality level of life. He no longer needs to feel that it is the nature of life to consist largely of low psychological points interspersed with only occasional high points of pleasure.

PLEASURABLE EXPERIENCES IN TIME

The feeling of pleasure an individual experiences is indeed dependent on each individual's perception of what constitutes this happy psychological reaction.

For purposes of defining the recreation experience, the pleasurable experience can be achieved in three different time frames:

1. In anticipation of the experience. A person, or a family collectively, may enjoy discussing or planning a vacation.

2. The experience. The vacation itself.

3. Reflection. After it is over, discussing and thinking about the vacation.

Of course, on the basis of a specific activity, all three functions need not always be pleasurable.

ENRICHMENT

The benefits a person receives from any experience can be generally categorized as being intellectual, physical, or emotional in nature. Similarly, any one, or combination, of these benefits must be present in the recreation experience and, most importantly, provide a sense of enrichment to the participant. They could include reading or study or chess as activities providing mental enrichment; walking or canoeing as physical enrichment; and the sight of towering trees or a pleasing painting as sources of emotional enrichment. Many recreation experiences have these in combination—the sight of towering trees on a shoreline while canoeing down a river evokes an aesthetic response (emotional) while engaging in skills (physical) necessary to keep the canoe afloat.

RATIONAL CHOICE

Rational choice is a function of the recreation experience if for no other reason than to exclude nonrational activities as being considered recreation. It is the only qualifier in the explanation of the nature of recreation that excludes the activities of people who are mentally unbalanced or intoxicated with drugs or alcohol. Those activities engaged in while a person is in one of these states of deviancy would qualify as being recreation except for the fact that they were not rationally chosen. A state of intoxication might be entered into as a matter of choice, but once drunk, the selection of activities cannot be undertaken rationally. Therefore, the person who gains pleasure from pounding his head against a brick wall or from any other such irrational activity is not engaging in a recreation activity.

The function of making a rational choice of the activity which one assumes will be recreation also assigns a useful definition to play. The joy of play is attributed largely to animals and the children who have not reached a point of mental maturity that permits a reasoned choice of whether or not an activity should be engaged in because the child cannot foresee the consequences of such activity. Play therefore remains a spontaneous, joyful activity without thought about consequences. When children push pointed sticks in each other's face it can be in the spirit of play. When an adult does this for fun, it is neither play nor recreation, merely an irrational and dangerous activity.

ETHICALLY NEUTRAL

Up to this point, this discourse on the nature of recreation does not address the matter of behavioral values. Indeed it is ethically neutral. As theory it is incomplete because it fails to recognize its social application. The most hedonistic and perversionary activities of man could qualify as recreation experiences on the basis of the functions described so far. But since man, by his nature, is forced to interact with others of his species and since such existence is regulated by ethics, systems of values, the recreation experience has to include the function of personal and social morality. In this context, it includes values accepted as being legal. This function of individual and social ethics, moral and legal, places limitations on what constitutes a recreation experience. But generally societies are free to make their own determinations about this and the individual is also generally free to choose the social groups that make these judgments—religion and church, community and country. In certain regions of the U.S., it has not been acceptable form for young people to engage in a dance in which the bodies of males and females were in contact, while ballroom dancing, as it is known, is perfectly acceptable in most other regions of the country. In other countries, the sale of pornographic material is legally acceptable which assures that for those who do not hold personal moral views in opposition, the experience associated with the consumption of pornography is therefore recreation.

The function of individual and social morality is that while the individual is still free to determine what activity and experiences he deems to be recreation, to practice the activity in a social context he is obligated to abide by the behavioral values in effect in his society.

THE RECREATION EQUATION

The following is an attempt to illustrate the various components and functions of the theory on the nature of recreation:

$$A + P_c + T + C \quad \rightarrow \quad P\,(\pm A_n\ \pm A_c\ \pm R_e) + En\,(\pm Mn\ \pm Phy\ \pm Em)$$
$$+ Ra + I_m \pm S_a = R$$

Any human activity (A), which may occur at any place (P_c), at any time (T), regardless of the circumstances (C) that results in a pleasurable response (P), that also provides and enriching experience (En), is rationally chosen (Ra) and fulfills either an individual's sense of morality or social acceptability (Im ± Sa) constitutes the recreation experience.

The pleasurable response (P) is further defined to include the experience of anticipation (An) or the actual activity (Ac) or reflection on the activity (Re); all three singly or in any combination (±).

The enriching experience (En) is further defined to include the enriching experiences gained from intellectual (Mn) or physical (Phy) or emotional (Em) benefits; all three singly or in any combination (±).

Chapter Three

History of Parks

THE BEGINNING

In the beginning there was the land.

In time some of this land was transformed into parks.

The genesis of park and recreation administration as practiced in the last quarter of the twentieth century lies in understanding why and how parks were invented in the very beginning. A continued search in subsequent history as to when, where, and by whom recreation places were developed and how recreation was practiced, all within the social and physical environment of the times, will result in a good understanding of the past as a foundation of a good chart for future administration.

Brief histories of parks are available covering the last two or three centuries and especially the last hundred or more years of American administrative efforts. To understand the developments of recent years, it is felt that the very beginning must be known, because a history of parks alone tends to divide the practice of park and recreation administration into two

A major portion of this chapter is extracted from Charles E. Doell and Gerald B. Fitzgerald, *A Brief History of Parks and Recreation,* 1954, by permission of the copyright owners, The Athletic Institute, Chicago.

parts: parks with a limited kind of recreation, and recreation as a separate discipline. Park and recreation administration as a single profession is the real objective. Nevertheless the brief histories referred to are important to our study.

The *Oxford English Dictionary* gives a definition of parks founded on historical evidences and is a good introduction for us. The *Encyclopedia of the Social Sciences* (Volume XI, "Parks," copyrighted 1933 by the Macmillan Company, New York) is a good general history. Still another reference worthy of reading is found in Chapter I of Volume II of Olmsted's *Forty Years of Landscape Architecture* (copyright 1928 by Frederick Law Olmsted; published by G. P. Putnam's Sons, New York).

One of the most illuminating works for our purpose is the monumental *A History of Garden Art* in two volumes, written by Luise Gothein at Heidelberg, Germany, in September 1913, edited by Walter P. Wright, and published in America by E. P. Dutton & Co., Inc., New York.

THE FIRST PARKS

Frau Gothein credited the Asiatics with being the real inventors of the park. The particular Asiatics the author had in mind were the Sumerians, a people even more ancient than the Egyptians. As evidence of the park idea, the author cites the "Epic of Gilgamesh," a story which was pieced together from inscribed tablets excavated in Mesopotamia. The Gilgamesh story antedates the writing of Genesis of the Bible, and is therefore the oldest story now known to mankind. The author quotes from part of this story, and after noting that there is no enclosure by wall or fence which differentiates parks from wood, says—

> All the same, this cedar wood of Humbaba's, so realistically described, with its straight, cared-for paths (the keeper of the wood is mentioned), and its bushy undergrowths and sweet-smelling plants, is a forerunner, the kind of starting-point for the park of history.

The author traces the western Asiatic parks from the vineyards and fishponds of the Sumerian King Gudea, about 2340 B.C., down through the the Hanging Gardens of Babylonia, about the ninth or tenth century B.C., past the introduction of flowers in the parks in the seventh century B.C., and concludes—

> This park is in its first intention the spectacular scene for a great man's hunting-ground, but is secondarily the place where feasts are given and where assemblies, and audiences granted to great princes, take place.

[1] Extracts from *A History of Garden Art* by Luise Gothein. 2 volumes. Edited by Walter P. Wright. London: J. M. Dent & Sons, Ltd., Publishers, 1913.

Centuries later, Plutarch and other Greeks tell of the parks and gardens of Persia. Socrates reports on how carefully the Persian kings guarded their gardens in their parks and placed the appellation "paradise" on them. Our author reports—

> We find from all accounts and from monuments also that these paradises were first and foremost hunting-parks, the fruit-trees grown for food, just as in the Babylonian-Assyrian sites. . . . The Persians were also familiar with the chase in the open country. A grand hunting-ground was given to the young Cyrus by his grandfather, in the hope that it would keep him at home, but he despised it, and, fired with longing, summoned his companions and went off, for in this park there were so many animals that he felt as though he was only shooting captive creatures.

The early gardens of the Israelites, as described in the Book of Genesis, (e.g., the Garden of Eden) are very similar to the old Assyrian and Babylonian gardens.

In India there were not only parks for the kings, but the communities as well were reported to have owned great recreation parks near cities. A description of a park in the twelfth century B.C. in the city of Polonnaruwa in Ceylon includes—

> . . . spouts of water, conveyed thither in pipes and machines, made the place appear as though clouds were incessantly pouring down drops of rain. There was a great array of different baths that delighted masters and men. We hear also of other parks and other baths, and even of gardens that the rich made for the recreation of the poor.

PARKS IN ANCIENT GREECE

In Greece we find the practice of surrounding the graves of important people with groves of trees, which were considered sacred. This sort of hero-worship brought on the famous Greek games which originally were a sort of wake. These games included chariot-races, and chariot-races produced the hippodrome. The need for practice of the Greek games established the outdoor gymnasium and one form of the gymnasium became the Academy, and the Academy became the seat of learning, actually the home of the Greek Philosophers. Hippodromes, gymnasiums, academies became parts of parks. Our author says—

> In Plato's time the gymnasium and the park were so closely connected that the philosopher wanted to have gymnasiums in such places only as were well-watered and specially favoured by Nature. In Rhegium such a zone was in existence in the Paradise of the elder Dionysius, and in Elis at an earlier date there was wild woodland round the gymnasium instead of garden. But we may be quite sure that gymnasiums were attached to hero sanctuaries, for the clear light of history gives us the origin of one that was set up in Syracuse: the town

raised a tomb in the Agora to Timoleon the liberator, and founded a Heroon with annual games. Hence arose later on a magnificent gymnasium with halls, exercise grounds, garden grounds, and an Odeon for musical performances.

Greece also had its public baths and some public parks in the days of the Republic, but these gradually gave way to those of a private nature. Under Alexander the Great, the large hunting parks came into their own, as did the private baths, gymnasiums, and academies, the latter now being more the place for intelligent discussion than the site for active sports.

Our author has this to say about a certain phase of Roman times—

In Roman times, Vitruvius is the first to describe the appearance of a building errected with a view to gymnastic sports. He calls it expressly Greek, not Roman, and palaestra, not gymnasium. He is mainly interested in the actual building, and it is only when he cannot help himself that he even mentions the garden sites. He first marks out a peristyle and round this are the different rooms which the philosophers used for their conversations. Here we get a wrestling school; a colonnade where in wintertime the games can be carried on in bad weather. It is called a "Xystos," and beside it there are walks under the open sky which the Greeks called sidepaths. The Romans, however, give the name Xysta to these walks where in the bright days of winter the athletes can go out and take their exercise. Their Xysta are a kind of thicket or plantation of plane-trees betwen two porticoes, and under the trees are seats to rest on; the stadion is generally at the end of the Xysta.

ROMAN PARKS

Wealthy Romans were great for having numerous villas, enough to each one so they could change their locale of living frequently, sometimes even from day to day. These villas at first were small, but later contained area enough for comparatively large gardens, and sometimes the size of small towns. Features of the park were in many of them. The hunting park was frequent. Speaking of one of them, *History of Garden Art* quotes—

... Quintus Hortensius had already made a park of fifty yokes of land, and enclosed it with a wall, and on this estate he had set up on the higher ground a shooting-box where he entertained his friends in a peculiar way. He had a slave dressed like Orpheus who sang before them, and then sounded a horn, whereupon a whole crowd of stags and boars and other quadrupeds came up, so that to him who told the tale the spectacle seemed more delightful than the hunt itself.

Generally speaking, throughout the Roman Empire, the villas were on the outskirts of the town or in the countryside, but in Rome, they invaded the city precincts themselves and became numerous, so that the entire city seemed like a garden except for the plebeian quarters which were indeed most squalid. Here was a move to bring the country to the city, much as was the purpose of Olmsted centuries later in the planning of Central Park in New York City.

The Romans seemed to be the ones who first used the floral greenhouse, using mica for window panes.

As the Roman Empire in the first centuries of the Christian era expanded northward into what is now France and Germany, their great villas and hunting parks went with them—some of them even as far as Great Britain. Again quoting from *A History of Garden Art*—

> Everything that the Romans did in these provinces, in the way of gardening and cultivation, was destined to perish when they were compelled to remove their troops under the German onslaughts. The open villas and gardens were the first victims and these Northern lands had to wait for hundreds of years before they could make a humble beginning with a new garden art. In the North the thread was broken, and only after wild, stormy years can we discover a new trace, again starting from the South.

There was only a slight thread remaining in western Italy, Spain, and southern France.

SUMMARY UP TO THE CHRISTIAN ERA

At this juncture in our history, it is well to pause and consider the elements of the park up to this time. It is quite evident that there were parks in or at the outskirts of several of the cities; a few may have been established by the people themselves; but most were established by noble and wealthy families, and only on occasion was the public invited to them. Some were given to the people at the time of a nobleman's death. Games, gardens, pleasant views (including water displays), music, and conversation were integral parts of these parks. The great hunting parks quite generally were a part of the large villas and country holdings of the provincial rulers. The animals were plentiful and not always wild.

As to motive for park development keep in mind that the development extended over a period of more than two thousand years before the Christian Era, a longer period than from the birth of Christ to 1970. The development was not confined to one location, or to one nation but was general throughout the known world. From one generation to the next the purpose was the same and the pattern was essentially the same except as it reflected the social life of the times. That purpose reached beyond the mere survival requirements into a universal and fundamental urge for something that was needed as a supplement to the activity necessary for mere existence. Today it is called recreation—recreation in physical activity, in contemplative posture amidst pleasing environment, in a general enrichment of life as discussed in Chapter 2 and referred to in Chapter 1 in the progression, "play, recreation, leisure, and the quality of life."

EARLY CHRISTIAN ERA AND MIDDLE AGES

If now we trace our steps into Byzantium and Islam and the Middle East in the early centuries of the Christian Era, we find some Greek influences. For instance in the fourth century, there were already stadiums, gymnasiums, and race-courses, and in the ninth century in the town of Samaria, we find ball-games and playgrounds (all private). The private hunting parks of nobility continued to be elaborate, most of them stocked with all sorts of animals—elephants, lions, giraffes, leopards—and in many cases a number of these were so tame they would eat out of a visitor's hand.

In later centuries when the Persians and Arabs spilled over into the West as far as Spain, we find their culture developing into grand palaces such as the Alhambra (thirteenth century) at Granada—most of them having parklike features.

Retracing our steps for a moment to the main continent of Europe, in the centuries succeeding the Fall of the Roman Empire, commonly known as the Middle Ages, we find the idea of parks barely kept alive—largely in the monasteries which frequently were the former villas of the nobility, which had been turned over to or became possessions of the church. These were meager times. Gradually some of the barons began to acquire sizeable estates and the art of gardening went from the chore of raising foodstuffs and plants for medicinal purposes to gardens of interest and beauty. By the time the thirteenth and fourteenth centuries came about, there were a number of such important villas and the one popular feature of most of these gardens was the maze, that labyrinth of hedges, which were interesting and intriguing to get into and out of. The maze was probably first used in Crete centuries before the Christian Era, but its adaptation to gardening took place on the Continent of Europe about the thirteenth and fourteenth centuries.

By the end of the thirteenth century, in Italy, and particularly in Florence, public grounds were established for the leisure of people. These took the form of walks and public squares, frequently decorated with statuary. Here is a significant quotation from the previously noted *A History of Garden Art,* which pertains to the thirteenth century.

A great advance in the development of gardens for the people is due to establishing Brotherhoods, both lay and clerical. They were highly approved of by the great of both kinds, and were constantly remembered in rich legacies and gifts. . . . The character of these Brotherhoods was half military and half religious: their patron was St. Sebastian, and naturally they were in high favour with the rich and great, for whom they trained good marksmen; and by them they were endowed with valuable privileges. They built fine club houses with large gardens, and had their shooting-stands set up in them, and it soon came about that the rest of the townsmen assembled there for recreation and amusement. . . .

. . . Not only for shooting, but for other sport, places were provided, and especially for ball games, which developed in the fifteenth century, chiefly in England; later they spread all over the Continent in the form of football, croquet, and lawn tennis, and when people had more room, these games were introduced in private gardens with properly laid-out squares and courts.

A sample of recreation as practiced in thirteenth-century England is given in the following quotation from Thomas B. Costain's *The Magnificent Century* (second in the Pageant of England series copyrighted by Costain in 1951, and published by Doubleday and Company, Inc., New York) beginning on page 343.[2]

There was a law that any yeoman with less than one hundred pence a year in land was obligated to have a bow and to practice regularly. This was no hardship, for one of the great pleasures of the common man was shooting at the butts. During the hours of leisure, sounds of loud laughter and approving cries of "Shotten!" would be heard from the archery grounds. The thud of arrows striking the clout squarely told the story of the skill English hands were developing with the mighty longbow. . . .

Boys, always eager to ape their elders, had bows of their own and would cover up their lack of skill by capering and singing. . . .

Younger children amused themselves on teeter-totters, although the name used then was merrytotter. They often played a game called Nine Men's Morris, which required a whole field.

The English, in fact, were great lovers of sport. In winter they fastened the bones of animals to their feet and skated on frozen ponds and streams. Those who could afford such luxuries, had a kind of skate with a metal edge, but they did not call them skates; they were termed scrick-shoes. A very popular game was known as bandy-ball, in which a crooked stick was used to clout a ball about a field. This form of amusement sired two quite different types of game, "goff" and shinny. Men bowled on the green and also played kayles or closh, a form of ninepins. They differed from most people in preferring games in which they could participate. Whole villages would turn to kick a ball or frisk around the Maypole.

At the same time they were avid followers of less healthy forms of sport in which they played the part of spectators—bear-baiting, bull-running, badger-baiting, and cockfighting.

The recreations of the nobility were somewhat more dignified. The tournament was the great amusement of the age and it drew all classes of people. Between joustings the brave knights kept the eye in for the next splintering of lances by practicing at the quintain, a special type of

[2]From *The Magnificent Century,* copyright 1951 by Thomas B. Costain. Reprinted by permission of Doubleday & Company, Inc.

target. Sometimes live quintains were used, men who covered themselves with a shield and defied the champions to bowl them over.

Hunting and hawking engaged most of the waking time of the nobility. Ladies of gentle blood took an active interest in both. Their participation sometimes took the form of sitting in an enclosure and shooting arrows at game driven past them. This, needless to state, did not suffice for the bolder ones who preferred to go into the field with their own harehounds. Ladies became expert hawkers and were seldom seen in the saddle without a hooded marlyon on wrist. The love of hawking, in fact, was universal. The poor man, with his tercel and the yeoman with his goshawk (a certain type of hawk was designated for each class) were seen as often as the earl with his falcon and the knight with his sacret.

The indoor amusements of the nobility included chess and an early form of backgammon. After supper in the great hall the minstrels would fill the hours with their ballades while the well-stuffed guests drank their wine. Minstrels were often well paid for their efforts, it being a not uncommon thing for the host to reward a particularly good performance with a gift of the cloak he was wearing or a drinking cup from the table.

RENAISSANCE

Beginning with the Italian Renaissance in the latter part of the fifteenth century, the private grounds and estates of the noble and the wealthy had developed in fabulous fashion. In the period between 1500 and the latter part of the eighteenth century, all over Europe, England, the Scandinavian countries, and even to some extent Russia, private parks became most elaborate developments. Topiary work (the art of keeping trees and shrubbery clipped in fantastic shapes) came into being in the fifteenth century. About this time, we find aviaries, fishponds, summer houses, grottoes, as well as hunting grounds and menageries finding their place in these parks. With the hunting grounds the hermitage was introduced (for real hermits or holy men), and these later developed into hide-aways for the weekend jaunts of the nobility. A feeling for antiques developed and bits of ancient ruins and replicas thereof were frequently used. Water displays, including canals and ponds, and most elaborate fountains (sometimes with statuary in which the water would come from "eyes, breasts, mouth, and ears") all became parts of one garden or another. Outdoor theaters were introduced as were facilities for certain games such as tennis courts, archery targets, playgrounds of various kinds, race-courses, and later (after the English influence), bowling-greens. Music became a part of the entertainment in all of these gardens. This was the period in which famous gardens such as the Tuileries and the Luxembourg in Paris, Sans Souci at Pottsdam, the Parque de Madrid were established and probably the most famous of them all, the Versailles outside of Paris.

Most of these places had their informal hunting parks, as well as their rigidly formal gardens which were the scene of gay festivities, including pastoral plays and exhibitions of jugglers and other entertainers. The development started in Italy, crept northward into France, the Low Countries, Germany, Scandinavian countries, and England.

Before proceeding in a strictly chronological sequence it is appropriate to consider Christopher Tunnard's article in the February 1951 issue of *The Magazine of Art* (published by the American Federation of Art) entitled "The Leaf and the Stone," taken from *The City of Man* by Christopher Tunnard, copyright 1953 by Charles Scribner's Sons, New York. He is discussing certain aspects of nature in a city plan extending over many centuries. In doing so, inevitably he must touch upon parks, and here he touches on the evolution of public parks from the private gardens of the high and mighty[3] —

> Green space as part of the organic structure of the city comes with the seventeenth century and the establishment of new forms based on changing social behavior. To a great extent, this development took place in France. Although the garden of Sixtus V's Villa Montalto at Rome had been almost as accessible as the Pontiff's person, the notion of opening pleasure gardens to the public is largely French; and although the French, like the Italians, based themselves on antique models, they soon adapted these to new uses. The grounds of Marie de Medici's Luxembourg Palace, built in 1620, have been open to the public for over three centuries; however, unlike the more popular forms of open space that were just then appearing, they were not specifically planned for public recreation.
>
> The idea of recreation for townspeople did not originate with the seventeenth century. It has been prompted throughout history by charitable motives, reforming impulse or the desire for public acclaim. Such recreational areas were usually on the outskirts of the town, however, and by the sixteenth century the use of "prairies" or meadows outside the walls was fairly common. In crowded Paris, still contained within its fifteenth-century walls, the margins of the Seine and the "quais" were in great demand. Bowing to public pressure for open space within the town, Henri IV began work on the Place Royale. A royal act of 1605 shows the idea of this plaza linked to that of a promenade under porticoes in the Roman manner; the Place Dauphine, begun in 1608 on the "Cité," was also then empty of verdure. Nevertheless, it was such innovations—public places growing out of the older palace-court designs—that placed France rather than Italy at the head of urban planning in this period.

And here Tunnard may have disclosed the embryo of the boulevard and cited its very conception—

---

[3]Excerpts from "The Leaf and the Stone" by Christopher Tunnard (copyright 1951 Charles Scribner's Sons) and used by permission of Charles Scribner's Sons from *The City of Man*.

Now came two inventions which slowly began to change the aspect of the city. One, a facility for sport of popular character, was the "mail," of which there were several in seventeenth-century Paris. The game was a species of croquet, played with a ball, mallet and wickets, and the courts, lying along the ramparts of the river, were always treed. The conditions of the 1597 lease for the land of two of the earliest, along the ramparts between the St. Honoré and St. Denis gates, stipulated that the allées were to be planted with elms having branches no lower than ten feet above the ground. By 1605 another long court had been made by the river near the Arsenal, and by the end of Henri IV's reign there was a circle of green under the ramparts from the river to the Bastille.

The other invention, much more important, was a form of promenade known as the "cours"—a word perhaps deriving from the Italian "corso." "Le Cours," wrote Sauval, "is a new word and a new thing, invented by Marie de Medicis. Before her regency there was no other way of taking the air save on foot and in gardens, but she introduced the habit of promenading "en carosse"* in the cool hours of the evening. To do this she planted allées of trees on the edge of the Seine, to the west of the Tuileries gardens." Actually, there had been earlier "cours," the difference being that the new Cours-la-Reine was planted. Four rows of elms enclosed a main allée and two side promenades, and there was a monumental gateway at either end. Although more fashionable than its forerunners, the Cours-la-Reine was frequented by the bourgeoisie of Paris also; it was in use forty years before the construction of the Parisian boulevards.

In highlighting his topic, "The Leaf and the Stone," and their adaptations to the city plan, Tunnard now clearly states the functional origin of the boulevard or the grand street:

This, then is the beginning of the marriage of nature with the urban complex—a union arranged by the French, as Sitte remarks, to suit their philosophy of human control in all things. We should remember, however, that the new city planning which was just appearing was based on social usage. The green allée was introduced not as decoration but as function; the "cours" and the "mail" were not tree-decorated avenues but recreation areas. The tree-lined avenue for traffic does not appear until the reign of Louis XIV, who, prompted by his planner-minister Colbert, laid out in 1670 on the site of Etienne Marcel's crumbling fortifications a boulevard connecting the quarter of the Bastille with that of the Madeleine—"to serve in all its length as a promenade," to quote from the official bulletin.

ENGLAND DEVELOPS NEW CONCEPT

By the latter part of the eighteenth century, England developed a park and garden character of its own, which in turn influenced the Continent

*The small horse-drawn carriage known as "carosse" may still be seen in Montreal and Quebec.

of Europe. In the time of Charles II of England, after many years of puritanical reign, the elaborate formalities of Continental Europe found very little appeal in England. Besides, the English were more active than the people of southern countries and preferred greater spaces for exercise. Their gardens assumed the appearance of informal walks and less formal plantings. Grass walks were developed and greens were provided for bowling. The bowling-green of England became the "boulingrin" of France where it gradually came to mean a sunken piece of grass which formed the center of a part of the garden.

By the last half of the eighteenth century, English estates were being developed in this entirely informal manner with natural landscapes, native shrubs, and trees being the essence of that sort of scheme. This was the era that witnessed the great ascendency of the common man which accelerated the trend of this type of design. In fact, it was during this period that true "people's parks" first came into existence. One must keep in mind that the American Revolution had taken place along with the French Revolution, and the great republican movement was in evidence all over Europe, including England. Our *A History of Garden Art* may well be quoted at this point to summarize the park situation as of the nineteenth century—

In the course of the nineteenth century it came about that princely gardens lost the special interest which attaches to the best models. Public gardens, which grew ever more important, and being every man's property alike, captured all hearts and all eyes, took their place. In the course of our history we have over and over again met with public gardens in towns, where all the people could go. When the Greek polis became democratic, the first real city park found its way into the gymnasium. Cimon embellished places like the agora with shady trees. In towns like Antioch and Alexandria, we have seen how Hellenistic cities developed in a modern spirit; they took over their inheritance from Greece and then extended it to a size and magnificence truly Oriental. In Rome the emperors were careful that round the narrow crowded dwellings of the townsfolk, free spaces for recreation should be provided in a belt of gardens and beautiful grounds. The development of the public garden took a different direction in the Middle Ages. No doubt the burghers found open walks in the gardens of the guild before the town gates, but they did not need them much, as the pasture-lands were so near at hand. Afterwards, in the days of the Italian Renaissance, the fine private gardens of the gentlefolk came into existence, and it became a point of honor to open them to the public. Travelers from northern countries, where the feeling of the Renaissance was not so fully active among the townsfolk as it was in Italy, and the love of private possessions was much stronger, recognized this with surprise, noting in Rome, above all other places, what they considered the liberality and magnanimity of the rich. It is seldom indeed that we hear of hospitality being extended to all comers in the patrician gardens of the great towns of the North, as it was in the Roman gardens of

Montaigne's day. However, northern princes became more and more imbued with the new spirit in the seventeenth and eighteenth centuries. Whenever possible the smaller princes made their residence in garden cities, and most of the parks were thrown open to all their subjects. The people were not, however, at home there—not the real masters. True, there were not many places where an inscription was put on the front gate threatening common people with a cudgelling if they presumed to sit down on a seat where some noble visitor wished to sit; but this was actually done at the entrance to the Herrenhausen garden; and particular gardens were often closed at the owner's pleasure. In Paris, for example, places which the people had supposed to be theirs by right were suddenly closed to them by some caprice of the actual owner. Thus, in 1781, the Duc de Chartres closed the Palais Royale Garden, which had been open ever since it was founded by Richelieu. In 1650, Sauval writes of the Luxembourg Garden, "It is often open and often closed, just as it may please the prince who is living at the castle."

The Duchesse de Berri had all the doors but one blocked up, so that she might be undisturbed at her gay parties.

In England, Queen Caroline, intelligent though she was, held the views of the despotic little court which she came from, and had the fancy to shut up Kensington Gardens. She inquired of Walpole, who was at that time her Minister, what it would cost, to which he gave the significant reply, "Only three crowns." In London the great parks were the property of the Crown, though in the eighteenth century they were completely given up to the use of the people. . . . By the middle of the nineteenth century, London seemed to set an unrivaled example in the size and beauty of these parks. A total area of 1,200 acres was covered by Kensington Gardens and Hyde Park, with the green park and St. James' adjoining, and Regent's Park on the north. But Paris also was very well off with the Tuileries Garden, the Champs Elysees, the Palais Royale, and the Parc Monceau on the right bank of the Seine, and the Jardin des Plantes and the Luxembourg on the left. In both towns the parks were Crown property.

In 1852, Paris took over the Bois de Boulogne from the Crown, on the understanding that in the next four years two million francs were to be expended on improvements. Many changes had the Bois seen since in 1528 Francis I erected the grand Chateau de Boulogne in the middle of the wood, since Henry II had put a wall around it to make a hunting-park, and since Margaret of Navarre had built the charming little castle of Muette. Louis XIV had had the wood pierced by wide avenues, with crosses at the intersection. The Revolution made its home there in terrible fashion. . . . [Later it was completely redesigned in confessed imitation of the parks of London.]

Paris intended to have parks at all four corners of the town. On the south, Monsouris was added. The Bois de Vincennes was restored, for the park attached to the ancient royal castle had come into the possession of the town.

In London the royal parks, great as they were, soon had to be added to. More and more thought and care were given to the subject, especially with a view to providing parks, great or small, for the districts east and south of the Thames, which hitherto had been much neglected. Victoria Park and Battersea Park were the largest, but a considerable number of smaller ones were added to these. A few figures will show how London was feeling the need of parks and was trying to meet it: in 1889 the whole area of town gardens and ornamental grounds, with the exception of royal parks, was 2,656 acres, whereas in 1898 it was 3,665 acres.

A peculiar system prevailed in the case of certain ornamental plots. Originally the so-called London squares were semi-private gardens to which nobody had the right of entrance except the people who lived around them.* For this reason they were generally enclosed in some way. There were hedges or at least bushes cutting them off from the streets; and within there was a garden of the picturesque type laid out with paths, groups of trees and shrubs, and even a small lake. There might also be a couple of carpet-beds on the lawn as the chief decoration. In many cases, however, the private character of the places was lost, passersby could go in, and the places were treated as ornamental appendages to the street. Paris adopted the name "square" as well as the style of laying out, and Alphand in particular planned a great many of these.

Germany did not hold aloof from the movement for making parks in the towns, and one of the smaller towns, Magdeburg, had the honor of being the first to come forward. As early as 1824 Lenne was commissioned to lay out a public park there. He replied in a letter that plainly shows how unusual this was: "It is nothing new to me that princes and wealthy private persons should spend large sums on the beautiful art of the garden. But an undertaking of this kind, which from a rough computation will cost, exclusive of buildings, no less a sum than $18,000, undertaken by the town authorities, is the first example I have ever encountered in the whole of my life as an artist." Berlin could not lag behind. At the centenary festival of Frederick the Great's succession, the town council at Berlin resolved to lay out a People's Park, to be called Friedrichshain, on the eastern side of the city. No happier occasion for an inaugurating of a town garden could have been found. It was a way of showing homage and gratitude to the creator of Sans Souci, who loved gardens, and also a proud demonstration of the growing spirit of citizenship, which now felt prepared to take out of the hands of royalty the ornamentation and the hygiene of the towns. But the Crown made a presentation to the people at the same time, handing over the garden for wild animals as a public park.

SUMMARY—PARKS IN THE OLD WORLD

Luise Gothein has traced the history of parks only as parks reflected the history of garden art which was her principal concern. To her parks were places where garden art developed rather than places where recreation inspired their beginning. To be sure, she knew parks were for recreation, but

*Note: There were some in America, too.

to her this meant a limited type such as that which comes from appreciation of art—not universal recreation.

Tunnard was interested in an art form but more particularly of an art form that was an integral part of the city plan. He too was aware of parks as a locale for recreation, but, again, recreation in a restricted sense.

Costain was reporting history and a part of history was what people did for recreation especially during leisure hours. Places were incidental.

However the feeling is developed that the study of parks up to this point has become a study of the history of how a natural resource was developed for human use with only incidental attention given to the reason for developing that resource in the first place. It was not until well into the twentieth century that the study of recreation became high-lighted as the motivation for park development.

PARKS IN AMERICA

The most widely known of the pioneers of park development in the United States was Frederick Law Olmsted, Sr., born in Hartford, Connecticut on April 26, 1822. His professional papers are published in two volumes titled *Forty Years of Landscape Architecture*, edited by Frederick Law Olmsted, Jr. and Theodora Kimball, published in 1928 by G. P. Putnam's Sons (Knicker-bocker Press) of New York, copyright by Frederick Law Olmsted. The following quotation begins on page 14 of Volume II.[4]

In America, as abroad, the municipal park was a late development. In the New England colonies the traditional largely utilitarian type of public ground known in the old country appeared again spontaneously in the new. Boston set aside a common as early as 1634, and in 1640 protected it from future diminution. In 1738 its improvement began in recognition of its long use as a recreation ground. The Lower Green at Newburyport is drawn out on the most ancient plat of the Old Town. Rowley Common was acquired about 1670 (by exchange of land) as a training field. All through Massachusetts, Connecticut, and New Hampshire numerous examples still exist of more or less beautiful village greens, of various origins, and in various states of preservation or retrogression from their original sizes and forms. But these commons were probably seldom, if ever, set aside by the colonists as any part of a conscious town planning scheme or predominantly for recreation.

In two of the English proprietary colonies, however, we find the same intelligent attention to the town of the future which the Spanish King and his advisors had shown in regard to their settlements in the New World. William Penn assigned five open squares in the plan for

---

[4]Reprinted by permission of G. P. Putnam's Sons from *Forty Years of Landscape Architecture,* edited by Frederick Law Olmsted, Jr., and Theodora Kimball. Copyright 1928 by Frederick Law Olmsted, Jr.

Philadelphia, drafted in 1682 by his Surveyor-General, Thomas Holme. . . .

General James Oglethorpe went much further in his plans for the principal city of the ideal colony of Georgia in 1733. Mr. Robert Wright thus describes the settlement of Savannah—

"Although the first settlers were but 120 in number, Oglethorpe thought of those who were to come after them, and their descendants. Acting on the motto of the Trustees, 'Not for themselves, but for others,' his imagination depicted a populous city, with a large square for markets and other public purposes in every quarter, wide and regular streets crossing each other at right angles and shaded by rows of noble trees. . . . Even in his own lifetime, his expectations were in a great degree realized, but not so completely as afterwards."

General Oglethorpe also had many of the fine forest trees spared when the site for the town was cleared.

When the proprietor re-visited his colony in 1736 he found substantial progress made in the carrying out of his plan: the streets were wide, the squares had been left, and each freeholder, besides his own town plot, had five acres outside the Common, to serve as garden and orchard. Oglethorpe was greatly pleased by the Public Gardens, which comprised ten acres of undulating ground in a delightful situation near the river. There is a charming description of this garden as he saw it in 1736 contained in Mr. Wright's *Memoir*.

A facsimile of the original plan for Savannah shows no less than twenty-four of the small squares and open spaces in addition to the Public Garden and Common. So generous a provision for the future needs has hardly a parallel in the early history of town planning. It is greatly to the credit of Savannah that a hundred and fifty years later when many cities were conspicuously lacking in public grounds, she had thirty-three acres in twenty-three public places, besides a ten-acre park and a twenty-acre parade ground.

When Major L'Enfant drew up the plan for the Federal City under the guidance of Washington and Jefferson, in 1791, again there was a vision of a future city with stately parks and pleasure gardens. The plan shows fifteen squares, intended to be developed by the fifteen states, a grand cascade, a public walk, grand avenues, a President's park, and so on. In the bustle and haste of a young democracy's super-abounding growth, many features of this generous plan for Washington were forgotten; and although some little attempt at park development was made in Downing's day, it was not until 1900 that the plan was rescued and given new life.

The Dutch colony of New Amsterdam was not unlike the New England colonies in their unthinking neglect of the future. The houses in old New York were built close together, the streets were narrow, and scarcely any open space was left in the oldest part of the town. One small place called the Bowling Green was kept free of buildings, its use having been granted since 1732 to various specified persons in consideration of its upkeep; and in the upper part of the settlement a rather extensive waste of land called "The Fields" (of which a part is now City Hall Park) had been used as a common from early days. No attempt had been made to improve this land or the pond it contained and various encroachments gradually decreased its size.

Such was the situation in New York at the beginning of the Republican period. If parks were ever to be provided for the people of a future great metropolis, it would not be through the preservation of legacies from early colonial days but by some conscious effort of a democratic body of citizens to meet a proven need.

LARGE PARKS ADVOCATED

It is not to be presumed that the above enumeration of public spaces in American cities was complete. For instance, Chicago had its park at the old Fort Dearborn site in 1839. Nevertheless, the picture presented is accurate enough to indicate the situation in America when large public parks were being advocated. The first of these, and the most important for a long time, was Central Park in New York. It is particularly significant because the philosophy on which it was based became the dominant influence in the design of the many large parks and parkway systems which were established in the latter part of the nineteenth and early twentieth centuries. And it might be added that later this movement in America outstripped that of the rest of the world in its various aspects. It is therefore desirable to consider the New York situation somewhat in detail. We quote from a letter printed in the *New York Packet* of August 15, 1785, a portion of a letter to the Mayor and Aldermen of the City of New York*—

> ... It is a very general complaint that there is not in this great city, nor in its environs, any one proper spot, where its numerous inhabitants can enjoy, with convenience, the exercise that is necessary for health and amusement.

After the letter goes on to say that some certain areas are provided in European cities, we have this paragraph—

> The size and consequence that this town must one day arrive at, ought strongly to impress the necessity of attending to this object, as well from a desire to contribute to the comfort and health of the inhabitants, as from the propriety of adding to the public ornaments of the city.

In 1807, the Commissioners of Streets and Roads were appointed, and in 1811, they submitted their plan for Manhattan Island. In it, they provided for "seven squares or places and a Parade Ground extending from 23rd Street to 34th Street and from Third Avenue to Seventh Avenue, these eight pieces of ground totaling about 450 acres." In their report, they said that few open spaces were now available, that they couldn't provide much

---

*Much of what follows was gleaned from *Forty Years of Landscape Architecture* as were the direct quotations.

more, and besides Manhattan Island was pretty well situated and probably wouldn't need to have as many open spaces as other locations, especially since the land cost was so great. Subsequently the idea of the Parade Ground was abandoned and by 1838, the area of the remaining squares had been reduced to less than 120 acres. Adding the Park (City Hall) and the Battery, both of which totaled 20 acres, and Washington Square and a small downtown triangle and enclosed residential parks, brought the total up to about 170 acres. However, by 1853 when the Act was passed authorizing the acquirement of Central Park, this total had been reduced to 117 acres.

In the early nineteenth century, there were a number of popular pleasure gardens in New York City, but these gradually gave way to buildings, and by 1855, there were none left. Then, quoting from page 21 of Olmsted—

> Other places of outdoor resort were the rural cemeteries rapidly springing up, following the tremendous popularity of Mt. Auburn near Boston, the first rural cemetery (1831) to be provided in America. Greenwood Cemetery had been laid out in New York, described by Downing in 1849 as "grand, dignified, and park-like." He estimated that something like sixty thousand people must have visited it in a season, many of these for the pleasures of its foliage and lawns. Lacking public gardens—he even went on to suggest—privately managed gardens might be laid out on the same plan as rural cemeteries, the proceeds of admission fees providing for their upkeep.

CENTRAL PARK, NEW YORK, IS ESTABLISHED

William Cullen Bryant seems to have been the first advocate of a public park for the central part of Manhattan. As early as 1836, he had discussed it with his family and after a trip to Europe in 1845, he became a very vocal advocate of such a park. By 1848, Andrew Jackson Downing, in his *Horticulturist*, was discussing public parks and gardens, and after his trip to Europe and experience in the London gardens and parks of 1850, he also became more vocal than ever.

It was on April 5, 1851, that Mayor Kingland (Ambrose C.) sent a favorable message to the Common Council. From then on there were the usual arguments pro and con, and indecisions as to ultimate locations, etc., but from 1853 to 1856 acquisition of the land was in actual progress.

Prior to the passage of any legislation for the government of the park, the Common Council of New York adopted an ordinance on May 19, 1856, giving the control and management to a Board of Commissioners consisting of the Mayor and Street Commissioner, to be termed "Commissioners of the Central Park." These Commissioners added to their number certain well-known citizens, and among them we find that Washington Irving was one member and was actually elected President. Their first Chief Engineer was Egbert L. Viele, a graduate of West Point, who later served in the Civil War, but was now in private consulting practice. Viele prepared a plan for the improvement of Central Park which was adopted by the Commissioners, and what little work was accomplished in the next year or two was done according to this plan. However, in 1857 the legislature passed an Act taking control of the park away from the city government and vesting it in so-called nonpartisan commissioners, and while Viele was reappointed Chief Engineer, it was the new board that advertised for plans for the laying out of the park and offered premiums for the four best. The political pot was boiling in those days and either in spite of it or on account of it, in 1857 Frederick Law Olmsted was appointed Superintendent of the park under the Chief Engineer. It is interesting to note that Mr. Olmsted believes that the signature of Washington Irving on his letter of application (Irving's was only one of many signatures, but Olmsted believes that his was the most potent) was the deciding factor in his obtaining the position.

OLMSTED AND VAUX PLAN CENTRAL PARK

It was while Mr. Olmsted was Superintendent of the park that Mr. Calvert Vaux asked him to collaborate in submitting a design for the park. Mr. Olmsted first declined, but after his superior, Mr. Viele, rather contemptuously indicated indifference, presumably on the ground that Olmsted wouldn't win it anyway, Olmsted agreed to collaborate with Vaux. It was their design known as "Greensward" which was awarded the top prize of $2,000. This was in the latter part of April 1858.

In the descriptive report submitted by Olmsted and Vaux, they called attention to the central motive back of the design by asking the question, why was such a large area set aside in the area of Manhattan? Their analysis was that some day in the future, all of Manhattan would be laid out in streets, and buildings would be placed on the intervening property; and that it would be impossible, except occasionally and at long intervals, for the inhabitants to obtain any other sort of view or encounter any surroundings other than this, were it not for such a park. In other words, the park should not only be an immunity from urban conditions, but in the laying out of its landscape features should provide the antithesis of urban conditions.

They point out that the hundreds of thousands of tired workers, who have no opportunity to spend their summers in the country, should be supplied with some semblance within the limits of the park. Their design, therefore, was based upon the fact that this bit of rural scenery ought to be featured within the park, and in their designs they had provided for the general outline to be pretty well wooded, so that one would necessarily get that effect from the inside. Since there were at least four crossings in the park for general traffic purposes, it was convenient to vary the type of landscape within these four areas, so that in effect the park seemed larger than it otherwise would have appeared. They also introduced structures for traffic separation, so that persons could walk, ride horseback, go in carriages, or escape the ordinary city traffic streets crosswise, without coming together or crossing at the same elevation.

In their rules for the competition, the Commissioners had already stipulated that there was to be a parade ground of from 20 to 40 acres, that there should be three playgrounds of from 3 to 10 acres each, that sites were to be reserved for a future hall for exhibitions and concerts, a principal fountain, a prospect tower, and a flower garden of from 2 to 3 acres in extent. All of these provisions were of course adhered to in the plan by Olmsted.

CENTRAL PARK ACTIVITIES AND OTHER VALUES

This being the first large public park in the United States, the influence of this concept on future designs of similar parks in other municipalities was quite apparent. How well did this park provide for the "comfort and health of the inhabitants" and act as an "ornament to the city," as the previously quoted *New York Packet* had suggested!

On page 65 of *Forty Years of Landscape Architecture—Central Park 1853-1895* it is noted—

As early as December 29, 1858, the first skating was permitted in the Park,—a sport then little practiced by the citizens.

In reviewing the tremendous growth of skating as a popular diversion, the Commissioners reported in 1866—

During the first season a scanty supply of commonplace American skates, with a few old-fashioned pairs of English manufacture, were all that could be discovered in the shop-windows. This matter of skating and the necessary implements had been fairly left to private enterprise from time immemorial, and the results showed that the varieties of skates were few and poor and the varieties of skaters still fewer and poorer.

A single year, however, developed a marked improvement. Ice there had always been; but ice preserved day after day in good order and order preserved day after day on good ice were attractive novelties, and the tide ... was fairly set in the direction of this health-giving amusement.

It is quite evident from what follows that skating in Central Park was probably the original incentive for the growing popularity of winter sports. One can readily understand why Currier and Ives used "Skating in Central Park" as one of their pictorial themes.

Saturday band concerts were instituted in July 1859, and thereafter given weekly during long summer seasons.

Here is a report of 1863—

Few landscapes present more attractive features than that of the Park on a music day. Thousands of brilliant equippages throng the drives. The waters of the Lake are studded with gaily-colored pleasure boats, appearing now and then in striking contrast with the green foliage that fringes its banks; the waterfowl float proudly over its surface; children play on the lawns; throngs of visitors from divers climes move among the trees, whose leaves, fanned with the soft lays of the music, wave silent approval; all seems full of life and enjoyment; and as some familiar strain breathes a sweet influence around, the whole appears like some enchanted scene.

On page 67 of Olmsted we read—

The recreations of driving and riding were almost immediately stimulated by the opening of the Park roads. No such good pavements had been known before and comparatively few carriages had been kept for pleasure driving, and still fewer horses for town riding.

It was suggested in another report that—

There is already many times as much pleasure driving as there was five years ago.

All this points up to the fact that Central Park was beginning to be a complete success from both scenic and recreational standpoints.

As to attendance in the park, we find on page 95 that—

During 1871 the number of visits to the park was over ten million, an average of about 30,000 per day. Actually the average number of visitors on the days other than Sundays, holidays, and concert days, was about twenty-three thousand, of which about nine thousand came on foot and fourteen thousand in carriages or on horseback. The number of women and girls was estimated to have been in fair weather about forty per cent of all; of children of both sexes when the schools were closed in summer, about forty per cent.

It was also noted thereafter that the weather had greatly affected the attendance—

... for instance, causing it to vary from about a thousand total visitors on an inclement day in winter to one hundred and nine thousand on a fine day in September.

These activities seemed to be carried on—skating in the winter time, carriage visitors, walking through the park, attending band concerts, boating on the lake (this was in 1872-73). The center of population had not reached as far north as Central Park. A report calls to the Commissioners' attention the fact that the park was designed to be the center of a population of about 2,000,000 and attendance was expected to increase when population had reached as far north as that. The center of population was then about two and one-half miles from Central Park.

PUBLIC BUILDINGS AND OTHER PARK ENCROACHMENTS FOUGHT OFF

It will be recalled that the main purpose of Central Park was to provide a rural landscape in the heart of the city. At various times attempts to place public buildings, or to otherwise obstruct this landscape effect, were promoted but for the most part denied. The construction of a speedway in the park was vigorously opposed by the public and fell through. During one of the political upheavals, some park superintendent thought it necessary to trim the border trees of the park so that the frequenters of the park could see the adjacent buildings. This was greatly decried by Olmsted and Vaux, but in later years, it became evident even to Olmsted that the plantings could not hide the adjacent skyscrapers which later came into being.

VALUES OF CENTRAL PARK CITED

In this Volume, II, the *Daily Press* and various reports are quoted to indicate the acceptance of the park idea in New York. Before the actual construction started in 1858, the *Herald* had prophesied that the establishment of the park and its construction would have a very bad effect upon the conduct of the people, and expected that it would be frequented mostly by rowdies. Some years after the park was established found the *Herald* on the other side of the fence. Through it and through others, we then learn that the presence of a park had a tendency to diminish crime.

On page 171, we quote—

At three or four points in the midst of the Park, beer, wine and cider are sold with other refreshments to visitors, not at bars, but served at tables where men sit in company with women. Whatever harm may have resulted, it has apparently had the good effect of preventing the establishment of drinking-places on the borders of the Park, these not having increased in number since it was opened, as it was originally supposed they would.

Later it was decided that the park had a good effect on the public health, and that many physicians advocated its frequent use. Quoting from page 172, says one—

Where I formerly ordered patients of a certain class to give up their business altogether and go out of town, I now often advise simply moderation, and prescribe a ride in the Park before going to their offices, and again a drive with their families before dinner.

It calls attention to the use of the park by the poor as well as the wealthy. It is reported that patients convalesce much more rapidly in the environment of the park than otherwise. The park had also made New York attractive to visitors and therefore had increased the business of the city.

Finally, it was reported that the investment itself had raised real estate values in its vicinity sufficiently to return increased taxes to the city in an amount greater by far than the actual cost of the project.

It is reported that the establishment of the park gave great impetus to outdoor recreation and cites as examples—skating, both horseback riding and carriage riding, a provision for the instruction of "harmless athletic out-of-door" sports, etc.

CONCEPT OF A "SYSTEM" OF PARKS AND PARKWAYS

On page 188, there appears a statement of the designer's conception of the function of Central Park as part of the city plan. Here it is—

> The dominant and justifying purpose of Central Park was conceived to be that of permanently affording, in the densely populated central portion of an immense metropolis, a means to certain kinds of refreshment of the mind and nerves which most city dwellers greatly need and which they are known to derive in large measure from the enjoyment of suitable scenery.

On page 189, there is discussion of Olmsted's vision of the growth of New York and the fact that Central Park was only one of a series of parks in New York and Brooklyn which would be necessary to meet the needs of a coming metropolis—

> Many references in the Brooklyn and New York reports of the sixties clearly outline in principle a mutually supplementary series of parks and subordinate recreation grounds widely dispersed throughout the metropolitan area and linked together by a system of connecting parkways (including one across the East River by high bridges at Blackwell's Island) of a width, capacity, and scenic quality of which there were then no examples in this country, the whole constituting a recreation service deliberately and comprehensively planned to meet in a well-balanced manner the fairly predictable needs of the entire metropolitan population—a service such as had not previously been envisaged anywhere.

And then it points out that this sort of scheme and plan was never thoroughly sold to the public. However, those in other metropolitan cities know that such a scheme of parks with connecting parkways was actually developed in their municipalities.

Olmsted and Vaux carried on a partnership more or less continuously until 1872, when by mutual consent they separated after a very successful career. However, Olmsted's career continued and he and his firm either designed or were consultants, in the establishment of their parks, to most of the important municipalities of the country. Here are some of the major cities served by this firm:

In the West—San Francisco and Oakland, California.

In the East—Boston, Hartford, and almost all the smaller cities in
Massachusetts; Brooklyn, Buffalo, Poughkeepsie, New York,
and Rochester in New York; Newark, New Jersey; Philadelphia, Pennsylvania; Providence, Rhode Island; Baltimore,
Maryland; Detroit, Michigan; the Capitol grounds at Washington, D.C.; Mount Royal Park at Montreal, Canada; Niagara
Falls State Park, New York (he was quite instrumental in the
establishment of the park on both sides of Niagara Falls).
In the South—Montgomery, Alabama; Atlanta, Georgia; Louisville,
Kentucky; Kansas City, Missouri; Cincinnati, Ohio; Knoxville
and Nashville, Tennessee; Richmond, Virginia.

In some cities, the job undertaken was simply one large park, and in others,
certainly the layout of the entire system. The firm also had great influence on
the design of a number of the estates of this country, perhaps the most
famous ones being the Biltmore Estate at Asheville, North Carolina; a number
of university grounds including that of Leland Stanford at Palo Alto,
California, and Amherst College at Amherst, Massachusetts. Some work also
was done for the State of California at Yosemite and the Mariposa Forest,
both of which are now a part of Yosemite National Park. Olmsted was
landscape architect to the Chicago World's Fair and for the capitol grounds at
Albany, New York.

Letters of comment and visitations too numerous to mention
broadened the influence of Olmsted and his firm to include the greater part
of park work in the last forty years of the nineteenth century. His philosophy
and underlying principles in design therefore give us a real clue to the
philosophy behind the establishment of the large park areas of this country.

OTHER FACTORS IN THE DEVELOPMENT OF PARKS

Even as American cities were establishing their individual parks, as
well as whole park systems after the Olmstedian manner, certain events took
place that were destined to influence the future concept and scope of park
development: the establishment of the first national park, the creation of
metropolitan park systems, and the introduction of the "playground movement."

In 1872 Congress established the first national park in northwestern
Wyoming, known as Yellowstone National Park. (Hot Springs National Park,
limited in scope, was established in 1832.) While this started the federal
government on the road to providing national recreation areas, that road was
too obscure and ill-defined for real notable achievements until after the turn
of the century, and so we shall leave that subject for the time being.

BOSTON SETS PATTERN FOR "METROPOLITAN" PARK SYSTEMS

The attention of park planners was still centered on the cities. The unfortunate city dweller in his confined, unnatural environment needed the peace and quiet that only a natural landscape of inspiring beauty could give. Now, as in ages past, parks were provided in or near a city. When established, Central Park was on the outskirts of the built-up area of New York and only now was it being surrounded by buildings. Boston, already largely built up and surrounded by suburban communities, must necessarily acquire property near the city, but was helpless without a new enabling vehicle. However, in 1892 such legislative authority was provided and thereupon Boston set a pattern, extensively followed in the twentieth century, by the formation of a metropolitan park commission.

CHARLES ELIOT, LANDSCAPE ARCHITECT

This first metropolitan park commission (Boston's) came into being through the efforts of another important pioneer park man. A wealth of material about him is to be found in a book entitled *Charles Eliot, Landscape Architect* published by Houghton, Mifflin and Company in 1903.

The book on Charles Eliot describes quite in detail much of Eliot's early life and his professional career, and reproduces many of his papers and official reports. It is interesting to learn that when he established himself as a landscape architect in his own business (1886), it was necessary for him to describe quite in detail just what kind of service he would render. It was consultation and planning, and exclusively professional in every way. He did no constructing; he was party to no contracts for the furnishing of material; his services were entirely of a personal nature to his own client.

THE BEGINNING OF THE BOSTON METROPOLITAN PARK SYSTEM—AND OTHERS

Clients were not numerous in the beginning, which left time for Eliot to expend his energies in advocating parks and open spaces at every opportunity. At one time he suggested the desirability of extensive, government-owned tracts along the entire shore of southern Maine, so as to preserve much of the rugged scenery and interesting coastline from human depredation. He called particular attention to the environs of Boston and the continuous loss of readily accessible landscape areas through the construction of homes and man-made appurtenances. He feared that in due time none of these previous rural scenes would be left to an ever increasing population of cities and suburbs. Eliot was instrumental in establishing a Board of Trustees "capable of acquiring and holding, for the benefit of the public, beautiful and historical places in Massachusetts." The Board did acquire some spots, but the limitations imposed through having only private financial support rendered it imperative that something further be done. Members of the park commissions of Boston and of the various suburban communities were called together for various meetings on problems of mutual interest.

Such a meeting was held on December 16, 1891, in the office of the Boston Park Commission where a number of inspiring speeches were made by some very prominent individuals. Charles Eliot was Secretary of the meeting. Petitions to the General Court and to the legislature followed, resulting in the establishment of a Metropolitan Park Commission with the bill signed by the Governor, June 2, 1892, the first in the United States.

Arguments for metropolitan park systems are well known today, but it is interesting to note that the basic reasons have changed but little since 1892. Here is the petition of the meeting of December 16, 1891, sent to the General Court.

> The undersigned petitioners respectfully represent that the sea-shores, the river-banks, the mountain-tops, and almost all the finest parts of the natural scenery of Massachusetts are possessed by private persons, whose private interests often dictate the destruction of said scenery or the exclusion of the public from the enjoyment thereof. In the opinion of the undersigned, the scenes of natural beauty to which the people of the Commonwealth are to-day of right entitled to resort for pleasure and refreshment are both too few in number and too small in area. . . .

Eliot's speech to the legislature, after emphasizing the foregoing, had this to say—

> It has been pointed out that the location of large public reserves should be determined chiefly with reference to the inclusion therein of the finest scenery of each region or district. Now, the park act limits the field of action of our park commissioners to the bounds of their respective towns and cities, while it is self-evident that these boundaries bear no relation to the scenery of the district they divide. Indeed, the boundaries of our towns are very apt to bisect the prettiest passages of scenery, as where the line follows the channel of a river or brook the banks of which are beautiful. In these cases it is at present practically certain that neither town would act to take the banks, for it would be senseless for one to act without the other, and one or the other is almost sure to feel that its burden of expense is out of proportion to the benefit to accrue to it. Under the park act, a board of park commissioners will seldom make open spaces near the boundary of their town or city, even though the best lands for the purpose are to be found there, and even though a dense population needs them there. Under the park act, no park board can take lands outside the arbitrary town boundary, even though a fine site for a park lies adjacent to the boundary near their own center of population, and so remote from the population of the adjacent township that its park board will never want to buy or take the place.

Within a very few years after the Massachusetts Act, New Jersey passed its first regional park Act, providing for county park systems. Pursuant to this Act, Essex County became the first county park system in the United States. Regional park systems, however, increased in number very slowly until about the second decade of the twentieth century.

PARKWAYS

With the coming of large municipal parks in several quarters of the larger cities and the establishment of metropolitan or regional park systems, boulevards and parkways began to receive more adequate attention. It will be recalled that the previously quoted Christopher Tunnard cited the Parisian beginning of the boulevard, which, as he points out, was introduced not as a decoration but as a function—" 'Cours' and the 'Mail' were not tree-decorated avenues but recreation areas." They became grand trafficways in connecting the larger park areas. Now, in the latter part of the nineteenth century, we are witnessing the beginning of the elongated park known as the parkway, and in his discussions concerning the boulevards and parkways of both Boston and the Metropolitan Park Commissions, we find Eliot struggling with a reconciliation of the two functions—that of recreation and as a means of transport. It is not at all certain that he succeeded any better than have numerous others since then.

ACTIVE RECREATION RAISES ITS HEAD
AND POSES PROBLEMS

Individual parks of sizeable area, designed after the Olmstedian principles, were located in the several quadrants of a municipality and connected by a parkway system to make up the typical municipal park system of the early 1900s. Very few of these large park areas contained much in the way of facilities for active recreation, such as ball grounds, tennis courts, etc. While it is true that at the time of its design certain playground areas were set aside in Central Park, New York, and a parade ground was also established, these were indeed but minor features of the general plan.

It was into this environment of passive recreation parks that the demand for active play, the result of the introduction of playgrounds and outdoor gymnasiums, began to usurp certain areas of these larger landscape parks. A distinct conflict arose between the advocates of active play in public grounds or parks, and those disciples of Olmsted and his contemporaries who wanted such areas preserved for the passive recreation of the people. This conflict often led to the establishment of separate recreation commissions in various cities of the country, especially where the acceptance of playgrounds by the existing park authorities was resisted. Playground leaders were recruited largely from those trained in physical education colleges, but with no deep-seated training in landscape architecture or in the art of general park design. On the other hand, the disciples of Olmsted frequently lacked the breadth of understanding to accept the new trend of recreation and to incorporate those demands into suitable designs. At least, that was the situation at first, so that for perhaps the first twenty or twenty-five years of the current century there was often great despoliation of previously well-designed park areas by the intrusion of active recreation facilities, improperly placed and improperly designed, and there were also a great many pretty barren-looking playgrounds established in many neighborhoods of many cities.

The late L. H. Weir, in the introduction to his two-volume *Manual on Parks* published in 1928, summarizes the situation in these words[5] —

THE CHANGING CONCEPTION OF PARKS

During the past twenty-five years the confusion in terminology has become even more marked. The word "park" came to be applied not only to plazas, squares, ovals, triangles, places, monument sites, promenades and public gardens, but to other kinds of properties which functionally were the direct opposite to the "peaceful enjoyment of an idealized rural landscape." Even the great masterpieces of idealized rural landscape created by Olmsted and others of the pioneers in park building had in many instances been transformed from places where "city dwellers could secure the genuine recreation coming from the peaceful enjoyment of an idealized rural landscape," to active recreation areas. Broad, open meadows had been appropriated for golf or baseball diamonds; the swift moving automobile had usurped the pleasant carriage driveway, destroying the restful atmosphere of the area, and in some rare instances even the amusement devices of the commercial amusement park had been permitted entrance. Intown parks had been appropriated either for children's playgrounds or for neighborhood playfields.

Both Eliot and Olmsted recognized that the supreme functional use of parks was for the recreation of the people, but the type of recreation they advocated was of a passive and semi-active kind, the dominant ideal being peaceful enjoyment amid beautiful surroundings of a naturalistic kind. There can be no doubt that this conception was fundamentally sound then, especially as applied to city dwelling people. It is of even greater importance today, as cities have grown larger and the stress and strain of living have become greater. This phase of the teachings of the great early planners should never be lost sight of in all present and future planning of parks. It so happens, however, that the life needs of people which can be expressed in their leisure are far wider than those comprehended in the early conception, and a wide range of active forms of recreation have come to be included.

[5] Reprinted by permission from *Manual on Parks* by L. H. Weir. 2 volumes. Copyright 1928, National Recreation Association, Washington, D.C.

Active Recreation Becomes a Part of Park Planning

Beginning in the eighties with sand courts for children and outdoor gymnasiums in the Charlesbank area of Boston, the so-called "playground movement for children," expanding into the "recreation movement" comprehending all age groups in the two succeeding decades, exerted a most profound effect on the entire pioneer conception of parks and their recreational functions. It was natural that with the expanding idea of recreation, people should turn to the agency then most closely identified with recreation for the facilities and supervisory services which the new movement demanded, and that there should be a strengthening of the feeling which had been growing up that properties then comprehended in existing park systems should be rendering greater dividends in service.

The effect was epochal both in regard to properties and to the functional services of park departments. The new movement for many forms of active recreation changed the functional uses of many existing park properties and at the same time brought into existence a number of new types, such as areas devoted more or less exclusively to playgrounds, playfields, athletic fields, stadiums, neighborhood recreation parks, swimming and boating centers, golf courses and boulevards and parkways. It added to the services of park administrating agencies a series of complex and difficult social problems involved in organizing for the people a wide range of recreational activities of a physical, cultural, social, and civic nature, involving co-operative relationships with other public and private agencies.

This change was not unattended by growing pains. It was not always easy for members of park governing authorities and park administrators deeply versed in the fine old traditions of park technique to absorb and apply the new and larger ideal of the new recreation service. The period from the late nineties to the present time (1926) has been a period of adjustment and development, and this process of adjustment between the old and simple concept of the functional services of parks and park authorities and the new and more complex functions is still going on. On the whole, however, the expanded recreation concept has been accepted by park authorities.

At the end of nearly three-quarters of a century of park development in the United States the term park has come to mean any area of land or water set aside for outdoor recreational purposes, whether it be recreation of a passive or active nature or any of the degrees between those two extremes, and "that the recreation is expected to come in part at least from beauty of appearance."

REEMPHASIS ON NATURAL SCENERY—THE NATIONAL PARK SERVICE

By way of indicating the great acceptance of the importance of natural scenery to the general welfare of people, one must note the great increase in the number of park systems of metropolitan, regional, and state proportions. Up to 1938, only eighty-six county and regional park systems were known. In 1952, certain staff members of the National Park Service estimated that the number now may reach 400. Now all states have a semblance of a park system, most of them quite well developed.

The National Park Service has kept pace with the requirements of a more mobile age. In establishing the National Park Service in 1916, Congress enjoined it "to conserve the scenery, the natural and historic objects, and the wild life," in the national parks and monuments, "and, to provide for enjoyment of the same in such manner and by such means as will leave them unimpaired for the enjoyment of future generations." This has been the objective of most Acts of Congress relating to the National Park Service, even in the establishment of the first national park at Yellowstone in 1872. The Antiquities Act, which antedated the establishment of the National Park Service by eleven years, gave the President authority to designate as national monuments "historic landmarks, historic and prehistoric structures, and other objects of historic or scientific interest" situated on lands owned or controlled by the United States. This idea was enlarged by the Historic Sites Act of 1935 which declared "that it is a national policy to preserve for public use historic sites, buildings and objects of national significance for the inspiration and benefit of the people of the United States." In 1936 the Park, Parkway, and Recreational Area Study Act was passed which placed in the National Park Service responsibility for cooperation with other federal agencies, and with the various states and their political subdivisions, in the planning of their parks, parkways, and recreational areas. Prior to that time (in 1933) the Re-organization Act authorized the President to transfer jurisdiction of all parks and monuments, previously administered by other departments, to the National Park Service.

In consequence of these Acts, the National Park Service has now the definite responsibility of coordinating on a national scale the preservation of scenic and historic sites throughout the country, either through its own efforts or through the cooperation and coordination of other agencies. To this end, hiking trails and parkways have been constructed, extending through scenic areas for hundred of miles, and extensive recreation and resort areas have been established, not only in national parks, but in various areas, acquired through the U.S. Bureau of Reclamation and other agencies of the federal government.

TRENDS IN THE PERIOD 1925 TO 1950

Perhaps it is too soon to summarize the 1925-to-1950 quarter century of municipal parks and recreation with an adequate appraisal of the situation. However, it can be said that the depression years of the thirties (during which the federal and local governments emphasized recreation in both facilities and leadership as suitable "made work" projects), served as a fine demonstration of the value of public recreation. Perhaps for the first time the promotion of active recreation was put to a real test and, generally speaking, was enthusiastically accepted by the people.

The succeeding war years brought a tightening of the belt, both as to public expenditure and as to active participation at home of a large part of our young male population that had gone to war. However, these same men experienced some recreation in the armed forces, and where possible, recreation was properly emphasized. With increased prosperity at the close of the war, and with restrictions on many things still unabated, further significant changes in our social life have taken place. Hours of leisure have increased tremendously; mobility of the people has been greatly extended; reasonably adequate pension plans have caused retirement from active work of many people beyond the age of sixty-five who now take part in recreational activities. Formal courses have appeared for the education of recreational leaders, as well as for park planners. A greater understanding has developed between the objectives of the playground movement and those of the old park planners. In many cities of the country, park and recreation administrations are being combined into one department. The unification of parks and recreation is recognized and is taking place. We seem to be entering an era of the establishment of new standards of recreation opportunities for the people, which will combine the recreation ideas of the Olmstedian era with those of the more recent so-called "playground movement." The design of properties is distinctly changing, so that both beauty and function are properly embodied in a single plan.

1950 TO 1970

The social developments of the 1950s and 1960s were both massive and dramatic, yet they had very little real influence on the basic patterns of the physical recreation resources that were available to previous decades. Local, regional, state, and federal properties, when designed and administered in conformity with altered public requirements, were still adequate to meet the challenge of an ever changing society.

The new challenge was abuse, overuse, and widespread lack of understanding of administrative objectives on the one hand and lack of public needs on the other. A great upsurge in population and affluence in money, leisure time, and mobility, particularly in the youthful segment of the population full of energy, inquisitiveness, and a zest for adventure overflowed available facilities.

These trends were first forecast in the latter part of the 1950 decade. A congressionally authorized committee to inventory outdoor recreation resources, the national Outdoor Recreation Resources Review Commission, submitted its report in 1962—the first overview ever made of regional, state, and federal resources. The urban scene, and the under-twelve-years-of-age segment of the population were not included in the survey. Besides forecasting future attendance trends and citing many other valuable statistics, the ORRRC report resulted in the creation of the Bureau of Outdoor Recreation as a division of the Department of the Interior. It was given the responsibility of coordinating all federal park and recreation activities, thus relieving the National Park Service of that duty which had been a rapidly enlarging function due to the many federal bureaus that were providing recreation resources only as secondary bureau function and the facilities of which were eagerly used by the people. BOR was also responsible for developing a national recreation plan which up to the early 1970 decade was still not ready for publication.

In the meantime, public pressure for more recreation resources in all government levels persuaded Congress to authorize federal financial assistance (usually about 50 per cent of project costs) to states and local subdivisions for acquisition and development of such projects and also increased appropriations for federal projects. This federal aid program was funnelled through BOR for nonurban projects and through the Bureau of Housing and Urban Development (HUD) for urban projects.

The demand for nonurban projects was easier to fulfill than the demand for suitable projects in the crowded cities. The pressure in the cities resulted in an increase in the importance of regional holdings which seemed a proper substitute for the large city park which was more and more losing its original appeal as havens for native scenery. This same sort of pressure for more resources of both the active and scenic variety was felt in state and federal properties of all kinds.

Even though there was a lack of the complete coordination of park and recreation efforts at the Washington level, the above-stated pressures resulted in overuse of the critical areas of national parks, forests, and other federal properties, so there gradually arose a sense of common cause among administrators of federal, state, metropolitan, and city systems. The old idea that national parks and forests had little in common, administratively, with state counterparts and almost none at all with municipal systems began to melt when problems in the heavily used portions of national parks were very like the problems prevalent in the large city parks. Rangers were no longer naturalists, interpreters, and tourist guides; they were called upon to devise recreation programs and often to act as police officers.

Originally, the large city parks of the Olmsted era sought to bring into the urban areas some of the soothing virtues of the natural landscape. City people (and three-fourths of the nation's people are city people) still search for that solace. That objective in any park situation—local or federal—can be attained when enough land is readily available to satisfy an equally urgent demand for active play which is always hard on scenery. Failure to do just that has resulted in the loss of native scenery in many of our large city parks, has altered their original intent and objectives, has caused critical areas in federal holdings to be overused and in some cases ruined.

The first half of the twentieth century proved that city park systems required park land for both native, scenic purposes and for active recreation in all forms. Another quarter century has demonstrated that state and federal holdings are subject to the same phenomena.

The development of the physical resources of a nation depends upon the traditions, customs, and immediate objectives of its people. Parks are included in that category of resources. The traditions, customs, and national objectives are being challenged.

Work as a catharsis for all that was evil, and industrial production as a measure of national progress, both received critical analysis as leisure time increased and as the environment that we all live in seemed to become alarmingly polluted before our very eyes. Quality of life assumed a national concern. The federal government established an agency, the Environmental Protection Administration, to concern itself with environment and gave it enough power to give a "stop-look-and-listen" effect to all resource developments including encroachment on park lands and the construction of industrial facilities that might adversely affect any factor of the environment. Such being the case, there is hope for optimism in future park and recreation development and administration. Unquestionably the seventh decade of the twentieth century is witnessing basic alterations of the conventions and mores of a new generation. American traditions are faltering in direction and quite probably may experience some significant deviation. Any leaning toward a greater moral acceptance of leisure as a co-equal of work among the ingredients of a generally suitable quality of life is bound to give increased emphasis to recreation and the quantity and quality of its required physical resources including parks.

IN SUMMARY

In the 1944 *Recreation Survey of the City of Minneapolis*, L. H. Weir gave the following grouping of natural interests, urges, impulses, and instincts of people which a program of recreation ought to satisfy to provide for the general welfare, or for what the Greeks called "the Good Life":

1. Interest in physical activities that use the fundamental muscle groups of the body—the physical play of children, organized sports and games are examples.

2. The constructive, creative interest giving rise to the many forms of handcrafts and handcraft art activities.

3. The interest in learning of the natural world in which we live and

of the world of people giving rise to the activities of learning in the fields of recreational science and of human society. This is the previous curiosity interest present to a high degree in every child and which should never be atrophied or stultified by any stilted methodology in education.

4. The interest in communication—the use of the mother tongue in conversation, discussion, debating, public speaking, storytelling, writing, etc.

5. Interests in expressing feelings, emotions, and mental concepts in beautiful ways are among the most important in making life enjoyable, rich, and full of satisfactions. This group or fields of activity springing out of this innate sense of beauty expressive of the emotions are sometimes called the "community arts." They include among the major arts:

a. Music in all its forms

b. The graphic and plastic arts

c. Dramatics in their many forms

d. Dancing as an art

e. Use of language as in poetry, literary prose, oratory, dramatics, etc., and many other forms of expression as in landscape architecture, architecture, etc.

(The wide field of handcraft arts or minor fine arts is also included under this category.)

6. The deep-rooted interest people have in mingling together and in doing things together as expressed in group organization of many kinds, through picnics, parties, celebrations, clubs, societies, etc., gives rise to the social activities program of the modern recreation department. It is this interest that is at the basis of all organized society.

7. The fundamental interest and instinct that give rise to the feeling of kinship with a Great Power outside oneself which in turn has given birth to all organized religious institutions of the world is one of the most important in human life.

A review of this historical sketch of parks will readily show that through the ages parks and parkways, both private and public, have encouraged and provided the setting for practically all of the "good life" cited by Mr. Weir. From time immemorial, parks and recreation have been inseparable. Only the emphasis on essential elements has varied from time to time.

Chapter Four

The Country's Physical Recreation Resources — The Cities and Their Suburbs

A GENERAL VIEW OF THE NATION'S RECREATION LAND RESOURCES

As noted under the subheading, "The Tools of Recreation" in Chapter 1, publicly owned land is the essential physical resource base for a recreation service. What, then, is the land situation in the United States? How much is available now for recreation? How much is actually used now? How much is needed? Where are the shortages, if any?

Of the total land area of the United States, estimated at 3,648 million acres,* 234 million acres are devoted to outdoor recreation according to the Outdoor Recreation Resources Review Commission report. Add another million acres for urban parks not included in the ORRRC report, bringing the total to 235 million acres. Major items in the total are as follows in millions of acres: National Park Service, 28; National Forests, 186; Sport

---

*One million acres=1560 square miles or a rectangle 40 miles by 39 miles, roughly, a little less than a 40-mile square.

Fisheries and Wildlife, 10; the balance in the Corps of Engineers, other federal agencies, and in the states. All told about 6 per cent or 7 per cent of the land area of the United States is government-owned land that can be considered to be a recreation resource. There are additional reserves that have not as yet been "discovered" to be of recreational potential.

The amount of land now actually used for recreation is considerably less than the above-stated 235 million acres, probably much less than 50 per cent. Because of various ways of interpretation, classification, and compilation, figures available are no more than estimates, but they are indicative nonetheless. With that in mind, we may estimate land used for recreation by cities and counties to be 1.5 million acres; states at various estimates from 10 to over 30 million, so let's say 20 million; national parks, 28 million; and that part of national forests which is actually devoted to recreation (aside from the very sparse use of all of it), 20 to 30 million; a total of about 80 million acres. Add to this, parts of state forests, wild life refuges, Corp of Engineers holdings and the total will be well over 100 million acres, 40 to 50 percent of available recreation land.*

Against the amount of land available and the 50 per cent of that total which is now used for recreation, how much land is needed? To get some idea of this we must resort to some rule-of-thumb standards, widely used, but known to be little more than general guides. Nevertheless we will use them for general approximation of needs.

For cities, counties, and regional parks in general, 20 acres per thousand population are required. About 150 million people live in metropolitan areas, so the total requirement for recreation land is 3 million acres. This is twice as much land as is now used, hence there is a distinct shortage in this category.

States require 65 acres per thousand population or a total of 13 million acres for a 200 million population. More than twice this amount is available.

The federal requirements, at 150 acres per thousand population, are only 30 million acres whereas many times that amount is now being used to some extent and more is available.

It would appear that while acute shortages seem apparent in the cities and counties, the states and federal government are amply provided for. But the latter assumption is not true for a number of reasons that are not disclosed by a general overview. The large land masses of scenic parks, forests, wild life refuges, and river impoundments are not and cannot be located with reference to large concentrations of population. Even with the great mobility

---

*The statistics for 1973 would vary from those given herein, but the variation would not materially alter the situations as stated.

of people, these resources cannot be intensively used; indeed their real recreational usefulness prohibits intensified use. Much like the introduction of neighborhood parks and community playfields in the Olmstedian scheme of municipal park systems of the late nineteenth and early twentieth century, so in recent years it has become desirable to introduce high and medium density recreation areas into the state and federal systems. This trend toward more active recreation areas, as distinguished from scenic and historic recreation areas, will continue for years to come. These active recreation areas must be located with reference to where people live, an altogether different requirement than existed for the large scenic parks and forests. A maldistribution of areas and perhaps some inefficient use of present areas alters the picture reflected by general statistics alone.

Partly to indicate the density of use mentioned above and partly to complete the national picture of recreation lands, some statistics on use are appropriate. Here again, figures are not at all precise, but are indicative enough to permit a general observation. City parks are used by the equivalent of the population they serve about once a week, state facilities about once in two months, and federal resources about once in six months. This is a descending ratio of attendance of one, to one-eighth, to one-twenty-fifth.

The present situation is such that the demand for adequate recreation satisfaction in metropolitan areas is now pressing enough to cause people to seek that satisfaction elsewhere—the state and federal facilities or at non-tax-supported facilities—provided time, money, and mobility are available to permit those alternatives. Lacking time, money, or mobility the inner city inhabitant is presently poorly served.

THE CITY AND ITS SUBURBS

Of the several park systems mentioned in Chapter 1, the city or municipal system is the first one that will be considered in this text. Incidentally, it is the oldest of the nation's park and recreations systems and, as previously mentioned, the one that is in the most advanced evolutionary stage of park and recreation systems. Particular attention is, therefore, drawn to its discussion which will probably be treated in more detail than the federal and state systems which follow.

A city of 50,000 population and upwards is composed of many features which become more numerous and more varied and more complicated with the increased size of the city. Some of the major items of the city's composition include business and commercial areas, industrial areas, and areas for living such as single family dwellings, duplexes, and apartment buildings. Zoning laws, based upon land use plans, usually designate these various areas in compact groups in an attempt to make the composition of the city more orderly. Residential areas are sometimes shown as being subdivided into neighborhoods, each bounded by such "barriers" as arterial streets, railroads, commercial and industrial districts. The purpose is to facilitate the placement of neighborhood services including neighborhood parks and elementary schools.

Woven into and among the areas set aside for the above purposes are parks to perform various kinds and degrees of service for the recreation of the people. It is obvious that systems of parks are a part of the city plan and hence neither city plan nor park system plan can be advantageously devised without concurrent attention to each. However, it is well to realize that the relative function of parks with regard to the city plan has changed in emphasis over the period of the last seventy-five years.

Before the introduction of active recreation parks (neighborhood and community) into the park systems, and before mammoth trafficways such as freeways and extensive concentrations of monumental commercial structures into the city plan, park and parkway systems embellished the city plan with works of spaciousness, dignity, prestige, and beauty, and hence often characterized the city plan itself.

But over time, economics and practical necessity have placed the greater emphasis on commercially and industrially oriented enterprises overshadowing the more cultural and recreational works of man. How long, or whether this situation will last is open to conjecture, but for the moment the former dominant place of the park system in the city plan is a thing of the past. Manifestation of public appreciation of recreation and culture in imposing public works must find a home in other than purely city systems.

Historically (see Chapter 3) American park systems emerged because of the inadequacies of such public recreation devices as commons, plazas, even cemeteries, and later of such large city parks as Central Park, New York. From these isolated and unrelated recreation grounds, whole systems of parks were built—commons, plazas, large city parks, parkways, neighborhood and community parks, and many variations of these.

It became desirable to classify as to purpose and content these components of such a possible park and recreation system and to establish standards of size and content of each class. In today's difficult planning situations professional planners have so often encountered wide variations from nationally publicized standards, have so often experienced complications in applying those standards among American cities, that some are inclined to throw up their hands in frustration and say "Why attempt standards? Why not just custom tailor each project according to our good planning sense."

We should custom tailor each park to fit the characteristics of the population it serves, but to do so without regard to a city-wide scheme of park classification would, indeed, be a step backward. That is about the way park systems were planned in the past; and that is one important reason why so many are now deficient in one or more categories. It is also a possible reason why our cities are now having to cope with such difficult planning situations. In spite of the variations in both standards and classifications, and in spite of the frustrations in applications it remains true that an analysis of or planning of, or administering of a system of parks without reference to some rather definite goals and limiting guidelines is a process of shifting objectives. A system of classification and standards is a must for the orderly administration of a park and recreation system in spite of its frustrations.

CLASSIFICATION AND STANDARDS

A. As a Means of Identification.

When parks have been classified in any given situation, the expression "neighborhood park," for example, brings to the mind's eye a picture of a definite thing to all people familiar with that system of classification. Communication has been firmly established. There is small chance of misunderstanding. How cumbersome it would be to have to describe in detail what is meant by "neighborhood park." How easy it is then for intelligent communication to break down.

B. As a Means of Analysis and Comparison.

Comparing one's park system with those of other cities is a constant practice of park administrators as well as of citizens' groups of taxpayers. Where do we stand? Are we above or below the average? If nationally accepted standards are available, comparison of our city with these standards is most significant; hence the desirability of having a set of classifications and standards that is as close to nationally accepted standards as possible.

C. As an Essential to Planning.

The planning of individual parks and of a whole system of parks could not be done in any sort of orderly way without assigning to each park a function, size limitation, radius of service or influence, and a general listing of facilities. There are still other matters which have to be considered in the planning process but without knowing the class which a given park is in, and hence what its purpose and general character is, the utility of the finished product is bound to be of low efficiency. Without due consideration for class, a system could be planned in a wholly unbalanced manner, e.g., all community playfields or none at all. Recreation service would be entirely at "sixes and sevens." A good system of classification and standards enables a whole system of parks to be planned in a balanced way for uniform and all-inclusive recreation service. All sections of the city can be properly served and all age groups and classes of citizens impartially provided for.

D. In the Formulation of Administrative Policies.

When parks are classified, the function of each is determined. It is planned accordingly and a feature of the plan is that its use in that particular instance is fixed and *noted* taking into account the character of recreation service (highly organized or entirely unorganized) intended for it. Noted, too, is the kind of maintenance that each of the various areas is to receive and what variations may be permitted in the future.

Maintenance, function, public use having been analyzed and noted on the plans or in text accompanying plans, a policy statement on these matters is now before the administrator. Reference to this statement will forestall impulsive decisions "off the cuff" or "off the top of the head" in the case of public use, policing, and the introduction of incompatible or inconsistent structures, devices, or uses. This information contained in a classification and standards system is an important feature for the adoption of such a system.

A case in point might be one in which persistent overuse has made satisfactory maintenance impossible. Such a situation often develops before the eyes of the administrator when he has made no reference to classification of the park and the policy statement that may accompany his plan. That policy statement could have named a maximum attendance per acre, as well as a notation as to the character of use, made as a result of previous careful analysis.

The resultant overuse and misuse, which take place gradually over a period of time, occur because both classification and the application of standards have not been periodically reviewed. If they had been reviewed, uses inconsistent with the park class and overuse would not have happened, because additional and suitable additions to park property would have been made elsewhere. At least the administrator would have had the firm basis for a concerted appeal for relief if he had used his classification and standards as a basis for his appeal.

It can be argued that in cases such as the foregoing, other suitable park lands are not obtainable. More often, the administrator permits the unfortunate situation to develop without recognition of what the consequences may be.

That situation would not happen to a successful Texas rancher. He knows that overgrazing results in poor cattle and worn out land which takes precious time and loss of production to recoup. His simple remedies are (1) reduce the herd, or (2) get more pasture land. Why can't park administrators advocate similar courses?

E. Factors That Complicate Application:

1. The shape and size of neighborhoods as bounded by such "barriers" as freeways and arterial streets, industrial districts, railroads, etc., are not of uniform size or of uniform shape; any neighborhood may be a half mile wide and a mile long instead of a nice three-fourth mile or mile square; it may be irregular in outline; it may contain the standard one square mile or only a small fraction of that. These situations must be studied for a suitable facility to serve the day-to-day needs of that particular neighborhood.

This search for substitutes requires a close examination of the existence of available school grounds, YMCA, and other buildings and open spaces for recreation use. Many churches now contain considerable indoor recreation facilities. Makeshift areas of the playlot size or small one-or-two acre playgrounds may have to be resorted to. Other possibilities will occur to an imaginative person.

2. School districts made up of several individual pockets, some quite remote from the school, can solve their peculiar resident problems by buses. Parks are not so equipped—hence school-park developments are not always possible, which often complicates recreation service to small neighborhoods.

3. Topographic features such as lakes, streams, steep hills, ravines, etc., break up the normal neighborhood pattern.

4. Abnormal age group patterns (predominately old or predominately young) affect the selection of appropriate recreation service. So, too, may ethnic, racial, and social groupings in concentrated patterns.

Population characteristics are not permanent neighborhood attributes; they change as often as every decade. The *suitability* of the neighborhood for certain classes of people is a similar factor but not quite the same. An eye to *suitability* is a more stable factor. Parks are often planned to fit the characteristics of the population of the neighborhood; the reverse has also been the frequent case, where the characteristics of the people to be served were influenced by the kind of park that was built. Parks often preceded the people. Many new private housing developments are made before any houses and lots are sold, and so the kind of people that inhabit the new subdivision is the kind that like the recreation and other facilities that are offered. The plan determines the kind of people; the people do not determine the kind of park, except after they move in, when it is often too late to do much altering.

5. Density of population has an overwhelming affect on the application of standards. The standards given in the text, page 72, will fit neighborhoods and communities having from five to as much as ten thousand people per square mile. They will not fit where the population density is much less or much more than that.

A great deal of observation, study, and experimentation still needs to be done on the total affect of this factor. In whatever direction such studies may take us, it would appear that the mind must be kept on the requirements of neighborhood, the day-to-day, hour-to-hour, short-period use by the neighborhood people whatever characteristics they may have—old or young, rich or poor, black or white. That "close to home" service is paramount, and if it takes facilities other than our standardized neighborhood park, suitable modifications must be made. The same goes for the study of a community (three to five) of neighborhoods.

6. The political organization of large metropolitan complexes consisting of a central city and numerous suburban satellites often precludes the application of the standards. The text has pointed out that two or more contiguous villages may jointly have sufficient population to justify large city parks, to name one example, but acting independently their populations do not justify it.

These and similar difficulties, compounded by jealous and chauvinistic attitudes, preclude sensible park and recreation development in the suburbs. The same is true for many other services necessary to an urban population; the whole problem of metropolitan political organization has assumed primary importance in those regions of the United States and Canada where suburban entities are a part of the metropolitan urban complex—and that includes most of the continent.

Experiments are being tried. In some large city complexes, the county is emerging as the metropolitan authority. Toronto, Canada, and others have created metropolitan authorities to assume those functions which are metropolitan in nature: water supply, sewage disposal, etc. In such instances, those classes of parks which are above the neighborhood and community playfield classes are governed by the Metro. The question of what predominant pattern of metropolitan government will ultimately be adopted in this country is still to be answered.

F. Future Trends:

In addition to the previously mentioned factors that affect the precise application of classifications and standards there are some future developments whose trends are now discernible that may have an effect on the classification and standards of the future. Some of these are:

1. *The redevelopment of the central parts of our cities.* In this process more open space is bound to result. Some open space will be in public parks. What kind? So-called "rest parks," "ornamental parks," parks for occasional exhibition or attraction (skating act, visiting musical organizations, a famed "personality," etc.)? We may even spawn a new class of park.

2. *Redevelopment of all or a large part of a city.* This possibility is not as remote as was once thought. There are small towns (10,000 to 25,000

population) and even larger sections of large cities which are old, obsolete, and yet healthy and apparently permanently important to a degree that could qualify under an expanded program of redevelopment. Such a situation might warrant a reexamination of present classification and standards.

3. *A solution to metropolitan political organization.* This has been discussed previously.

4. *"Surrounded by parks."* Some progressive planners have envisaged a locale for living set in the midst of parks—parks surrounding the home, parks as ways to and from school, shopping, and church, parkways to and from work. Surely such a profusion of park land could take place only in a few special places and would be in accordance with new standards.

5. *New ideas in subdivision plan.* This is a modification of the foregoing and occurs when open space and building space are each planned as more concentrated areas but not necessarily changing the proportion of each. Often this permits a more useful park space instead of such space being cut up into smaller yards. Also more park area may be made available at the expense of streets and alleys.

6. *Move from suburbs to city.* This trend is significant but not large so far. When it happens it usually means that older age groups have moved to apartments (usually the better class) thereby creating a denser population. When whole neighborhoods are thus reconstructed, the possibility of a new class and a new standard of parks may be in the offing.

7. *County and state zoning.* It appears logical that with a continued expansion of urban centers more attention will be given county and state zoning. The requirements for recreation areas in less dense population requires revision of standards.

8. *Five- to ten-acre tracts for the ex-urbanite.* This is akin to point 7.

9. *"Green belts in future planning."* Presently we are not sure how economically feasible green belts about our urban areas are. If they become prevalent they will affect both standards and classification.

10. *The effect of private enterprise.* As the people become more affluent and are willing to spend more for recreation, the private entrepreneur is encouraged to provide such facilities as bowling alley complexes that simulate the community center; deluxe motels cater to more than the traveler; whole cities are built about a large industrial or commercial undertaking; family resorts, ski areas, and similar recreation areas, even county and state park facilities may in the future affect neighborhood and community recreation standards.

THE SIMPLE APPLICATION OF STANDARDS

The application of a set of standards to present cities that change their physical structure as rapidly as they do in this era, and to the great variety of satellite towns that spring up, sometimes even as a whole new, planned and developed city by a single organization, may seem at first to be an exercise in futility. But it need not be so. One should keep in mind that all new attempts at town planning are attempts to produce something that is more adaptable than what was previously available in the way of happy living—and at less expense. Innovation itself is a pretty good sales pitch. Considering that many cities in the past have done less than an adequate job of providing an efficient park and recreation system, there is ample room for innovation—both good and of questionable merit.

The simple fact remains that there is always a need for parks within a short walk from where people live (neighborhood parks) and near where they leisurely stroll (the rest park, a variation of the neighborhood park). Older teenagers, young adults, and hobbyists will always need facilities within easy "biking" distance or within a short driving distance—the community park or playfield with its pool and community center building. There will be a need for a place to get a feel of open space, different than the crowded home environment. Needed will be picnic facilities and some attractions and entertainment—the large city park and the special use parks with floral displays, pretty landscapes, a zoo, a museum, golf course, even large sports centers and outdoor theaters, perhaps parkways to drive over to get to these attractions. Such facilities are fundamental needs; it is only a matter of providing for them in a variety of ingenious ways, or even under the guise of alluring names that tend to make the simple pattern of a park system seem obsolete. The wants are unchanged from those shown on the table on page 72.

Imagination in application is the challenge and indeed many administrators of the recent past have had their ideas about modifying the standards first published many years ago by the National Recreation Association.

There never was a single standard of classification adopted by all national organizations and accepted and adhered to by all authorities throughout the continent. In spite of this, there was great similarity in all of these classifications, the difference being mostly in nomenclature and in the degree to which the list of all possible characteristics of parks is broken down into finer subdivisions. For our purpose nothing is gained by reviewing a lengthy and minutely detailed classification if a shorter one will serve our purpose. The one reproduced here is one which was used in a study several years ago involving the Dallas, Texas, park and recreation system. It is representative of the average of all such classifications and standards expressed in a reasonably brief way.

The major categories of the Dallas schedule mention play lots, but suggest that, in the main, they should be operated by private persons and organizations, and ordinarily should not be included in the parks operated by the municipal government. Although this is generally true, there is scarcely a city in the country that has not found it necessary to become involved in that sort of operation. Even in a new situation, instances may arise in small and congested areas in which this type of park is the best solution available to provide some degree of recreation service. This does not alter the conclusion of the Dallas schedule that these situations should be minimized and, if possible, eliminated. No definite acreage per thousand population is consequently attributed to this classification.

Otherwise, then, the smallest and most elemental classification is the neighborhood park of one to two acres per thousand population. Playfields are expected to service two or more neighborhoods, usually three or four with a radius of influence of a mile and a half to two miles. Again one to two acres per thousand population are required. Large park areas constitute the next category to which has been attributed five acres per thousand population, and the character of which is noted in general terms on the schedule. Special use parks follow, with two acres per thousand population attributed to them. This makes a total of ten acres per thousand population for the entire park and recreation system of the municipality. The table does go beyond that by suggesting that any metropolitan or regional park system ought to contain an additional ten acres per thousand population, but for the moment we will confine our consideration to that of the municipality proper.

The widely publicized standards published by the National Recreation Association are substantially the same as those of the Dallas survey, but expressed as one acre of neighborhood park space for a population of 800 and one acre of community playfield for a population of 800. The Dallas classification and set of standards have been chosen here because of their brevity and simplicity as compared to the more extended and detailed NRA compilation. There is no appreciable differences in values. (See expanded list, page 83, etc.)

As a matter of clarification of the material which follows, it is well to pause here and make some observation as to the predominant character of the various classifications. The first two—neighborhood parks and playfields—are predominantly characterized and influenced by active recreation for the age groups from about eight to the early twenties not ignoring, however, both younger and older age groups. The neighborhood parks are the parks which can be reached by walking to them; the playfield type requires the use of bicycles and cars although a fair number can walk to the location. The younger children and the adults use these facilities but not to the extent that other age groups use them. Areas for athletics, games, amusement, club gatherings, and the like become the controlling feature of the design. Pleasing patterns, beauty of landscape, and peaceful environment are part of the designs, but are not the controlling factors. The influence of the recreation

PARK AREA & SERVICE STANDARDS

RECOMMENDED

Type of Park Area	Size	Area per 1000 Persons	Service Area	Location	Usual Facilities & Remarks
Playlot	Less than 1 acre	Special Facility	Usually limited to single block or project	High density neighborhood where usual private yards do not exist	Paved areas, sitting area and play equipment for small children. Usually private responsibility.
Playground (Neighborhood Park)	6 acre minimum additional for parking & natural scenic areas desirable	1 to 2 acres per 1000 persons depending upon shape & intensity of development	Approximately 1/2 mi. or a 1 sq. mi. neighborhood same as elementary school	Preferably adjoining the elementary school near center of neighborhood unit	Softball & other games, play equipment, multiple use paved areas, turf areas & planting, some rustic & passive areas desirable, minimum of automobile parking
Playfield (Includes Athletic Field)	15 to 25 acres may be part of larger scenic area if location provides convenient service.	1 to 2 acres per 1000 persons with at least 1 acre active play area per 1000 people	Approximately 1 mi. or 4 or 5 neighborhood units. Similar service area to high school	At or near the intersection of major or secondary thoroughfares near center of 4 or 5 square mile service area	Baseball, football, softball, tennis and other active athletic areas, possible field house community center & swimming pool. Some facilities may be lighted for night use substantial automobile parking required. May include playground type area
Large Park	Minimum of 100 acres, preferably several hundred acres	Approximately 5 acres per 1000 persons	3 miles or more with good accessibility by auto	Where appropriate sites can be obtained incorporating natural features, one area for each 50,000 to 100,000 persons desirable within urbanized area or on the periphery	Active athletic areas similar to playfield but at least 1/2 area should be rustic & provide picnicking, hiking, archery, etc., golf courses, fishing, boating, & water sports may be included. Much off street parking required. Shelters, swimming pools & quiet, passive areas desirable
Parkways Ornamental Areas Special Parks	Size varies depending on conditions & nature of area	Approximately 2 acres per 1000 persons	No specific service areas as most facilities serve entire urban area	Along waterways, as esthetic treatment for civic buildings, subdivision, etc., zoos. Botanical museums & gardens. Exhibitions should be near center of urban area	Largely scenic areas but may include picnicking & play facilities. Special parks may include golf courses, hobby centers, zoo, monuments, fair grounds, & a variety of special functions
Reservations & Preserves	Several hundred to a thousand or more acres	10 acres per 1000 persons. May include some close-in regional recreation areas	Entire urban area	Usually on fringe of urban development at appropriate sites	Rustic & wild areas, camping, nature & hiking trails, bridle paths, bird sanctuary, boating, fishing, and similar uses not requiring intensive development
Regional Recreation Areas	Several thousand acres	No specific standard. May be partially included in area of reservations & preserves	Entire region	Within 1 to 3 hours driving time of urban center	Lake, river or reservoir providing fishing, boating, water sports, picnicking, hunting, camping & similar facilities

directors and the recreation program not only influence but actually dictate the character of the parks in these two classifications.

It is noted that neighborhood parks and playfields are relatively new introductions into the pattern of municipal park systems. Prior to 1900 or even 1910, park systems were constructed in the best tradition of the "founding fathers." They consisted of several large parks (100 acres or more) in the several radial portions of the city, connected by a parkway system. Parks not on the parkway system were still relatively large, widely spaced and, like all other parks, were designed for rest, contemplation, appreciation of scenery, and sedate use rather than for active play. Indeed the responsibility for either sports or complete recreation programs had not generally been assumed by government, and hence, there was no need for an extensive system of playgrounds and sports fields. Since the city pattern was by that time pretty well fixed and the city largely developed, the introduction of the neighborhood parks and playfields posed a difficult problem and an expensive one to solve. In the older cities such is still the case. It is not too surprising that the use of numerous playlots has been resorted to in some cases, and in others the absence of neighborhood parks allowed to continue.

Recreation and park planning is greatly influenced by the degree to which school districts are involved in providing neighborhoods and communities with recreation facilities and services, and how well coordinated are the efforts of the district and the recreation and park authorities. In some states both school and park agencies are authorized and financed to provide community recreation, while in other states it is the practice, if not the law, for schools to provide athletic fields for community use. Planning must conform to the existing situation in each individual case.

The functions and features which distinguish large city parks from special use parks are often vague. In most situations special use functions have been separated from the formerly large city parks and given a home of their own—conservatories and flower gardens, zoos, arboretums, outdoor theaters, museum sites, golf courses, large municipal stadiums, and sport centers. That is because so often the space required for such functions under present standards is too great to be put "in a corner" of a large city park. But many large city parks are still extensive enough to encompass land required for one or more of these functions and for the most part such functions are not incompatible with the original idea of a large city park.

Olmsted and Vaux set the pattern for the large city park when they designed Central Park in New York City over a century ago. As Olmsted himself once put it, "The kind of recreation that these large parks supply, and nothing but these large parks supply near a city, is that which a man insensibly obtains when he puts the city behind him and out of his sight and goes where he will be under the undisturbed influence of pleasing natural scenery."

"Pleasing natural scenery" not being available at the site of the proposed Central Park, it had to be reporduced by the landscape artists' ingenuity. The surface of the earth was molded, trees and shrubs were planted, carriageways and paths constructed, service buildings placed in unobtrusive places, broad meadows and "parade grounds" provided to permit the feeling of countryside distances. The rules for the Central Park competition had provided that there should be a parade ground of from 20 to 40 acres, three playgrounds of from 3 to 10 acres each, and sites provided for a hall for exhibitions and concerts, a principal fountain, a prospect tower, and a flower garden of from 2 to 3 acres.

One can understand from such descriptions that the mood of the large city park was one of sedate leisure, quiet contemplation, and when activities were provided for, they were not of the sports or competitive, noisy type activities that might mar the landscape. Later, evolution in design brought to the large city park picnic areas, day camps, water activities, and such other innovations as would not disturb the relative tranquillity of the environment or mar the beauty and scope of the landscape. Such is still the theoretical nature of the large city park; unfortunately, competition for open space in large cities has reduced many former large city parks from spacious, landscaped parks to mammoth outdoor playgrounds.

With that sort of historical background in mind one can readily understand the difficulty of drawing a hard and fast line between the large city park and the park of special uses. Except for special purposes and for matters of verification, the two classifications might well be considered as one, using 7 acres per 1000 population as a standard for the combined classification.

The above classification includes parkways and boulevards which have a different background and in some respects, a different function. Parkways are roadways through parks or through such an environment as to constitute an elongated park. Boulevards have less horticultural embellishment, a more restricted right of way, and are like a grand tree-lined avenue. The function of boulevards is simply to provide an attractive way from one place to another. To some extent the same may be said for parkways, except that in the case of parkways there is a much greater degree of scenic and horticultural effectiveness about them.

As has been noted, the important function of parkways in the early plans for park systems of municipalities was that of connecting one large park with another, providing a continuous, pleasant tour through and between parks. Not a few of the fine parkways of the country have since been debased by permitting on them commercial truck traffic as well as passenger traffic, and using them as general trafficways rather than as a leisurely and pleasant way of getting from one place to another. This has tended to restrict the introduction of parkways into new city plans. While parkways also were an important feature of some of the early and more famous county and metropolitan park systems, the use of parkways and boulevards in present-day design for county park systems seems questionable, except bordering lakes and streams where they are effective in several ways. Rapid transit from home to regional or state parks along a system of adequate highways tends to be more significant than providing for slower and more leisurely ways of getting from home to the scene of our outdoor recreation desires except as noted.

However, on a much larger scale there have been built, and still are being planned, national parkways traversing more or less continuous open country of pleasing scenery. These parkways have ample rights-of-way, do not follow a straight line, but tend to fit the landscape in pleasing curves both vertical and horizontal. They are built for leisurely driving and not for speed. Sometimes easement rights have been acquired beyond the right-of-way in order to preserve the adjacent territory in status quo.

With these general observations in mind, an attempt to apply these characteristic and classifications and standards to specific cases will prove interesting and revealing.

STANDARDS APPLIED IN THEORY

In the accompanying diagram (Figure 1), there is shown an 80,000 population city, 3 miles wide by 5 miles long, containing 15 square miles or 9,600 acres. The 80,000 population is assumed to be the potential maximum which the city will reach in approximately 25 years. If the standards for various types of recreation areas are applied to this city, the following would be the result:

Applying the standards to the foregoing yields these requirements

Neighborhoods . . . .   1-2 acres per 1,000 = 80 x 1 1/2 = 120 acres
Playfields   . . . .   1-2 acres per 1,000 = 80 x 1 1/2 = 120 acres
Large City Parks . . . .   5 acres per 1,000 = 80 x 5   = 400 acres
Special Use Areas   . . . .   2 acres per 1,000 = 80 x 2   = 160 acres
                                                             Total . . . . = 800 acres

The total acreage arrived at in this manner is sometimes compared with 10 per cent of the area of the city, which in this case is 960 acres. We therefore come to the conclusion that a park and recreation system properly distributed for this city of 80,000 ought to be somewhere between 800 and 960 acres in total.

Now, mark off our city of 3 miles wide by 5 miles in length into 15 equal areas each one mile square (Figure 1). Since a neighborhood is to be presumed to be three-quarters of a mile to a mile across, we can in this case

Michigan State University
Dept. of Resource Development
Park Management

A SYSTEM OF PARKS
LAID OUT ACCORDING TO STANDARDS

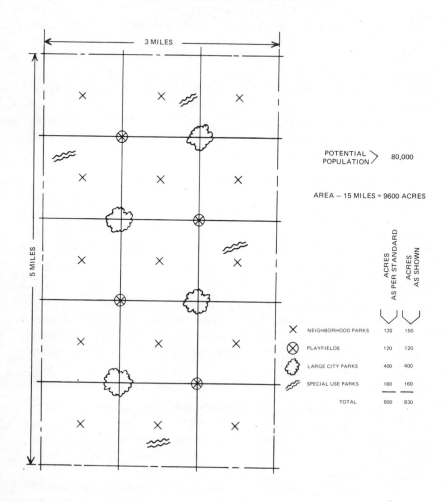

Figure 1

assume 15 neighborhood parks at about 10 acres each or a total of 150 acres. Playfields are to serve two or more neighborhoods or an area from a mile and a half to two miles across. With 15 neighborhoods to accommodate, we can nicely assume that four playfields will satisfy the requirements yielding four times about 30 acres, or 120 acres. In the category of large city parks we require 400 acres and, since our diagram does not reveal any topographic or other features, we can assume about four such parks at 100 acres each or a total of 400 acres. In a similar manner, we might assume the special use parks to number about four at 40 acres each or a total of 160 acres. All this totals up to 830 acres which is within the requirements of 800 to 960 acres previously calculated.

STANDARDS APPLIED TO ACTUAL CASE

This assumed diagrammatic city very probably does not exist. To indicate the necessity of adjusting our ideals and compromising with the schedule of requirements, let us assume an actual city 3 miles wide and 5 miles long. The kind of map or maps which will be needed for our study of a park and recreation system include the following: a map showing the streets, the highways, the arterial streets as distinguished from ordinary residential streets; a map showing the topographical features, including vacant areas and wooded areas; a city master plan if it is available showing the future development of the city; maps indicating the locations of schools and a possible allocation of future school sites. All of the foregoing are basic and essential. If the study which we are about to undertake gets down to details, other factors become important. These include land values, characteristics of the population, local history, extent ownership of facilities which may be used by a recreation service, the extent of museum and library services, and similar factors.

The fact that so much related material is necessary to intelligently explore the possibilities of a park and recreation system highlights the desirability of friendly and amicable relations with all the foregoing agencies that have to do with the matters in hand. It also points up the fact that the park administrator must be equipped with some general knowledge of the operation of the related functions which we have enumerated.

Figure 2 of our 15 square mile 80,000 population city has been drawn with some of the important features in it. For example, the state highway coming through the town has been shown as well as the interstate freeway which by-passes the town. The assumption is made that each of the section lines will have rather important arterial streets on them. A central business section has been shown. A possible industrial area alongside a railroad track has been shown; topographic features such as rivers, streams, lakes, a couple of hills, some wooded area, a country club, have also been

APPLICATION OF PARK STANDARDS
TO
SIMPLIFIED TOWNSITE

3 Miles by 5 Miles = 15 Sq. Mi. Potential Population = 80,000

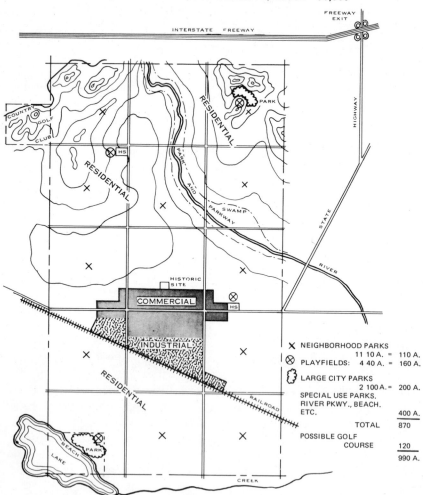

Figure 2

indicated. But as a whole, the city has been drawn rather simply, leaving out a number of the more complicated and frustrating situations.

In selecting our park sites in this situation, we look first for those features which are of special scenic, topographical, or historic interest or are otherwise unique; and secondly, those areas which may prove most beneficial for some special uses.

In the example shown in the diagram the logical first step is to establish control of the river which flows through the town together with sufficient area in some locations to provide for a large city park. Secondly, we are assuming that the lake in the southwest corner of the city has some swimming beach possibilities and, consequently, we set aside some area for that. Next, we find that at least two of the high schools have been located, and assuming that areas adjacent to them are available, we pick those out as being suitable for playfields. Inasmuch as we probably will need more than two playfields for the population, served by the two schools, we will tentatively locate one in the northeast section of the city. We have discovered the possibility of an additional playfield in the southwest part of the town primarily because of the intervening railroad which seems to separate approximately four square miles from the rest of the town.

In locating neighborhood parks, we encounter the usual situation that the neighborhoods are of neither uniform nor of standardized size, but still the situation is not complicated enough to prevent us from placing neighborhood parks in most of the square-mile neighborhoods of the town. It is assumed that these will be where elementary schools are located, but this is not always so.

Now, if a tentative summary is made, we find that we have eleven neighborhood parks at 10 acres each for about 110 acres; four playfields at about 30 acres each for 120 acres; we can assume that our park along the river is mostly parkway, and that there is a possibility of enlarging the area along the swimming beach to considerably more than is required for a beach alone, probably even enough to combine this with our playfield area so that the total of special use areas might be 400 acres or more. The northeast corner of the city, because of its interesting topography, provides the basis of a very interesting community study. This might disclose the possibility of a fairly large park together with a playfield with a portion set aside for a neighborhood park—all in one general territory, or all in one piece of land. Such a large park, in addition to the one in the southwest part of the city, could easily amount to a couple of hundred acres.

The matter of a golf course for the city is open to question. A country club has been located just outside of the city on the northwest section, and while this is privately owned and operated, it goes a long way towards satisfying the golfing demands for the city. If this course should be a privately owned public fee course, it would satisfy the wants of the city entirely. However, there is the bare possibility that a golf course may be desirable, and the people might be willing to pay for the cost of operation over and above the income from fees, the acquisition of which would add to the acreage set aside for special use parks. Incidentally, the northwest section of the city, adjacent to the country club, apparently has topographic features of enough interest to provide the basis of another very interesting study as to the development of the entire two or three square miles.

There is a small historic site adjacent to the central business district which needs to be preserved. While no neighborhood parks have been shown near the central business district, it is barely possible that there are enough living quarters of one kind or another—be they over commercial buildings or in apartment houses—to justify the location or the establishment of one or two playlots.

A breakdown of our total acreage now looks something like this:

Neighborhood parks . . . .   11 at 10 acres=110 acres
Playfields   . . . .   4 at 30 acres=120 acres
Large parks . . . .   2 at 100 acres=200 acres
Special Use areas—
river parkway,
possible golf course,
and others   . . . . 520 acres
                                    Total . . . . 970 acres

If we compare this 970 acres and its breakdown to the 830-acre total of the idealized city of Figure 1, it will be noted that we actually have exceeded our 10 per cent of our gross area of the city; if the golf course, (which is a questionable item) is eliminated, we reduce the figure to approximately 850 acres which is not too far from the 830 acres of our idealized situation. However, comparing the two tabulations more in detail, we find that we have set aside less playground area, more playfield type area, and more large parks and special use area in our Figure 2 than in Figure 1. Were it not for the river parkway and the desirability of controlling the banks of the river and the existence of unusual topographic features in the northeast section of the city, and the bathing facilities at the lake southwest of the city, our condition would have been entirely changed and we probably would have less than 800 acres set aside for park purposes.

VALUE OF STANDARDS

The foregoing discussion shows that precise application of accepted standards is impractical; deviations are necessary to secure and preserve natural topographic features and to adjust for odd-shaped neighborhoods and interfering but essential elements of the city plan. The deviations are not great enough to destroy the essential validity of the standards and yet their application should be flexible enough to allow for differences in population density (more about this later), unusual amounts of scenic topography, and unusual extent of commercial and industrial development and other similar peculiarities of a given city. In the final appraisal of its worth, a park and recreation system must be adequate enough to serve the recreation needs of the people and extensive and attractive enough to enhance the aesthetic, social, and economic values of the city.

In summary, let it be said concerning park classifications and corresponding standards that however inexact they may be, how general the need is for modifications in applying them, how subject they may be to criticism because of the unscientific way in which they have been compiled and the empirical experiences on which most reliance is placed, there is enough inherent merit to them to justify a high place in the list of tools which are used in evaluating and planning a park and recreation system. Classifications and schedules are essential to the park administrator.

THE SUBURBS

As was previously stated, the 80,000 population city just studied (with all its urban area within the city's corporate limits) has not included "a number of the more complicated and frustrating situations." Let us now explore some of these complications while we examine the situation in the suburbs, keeping in mind that suburbs have much the same physical characteristics as the city except that any one suburb may not contain all the characteristics of the city. The population of a suburb is smaller. The area may or may not be less, the density of population differs, some suburbs are almost exclusively residential, others almost wholly industrial. Collectively, the suburbs may be much like the city or conversely the city much like the collection of suburbs if the city were broken up into a number of separate governmental units, each with its own independent municipal services.

Many metropolitan areas of the country which have taken their names from the central city are actually aggregations of a number of municipalities, composed of the central city and a number of satellite towns and villages usually known as suburbs. Even these suburban communities have attached onto themselves other towns and villages of like characteristics. Annexations of suburbs by the central city are reasonably simple in some parts of the country where the demand for adequate water supply and other situations invoke the necessity of amalgamation, but there are other areas of the country in which there is no such inducement and where the destiny of each of the satellite towns and villages rests upon its own resources. The

Michigan State University
Dept. of Resource Development
Park Management

ARRANGEMENT OF SUBURBS
ABOUT THE CENTRAL CITY

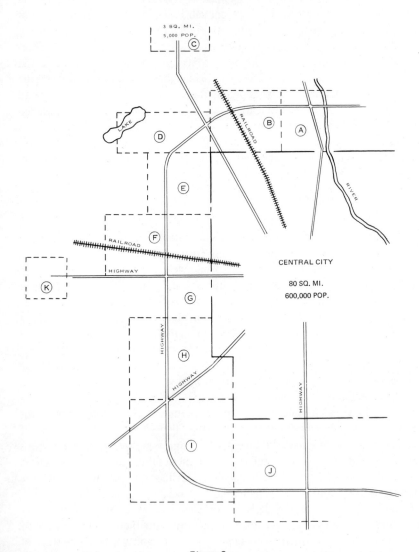

Figure 3

application of park standards to some of these individual localities and to a number of them taken collectively reveals a situation much more complex than that of cities. We are dealing with a much more complicated jurisdictional structure than the central city.

There has been prepared, and included herein, a diagram of a portion of the outlying district adjoining a central city (Figure 3). It is assumed that the central city has a population of one-half million or more. Towns and villages have been shown on the outskirts of the central city; these towns and villages are of various sizes and characteristics. A table has been prepared showing the probable area of parks in the various classifications which would reasonably take care of the park and recreation service required of each of those towns and villages (Table I, page 84 and Table II page 84). Some of the figures contained therein prove to be interesting.

It will be observed that the table shows there is not the same number of neighborhoods in towns of equal population. This comes about by reason of the character of the town itself. Some of the communities are heavily industrialized and commercialized while others are predominantly or wholly of the residential character. Some of the towns have distinctive features brought about by other circumstances. Consequently, variations of figures attributed to towns of comparable population size must be taken for granted by the student. It can be authoritatively stated that the circumstances resulting in the tabulation are not farfetched but are quite realistic. In other words, the situation revealed here is quite usual.

Now in judging the adequacy of some of these park and recreation systems, it is well to give some thought to a few additional generalized standards in order to illustrate the points to be made. The National Recreation Association* has suggested for neighborhood parks and community playfields one acre of each for each 800 population. This differs slightly but not materially from the Dallas table on page 72. In addition to the foregoing, NRA suggests the following standards:

1 baseball diamond for each 6000 population
1 softball diamond for each 3000 population
1 tennis court for each 2000 population
1 hole of golf for each 3000 population
15 square feet of swimming pool or beach wading area for each 1 to 3 per cent of the total population (a 50-by-165-foot pool having an area of 8000 to 9000 square feet would accommodate a population of about 20,000).

*National Recreation Association has now been absorbed by the National Recreation and Park Association, 1601 North Kent Street, Arlington, VA 22209.

TABLE I

PROBABLE STATISTICS OF SUBURBS SHOWN IN FIGURE 3

(Arranged alphabetically)

Suburbs	Area Sq. Miles	Potential Population	Neighborhood Parks Number/Acreage	Playfields	Large City Parks	Sp. Use Parks	Total Acres Theory	Total Acres Actual
A	7	24,000	5/50	2/40	1/120	1/48	240	258
B	10-1/2	38,000	4/40	2/60	x	1/30	380	130
C	3	8,000	1/15	x	x	x	80	15
D	6	20,000	4/40	1/30	100	100	200	170
E	7	24,000	4/40	1/40	x	1/50	240	130
F	13	44,000	10/100	2/60	200	200	440	360
G	4	10,000	2/30	x	x	x	100	30
H	14	48,000	10/100	3/100	2/200	1/80	480	480
I	20	65,000	15/120	4/120	2/200	2/150	650	590
J	48	100,000	25/250	7/210	2/400	2/400	1000	1060
K	3	7,000	2/30	x	x	x	70	30
Actual		388,000	805 acres	660 acres	1070 a.	708 a.		3253
Theory			582 acres	582 acres	1940 a.	776 a.	3880	

ACTUAL EXCESS   ACTUAL SHORTAGE

Standards
Neighborhood Parks   1 to 2 acres per 1000 population
Playfields   1 to 2 acres per 1000 population
Large City Parks   5 acres per 1000 population
Special Use Parks   2 acres per 1000 population
TOTAL   10 acres per 1000 population

TABLE II

PROBABLE STATISTICS OF SUBURBS SHOWN IN FIGURE 3

(Arranged according to population size)

Suburbs	Area Sq. Miles	Potential Population	Neighborhood Parks Number/Acreage	Playfields	Large City Parks	Sp. Use Parks	Total Acres Theory	Total Acres Actual
K	3	7,000	2/30	x	x	x	70	30
C	3	8,000	1/15	x	x	x	80	15
G	4	10,000	2/30	x	x	x	100	30
D	6	20,000	4/40	1/30	100	100	200	170
A	7	24,000	5/50	2/40	1/120	1/48	240	258
E	7	24,000	4/40	1/40	50	50	240	130
B	10-1/2	38,000	4/40	2/60	x	1/30	380	130
F	13	44,000	10/100	2/60	200	200	440	360
H	14	48,000	10/100	3/100	2/200	1/80	480	480
I	20	65,000	15/120	4/120	2/200	2/150	650	590
J	48	100,000	25/250	7/210	2/400	2/200	1000	1060

A selection from the following group of facilities should be provided at the rate of one for each 1500 population:

Archery range	Hard surfaced, multiple
Boccie court	use areas
Bowling greens	Roque courts
Fields for soccer, football,	Shuffleboard courts
field hockey, etc.	Shooting ranges
Handball courts	Golf driving ranges

A selection from the following group of facilities should be provided at the rate of one for each 2500 population:

Bicycle trails	Recreation piers
Bridle paths	Ski jumps
Boating facilities	Toboggan slides
Casting pools	Tracks, running, skating,
Ice skating areas	or bicycles
Model yacht basins	Wading pools
Picnic centers	Yacht harbors

A selection from the following special recreation features should be provided at the rate of one for each 10,000 population:

Band shell	Nature trail
Botanical garden	Outdoor theater
Camp	Arboretum
Community garden	Stadium seating 1000 or
	more

A neighborhood in a central city with single family dwellings on fifty-foot lots will contain 6000 to 8000 people. According to the standards previously enumerated, it should have a neighborhood park of about eight to ten acres. This is sufficient to justify, too, a baseball diamond, two softball diamonds, three tennis courts, and a number of other things. Suppose now we have a one square mile neighborhood in the suburbs with only 3000 population, requiring theoretically only four acres of ground for a neighborhood park. We are now limited to one softball field, one tennis court, and no baseball field. Such a limitation of acreage has several disadvantages:

The size itself is too small to permit sufficient embellishment to raise the play area from a neighborhood nuisance to one which enhances property values.

The elimination of a baseball diamond is open to question. Its elimination tends to limit the use of the neighborhood park to a lower age group, probably under thirteen or fourteen years of age. While it is true that the older children can go some distance for full-sized regulation ballfields, it is also true that for full neighborhood use the athletic fields are used for more than just athletics. Most of the other essential facilities can probably be provided in the more commodious private yards.

The construction of single tennis courts is more expensive than the construction of tennis courts in batteries of two or more.

Altogether, it would seem that four acres is really too small an area for a neighborhood, even though the neighborhood is of low density population. Although there are many neighborhood parks that are of no more than four acres in extent, this is hardly a goal to shoot at. Our minimum ought to be close to twice that figure. Failing that, the variety of uses provided for should be so limited as to permit enough lawn and plantings to make it pleasing in appearance.

A neighborhood in a section of the city which is wholly built up in multiple dwellings, particularly large apartment buildings, might have a square-mile population of 30,000 or 40,000 people. This would call for a neighborhood park of over thirty acres. Theoretically there should be six baseball fields, ten or more softball fields, sixteen or more tennis courts, and other items in proportion. In addition thereto, we now have a population to contend with which is sufficient to support a full-size community center building with probably two gymnasiums. Applying our theoretical standards to a situation of this kind will produce design problems of great complexity and the cost of acquisition of the land in places that would in all probability be prohibitive. This is an example of the other extreme of the effect of population density.

The foregoing two examples are sufficient to indicate that both density of population and area requirements for facilities present problems of necessary deviation from the application of general standards that apply to the average.

It takes a population of approximately 20,000 to justify adequate expenditure for major swimming facilities. In the case of isolated towns in the plains states of the country, or in arid regions lesser populations can frequently support a swimming pool. But normally, in satellite towns and villages, as well as in built-up areas of any urban community, it usually requires 20,000 to justify a 50-by-165-foot swimming pool. Consequently, in suburban communities of 10,000 to 15,000, there is little justification for setting aside areas for swimming pools which normally are included in the playfield type of park.

Playfields themselves are justified when two or more neighborhoods are involved, preferably three or four neighborhoods. Residential neighborhoods vary in population from 3,000 to 10,000; consequently, in a 15,000 to even 20,000 population town the establishment of playfields can be doubtful. Generally speaking, playfields with community center buildings in them can be justified only with population extending from 30,000 to 50,000.

Eighteen-hole golf courses are not justifiable except for populations ranging from 60,000 to 100,000.

Large city parks of a size justifying the name can extend for a mile and a half to three miles away from the center of population. Therefore, in towns smaller in area than three to five miles across, the desirability and the necessity of establishing large park areas is doubtful. On the other hand, some towns of the above size may have unusual amounts of natural recreation possibilities—lake and river shores which ought to be publicly owned but cannot be locally justified.

Summarizing the factors that cause deviations from the general standards, the following may be considered some of the more usual causes:

Density of population.

Facility area requirements, the shape of neighborhoods, neighborhood physical characteristics such as possible changes in zoning, the effect of rehabilitation and redevelopment programs, topography, land values.

Neighborhood population characteristics such as age groups and the trend of change, traditional and ethnic background, racial characteristics.

Climatic conditions. (This has a close relationship to geographic location which in turn affects some of the factors in neighborhood population characteristics.)

Permanence of other community recreation assets such as churches, schools, volunteer agencies, such as YMCAs, Scouts, and so forth.

Private and commercial recreation—their relative permanence and community effectiveness.

The foregoing should suffice to indicate why there is an absence of some of the park classes listed in the accompanying tabulations. When we consider that no mention has been made of occasional and distinctive features of large cities that are usually absent in the suburbs such as municipal stadiums, large outdoor amphitheaters, museums of various kinds, zoos, planetariums, aquariums, arboretums, horticultural conservatories, marinas, we can understand why small cities have fewer purposes for the establishment of park and recreation areas than do large cities. It is an anomaly, but a fact, that the larger the city, the larger per capita area that should be devoted to parks and recreation, and that the larger the city, the larger amount of money that should be spent per capita.

The accompanying tabulation according to size of suburb (Table II) leads us to conclude that cities under 25,000 can do little more than provide neighborhood parks. Yet, if we total the entire population of the surrounding towns and villages, we find that the total is more than half that of the city. In fact, if we totaled the population of all of the towns and villages completely surrounding the city, we might find that the population was more than that of the central city. Collectively, these suburban towns require the same sort of service that is encountered in the city; however, if there are a number of towns under 25,000 population, we are bound to be deficient in all categories of park areas above the neighborhood level. In less than 50,000 population, there is going to be a deficiency of everything above the playfield type of area. In the total suburban complex, there is bound to be a deficiency of areas set aside for park and recreation purposes, and yet, every citizen in every part of the urban area of this metropolis ought to have access to the same sort of park and recreation service.

Something akin to this situation sometimes prevails between the central city and any one or all of the suburbs. In the initial stages of development, the central city is often disposed to act as a tolerant parent to the suburbs in helping them plan their development in many ways, but as time goes on, the "children" become numerous and tend to "grow," taking advantage of the facilities in the central city which they cannot provide for themselves. "Parents" get tired of being imposed upon and retaliation sets in. Shall the central city shoulder the entire cost of such metropolitan facilities as zoos and other of the big city park facilities enumerated above?

Will schools help? School districts usually are not coterminous with suburban areas. This comes about because of the early establishment of school districts encompassing enough area of sparse population to justify the construction of a school. Children are probably transported to the school in the first instance and the school buildings are built upon land which is oriented and intended, exclusively, for educational purposes. Because school boundaries do overlap into more than one suburb, there does exist a possible vehicle for community coordination between villages. Sometimes this happens in the early stages of a recreation program where a school district employs a part-time or even full-time recreation leader and conducts the recreation program for the entire school district. The long-range effectiveness of such an operation, however, is quite limited, for it does not satisfy the situation of park area or of proximity to the individual neighborhoods. A large school might go a little way towards satisfying some of the requirements of the community center building, but the total athletic requirements of the community exceed that required by the educational process both in quantity and in extent. Even indoor swimming pools established for the physical education program of the schools are generally far too inadequate in size to care for the requirement of 20,000 people. The fact is, too, that the actual pool is only part of the recreational value of pool sites. Utilization of school districts to accomplish any degree of cooperation between the suburbs is without much long range hope.

It would appear that political organization on a metropolitan or urban basis, encompassing the central city and all of its suburbs, might solve our difficulty. A few experimentations along that line are proceeding, but the results, so far, are inconclusive.

Our hope, then, may have to rest upon the possibility that a regional park system could take up the slack and supplement for the suburban towns those services which the individual cities and villages cannot seem to provide. Unquestionably, this is going to produce some complications in finance and some pretty neat maneuvering on the part of pressure groups within these communities. There is liable to be considerable heeing and hawing in spite of the fact that the vehicle seems to be present. It is barely possible that this function is one which might be assigned to the regional or metropolitan park systems, a subject upon which we are now about to embark.

Chapter Five

The Country's Physical
Recreation Resources —
The Metropolitan and County

PRELIMINARY AND HISTORICAL

Three-fourths of this country's population is concentrated in metropolitan complexes ranging in size from 50,000 people to many millions of people. For quite a long time people have been migrating to the metropolitan centers in quest of the benefits which mass markets and mass opportunities offer. At the same time there has been a mass movement away from the core of the metropolis to the suburban periphery in an attempt to gain more of what was insufficient or lacking in the central city: space, quiet, peace, and privacy. Slowly at first, the urban area merely expanded to the open countryside, except for the expensive country villas and estates of the wealthy which used the more carefully chosen scenic and probably more remote locations. Recently a much more accelerated movement of a different pattern (or patterns) has characterized the expansion—something like a seething cauldron of viscous and boiling fluid that spatters large globs of stuff outside and away from the kettle's edge. Each glob forms a separate self-contained community of homes and businesses, and each glob, in turn, overflows to fill up surrounding vacant space. Sometimes the pattern is that of a fissured container releasing rivers of stuff to flow along the paths of arterial highways, at intervals forming nodules that are the centers for homes and business; these, too, expand to urbanize adjacent vacant space.

Accompanying this massive population adjustment has been the development of non-urban park systems, each arising in its time and place to fulfill a current local need. Because the precise needs were evident at different places and in different decades it should be apparent that there was no standardized form or even a common motivation for the formation of each. These park systems were caught up in an evolutionary process which still continues in response to new motivations. A quick look at some of the more significant of these older systems is a good starting point for this chapter's discussion.

SOME TYPICAL SYSTEMS

First note that a county, metropolitan, or regional park system is known by any one of a number of names; for example, regional park systems, metropolitan park systems, county forest preserves, park districts, park reserve districts, regional park and planning commissions, and metropolitan authorities. Each name is an attempt to distinguish each from a city park system and, at the same time, to provide a name that will characterize the objective of the service to be offered. Regardless of variations in primary purposes, each does attempt to provide a recreation service somewhere between that offered by the city and that offered by the state.

The earliest such system was the metropolitan park system of Boston, which was established as a sort of made work project in the early 1890s. For several years, the noted landscape architect, Charles Eliot, had been badgering public authorities on the subject of preserving for public use some of the fine areas about Boston (and in New England generally), which were very rapidly being purchased by individuals for the establishment of private mansions and estates. The many arguments he advanced in support of his views can be profitably reviewed by present-day conservationists, so appropriate do they seem. The primary purpose of a system of metropolitan parks (the system included parkways for pleasing connections between parks) was to preserve some of the best naturally scenic and topographic features of the Boston environment. It should be kept in mind that in Eliot's day and from his personal viewpoint only undisturbed nature was the antidote for the damaged health of city inhabitants. The contaminations of foul air, polluted streams, and unsavory city slums are still with us.

Within a year or so of the establishment of the Boston Metropolitan Park System, the first county park system was established in Essex County,

New Jersey. The purpose here was somewhat different than the Boston system. The Essex system was to provide for *all* the park needs of the entire county including its cities and towns. This objective should be kept in mind, for as matters developed in later years, it might have been well for all counties having metropolitan potential to adopt the same type of managerial authority, thus obviating to some extent the difficulties encountered by the systems of peripheral suburbs which became attached to growing cities. However, it was not until a half century had passed that this virtue was generally realized, and by that time some of the shortcomings of the first type of county systems had developed, as noted later herein.

Adjacent to Essex County is Union County; its county park system was established thirty years after the Essex system but it had the same general authority and purpose. Active recreation services by this time had become an accepted responsibility of cities so Union County supplied such services as horseback riding, bridle trails and horse stables, skeet and trap shooting, day camping, skating ponds and winter sports centers, nature trails and small nature museums. Like the Essex system, Union County supplied the park and recreation needs of the whole county including its cities, but cursory examination leads one to believe that much more attention has been given to nonurban service leaving its principal city of Elizabeth sparsely supplied with urban facilities. Likewise, Essex County has left its principal city of Newark in a similar situation. In 1965, Essex County had 5151 acres of parks for one million people; Union County had 5031 acres for 530,000 people; statistics in both cases include cities.

Following the establishment of a few other such systems prior to 1900, little was done toward the establishment of regional park systems until approximately 1920, to use a convenient date.

In some states, permissive legislation had been passed by means of which the organization of park districts was encouraged. The park district law of Illinois was an old one and there, park districts were organized about almost any individual park—actually any district of less than 500,000 population. At one time, Chicago had in excess of twenty such districts which later were combined into one Chicago Park District. However, other districts involved not only municipal parks but large parks and sometimes systems of parks along the streams and throughout the countryside. The law permits (1) Park Districts, (2) Pleasure Parkway and Park Districts, and (3) Township Parks.

Ohio has a park district law permitting the establishment of regional park districts. Perhaps the most important of such Ohio Districts are those of Cleveland Metropolitan Park District and the Akron Metropolitan Park District, but there are others of similar nature.

Being on the south shore of Lake Erie, Cleveland services a

population which is spread out in a semicircle to the south. Following a definite plan for the metropolitan park district, a number of rather large-sized parks were established in a rough semicircular route about the city. It was intended that these large parks would be connected by parkways and several important stretches of the parkways were actually constructed. It will be noted that this sort of pattern was not unlike the pattern of the city park systems of previous generations. The individual parks were chosen for their scenic and topographic interest and were intended to supply a demand for native reservations and native landscapes, together with the ordinary means by which such features could be enjoyed, that is, roadways, hiking trails (particularly hiking trails with nature study possibilities) throughout the entire route, nature museums, and similar facilities. Provision was made for a certain amount of camping; certain volunteer agencies such as Boy Scouts, Kiwanis Clubs, and so forth were permitted to build their own structures on various sites in some of the parks, a practice later regretted and discontinued. The 1965 acreage was 17,000 and population was 1.7 million.

The park system of Westchester County, New York, drew nation-wide attention when it was developed in the early twenties. (It was created in 1922.) Some of the distinguishing features of it included the elimination of dumps and neglected and polluted areas along the streams leading through Westchester County down to Long Island Sound. The establishment of parkways along these river banks, the establishment of large parks in which were developed recreation areas similar to those of large city parks, as well as the purchase of large native tracts in the more remote sections of the county established the Westchester system as having the characteristics of a model city system on a county scale. The purchase and rehabilitation of an old amusement park at Rye, New York, its redesign and operation, set a model for such amusement areas, both public and private. At the time of its establishment, it was the first and only such area in the park systems of the country. Some of its features have since been incorporated in other parks, but so far none has equaled the operation at Rye.

Certainly the system at Westchester went much further in some respects than any similar metropolitan system had previously attempted. The man-made parks of a large city park character, including swimming pools, athletic fields, children's playgrounds, and similar recreational facilities, were more a transplant of city facilities into the county than any regional park system had previously attempted. The parkways along the Hutchinson River, Sawmill River, and Bronx River were models of their kind, and the transformation of poor property into attractive park areas created considerable additional private property values and highlighted the effect of creating such values by the establishment of parks and parkways.

In more recent years, Westchester has been squeezed in at least two directions and this has altered the picture considerably. The parkways, being such convenient facilities for traffic into and out of New York City, have, to a large degree, become passenger trafficways rather than parkways, and in 1961 the Hutchinson River, Sawmill River, and Cross County Parkways were turned over to a state agency. The tug of war between the county and the municipalities within the county as to who is to support what in the way of recreation has caused a downgrading of the recreational features in some of the large parks. In some cases playgrounds have actually been removed because of the unwillingness of the county to maintain facilities for the benefit of nearby cities. The use of some of the golf courses in the county parks was restricted to residents of the county in order to reduce or eliminate the influx of New Yorkers. Fees were established for the use of picnic areas with some discrimination in the amount of the fee in favor of Westchester County residents. These and similar factors have tended to downgrade what originally seemed a fine example of applying to the county the principles of city park requirements in vogue during and immediately following the Olmsted era. In 1965 Westchester County had 11,658 acres of parks for 950,000 people.

The Cook County Forest Preserve about the city of Chicago has adopted and pretty well adhered to a definite land policy. This is not called a park system, but a system of preserves—forest preserves, to be more exact. In 1965 it encompassed 54,089 acres for 5½ million people and has continued to expand acreage commensurate with increases in population. It almost encircles the city of Chicago. It has followed a consistent course of acquiring forests wherever they were, preserving those areas and rehabilitating many with additional forest plantings. They have kept facilities for active use to a minimum, largely to picnicking, nature trails, bridle paths, some wayside developments, and a very few athletic fields. Sometimes the latter have been close to adjacent villages and towns, but officially the department insists that these areas have been located not with reference to the town locations but to the use of all of Cook County.

Perhaps no system has been so diligent and probably none quite so successful as Cook County in adhering to its original policies of forest preserves. While this has appeared to the officials and residents of Cook County as being the major purpose and justification for the establishment of this system, the officials and students of urban development are inclined to think that a by-product which was originally unforeseen may now equal the original purpose in importance. Reference is made to the Green Belt area, for it so happens that the locations of the forest preserves are in such geographical shape as to form an almost continuous belt of forest preserve properties about Chicago. Its function in interrupting the continuous urbanization of land outside of the city of Chicago is looked upon as something of great merit. Incidentally, one can almost compare this with the situation in Cleveland where their system is often given the name of the "Green Necklace of Cleveland." Cleveland's is not nearly as extensive in width as that of Cook County nor does it cover such a long stretch as Chicago's.

The city of Milwaukee for a long time has concentrated many people in a relatively small area. Quite early in its history, a large number of suburban towns were attached to the rim of Milwaukee so that the urban metropolis was far greater than the city proper. At one time the city of Milwaukee had about a thousand or eleven hundred acres of park land for a 600,000 population. Milwaukee County established a county park system in 1907, but its major developments took place in earnest in the 1920s.

The original planners planned well in acquiring a number of large park areas and developed a fine system of parkways. The developments within these large park areas were not dissimilar from the old type large city parks with their well-designed, horticulturally improved scenes and gardenlike devices. Swimming pools were frequent. Today, the Milwaukee County park system, which in recent years absorbed the park system of the city of Milwaukee (and all other incorporated towns in the county), has more of the characteristics of an urban system than of a regional system. All of Milwaukee County is now incorporated into towns and not much is not urbanized. The whole county is now virtually one metropolis served by one park department. It contained 12,836 acres for 1,109,460 people in 1965.

Geographically, Los Angeles is a mess. On occasion, its frontiers reach out in long tentacles between well built-up adjacent towns and villages; in some cases the city completely surrounds other towns and in still other cases patches of the county still remain completely surrounded by the city. In such a situation, a division of jurisdictions and jurisdictional functions is complicated. It is not surprising, therefore, that the ownership of the individual parks anywhere in the urban area of Los Angeles is a continual source of curiosity to the visitor. Many of the county parks are no different than city parks and perform the same functions. Generally speaking, the systems of the county and the city tend to complement each other in providing recreational service. The county is attempting to acquire the larger park areas to supplement the systems of the smaller cities of the county in cases where the local governments "can't afford it."

The Maryland National Capital Park and Planning Commission has planning and zoning functions as well as the responsibility of providing parks for two counties adjacent to the District of Columbia. Certain Acts of Congress have facilitated the acquisition of stream beds leading into the District. Otherwise, the Commission properties have characteristics similar to the large parks and local playgrounds of a city system.

Detroit is a city typical of a number of American cities that did not provide sufficient parks after the Olmsted-Eliot era to keep pace with its rapidly growing population. By 1965 it had only 5848 acres for its 1,671,062 inhabitants, less than four acres per thousand. Some years ago, Wayne County in which Detroit is located formed a park system under a Michigan law that permits county boards of supervisors to establish park systems. By 1965 it had 4330 acres to help offset the inadequacy of Detroit's system, but that still was not enough. Under a special legislative act five counties (including Wayne) banded together to set up the Huron-Clinton Metropolitan Authority. It has (1971) 17,857 acres, but in the meantime population in the five counties has grown to 4,493,000. Even though the many suburbs have added their own systems to the total, making an estimated 30,000 acres, the ratio of parks still is only about six acres per thousand population. This is an example of rapid expansion of park acreage in a metropolitan complex barely keeping pace with the population—running fast to stand still. And the Huron-Clinton system has some fine properties containing swimming, fishing, boating, golf, picnicking, and a number of large city park facilities in a more native environment than Detroit can possibly provide. In a recent and prophetically significant move, the Huron-Clinton Metropolitan Authority is currently seeking jurisdiction over Detroit's nationally famous Belle Isle Park.

A few more regional park systems are of significance. San Francisco-Oakland area has its East Bay Regional Park District that has added enough acreage in recent years (prior to 1965) to bring its total to 25,000 acres, serving a population of 2,500,000. This system is largely of a native character but by no means exclusively so. Phoenix, Arizona, has its Maricopa County system of mostly mountain parks with the impressive acreage of 91,538 acres. The Muskingum Conservancy District of Ohio, as its name implies, is a native area of 52,000 acres featuring the ecology of animals and birdlife around its water areas. There are a number of other rather large and locally important park systems of the regional category, but the foregoing sufficiently illustrate the scope of purpose and cause of development of these systems.

COMMENTS ON TYPICAL SYSTEMS

Perhaps the characteristic most common to all of these systems is that they were conceived and established for a recreation purpose that the founders believed answered a current or potential need in each of the local situations. They were opportunistic in conception, individual in purpose, and individual in design. They were needed, each in its own way, and built and operated to fulfill a current vacancy in recreation service. That vacancy represented services which the incorporated cities and villages either could not or would not provide. The demand led to the creation of a park and recreation service outside the cities and the urbanized periphery.

In almost all cases, the underlying service that county and regional parks attempt to supply is a sense of spaciousness which is difficult to provide in a completely urban environment. The functions are akin to those of large city parks such as Olmsted saw them to be plus a more recent development of the large city parks as the setting for a wide variety of special uses and attractions such as museum sites, sports stadiums, cultural complexes, arboretums and floral conservatories, and so on.

Olmsted conceived the large city park "in and near" a city (Central Park was then on the outskirts of New York) as a piece of native landscape in which peace and quiet could be experienced in distinct relief from city conditions. As large and as well designed as was Central Park, it could not fully retain its original purpose in spite of the many heroic measures taken by its past administrators to "save" it. The dense population of its environs was inadequately supplied with recreation grounds and of necessity overflowed into the park, upsetting its previous restricted purpose and design. To a more or less extent this typifies the large city parks laid out in the Olmstedian era extending into the first decade of the twentieth century. Extensive native areas, never extensive enough for present-day mobility of person, are fast dwindling in our growing cities to make room for more sophisticated uses and a more "polished" type of maintenance. Most of them are not extensive enough to harbor modern zoological gardens or any of the wide variety of special uses previously mentioned without complete usurpation of native scenery. Moreover, many of these special facilities require a broader base of financial support than can be supplied by only one of a large number of municipalities comprising the entire metropolis. These trends call for a county, regional, or metropolitan park authority.

A MINNESOTA EXPERIENCE

While Huron-Clinton, Cook County, East Bay, and the other regional systems were busy enlarging their holdings and adapting developments to meet prevailing and ever-changing social and political demands, a more recent adventure in metropolitan park systems and metropolitan political organization was taking place in Minnesota. At first, it was only another county park system trying to establish itself as an improvement of the best practices of other and older systems—higher space standards, a long-range plan of zoned development and policy statements to ensure continuity of operation for at least a decade or two. But soon that process was overtaken by a movement to organize and implement a comprehensive seven-county metropolitan government. Both projects plowed a little new ground worth examining.

As to the county park movement, it got under way a generation after the talking first began, when in 1957 the state legislature authorized the formation of a Hennepin County (Minneapolis and environs) park system. It came to be known as the Hennepin County Park Reserve District in a salute to the Cook County Forest Preserve District which the new system took as a suitable example.

In a little over a decade the Hennepin system had acquired and partially developed 15,000 acres in six "Reserves" varying in size from 1000 to 5000 acres each and every one possessed such potential recreation resources as lakes, streams, marsh land, woods, and rolling open country. Acquisition still proceeds to keep pace with a growing population aimed at 15 acres per 1000 population of 1¼ million.

In its determination to retain a substantial amount of native land of low density use but still provide for active daytime use, the acquisition of tracts of less than 1000 acres was consistently avoided. Limited finances induced the District Commissioners to gamble that they could convince the rapidly developing suburban cities and towns to provide the local parks (neighborhood to large city parks) in sufficient amount and diversity (say 10 acres per 1000 population) to keep the pressure for such parks off the county system. This would permit the County Reserve to retain 80 per cent of its areas as native low density zones and to develop only 20 per cent for active daytime use.

Such a scheme will work only when the total county recreational plan is accepted and each town, city, as well as the county, working together is willing and able to fulfill its purpose. A generation earlier when county parks were first proposed the scheme could not have been devised because the facts of park and recreation service were not known and the problems of population growth, extent of mobility, affluence of leisure time and money were not anticipated. In such a circumstance some would say it was a good thing that the formation of the county system was delayed; others would recall the many beautiful gems which were forever lost to say nothing of what joyful recreation experiences were missed. But time and human progress does not stand still; we begin when we can and we accept the current conditions as they are and proceed to build from there.

In the meantime, while the HCPR District was making excellent progress, another development suddenly appeared which had great promise but also produced some complications. The state legislature transformed a Twin City Planning Commission (seven counties) which had been only a data-gathering body with advisory powers into an administrative body endowed with legal authority to govern the Twin City Metropolitan Statistical Area (Minneapolis-St. Paul and environs) in all metropolitan matters—sewage disposal, water supply, parks and open space, the "works."

This bold move by the state, heralded as an example of how the knotty problems of a metropolitan entity should be attacked, was too sudden for its 2 million people organized into seven county governments and many local governments involving a great number of politicians with special interests and the chauvinistic inclinations of its civic bodies, to swallow in one big gulp. Several more legislative sessions struggled with details including that of parks and open space.

The Hennepin County Park Reserve District had always looked upon its system as only a part of a future metropolitan park system. Legal provision had been made for additions of other counties into the District in the original park act. The spirit in all succeeding attempts at enlargement was ever willing but matters of finance and political chauvinism thwarted every overture that was made. The new metropolitan government Act now offered solution. However, the District had spent too much time, thought, and critical expertise all with too much solid progress to blithely trust a new untried administrative body, no matter how well intentioned it might be, to carry on the policies and future plans so carefully worked out during its lifetime. To secure these objectives has taken several sessions of the legislature and at this writing the matter is still not settled. But compromises will be made and a new Twin City Metropolitan Park System will be born about forty years after its original proposal.

Such is a sample history of the birth of metropolitan park systems.

AREA REQUIRED

In the discussion of rule-of-thumb requirements for a city park system a ratio of acres of land to population was set at 10 acres per thousand population. The present discussion seems to say that this ratio is not enough, especially for large city parks, and in some respects it is not. The ratio is adequate only if the city system is supplemented by a regional park system that has a ratio high enough to compensate for the inevitable future "squeeze" of the city parks and at the same time provide a future metropolitan population expansion with an adequacy to satisfy a future generation. This means not only 10 acres per thousand population for regional parks (as is the case for cities) but somewhat more, in order to have the extensiveness for native environment and other special developments. The required ratio is more like 15 to 20 acres per 1000 population in addition to whatever is required for neighborhood and community facilities that local suburbs do not provide for themselves.

The size of these parks ought to be in thousands of acres rather than in hundreds or tens of acres.

The area to be served should be a metropolitan area regardless of political subdivisions, if at all possible. Under present circumstances of traffic a distance of 25 to 30 miles from the center of the metropolitan area should be a sufficient distance outward.

The land acquired should have the characteristics of uniqueness in scenery, history, archaeology, geology, and the scientific values as much as possible. But if the native areas are not conveniently located, other areas must be acquired and the native characteristics which are missing must be supplied by human hands.

Stream valleys and other topographic or scenic features should determine parkway locations, if they are provided at all.

A SYSTEM OF CLASSIFICATION AND USE-ZONING

Like city parks, regional parks serve several purposes and are subject to classification as are city parks. In the city systems described in Chapter 2 it will be observed that functional classification has the earmarks of a system of use-zoning. Neighborhood parks and community playfields are planned to fit certain compatible situations—those found in specific neighborhoods and communities of neighborhoods. With reasonable attention to administration, the uses will automatically be consistent with the design. The uses of the large city parks will also be consistent with its planned purposes so long as the administration does not misinterpret demand for additional functions and space as a demand for substitute uses that need a home of their own. This principle of design by zoning is applicable to other park systems—regional, state, and federal.

A logical classification of county or regional properties may be as follows:

1. The *large reservation* of native land containing 1000 or more acres. These may be zoned according to intensity of use, e.g., (a) Native sanctuaries which are rarely invaded and in which native ecology is to be maintained as much as possible, (b) Native areas for light intensity use—trails for hiking, horseback riding, for nature centers, very light picnicking and camping, (c) Intense daytime use for swimming and boating, intense picnicking and similar active recreation. Only about one-fifth of the total area would be subject to development for intense use.

2. *Recreation areas or parks.* These are in the hundreds of acres in size—they may be largely developed for active daytime use but with a native environment predominant. These may be closer to the urban areas than the reservations.

3. *Special use parks* include any of the numerous facilities mentioned previously such as zoos, stadiums, museums, cultural complexes, all of which are located after special study of the factors involved in such undertakings.

4. *Parkways or scenic highways* are really part of No. 3 but with special parklike characteristics. These will be discussed more explicitly in the following chapters.

5. *Historical parks* of no particular size except large enough to encompass the items of historical significance without crowding; of course, they occur where history was made.

PARKWAYS AND BOULEVARDS

Boulevard—Originally the flat top of a rampart, hence a broad avenue or thoroughfare.

Parkway—A broad thoroughfare beautified with trees and turf.

The above brief definitions found in a college dictionary need a little more clarification according to professional park people:

A parkway is a roadway through a park or a roadway with a generous enough right-of-way to permit parklike embellishment so that it looks like a park.

A boulevard has a much more limited right-of-way but it too is beautified by turf and trees but is more like a grand avenue than an elongated park.

To be part of a park system, both parkway and boulevard must carry only noncommercial vehicles.

A third form of parklike thoroughfare that has recently come into prominence is the scenic highway. It passes through attractive native scenery and differs from a parkway in that mixed traffic—commercial and non-commercial—is permitted because it is a part of the highway system. As discussed later, closer study has emphasized some of the weaknesses of the boulevards of the Olmsted era.

Parkways and boulevards were the sinews that bound together the Olmstedian parks to form a unified park system. After seventy-five years or more, the sinews have become frayed, broken and their binding power too often is only in name. Those that remain vigorous are along streams and lake shores, yet the idea of a system of parklike ways strongly persists in the minds of planners. A new factor that adds spark to the parkway embers is a realization that automobile driving for pleasure is the most frequently used form of recreation. Since this was noted in the ORRRC report of 1962, every state highway department has been instructed to map out a system of state scenic highways. The National Park Service has planned both state and national scenic highways—some have been constructed. The idea is a carry-over from the old parkway systems of the cities, but with important differences.

The differences come about because of changed design factors and high cost of lengthened right-of-way. Travel on the old parkways and boulevards was at a horse's pace of 5 to spurts of 15 miles an hour. Sharp curves, short forward as well as side vision meant meager rights-of-way. Even in the early twenties, when parkways were often used in county and regional systems, speeds of 25 to 35 miles per hour were common. Today the speeds are twice that; both horizontal and vertical curves must be lengthened accordingly. This is all very admirably explained in the excellent chapter on highways in the book, *Man-Made America*, by Tunnard of Yale and Pushkarev of Regional Plan Association of New York.

Some of the old boulevards were no more than 100 feet wide. Their apparent "grandeur" induced the construction of fine residences, mansions, and first class apartment buildings fronting on them. Time depreciated the environment and mixed traffic did the rest to reduce the boulevard to an ordinary city street. Parkways fared better where their scenic corridors were wide enough to provide a park scene at relatively high vehicular speed; hence the advantage of an extensive body of water on at least one side. In the design of scenic highways, these factors are all important and have been instrumental in halting many proposals. Corridors of a half mile to a mile or more are often necessary and distances in length are likewise formidable. Resulting large right-of-way costs could not be legally financed out of taxes that were levied for exclusively transportation purposes. Significantly the newer county and regional park systems are without connecting parkways—Huron-Clinton Metropolitan, East Bay Regional, Cook County, and a host of lesser ones.

In summary, what failure there has been in the connecting boulevards and parkways of the past is due to their inadequate size of scale; failure to own or otherwise control a wide enough scenic corridor to preserve the parklike aspect in the face of increasing speeds of travel on the roadway, and the length of forward vision to accomplish the same purpose. Contributing to the hesitancy in incorporating the encircling parkway scheme into present-day county, state, and national park system plans is the cost of acquiring and difficulty of otherwise controlling the necessary scenic corridor. But the attractiveness of the encircling parkway plan has great appeal and where the inhibitions above referred to are not present, parkways and scenic highways will be used—even though the "encircling" feature has to be sacrificed for only "stretches" of parkways.

Chapter Six

The Country's Physical Recreation Resources — State and Federal

PRELIMINARY OBSERVATIONS

SIMILARITY OF STATE AND FEDERAL SERVICES

The recreation resources of the state and federal governments have so much in common by way of origin, purpose, physical characteristics, and variety of administrative agencies, and both are so distinctive from the local aspects of recreation service that treating them in a single chapter makes for overall clarity. These two services share a late blooming appreciation of the full scope of recreation which, at long last, recognizes the singleness of purpose of the recreation of children in the neighborhood parks of the city and the fisherman, hunter, and camper in our great national forests. This concept must henceforth be embodied in any national recreation plan.

TRANSITION FACTORS OF RECREATION SERVICE, LOCAL TO FEDERAL

As the horizon of the study of parks extends from the local neighborhood park through the other parks of the city and the county and then into state and national parks, the emphasis placed on certain factors and functions common to all classes of parks is continually shifting. These factors are: the degree and variety of organized and supervised recreation programs, the proportional amount of native environment to active recreation areas, the distance from home, the length of stay, the expense per visit, the frequency of visit, and other factors of lesser importance.

Although there is much free play and unsupervised use of local neighborhood parks and community playfields, even by children, the facilities provided in these parks, and frequently their arrangement into the park design, are dominated by the kind and content of the supervised recreation program offered by the city, and to some degree, the way in which it is administered. We have previously spoken of the fact that active recreation dominates the design of these local parks, leaving such things as aesthetics to be expressed by arrangement and the subtle use of materials and colors and a minimum amount of landscaping.

Organized and supervised recreation becomes progressively less dominant and less influential in the park design as our study progresses through the large city parks, most of the special use parks, the county parks, the state parks, until on the national level, supervised recreation has only recently appeared, unless one includes in supervised recreation the long-standing interpretive programs of the state and federal park services. Originally the interpretive programs were considered to have as much kinship with education as with recreation.

More space, space per occupant, space for native environment, for longer views, for inspection and appreciation of individual plants and animals and the ecology of the environment—all these grow to an ever increasing degree as attention is drawn from the local scene to the national scene. The form of recreation, therefore, changes from something which needs direction to something which comes from within, is more contemplative, more peaceful, more inspiring, and more edifying. Space for tranquillity and a relief from a busyness caused by urban living is the great appeal. This is an even greater escape from urban life than Olmsted expressed, but then, in his day, the countryside was much more accessible.

The experiences of state and federal park visitation are not daily ones, as is the case in city parks. The visits are much less frequent, but the length of visits are much greater. A visit to a city park may be just a "passing through," or a half-hour or an hour's time with children, or a couple of hours by the children alone. A visit to a state park may last for half a day or, on occasion, an overnight stay, possibly even several days for a camping trip. Visits to federal resources are often longer.

For such an experience the visitor will travel much farther from home—a matter of a half-day or more to state parks, maybe a week or more to federal parks. This, in itself, costs more than a local visit to a city park; but especially is the expense greater when camping equipment, boats, winter sports equipment, special clothing, etc., are required.

THE DEVELOPMENT AND PURPOSE OF STATE AND FEDERAL PARKS

When Congress established national parks, it imposed upon them a function which is not imposed upon city and county parks. National parks, being made up of nationally unique features, were to be *preserved* because of those very features. Access to these parks was to be permitted and provided for so that people could see and enjoy them, but these unique features were to be preserved at all costs. Use (active recreation) and preservation are not always compatible. Consequently, as demand for more use became evident (a situation which would endanger the superlative qualities of the national and state parks), it was apparent that more land was needed and that this land could be less than superlative in quality (although far better than the average), and that it could be devoted more extensively to such activities as picnicking, camping, water sports, nature lore, and others. Also, it was apparent that these new recreation areas ought to be located with reference to centers of population. Hence, these areas could then satisfy the popular demand for national and state parks closer to home than the traditional state and national parks had been.

State parks, as was noted in Chapter 3, are a more recent invention than national parks. Consequently, the function of state parks was at first conceived to be substantially that of the National Park Service transferred to a state level. The policy of the National Park Service had been to set aside and to preserve, while at the same time making accessible for public enjoyment large areas of the superlative in scenery, geology, archaeology, history, uniqueness in flora and fauna. States followed suit by doing likewise for the unique areas of each state. Such areas were wherever they were found and were not located with reference to centers of population. This accounts for the situation noted in Chapter 4: plenty of recreation resource land for state and federal parks if it were more accessible to centers of population. In the ensuing years, the National Park Service was perhaps more successful in adhering to high standards of quality in their selections than the states, which were often importuned to acquire state parks closer to their principle cities. Ultimately the maldistribution of the country's unique and superb areas also gave rise to the introduction of National Recreation Areas into the system of National Parks as well as to the utilization of other federal lands—national forests, wildlife refuges, Army Engineer impoundments, and others.

Following some early and significant federal and state recreation holdings, actual consolidation of these must be characterized by the birth of the National Park Service in 1916 and the organization of the National

Conference on State Parks five years later. Let us now trace some of this history with a view to following the development of policy in which we are as much concerned as in areas and budgets. Bear in mind that as the federal park service leads, the states generally follow.

NATIONAL PARKS BEFORE 1916

There was very little professional theorizing behind the congressional Act which established Yellowstone as the first national park in 1872. Very simply, Yellowstone was thought of as a large area containing the most wonderful, the most incredible, and the most fantastic and spectacular geological and scientific features of this wonderful country of ours, and "we ought to protect it within government ownership for all posterity." It is improbable that appreciation of these wonders was considered to be a part of recreation, as we view recreation today. Yellowstone was something too wonderful to permit it to be destroyed. It was precious and it should be preserved.

In succeeding years a number of other historical, scenic, and scientific sites were thought to be important enough to maintain intact, and some even important enough to acquire. A number of archaeological and some historical treasures, some even in the public domain, were being plundered, ravaged, and destroyed. In 1906 the so-called Antiquities Act was passed by Congress which authorized the levying of a fine or imprisonment penalty on anyone mutilating or destroying any object of antiquity in the public domain. It also authorized the President to set aside by proclamation historic spots, landmarks, and other sites and objects of the nature of an antiquity, and to receive gifts of such sites. This was an important step forward from a preservation standpoint, but still in all likelihood there was little conscious connection between preservation and recreation. At any rate the government continued to acquire properties of national significance, and in 1916 it created the National Park Service to administer all these holdings and to do a lot more.

THE NATIONAL PARK SERVICE

As noted above, the National Park Service Act and subsequent supplementary Acts brought together under one administration not only the then existing national parks, but also a number of other miscellaneous holdings. These included monuments, military parks, memorial parks, battlefield parks, battlefield sites, and others. By 1971 the total number of administrative units had been extended to 283, and the total acreage involved was 30 million acres including nonfederal inholdings of 1.242 million acres, Included in the above were 36 national parks with 14.3 million acres, 84 national monuments of about 10 million acres, 5 national parkways of over

130 thousand acres, the park system of the national capitol at Washington, D.C., totaling 45 thousand acres, six national seashore areas of 130 thousand acres, and 13 national recreation areas totaling 3.6 million acres. The attendance at all these areas was almost 164 million in 1970. Total budget for 1969 was $164 million. the federal government has spent so little money for the acquisition of land that appropriation of some federal funds for the recently established Cape Cod Seashore Recreation Area marked a new trend.

As to congressional instructions to the administration regarding purpose and general administrative objectives, the National Parks Act gives this often quoted statement:

> The service thus established shall promote and regulate the use of federal areas known as national parks, monuments, reservations hereinafter specified by such means and measures as conform to the fundamental purpose of said parks, monuments, and reservations, which purpose is to conserve the scenery and the natural and historic objects and the wildlife therein, and to provide for the enjoyment of the same in such manner and by such means as will leave them unimpaired for the enjoyment of future generations.

Park administrators often place emphasis on the apparent inconsistency of the two stated objectives of conservation and enjoyable use. The point is that if uncontrolled access and unlimited enjoyment of the natural recreation resources are permitted, preservation to the point of unimpairment of the natural asset becomes an impossibility. In actual practice and with some few exceptions, the National Park Service has done a creditable job of preservation while at the same time providing access for public enjoyment. Part of this is due to the large areas involved as well as the responsive administration of the Service. Today's excessive use in localized spots together with estimates of future public demand now seem to be so impressively large as to demand even further adjustments of the administrative policies.

For our present purpose it is interesting that in 1916 Congress was thinking not only in terms of preservation with a sort of nebulous objective, but was also concerned with the preservation of these unique things for the purpose of providing pleasure to the people, and it charged that these objects and their environment which give pleasure (recreation) to the people shall be preserved for all times so that the pleasure they give can always be present for the people of future generations. In other words, we have something here which by itself and standing alone provides recreation to the individual, and Congress said that "that something" must be retained forever so that the pleasure and inspiration which it exudes shall be there for all times.

How has this policy been interpreted by the various administrations since the enactment of the Act in 1916?

Stephen Mather was the first of a succession of able administrators. Professor. John Ise, in his *Our National Park Policy* published by the Johns Hopkins Press in 1961 for Resources for the Future, reports a letter dated May 13, 1918 from the then Secretary of the Interior, Franklin K. Lane, to Mr. Mather in which an administrative policy is outlined:

> First that the national parks must be maintained in absolutely unimpaired form for the use of future generations as well as those of our own time; second, that they are set aside for the use, observation, health, and pleasure of the people; and third, that the national interests must dictate all decisions affecting public or private enterprise in the parks.

Then he goes on to make note of several other policies:

The grazing by cattle, but not sheep might be permitted.

There should be no leasing for summer homes.

No cutting of trees except for buildings and where it would not impair the landscape.

Roads must harmonize with the landscape.

Private holdings and exclusive jurisdictions ought to be eliminated.

All outdoor sports including winter sports should be encouraged.

Low priced camps should be maintained, and high class hotels.

Concessionaires should be protected against competition if they were giving good service, and they should yield a revenue to the government, but the development of revenue should not impose a burden on visitors.

Auto fees should be reduced as motor travel increases.

Advise was given as to the publicizing of the national parks.

The Service should keep informed as to municipal, county, and state parks and cooperate with them as well as with the Canadian Park Service.

In setting up new projects, the Service should seek to find "scenery of supreme and distinctive quality or some natural features so extraordinary or unique as to be of national interest and importance." The national parks system as now constituted "should not be lowered in standard, dignity, and prestige by the inclusion of areas which express in less than the highest terms, the particular class or kind of exhibit which they represent."

The first paragraph in Secretary Lane's letter simply repeats what was placed in the law together with a rather obvious statement that the national interests must dictate all decisions. Other important points suggest the elimination of private holdings or vested interests in public areas, encouragement of educational and recreational use of the parks, and the establishment of services which would aid in that direction. Cooperation with other levels of government was stressed and admonition given toward maintaining the high standard to a superlative degree in all future additions to the system. It is a noble statement and, by and large, it was lived up to except in those few instances where inferior parks were acquired because the people, through their congressional representatives, said they were entitled to some of these national benefits which for the most part were concentrated in the western part of the country. The establishment of National Recreation Areas, State Parks, and State Recreation Areas, indeed the beginning of a unified National Recreation Plan by the Bureau of Outdoor Recreation have not obviated much of this difficulty.

Times and conditions change and in retrospect now we can see that even such an able man as Mather could not clearly anticipate the situation fifty years in the future from his time. Congressional support for adequate appropriations was hard to come by so considerable attention was given to informing the public, important people, and especially the Congress about the wonders in the national park system. Mather and his successors continued on that theme until their efforts, supplemented by other startling developments, made the Park Service think of ways of relieving the pressure of excess attendance at the more famous of the national parks.

Early emphasis placed upon the desirability of using national parks for sports and other active recreation purposes is not exactly what is being advocated today. That is the kind of activity that we now wish could be diverted to other less precious areas of the nation's fine scenery (e.g., National Recreation Areas) so that the best areas may remain unimpaired and preserved for the one kind of recreational use for which they are best fitted.

Mather's great interest in promoting the establishment of state parks (he was the principal promoter) was probably less motivated by the idea of providing state parks as a relief from the pressure of attendance at national parks than by the hope of inducing states to acquire inspiring areas in their own states because of their value to the people of the respective states. There might have been a feeling, too, that if the states acquired the areas of secondary importance, there was less chance of those areas being foisted upon the federal government. Today both objectives are valid and in this respect Mather operated probably better than he knew or could foretell.

The National Parks Service Act of 1916 did not give to the National Park Service administrative control over a number of miscellaneous properties. A number of military parks, battlefield sites, military and historical national monuments, miscellaneous memorials in the cemeteries were turned over to the National Park Service by presidential executive order which was authorized by Congress in 1933. It was during this reorganization process that the parks of the District of Columbia (the National Capitol Parks) were placed under the jurisdiction of the National Park Service. Between 1916 and 1933, several important national parks were added to the list of properties and some thoughts on administration policies as well as purposes involved in the acquisition of the new properties were expressed. Let us examine some, using as our principal authority the aforementioned Professor John Ise and his book on *Our National Park Policy*.

Ise reports that in November 1916, Mather wrote, referring to Yellowstone, "Golf links, tennis courts, swimming pools, and other equipment for outdoor pastime and exercise should be provided by concessions, and the park should be extensively advertised as a place to spend the summer instead of five or six days of hurried sightseeing under constant pressure to keep moving... there are no national parks better suited by nature for spending leisurely vacations." Ise further comments in his own words as follows: "At the time, this was not bad, perhaps, but it involved a confusion of two functions of parks which should have been and later were distinguished—the function of preserving the natural wonders and making them accessible to the public, and the function of mere recreation, which is appropriate not to national parks, but to state, municipal, and county parks and private recreational agencies. A criticism often aimed at Yosemite was that it was devoted too largely to recreational activities, mere amusements, while the scenic wonders were too little considered."*

Nearly all park administrators today would agree that if Mather's idea had been pursued to the present time, the functioning of our national parks for their fundamental purposes would be greatly impaired. The guidance that can be given by a park administrator toward the appropriate uses of our national parks must be buttressed by the establishment of other public recreation grounds in such amounts and in such locations as to make compliance with the restrictions in our national parks an automatic thing. Even so, let us not be too surprised if on rare occasions public pressure has caused the introduction in national parks of some of the features mentioned by Mather, or, still more probable, contracts with private entrepreneurs for just such facilities and services.

It is interesting to note that entrance fees to some national parks in the early days were high—made high partly because of the needed revenue. Over a period of time the entrance fees have been reduced but are now charged to enter, with a few exceptions, all National Parks and Recreation Areas.

The history of the National Park Service is replete with administrative difficulties such as vandalism, various aspects of the concessionaire problem, fending off inroads by power, timber, and grazing interest, all of which can be treated more appropriately elsewhere. For our present purpose here, one of the more interesting difficulties encountered was to fend off the establishment of so-called inferior national parks—those that did not

---

*This lack of suitable classification and segregation of purposes now has been somewhat alleviated by BOR but public demand still keeps the question open.

live up to the standard of excellence that park enthusiasts thought proper.

The preservation responsibility of the National Park Service received quite an impetus when there was passed in 1935 an Act calling for the preservation of historical sites, buildings, objects, and antiquities of national importance, known generally as the Historic Sites and Buildings Act. The Antiquities Act of 1906 had been applied largely to the preservation of archaeological sites and structures, although its authorization was somewhat broader than that. The Act of 1935 supplemented this authorization by being more specific concerning historic sites, particularly buildings. Under this authority it was possible to expend money to learn all about these historic structures, to reconstruct them, restore them, to preserve them, and maintain them and charge fees for admission to them. It was also possible to contract and make cooperative agreements with states and their political subdivisions and with associations and individuals.

This museum type responsibility of discovering, restoring, and maintaining the visual parts of American history has a combination of purposes: the fostering of national pride, education, and recreation if one approaches this study with recreation as the major motive. The element of recreation is there but certainly not predominant, but it has its parallel in the functioning of almost all park departments, local and state. Almost all park departments have found it expedient to respond to the public's desire to have historic sites and objects suitably preserved or commemorated. Accepting such responsibility, the park departments are not acting illogically because historically and traditionally they have generally accepted this responsibility and it is not unrelated to their major responsibility of providing recreation service to the public.

More important to the purely recreational aspects of the National Park Service's responsibility was the passage in 1936 of the Park, Parkway and Recreation Area Study Act which directed the Park Service to cooperate with practically all other governmental agencies in the various levels of government to prepare a study of the whole problem of recreation in the national, state, municipal, and county parks of the nation. The authority for actual study was of no greater impetus to the park movement than was the inspiration it gave to the general ideal of park planning everywhere, and particularly to the state systems. (This function has been transferred to the Bureau of Outdoor Recreation of the Department of the Interior established in April 1962.)

It was during this depression period, too, that a great deal of help in park development was given particularly to the states and to county and metropolitan park systems. Then probably for the first time in the history of the country there was provided through federal aid a sufficient amount of recreation leadership in all levels of government to demonstrate to the public that recreation included many things other than summer playgrounds and sports—e.g., music, drama, art, and cultural pursuits in general.

In 1936 a number of the so-called Recreation Demonstration Projects were turned over to the National Park Service as a part of its responsibility. These areas had been established on lands which were submarginal from an agricultural standpoint, but had recreational possibilities. Through the Civilian Conservation Corps under the direction of the National Park Service, a number of these areas were developed for recreation purposes on a regional scale—actually, a new type of development for that period. For the most part, they were not far away from large concentrations of population and those population centers were not always in a single state. The service that these areas rendered often extended beyond metropolitan or county lines and yet were not typical of state park service. These were true demonstration areas suggesting a more varied development for active recreation than was then prevalent in other metropolitan or state parks. However, the National Park Service did not retain them as a part of its system, as they were later transferred to the lesser levels of government.

National recreation areas, however, emerged, probably as a result of the experience of the National Park Service in their demonstration areas as well as the gradual unfolding of an enlarged recreation responsibility felt by the National Park Service. Perhaps it *was* their responsibility to provide areas of national significance more suited to more active recreation than the superlatively unique areas of national parks. At any rate NPS accepted responsibility for the Demonstration Area around Lake Mead created on the Colorado River when the Reclamation Bureau built Hoover Dam. Others followed in the wake of the construction of other large reservoir lakes.

In the thirties the National Park Service became interested in the acquisition of wilderness areas (the Everglades in Florida) and began surveys of the shorelines of the country, the Great Lakes as well as the ocean shorelines.

The NPS was being criticized from both extremes—those who believed that there was a gradual deterioration of the high standards for national parks and those who believed the Service was not providing enough in the way of recreation. According to Professor Ise, the National Parks Association criticized the confusion in the classification of park areas. "State parks, recreation areas, national parks, and primeval national parks have been shuffled and jumbled until today a confused American public scarcely knows which is which." Later administrations have been similarly criticized by the same association and others on the ground that recreation and general development have been stressed too much to the neglect of "fundamental national park principles and of rigorous protection of scenic values." Professor Ise continues, "It is easy to see how a director might do this, for

most of the forces operating push him in this direction, particularly if he is
ambitious and anxious to see his department grow. Albright and Cammerer
were accused of the same sin—if it is a sin. There may be honest differences of
opinion of this point."

These differences in opinion soon developed into a mounting
realization that somehow there must be established a much more realistic
approach to what the federal government and the states should do about the
great increase in recreation demand that became apparent after World War II
and the alarming forecasts that were made of demands to come. Other federal
and state agencies had already begun to respond to public demand for
recreation use of their properties for camping, fishing and water sports,
hunting, picnicking, and some forms of recreation to which such properties
had not been previously subjected. These agencies included federal and state
forests, wildlife refuges, huge reservoir lakes impounded by Army Engineers
and state water conservancy districts and many others. The 1966 Recreation
and Park Yearbook of the National Recreation and Park Association mentions seventy-two federal agencies that have some interest in recreation
service. Only a few need special attention here. The reader is referred to the
above publication for more detailed information.

FOREST SERVICE—DEPARTMENT OF AGRICULTURE*

"The management of forest and grasslands administered by the
Forest Service is governed by the Multiple-Use, Sustained Yield Act of 1960
under which resources are appraised, evaluated and then administered to yield
the greatest public benefit." Public benefit includes recreation.

The Forest Service had actually been in the business of providing
facilities for camping and other recreation purposes long before 1960, but
only in the last decade has recreation commanded important attention. By
1966 there were 154 national forest and 19 national grasslands located in 41
states and totaling 186.3 million acres and having over 160 million visitor
days of use. Facilities can accommodate 800,000 people at one time. The
1967 budget for outdoor recreation was $74 million.

"Virtually all National Forest lands and waters are available for
public use and activities are typically unrestricted. . . . Only those types of
recreation appropriate to the forest environment are encouraged." This
indicates the complete absence of recreation "supervision" or "guidance" so
prevalent at urban city parks and even of the interpretive programs of the
National Park Service—literally the "end of the line" in the retrogression of
recreation guidance previously referred to.** Another note of the prevalence

---

*Quotations are from the 1966 Recreation and Park Yearbook of NRPA.
**By 1970, interpretive service, guidance in trail use, and permits for public and
quasi-public resident camps were prevalent.

of principles in all recreation administrative and physical design factors is the "zoning" factor suggested in the following quotation.

"The most pristine type of recreational experience is to be found in the wilderness and primitive areas of our National Forests." The status of the National Wilderness Preservation System, established by the Wilderness Act of September 2, 1964, is noted in the following table.

National Forest Wilderness and Primitive Areas, Dec.31, 1965

Types of Area	No. of Areas	Acres	Visitor Days
National Forest Wilderness Area	54	9,108,082	3,129,100
Primitive Areas	34	5,474,987	1,393,000
Scenic Type Areas	92	726,000	- - -

CORPS OF ARMY ENGINEERS

Recreation has not been one of the essential functions of the Army Engineers. In fact only in the last fifteen years have values of recreation use been recognized in the economic justification for the many projects of water supply, flood control, navigation, or power development which are the primary purposes of the Corps. But once great river impoundments were created and water surfaces used, the available shorelands became useful for picnic grounds and many other recreation uses. The value of these resources for recreation became apparent, so the Corps found itself in the recreation business and began to capitalize on its virtues. Facilities and annual use are now impressive.

The Corps administers over 8 million acres of federal land. Besides its 28,000 miles of improved inland and coastal waterways, it operates 350 reservoirs in 44 states. Principal uses are fishing, hunting, boating, camping, and picnicking. Many of its land facilities are leased to other governmental agencies and some to commercial concessionaires, while some are operated by the Corps. Annual visitation is about 130 million. The budget for construction and development of recreation facilities was $31 million for 1967.

FISH AND WILDLIFE SERVICE

This department's role in recreation is to protect, conserve, and restore our fish and wildlife resources. They report that in 1965 there were over 33 million anglers and hunters who spent 700 million recreation days (or some part of a day) at their favorite recreation.

The functions of the department are varied and many, and they manage many acres of land and marsh for game production; also 312 game refuges in all but five of the states, covering 28.5 million acres. Compared to attendance figures of other recreation agencies its annual attendance of about 13 million seems small but this has more than doubled in the last 10 years.

BOR AND HUD

From the standpoint of the park and recreation administrator in all levels of government and in all phases of work, the two most important and influential federal agencies are the Bureau of Outdoor Recreation (BOR) of the Department of the Interior, and the Department of Housing and Urban Development (HUD). Among the many functions of the former is the responsibility of preparing a national recreation plan (formerly a function of the National Park Service) and the allocation of federal recreation funds to other federal agencies and of grants-in-aid to the states and through them to political subdivisions of the states. HUD, having responsibility for urban affairs, allocates grants-in-aid to urban communities from funds raised for urban development. These two agencies, together with all other federal agencies that have an interest in recreation, are brought together at Cabinet level by the President's Council on Recreation and Natural Beauty.

Neither BOR nor HUD have any responsibility in land management for recreation because they are not operating agencies. Their immense influence stems from two main sources: (1) the formulation and promulgation of national policy, and (2), the allocation of grants-in-aid to recreation, mainly for land acquisition and development. BOR aids nonurban projects as well as urban projects, while HUD is restricted to aiding only urban projects.

BUREAU OF OUTDOOR RECREATION

The Bureau was created as a result of recommendations which the Outdoor Recreation Resources Review Commission (ORRRC) submitted to the President and Congress on January 31,1962, after a three-year study of the nation's outdoor recreation resources and needs. The twenty-seven-volume report is available from the Superintendent of Documents either in single volumes or in a total at $2.00 a volume. The summary is titled "Outdoor Recreation for America." This report has had a profound effect on recreation planning and administration due to a documentation of evidence pertaining to recreation preference, degree of use, and an inventory of resources.

By virtue of several public laws enacted since the BOR was established April 1, 1962, the Bureau is authorized to—

Prepare and maintain a continuing inventory and evaluation of the nation's outdoor recreation needs and resources.

Formulate and maintain a comprehensive nationwide outdoor recreation plan.

Provide technical assistance to and cooperate with states, their political subdivisions, and private outdoor recreation interests.

Sponsor, engage in, and assist in outdoor recreation research.

Promote coordination of federal outdoor recreation plans and activities.

Administer a program of financial assistance to the states, and through the states to local public agencies, for planning, acquiring, and developing public outdoor recreation resources.

Coordinate a program of recreation and acquisition by the National Park Service, Forest Service, and Bureau of Sport Fisheries and Wildlife.

Provide outdoor planning assistance to federal water projects.

Provide the Executive Director to the President's Council on Recreation and Natural Beauty.

The BOR has requested state recreation plans from all of the states and has provided a method by which these plans shall be made. It was directed to submit its Nationwide Recreation Plan to Congress by 1968. However by 1972 such a plan had not been made public.

Since its inception and including 1967 BOR has provided funds for the acquisition of 9393 acres of land totaling almost $15 million and 101,878 acres for over $15 million for the Forest Service. States have been allocated $152 million for the fiscal years 1965, 1966, and 1967. This latter allocation of funds is predicated upon the approval of a comprehensive state outdoor recreation plan.

As a point of interest in our underlying premise that area zoning in recreation resource planning is a key factor, this classification by BOR is presented: Class I, High Density Recreation Areas; Class II, General Outdoor Recreation; Class III, Natural Environment; Class IV, Outstanding Natural Feature; Class V, Primitive Area; Class VI, Historic and Cultural Sites. A single property, if it is large and varied enough, might contain several or even all of the classes. Since classification affects both plan and administration, a zoning process has taken place in which use and physical characteristics are harmonized. This process was seen in the classification of the Wilderness areas of the Forest Service; it appears in the more recent state plans of state systems as well as in individual parks and it is in evidence in plans of local systems and local parks.

DEPARTMENT OF HOUSING AND URBAN DEVELOPMENT

This department, created in 1965 by combining several other agencies with new and additional functions, administers federal programs for urban renewal, public housing, urban planning, open space land, mass transit, and community facilities. Open space grants-in-aid to urban agencies are available up to 50 per cent of total cost. Planning assistance up to two-thirds of cost is also available for comprehensive planning of urban needs including parks and recreation. Estimated grants for fiscal 1968 are $90 million for the acquisition of 72,000 acres of land.

Inasmuch as all requests for grants-in-aid are predicated upon plans validated by planning agencies having larger jurisdiction than that of the applicant, it becomes apparent that approved plans must be integrated with plans of greater area scope.

In the discussion of BOR and HUD the full scope of available aid programs, or of authority and influence of the agencies themselves have not been enumerated. Now programs have appeared with fascinating frequency; the federal government is deeply concerned and reasonably responsive to park and recreation problems, once the case is made clear and urgent. This discussion of other federal agencies has not exposed all of their responsibilities and all agencies having an interest in recreation have not been mentioned. Enough has been presented to reveal the major resources and to indicate the general pattern of administrative policy prevalent in the federal government.

The states have administrative departments paralleling the major federal services, often combining several services under one administrative head, called, for example, State Resources Department or Conservation Department. Within such a department one usually finds divisions of State Parks, State Forests, State Minerals, Waters and Drainage; and also a BOR and State Planning. Each of the divisions may or may not have divisional planning sections, but if so, these are coordinated in the State Planning Division. In recent years, some states have recognized the recreation function by including it as part of the State Parks division. The state Division or Bureau of Outdoor Recreation with liaison functions attuned to the federal BOR usually coordinates the federal and state recreation programs and oversees the allocation of state funds to its political subdivisions.

Federal grants-in-aid are not expected to wholly finance recreation facility projects, but to act as an incentive for the states and local communities to wake up and do something for themselves. As of early 1967 over $100 million in qualified projects had been received by the BOR from the states, which means that the states (or subdivisions) were prepared to spend an equal amount. A number of states had authorized bonds ranging from $1.5 million to $200 million. In addition an untold amount of financing took place by cities and counties through HUD aid.

To keep abreast of these fast moving programs, states and urban communities have had to add administrative personnel.

RATIO OF ACRES TO POPULATION

ITS APPLICABILITY

In Chapter 2 it was mentioned that ratios of park acreage to units of population are but rule-of-thumb guides in assessing the adequacy of park lands in a given situation, It has been noted that certain factors involved in park statistics show either progression or retrogression as one considers the transition from city parks to national resources. The ratio we now discuss is one of those factors. The ratio is more meaningful when applied to the local scene, less so to the state resources, and most difficult when applied to federal resources.

The reasons for this seem obvious:

1. A major part of nonurban recreation resource area is made up of outstanding natural features which are not uniformly distributed over the nation or uniformly over the individual states. The great national parks and forests are predominantly in the West where some states are "overrun" with them. Some states also have large areas of state significant resources while others have very little. Hence, a ratio of acres to thousand population applied to states like Idaho or Nevada with large national holdings would not be anything like the results as applied to Kansas or Nebraska where there are few such national assets.

2. Federal resources, occurring as they do in much larger units than do state resources, tend to increase the disparity noted in Paragraph 1.

However, in some instances, e.g., State and National Recreation Areas, the ratio analysis does have some merit.

Several sources suggest that the states should have about 65 acres of parks per thousand population. If the acreage of recreation resources found in forests and wildlife refuges were included, a much higher ratio of park and recreation acreage might be justified. Actually, as of 1966, states already possessed more than twice the ratio of 65 a/1000 pop. but still were pinched for the right kind of space in the proper locations. The following table illustrates the point. The classes listed on the table are those used by BOR as being applicable to state and federal resources; Class I, High Density Recreation; Class II, General Outdoor Recreation; Class III, Natural Environment; Class IV, Outstanding Natural Features; Class V, Primitive Areas; Class VI, Historical and Cultural Sites. Primary statistics are from the 1966 NRPA Yearbook.

There can be some difference of opinion concerning the breakdown of the ratio as shown, but not in great enough degree to alter the general conclusion that the important shortage of area is in the active recreation categories of Classes I and II which are located with reference to population centers. Any surplus areas occur in Class III, which is 90 per cent made up of the state forest and wildlife refuges which are not exclusively recreation resources. The inadequacy of Classes I and II is a current state recreation problem. The usefulness of the ratio technique makes it apparent.

As a whole, federal resources are less susceptible to analysis by the acres to population ratio than the states, as has already been noted. However, National Recreation Areas, like their state counterparts, do find such analysis if not altogether relevant at least helpful. The National Park Service seeks to

STATE RECREATION RESOURCES BY BOR CLASS

CLASS	DESCRIPTION	ACTUAL 1966-AREA	Acre per 1000 pop. for 190,000,000 *Ratio	Computed Acres
I	High Density Recreation	67,291	10	1,900,000
II	General Outdoor Recreation	2,281,927	35	6,650,000
III	Natural Environment	+30,142,298	15	2,850,000
IV	Outstanding Natural Features	671,358	7.5	1,430,000
V	Primitive Areas	1,492,796	7.5	1,430,000
VI	Historical and Cultural Sites	39,272	Small	40,000
TOTALS		34,794,942	75+	14,300,000

*Author's personal suggestion.
+90% Forests, Fisheries, and Wildlife.

establish Recreation Areas, each not less than 20,000 acres and usually much more extensive, within 250 miles of centers of population of about 25 million people. This makes a minimum of 10 a/1000 pop. with usual results far higher. Then, too, a more careful scouting of possible sites for National Scenic Parks, Wild Rivers, Seashore Recreation Areas continues in the regions of the country harboring large centers of population—and a number of qualified national parks are being found. This is a concerted effort to correct, so far as is practical, the natural maldistribution of recreation resources, and in doing so a furtive eye is cast in the direction of the ratio, acres to population.

There is one more vulnerability to the acre/population ratio and that is use by visitation—or rather overuse of critical areas. If annual visitation continues to increase faster than the population, time may come when overuse becomes general. Only two alternatives exist. As the old rancher says, "When the land is overgrazed, reduce the herd or get more pasture land." In our case that additional land must come from new additions to Classes I and II or we rob Class III if any of its lands are accessible. More probably, we may sacrifice the native areas within Class II—a real recreation tragedy. Logically, the ratio of land to population should be revised upward.

In actual practice, no rule-of-thumb ratio is entirely adequate for land acquisition and design purposes. A very careful "market survey" must precede both acquisition and development to ensure an efficient result. More will be said about this later.

Chapter Seven

The Country's Physical
Recreation Resources –
Summary

There is now in government ownership (federal, state, and local) impressive array of diverse land characteristics in great enough quantity to satisfy present recreation needs, *if* the land and its natural superlatives were uniformly distributed, and *if* these were supplemented by other appropriately developed properties at strategic locations so as to be readily available to the whole population, or rather, to all segments of the population at all times. That is not the case and therein lies a fundamental recreation problem: how to produce an adequate and effective national system of physical recreation resources.

Looking at the matter of the maldistribution of the unusual land forms, the most unique are concentrated pretty much in the western part of the country. Each state has attempted to improve this situation by setting aside the best scenic areas, each within its own borders; but generally such superlative values are likewise concentrated—usually at considerable distance from the cities. The cities themselves have all too few naturally scenic parks and, in most cases, have never set aside enough ordinary land for neighborhood and community parks. Too many people find present parks and other recreation areas too remote or too crowded to fully enjoy.

Cities have undertaken redevelopment of their worn-out parts and experimented with model city projects; suburban new towns have sprung up offering new ideas of space allocation for parks and recreation; metropolitan park systems have been created with large recreation parks serving as substitutes for the old large city parks; states have supplemented scenic parks with state recreation areas, as has the National Park Service; the NPS has acquired seashore Recreation Areas, Wilderness Areas, Wild Rivers; the Forest Service has opened new areas for camping, permitted the establishment of resident camp sites by volunteer welfare agencies, has cooperated with local public and quasi-public agencies in constructing and operating ski centers; the river impoundments of the Army Engineers have been made available for recreation; such agencies as BOR and HUD have dispensed millions in grants-in-aid financing. Still the problem of inadequacy persists.

It persists (and probably will continue to persist) because people are not static as to their location or constant as to their quantitative and qualitative appetite for recreation. They travel hither and yon in all directions and in all manner of conveyances; they readily change their places of residence and today they want something different in the way of recreation from that which they enjoyed yesterday. As a society they are mobile, fluid, flexible, whimsical, and hard to classify in any way that will be long lasting.

However, since recreation resources are to be acquired (in the natural state) and developed for people, no solution to the inadequacy problem can be successfully attacked without studying people and their motivations. (Rule-of-thumb standards are not precise enough for careful analysis.)

While the inherent instincts of human behavior are relatively, if not absolutely, constant, their manifestations vary with time and circumstance, with changing social habits and changing mores. A study of the causal factors of social change is crucial to any attempt to supply appropriate recreation resources to all people and to each and every segment of the population at a given period of time, a period of time which is more than transient in extent.

These causal factors are myriad in number, often subtle in character, dynamic rather than static in nature, and sometimes hard to recognize and identify. They affect each other as well as the resources and the people. They are variables in any attempt at devising a mathematical equation. The accompanying enumeration of some of the more significant and easily recognized factors is presented as a suggestion of the scope of the problem at hand.

1. Population Growth. The more people, the more recreation resources that are needed. Determination of *rate* of growth is needed to

forecast the population at a given time—the time at which the resources will be needed.

2. Change in Population Characteristics. Age groups; sex; racial and ethnic groupings and percentages of total; identification of concentrations, all to help fix location of resources and give some initial clues to required attributes of the resource.

3. Economic Status. A measure of disposable income after survival requirements, by social and ethnic groupings and relative to geographic location. Helps fix the nature and amount of recreation resources required. Has an effect on mobility. Economic and social status—prestige—has a subtle but powerful and pervasive affect upon both physical recreation resources and recreation service in general.

4. Leisure Time. For simplification this means the amount of time not needed for survival purposes and other time related thereto. It measures the time available for personal choice of alternative activities—recreation in all its varied forms. It affects mobility and presents alternative recreation resources required for alternative recreation pursuits.

5. Changing Ethics and Moral Attitudes. This affects amount, quality, and character of recreation pursuits and hence the required resources.

6. Quality of the Environment. This affects quality, quantity, and location of actual and potential recreation resources.

7. Ecology of People with relation to nature, its plants and animals, with other people, and with industrial production and its necessary adjuncts. The alternative of land development vis-a-vis land conservation is an almost constant confrontation with unpredictable results. Here might be considered the matter of complete racial integration versus the emergence of racial and ethnic enclaves or socioeconomic groupings in urban areas.

8. Mobility of People. This is perhaps the most pervasive of all the factors bearing on the determination of adequate recreation resources in all their categories. People not only travel about with astonishing ease, they change residence location about once every six or seven years. The physical aspects of neighborhoods consequently change, introducing different kinds of people for each decade of change.

The travel propensities are almost impossible to keep up with—foreign travel, family vacation travel; camper vehicles are often more numerous on the highways than passenger cars. People travel by car, bus, bicycle and motorcycle, by plane, hitch-hiking and ordinary hiking. Dune buggies and other off-the-road vehicles are carried in trailers and trucks for use at some temporary destination. Literally hordes of youths may invade a national park, forest, or some prearranged camp site with surprisingly short notice and, like ants, they suddenly overwhelm everything.

9. The Inner City. This has some unique situations of its own. Its

existence has an impact on other municipal recreation resources, and, because of its potentially explosive social nature, it is of extreme significance to all organized society. City slums and havens of the poor and nonconformists, the destitute and often the dangerous, have been a part of urban communities for hundreds of years. These ghettos are being constantly studied and also served by sociologists and social workers, police authorities as well as by recreation workers. Somehow, so far as meaningful recreation resources are concerned, there is still much to be learned. The inner city may be remote and somewhat apart from other phases of our study, but its influence on the whole subject of adequate recreation resources is real; it could be the focus of some great unforeseeable social crisis.

10. The Private Sector. The appetite for the fruits of recreation makes no distinction between that which is publicly owned and that which is private. Price in its various aspects may cause a choice to be made, but the desire for the costly or unattainable is ever present; therefore to consider only the private or the publicly owned is to consider only part of the whole, for each part affects the other part as well as the whole.

The main attention in this book is directed toward the public sector. In the eyes of the consuming public it is only part of the market. A person may sample the publicly owned recreation resources, but if he is not satisfied he begins to seek alternatives. If neighborhood services are inadequate, he looks for the resources of churches, public welfare agencies, commercial substitutes. If tennis courts, golf, swimming facilities are nonexistent nearby, he must spend time and money to go farther away. He may forego boating except on infrequent occasions unless facilities are nearby and of reasonable price. Theaters, movies, museums, libraries (public and private), spas, ski resorts, amusement centers on the order of Disneylands—literally a host of recreation attractions either in competition with or in supplement to publicly owned recreation resources must be considered in the location and development of publicly owned facilities.

In Chapters 4, 5, and 6, there was pictured in a general way the presently available physical recreation resources (principally land) and, by using a land-population ratio, a rough measure of the adequacy of those resources was made for each of the major categories. The function of land in a recreation service was dealt with in a general way which led to a consideration of the development of the natural land for appropriate recreation services. Land and its development became "recreation resources." The most detailed aspects of land development were dealt with in Chapter 4. In Chapter 6, the development aspect was least important but it was certainly still present.

In this summary, Chapter 7, let it now be stated that the physical recreation resource dealt with throughout is land and its development; natural land is more in evidence in the federal properties and less in evidence in municipal properties but in all public properties both land and its development each play a part—always, even in Wilderness areas.

Let it also be now stated that measuring the adequacy of recreation resources (either as a single unit or a complete system of units) cannot be done with accuracy by the land area-population ratio method. A review of the imposing list (incomplete as it is) of the social factors having marked influence on the adequacy of recreation resources makes this apparent.

Even a cursory examination of the aforementioned list leads to the conclusion that if an accurate measurement of the adequacy of recreation resources *could* be made it would be relevant for only a short "moment" in time. Times and conditions change much too rapidly. By identifying some of the numerous factors involved in that rapid change, one can begin to penetrate the complexity and enormity of determining the adequate recreation services for any given period of time. The key, then, is to be aware of the social trends, to identify them, measure the effect of each on the requirements of recreation service (land development and recreation management), and then locate its focus in time. This is like firing at a moving target from a moving base using ammunition variable in both speed and substance.

There is no one formula for solving the problems outlined above. What is needed is the ability to think, i.e., to identify and collect pertinent facts, to analyze them with reference to the problem, and to make decisions. That is also the ultimate objective of education, for study is a continuous process throughout life—not just an exercise at a university.

In view of the conditions noted, it is not surprising that a very fertile field has opened up for all sorts of planners and analysts—architects, engineers, sociologists, ecologists, economists, statisticians, philosophers, and various combinations thereof. Large sums of money have been spent on plans and reports for local, state, and federal bureaus. Only a few of them have been pertinent long enough to be translated into action. Those projects that have survived have usually been of limited scope and timed for prompt execution. It is more typical than otherwise that the national recreation plan of BOR, originally scheduled for 1968 disclosure should, five years later, be shuttled from bureau to bureau and then declared to be incomplete and now untimely. "A little longer wait will result in a better plan," so it is said. The perfect and timely plan is all but impossible. A deadline must be set and met and matters progressed from that point on.

In the meantime history is being made, on the one hand by the inexperienced and scantily schooled innovator who does not yet know what is "impossible" and on the other hand by the knowledgeable practitioner who is confident and bold enough to stake his all on his own reasoning. Small, but significant gains are being made. The sum total progress is appreciable.

Chapter Eight

The Making of
a Park Plan

It was noted in Chapter 1 that the administration of park and other recreation resources required the use of a rather extensive number of specialists—professionals, scientists, technicians, skilled and unskilled workmen. The administrator obviously cannot be a specialist in all the ramified functions within his department; he must assign duties, receive responses, consider findings of investigations, make decisions, and delegate responsibility in as broad terms as possible. Otherwise he will become bogged down in detail with little time to think and to plan strategy of operation.

Nevertheless, the administrator must have some knowledge of the specialized fields under his command at least to a degree that will permit an intelligent appraisal of the value of the specialized operations. Three of these special fields most often discussed among young executives—planning, budgeting, and organization—are given some treatment in the following three chapters. The discussions are not complete but enough detail is given to expose the nature of the functions, how they are handled, and what an administrator may look for to appraise the efficiency. Other departmental functions may be touched upon from time to time in other chapters. In all cases the future administrator should look for generalities rather than specific details (better left to the specialist), keeping in mind that the broader the horizon of knowledge the better equipped he becomes to make the far-reaching decisions.

The future administrator (and present ones too) must always have in mind the central purpose of all recreation resource operations: to provide a service that will afford the greatest opportunity for the life enrichment of the user and encourage him to utilize his leisure time for the development of his own potential and the betterment of society. Only a radical change in social values of civilized people can change that.

That kind of service is made up of appropriate physical recreation facilities together with a well-conceived guidance and protection service for the best use of those facilities. Hence, the physical resources are chosen, and the use directed in accordance with the needs and desires of the using public, all within the budget limits set by the people's representatives for that service.

The public service is only part of the total recreation service that the public utilizes and the physical park and recreation grounds are only part of that public service. Therefore, while the making of a park plan is being considered an eye must be kept open for the service available through private and quasi-public agencies. Such a reminder as this needs frequent repetition.

THE MAKING OF A PARK PLAN

To make a plan for an individual park, even a small one, is a very technical matter. It looks disarmingly simple to make a layout for the ball diamond here and the tennis court there, and the hard surface area, playground apparatus, horseshoe courts, building, wading pool or swimming pool in various other locations, and to put them together so that they form a decent pattern. Be assured that while this can be done on paper and look reasonably simple, much more needs to be done.

The student will feel that this sort of simple operation may be learned in a short time—certainly within the scope of one semester. Such is not the case. If a student has a background in simple architecture or the use of drafting instruments and the techniques of delineation; if he has studied surveying and the techniques of topographical mapping; if he has a background in plant materials and simple engineering construction; if he understands all that is being taught in this course pertaining to park administration of recreation resources; if he understands the technique of simple research; if some landscape planning has been included in his curriculum—then he is prepared to begin a course in park and other recreation area design. Until then he is not ready.

This should not be entirely discouraging—the graduate in Landscape Architecture and the graduate in Recreation or Forestry are no better off. The landscape architect has the skills in planning, delineation, and representation, the Forestry student in the preservation of forest ecology and timber production and other techniques, but none is a specialist in park design or recreation resource administration. The Recreation graduate and the Park Management graduate, the Forestry graduate, and the Engineer can provide to the planner the special insight into park and recreation service which the planner does not have. Pooling their talents and working together they are capable of producing good results. In short, the creation of a sound, functional, beautiful park design is a cooperative effort involving more than one professional.

Park planning is, therefore, a specialized field in the overall operation of the park and recreation organization. The park administrator must recognize that fact. He must necessarily be very close to the planning operation, but he need not be a specialist in that operation. In view of this, no effort will be made in this chapter to give detailed instructions in park planning. There will be included, however, some discussion on resource material, relationships in the design process, and some general criteria for judging the worth of the final plan.

DESCRIPTION OF SOME BASIC RESOURCE MATERIAL— PARTICULARLY PLANS

There are two general definitions of a plan:

1. *A plan is the representation of an object drawn on a single plane.* A single map is a plan, but a single map as a final product is seldom sufficient in park administration. It may be a step toward the final product or it may be one of a series of maps the whole of which may suit the purpose. A floor plan of a building likewise reflects only one piece of the total information we need to judge the worth of the project, to construct it, or to operate it.

2. *A plan is a method or scheme of action.*

A budget is a plan of action: the action involves expenditure of funds.

A report may encompass a plan of action or it may be only a part of a plan of action.

A plan for construction of a building includes a number of plans (called working drawings) and a descriptive report (called specifications).

Plans for the construction of a park or other recreation facility include working drawings (often simply called plans) and specifications.

A plan of operation for recreation facilities includes maps of parks and a report of instructions as to methods of maintenance and use of the properties after the park has been constructed.

An organization chart is a plan of personnel responsibilities in the operation of an organization.

Other examples are numerous.

In speaking of plans we often use the expressions "plats" and "maps." A plan of a piece of land is usually called a plat (generally applied to a land subdivision or property survey), or a map.

Plans may refer to operational plans or plans of physical things for actual or proposed construction or execution. In this chapter we will deal mostly, but not exclusively, with plans of construction. Reference will be made to "plats" showing property ownership and "maps" showing land characteristics. Reports in connection with these plans will usually be strictly reportorial (reporting facts), analytical, and descriptive (specifications).

Property surveys on which land plats are based are made by land surveyors registered by the state and authorized by law to practice in a particular state. Civil engineers are also legally registered (as are architects) and are often also registered land surveyors. Land descriptions as a basis for plats and for the conveyance of land titles can be made by land surveyors, but before they are used in legal instruments, they should be verified by lawyers specializing in title investigation (title search or examining title abstracts) because the exact wording used is often necessary to ensure contiguity of adjoining parcels, and for other reasons. Land descriptions as used in deeds can present some rather tricky problems; consequently, the employment of both lawyer and land surveyor is often advisable.

Land plats or the information for making them are usually obtainable in the office of the county registrar of deeds.

Topographic maps show land topography (variation in land heights), location of physical characteristics such as woods (sometimes individual trees with size and species given, for example, 24-inch elm), lakes, water courses, buildings, roads, trails, power transmission lines, underground utilities (sewer, water, and drainage lines), and all other features that will clarify the character of the land. Land plats and topographic maps are sometimes superimposed on each other; this combination is the most basic material for the park planner.

Sometimes suitable topographic maps can be purchased, but often special topographic surveys and maps must be made. Even when maps can be purchased they usually have to undergo processes which will either reduce or enlarge the scale to fit a particular requirement.

The most complete and accurate of purchasable maps are those of the United States Geological Survey. These are available for most of the country. They show complete topographic information as well as geological characteristics of the underground with appropriate texts. Sometimes the maps of only the earth's surface may be purchased separately.

The United States Department of Agriculture sells aerial maps which are aerial photos and show what can be seen from the air. Their accuracy depends upon how much overlay or duplication of adjoining photos takes place. These are excellent for reconnaissance work.

Local aerial survey companies can often provide aerial maps. Usually these companies can also supply topographic information on the maps, the land elevations being supplied by a stereoscopic procedure. They are available in various scale sizes.

Other government agencies—state highway departments, county highway departments, planning commissions—can often supply basic maps. These agencies can also supply plans for future development of their particular phase of work.

Still other federal agencies are making advances in more and more sophisticated aerial photography (notably infrared) that make possible the detection of various land cover characteristics of value in planning. The student is advised to keep abreast of these developments.

Informative maps, particularly those pertaining to the ecology of a region, can usually be obtained from the state conservation or natural resource department. These maps show soil conditions, lake and stream characteristics, forest areas and tree species, wildlife distribution and characteristics, mineral resources, and others.

Universities (land-grant colleges in particular) may also have similar maps as well as maps showing the results of special studies related or important to park administration.

DEVELOPING A PLAN FOR A PARK

The general planning process consists of these major steps: (1) the preparation of an investigative report; (2) topographic survey and map; (3) the preparation of diagrammatic sketches; (4) design of a preliminary plan; (5) the preparation of working drawings and specifications; (6) the report and plan for the method of maintenance and operation when the construction is completed.

PARK PLANS A PART OF DEPARTMENTAL POLICY

A park plan may be considered a declaration of intent to do something at some future time. That *something* must be a part of the total purpose of providing that kind of recreation service which that particular public agency in that particular level of government is organized to provide. The plan of a park (or other recreation facility) is a declaration of po icy just as thoroughly as is any written document. The things called for in that plan must, therefore, be consistent with the policies of administration because it is a part of such policies.

For plans that have the immediate prospect of execution into finished jobs, all the previously named six steps must be carried through. For projects which might be included in a five-year program, the steps up, through, and including the preliminary design may be sufficient. For projects more remote than five years, it is possible that the steps may not go much beyond the making of the diagrammatic sketches. In all these cases, estimates of cost should be included, but these again are in the several stages of exactness depending upon how soon the project is to be carried out.

In all cases, the park plan, however sketchy, should always carry with it a declaration of intent of how it is to function. This statement may be in general terms for projects quite remote in time, but for projects being carried out promptly, this statement should be quite exact.

Once a plan for the development of each park in the whole system of parks has been made, we have a total declaration of intent stating how the planners expect to develop parks individually, and the system as a whole. This total plan of development becomes a part of the total future policy of the board or the department and must be consistent with the development plans of each of the other divisions of the department, with the standards of requirement nationally accepted, with plans for future financing of development, maintenance and operation, methods of administration, and all else that goes to make up the total operational intent of the entire department.

From what has been written of the BOR and the nationwide plan and of HUD and its regulations, it is obvious that any plan for acquisition or development of a whole park and recreation system, or of a single part of such a system, must be consistent with the federal requirements as a matter of both prudence and the necessity of qualifying for grants-in-aid.

It has been noted before that the making of a park plan, that is, the design of an actual park, is a cooperative procedure requiring the talents of expert planners, the engineer, recreation director, the maintenance supervisor, and perhaps a number of others who will have a hand in either operating or maintaining the project after it is completed. There are also administrative policies that are woven into each plan, such as the standard of excellence, the durability of construction, the method of handling certain types of recreation services, and similar considerations and there are still others that, in the ultimate, may have an important influence on the suitability of the plan. All of these should be consulted.

It would be a mistake if the governing body of the park department were not apprised of the whole volume of plans for proposed development. Final and formal approval may not be necessary until the project is about to be executed, but preknowledge of the intent of all of the plans ought to be given to, for instance, members of the park board or anyone who is superior to the director of parks and recreation. Inasmuch as this declaration of intent is a part of the declaration of policy of the entire level of government in which we are operating (the city, state, or for that matter, the nation), it calls for coordination with the plans and aspirations of other departments of that level of government. In the city, that means that the urban planners must be aware of the existence of such a plan and must have knowledge of the overall policy intent and be able to refer to specific parts whenever that becomes important in the development of a city plan. If a total city plan is developed, the agreed-upon park and recreation plan becomes a part of the total city plan. The country and state situations are analogous.

The question of if, when, and under what circumstances the public is to be taken into confidence in planning matters has long been a matter of inconsistent departmental policy. As the public has become more knowledgeable, more vocal, and more critical of decisions of government, that of "if" has all but disappeared. The general public must be consulted.

A new dimension has now been added. Recent legal requirements are that a report on the impact on the environment must precede the construction of any public work—and very likely of any private work as well. The public is being accorded a voice—even a final voice—in determining what kind of an environment it chooses to live in. At what stage of planning the public is to be consulted is an open question, but they, the people, must be part of that planning.

INVESTIGATIVE REPORTS OR ANALYSES

In all cases in this discussion it is assumed that the particular park or other facility which is about to be planned fits into an overall park plan involving the city, the county or metropolitan region, the state, or the federal government, whichever has control of the park district in which this particular park lies. It is essential that this park and the purpose for which it was acquired be related to the entire park system of which it is a part. It is from that point on that the investigation proceeds.

This report, or analysis of conditions, is a listing of, and comments on, all matters that are needed to make a facility plan which properly accommodates itself to the uses it is expected to get. Obviously, there must be an analysis of the characteristics and recreation habits of the people who live within the zone of influence of the park and who will use the facility. The contents of the park and space needed for each item are determined from this analysis.

The site must be visited, not once but perhaps often, preferably with the topographic map in hand. At this time, all information about the site which has a bearing on the arrangement of facilities within the proposed park and which has not been shown on the topographic map must be noted—ground cover, soil inspection, how drainage runs, highways and roadways bordering or near the site, the character of buildings in the vicinity, presence of water supply, power lines, municipal sewer lines, etc. It is probably necessary to visit local public offices for information on underground services not apparent by site inspection, future plans for roads and highways, building zoning regulations, police and fire protection, etc.

The following are some suggestions for specific information for each of the major classes of parks. Keep in mind that in each case the environmental impact on this development must be investigated. It is well to remember, too, that while people and their propensities are the basis for the plan, the plan itself may affect the nature of the use of that plan when it becomes a reality. In other words, the people influence the plan, but the plan also may dictate the kind of clientele.

Neighborhood Parks and Community Playfields: A knowledge of the exact character of municipal recreation program for which these parks are essentially used becomes the first thing to be determined. This is followed by population analysis including trends of growth, age groups, ethnic groups, social and economic groups. Make note of any trend in possible change in the population characteristics, present and proposed land use of the area which this park is to serve, the age of buildings and structures, the possibility of rehabilitation and redevelopment; land values may or may not be important enough for special attention. The relationship of the location of this park to the area which it serves and to schools, streets, and highways (all present and proposed) are to be noted. In considering the recreation program (a necessary element in the investigation) certain local basic policies must be known: Is swimming being provided by natural beaches, by pools, and if by pools, are there fewer large ones or more smaller ones? Does the department favor wading pools or spray pools? What is the policy as to the function of buildings in both neighborhood parks and community playfields? To what extent are school buildings and school grounds available for community recreation? Must provision be made for skating either on artificial rinks or natural ice? What recreation functions and what space are required for those activities that are peculiar to this city? Other similar and related matters pertinent to the investigation will suggest themselves as the process continues.

Large City Parks: These are susceptible to many uses and the tendency over time is to utilize every "vacant" area with some special facility such as a building (outdoor theater, museum, auditorium, even fire station or municipal parking lot) or an active play area. This eroding process changes the original intent of the park; its original plan and charm are violated and there is little left for native or simulated native landscape. Many of these facilities should have a home of their own. Be careful not to crowd too many diverse uses and too little landscape into the original design.

As to the investigative report, what special features does this site have—stream, lake, waterfall, hills, valleys, woods, special views, archaeological or historic items, and so forth? What is its relationship to other similar parks in distance, zone of influence, other land uses in the vicinity, access, location of streets and highways? Is it necessary to provide for neighborhood park or community playfield within this larger park area? Is this area large enough to be suitable for such special uses as zoos, arboretums, garden centers, museum sites, day camping, picnicking, swimming, tennis or athletic centers, stadiums, outdoor theaters, golf, parkways? Which of these areas must be provided for and which other uses may it be adaptable for if found advantageous? What is the probable zone of influence of each of the *functions*? What will be the attendance at the various use areas, and how will that attendance be distributed by the hour on peak days, by the days of the week, by the seasons of the year? Compare the required space with the available space and make suitable adjustments of number and kind of uses or adjustment of maximum capacity permitted. Most of the information required for community playfield and neighborhood parks such as population characteristics, zoning, types of buildings, and so forth will be needed within the zone of influence of this large city park.

County or Metropolitan Parks: Area use-zoning is more apparent in these parks than in city parks where the zoning is apparent only when the idea is applied to the entire park system, although in reality and on a small scale it exists in the smallest park. In county parks, however, the planner is conscious of the need of applying zoning to all parks; in fact the classification system itself is a zoning process pertaining to the entire park system.

The investigative report is based on the assumption that the county's parks are classified as to preserves, active recreation parks, and historical and cultural sites. It is also assumed that a ratio of permissible developed area to native area has been established as park district policy. In such an overall view of the entire park system, a determination of the radius of use must be made for all parks, or an origin and destination analysis of the park users. If this has not been done, it becomes the first objective of the present investigative report. The radius of influence, the distance and origin of the user, the socioeconomic characteristics of the population within this zone of influence, and their habits of recreation are not easy or inexpensive to determine. It should be realized that several studies have been made applying a process to a specific location and many more will be made in the future. So the admonition here is to refer to these investigations and apply the improved principles to the situation. In any event, some determinations, however approximate, must be made.

As previously noted, sometimes the suburban towns have difficulty in providing large city parks so the county or metropolitan district has filled in the gaps.

If the county or metropolitan district policy prescribes that the park now being planned is in the nature of a large city park acquired to complement the park system of suburban communities, then the investigation is similar to the investigation outlined above for large city parks. More likely, the park district policy prescribed for this particular park includes functions more typical of the usual functions of county and metropolitan parks; uses similar to those of a large city park will be prevalent, but in a more spacious environment of a more native character; hence more information on the ecology of the area, character of soils, tree and shrubbery growth, topography, geology, water characteristics become essential. More information is required on accessibility, distance to centers of population, presence of highways and county roads, probable radius of influence, and the general nature of everything that is within that radial zone. Inasmuch as this park is probably outside of the service area of municipal utilities, factors pertaining to them become important—the source of water supply, the possibility of sewage disposal, accessibility to electric power and possibly even to natural gas. The same investigation as to space required for the functions that must be performed, the adaptability of this piece of property to other functions, and how much space each will require needs to be made.

County parks of the preserve classification are the insurance for retaining native areas of the county for a long, long time. Hence it is necessary to preserve these areas. This is done, it is hoped, by permitting only about one-fifth to be developed for active use. This is one of the reasons for the acreage to be in thousands instead of in hundreds. Because of its size it can be readily zoned for areas of various intensities of use. The prime native areas will have lowest use density, and access to them will be limited to horseback riding, hiking, and possibly a parkway or scenic drive with no parking areas except for small turnouts for outstanding views. This sort of arrangement makes compliance with low density use almost automatic.

Assuming one-fifth of the park is to be developed for active use, that portion can also be zoned variously from high density use to medium; the former would include the swimming beach and boat launch with adjacent area for high density picnicking while the latter zoning would include overnight camping and incidental picnicking.

In making the investigative report, appropriate areas for these use-zones may be noted as a preliminary suggestion to the planner with the reasons for making these suggestions.

The active recreation parks do not carry the same burden of perpetual preservation that the preserves do. By their very nature of being largely developed, they protect the preserves from suffering, the native areas from being encroached upon by active use. Consequently, these recreation parks can be in hundreds of acres instead of in thousands and can be quite fully developed, keeping in mind that the lure of all metropolitan parks is the sense of space in a natural setting that is difficult to find in city parks. The zoning concept is here present as in the preserves except that the low use density of the preserve may be present very little if at all. Allocation of these density zones may be made in the investigative report as mentioned before.

State Parks and Other Recreation Resources: State parks are of two general types—(1) those that are unique and, consequently, resource based, the areas which need to be preserved in their native state, and still to be made accessible, and (2) those state parks which carry the classification of state recreation areas, the main purpose of which is to provide outdoor recreation in a natural environment readily accessible to centers of population. It is presumed that the state policy has determined which functions are to be performed by the particular park being investigated. It will have been determined previous to the investigation what proportion of the total area of the park should be left native or made native in character and which proportion of the park might be devoted to the active types of recreation appropriate to state parks. As was true in county parks, the character of soils, tree growth, vegetation of all kinds, geological features, the characteristics of lakes and streams, possibilities of water supply and sewage disposal, presence of wildlife (state policy will have determined whether hunting and fishing are to be permitted), the necessity of control measures for wildlife, highway accessibility, distance from centers of population, estimates of probable use of the various possible outdoor recreation facilities are all matters of concern. Archaeological and historical treasures must be thoroughly documented as to exact location, and all information pertaining to the events which make this site significant must be investigated.

State parks are not the only class of recreation resources available on the state level. State forests, wildlife refuges, some national forests, reservoirs of the Corps of Engineers and the Reclamation Service are also present. Then, too, a greater array of recreation pursuits must be dealt with: hunting, fishing, motoring for pleasure, overnight accommodations are examples. Privately owned facilities either complement or compete; hunting and fishing camps and preserves, campgrounds and resorts, and ski runs are examples.

These facilities and recreation pursuits complicate the preparation of an investigative report and all of these should be carefully noted. But their presence need not discourage the necessary process of determining the socioeconomic characteristics of potential clientele: who they are, how many of them, how often do they come, how long will they stay, how much space will they need for various purposes, and the degree of sophistication they might expect in the accommodations. Zones of influence of the individual facilities being planned should be determined in much the same way as in other cases, but there may be more factors to contend with. The general principles heretofore outlined remain unchanged.

The factor of preservation of the native and unique resources of the state is more pronounced and of greater importance than it was in the county situation. Greater attention must be paid to the ecology of plant and animal life in the face of human invasion. Hence the extent of subject matter contained in the investigative analysis is greater than in any of the city or county settings.

National Recreation Resources: There is only one National Park Service. Since its organization in 1916 it has been functioning and has developed its methods of preliminary investigations for proposed acquisition and facility development quite thoroughly and systematically. Many examples of its reports are available. These should show the young administrator the process on the national level and provide suggestions for carrying on investigations in his own field. He will notice that in all NPS investigations great emphasis is given to the native recreation assets even for potential Recreation Areas, and to the desirability of including all those assets in a given area within the boundaries of the proposed acquisition.

In general, the planning of national parks and other recreation resources parallels the procedure outlined for the states with expected increase or decrease of emphasis on certain factors: lesser percentage of developed to total area, element of preservation more pronounced, a greater number of use-zones in any one park. Although the radius of influence of national scenic parks is nationwide, experience has shown that the bulk of the visits (because of repeaters) come from within 200 to 250 miles of the park. Scenic parks are where nature put them—resource based without reference to centers of population. But National Recreation Areas are usually located where there is a population of about 25 million within a 250 mile radius. Hence the socioeconomic status and recreation habits of the population within the 250 mile radius of influence will determine the use pattern of Recreation Areas and will greatly influence the use pattern of the traditional National Parks like Yosemite and Grand Canyon.

Other federal recreation resources are of as great a variety and exceed in numbers those of the states. Again, the principles of determining the factors governing planning (investigative reports) are the same as in previous cases. Both on the federal and the state levels, a tie-in with the nationwide recreation plan of BOR should be made.

Summary of Investigative Reports: In summary, the investigative report provides the necessary instruction for the planner to make his plan by providing these elements:

√   The purpose for which the park is provided.

√   The uses to which the park is to be put.

√   The probable amount and character of the various uses and, consequently, the space required for each.

√   The source of expected attendance: from which directions, at what times, and in what amounts.

√   The permanency of the present pattern of use, as to use character, quantity, and timing.

√   The land characteristics (topography, biology, etc.).

√   Special foundation conditions for buildings and other structures, soil conditions for vegetation, soil conditions for sewage disposal systems, possible underground source for potable water supply assuming public utility services are unavailable.

√   And all departmental policy statements that affect park planning; some general description of any program for organized recreation or park interpretation, nature programs, etc.

√   Any other information which will help the planner determine space requirements and space location.

As a part of the planning process the investigative report will probably consume almost as much time as the preparation of the preliminary plan, and the time required increases as the attention proceeds from neighborhood parks to the great national resources. In cases where the park site and its environment are well known because of previous experience with that locality, short cuts may present themselves either by eliminating some elements of the formal report or by investigation of only those elements which present themselves as the preliminary plan is being prepared. However, such short cuts are not recommended to anyone except the most experienced planners and even in those cases their continued practice is fraught with possible gross errors.

In the determination of probable amount and character of use the proposed facility is to be planned for, an analysis of the socioeconomic status of the expected users, matched with what these kinds of people expect and require in the way of recreation facilities, form the basis of any such approximation. The necessity of precision in this analysis is greatest in the metropolis and less so in the cases of federal resources. Information and methodology at this writing may be sufficient to approximate requirements for state and national parks, but in planning recreation facilities for urban living much more precise information is needed. Urbanologists (including sociologists and psychologist specialists) are busy finding out what social amenities (including parks and recreation services) are necessary, not only the minimum that can be tolerated but what in kind and quantity are needed for happy urban living. This fitting together of socioeconomic groupings and recreation needs must go on in many situations if the more or less intuitive or rule-of-thumb methods of the past are to be improved upon. In preparing investigative reports on urban proposals, the closer the ideal can be reached the more successful will be the result.

THE DRAWING OF THE PLAN

The first stage of the actual drafting process consists of several cut-and-try attempts at producing a diagrammatic sketch in which each of the functional space areas is blocked out, the size of those spaces having been determined from the investigative report. This is usually done on an overlay on the topographic map of the site. No attempt is made to fill in the details. Even at this first stage, consultation between the planner and the administrator is important because of the functional relationships between the various areas set aside for each of the functions. A number of diagrammatic sketches of this sort will be produced before one is chosen as the basis of the preliminary plan. Some of the more important criteria to watch out for are listed below in each of the major park categories.

1. Neighborhood Parks, 10 acres more or less. The athletic field should fit the topography as closely as possible in order to avoid excessive grading and to permit the salvaging of as many trees and other useful, scenic features as possible. If the building is to be used as a skating shelter, it should be close to the athletic field assuming that the athletic field will be flooded for skating. However, that location ought to be far enough away from home base to be safe from batted balls. If the athletic field is not to be used for skating, the building may be removed a little farther from the athletic field but still in its general proximity. Faulty foundation conditions may influence the placing of the building to more suitable locations and this in turn will have an effect on the location of the athletic field and related facilities. The building will function as a shelter building with toilet facilities and probably headquarters for both playground leader and maintenance man. Facilities for the smaller children should be in the vicinity of the building for closer supervision. These facilities include general hard-surfaced area, apparatus area, wading pools, etc. Sports areas for groups of older children and adults, such as basketball, volleyball, horseshoe, tennis, shuffleboard, bowls, etc., can be a little bit farther away from the building. All lawn spaces should be located to make their limited use and preservation (devoid of paths and worn-out spots) almost automatic through proper design of trafficways. The overall aspect should be susceptible of being developed into a pleasing pattern—a real aesthetic asset to the neighborhood.

When neighborhood parks are adjacent to schools and the grounds of both can be planned as one, certain other guides may be noted. First it must be determined if a separate park building is necessary or will the needed conveniences be provided in the school. If a separate building is required, sufficient dispersal space should be allowed between school and park to permit placing of the facilities for smaller children convenient to the park building but close enough to the school for convenient recess use. The athletic field can be a reasonable distance from the school but not too far. Provision for some auto parking is necessary for teachers and public use. Some of this parking can be used for recreation daytimes and some evenings, but provision for blocking off a part of it is necessary. No other parking area is necessary because this is a park that is "walked to" and not "driven to."

Neighborhoods and planned communities are no longer stereotypes. Density of population is often the factor that characterizes the variation from the usual neighborhood facility. An apartment house neighborhood may be void of children and overloaded with adults and senior citizens having no use for a regulation baseball field. On the other hand such a neighborhood could be overloaded with children of all ages with a minority of adults. An unusual amount of active play facilities—indoor and outdoor—with much more acreage is needed. Planned communities in other variable situations have neighborhood facilities in keeping with the more spacious home lots, and other recreation facilities befitting the needs of a special kind of inhabitant. Likewise, if "cluster" planning takes place the distribution of park space is quite special.

Other variations from the stereotype result from departmental policy in providing such services as swimming, tennis, indoor programs, and others. Examples: Is swimming provided in only Olympic size pools at community centers or supplemented by smaller pools (or wading pools) at almost all neighborhood parks? Are tennis courts provided at all local parks or are they concentrated mostly at special tennis centers? Are small gyms or games rooms provided at all local parks or are such indoor activities limited to large gyms and community centers? These and similar matters must be considered in neighborhood park planning.

2. Community Play Fields, 20 or more acres. The space allocation in this situation undergoes the same process as in the case of neighborhood parks, but there is more athletic area and also the possibility of other elements such as community building including gymnasiums or large social room with several club rooms, swimming pool which may or may not be developed in conjunction with the community building, auto parking areas, a separate tot lot area, some area devoted to neighborhood picnicking, and quiet unorganized use, more chance for plantings. The relationship of the "functional blocks" of the diagrammatic sketch has more possible patterns than in the neighborhood park case, and hence the greater importance of

operational advice or criticism to the planner. It should be kept in mind that recreational functioning in both neighborhood parks and community play fields are paramount to topographical and horticultural features some of which may have to be sacrificed to permit good operation. Nevertheless, the final design should present a very pleasing pattern which again will be an asset to the entire community; hence the diagram should be susceptible of being developed into such a scheme.

3. Large City Parks, 100 acres or more. Scenic beauty and topographic interest dominate the large city park. Every effort is made, therefore, to preserve existing features of this sort. Provisions are usually made for a variety of special uses both in kind and in number such as the neighborhood park, a central athletic area, zoos, golf courses, sites for buildings, horticultural displays, etc. Each of these uses constitutes a separate block in our diagram. Each should be segregated and yet placed to not interfere with an overall aspect of spaciousness and scenic interest. Necessary roadways should be kept to the minimum. Obviously, large auto parking lots will be necessary but ought to be placed to serve more than one purpose if at all possible.

In the large city park the planner will assume a more dominant role than in the case of community playfields and neighborhood parks. Important considerations here are the proper placing of access points, the circulation of traffic, the preservation or development of a pleasing landscape while serving a variety of unsupervised recreation activities.

4. County Parks and State Recreational Areas, hundreds to thousands of acres. These parks are much in the nature of the large city park with diminishing amounts and variety of recreation facilities and increasing amounts of spaciousness and native areas. Picnicking, camping, boating and water sports, winter sports in appropriate locations, native hiking trails and bridle paths, are the usual recreational activities provided for. Again the investigative reports will determine the space requirements of each of these activities, which are incorporated into the blocks of our diagrammatic sketch. These are either concentrated in one rather large general location that separates the park from the native areas, or they are provided in several locations which do not destroy existing scenic and wilderness features. Preservation of these features comes into the picture here a little bit more prominently than in large city parks but still does not assume the importance that it does in what were previously conceived to be traditional state parks. Area zoning based upon intensity of use is effective in these plans.

Important things to watch out for include traffic circulation (which should be reduced to as few roadways as possible), the care with which estimates of space have been made, the possibility of enlarging these spaces in case the estimates prove to be low, and the keeping of developed areas to about one-fifth the total area of the park. The whole should be consistent with the biological facts contained in the investigative report and should ensure a beautiful landscape.

5. Traditional State Parks, hundreds to thousands of acres. These parks, which were selected for their unique characteristics, bring preservation of the native assets to the fore. Here preservation is the dominant purpose of any plan. Consequently, in blocking out areas for possible use, none of the preserved areas are to be encroached upon. Roads, parking places, picnic areas, and the like, must be located and limited to leave the native assets unimpaired.

There is more leeway for expression of the planners' imagination in the larger and more native of the state and federal holdings than there is when planning city and county parks. Use-zoning has more apparent application in allocating various use-densities; it is not unusual for large state and federal parks and forests to include two, three, or more of BOR's resource classifications.

Possibility of introducing parkways and scenic highways in state and federal properties has appeal, especially in satisfying the large interest in motoring for pleasure—sightseeing. Historical and cultural sights may be linked by such means with parks and private motels, resorts, and other such accommodations and attractions to improve the tourist interest of a region. On a larger and more comprehensive scale, some thought-provoking studies have been made of regional development for recreational, industrial, and residential complexes of, for example, whole river watersheds, with the hope that all three interests may live together in peace and harmony to the advantage of all.

DEVELOPMENT OF THE PRELIMINARY PLAN

The next step in the design process is the preparation of the preliminary plan. This is based upon the diagrammatic sketch and consists of filling in the details of the various blocks of the diagram. It is here that the ingenuity of the planner can be exercised with some freedom of his own expression. In consultation with operating specialists he can exercise his imagination with form, color, texture, and materials to produce a variety of pleasing visual experiences. Freedom of expression is highly desirable but it should not constitute a license to go "hog-wild" to the extremes of color and form. Sensible restraint is necessary and that may become an important function of the administrator. His good judgment may have to limit the extent to which experimentation takes place.

The preliminary plan should go through a very extensive and critical analysis by all those who will have anything to do with the operation of the park upon its completion. For city parks, this is the time to bring in the recreation directors and the play leaders, the maintenance superintendent and his specialists in turf management, horticulture, building maintenance, the engineer as to practical construction and the use of materials, and, not infrequently, representatives of the using public. The preliminary plan becomes the final picture of the ultimate park and will be altered only by minor details encountered during the preparation of working drawings and specifications.

WORKING DRAWINGS

The final stage in the design process is the making of the working drawings and the preparation of the specifications, prior to the letting of the contract. The planner has now turned over his preliminary plan to the engineering staff which now indicates by drawings how the preliminary plan is to be executed. Plans will show all underground construction such as sewers, both sanitary and storm drains, water supply and water lines, electric lines, all in their exact location and proper depths. It will show all the physical features such as roads, walks, curbs, tennis courts, hard-surface areas, fencing, playground apparatus, and whatnot, all specifically located. It will give the detailed elevations, often down to a 100th of a foot. It will show cross sections at various locations indicating the exact amount of earth to be moved, and where it is to be moved. It will show the locations of all plantings by the preparation of a planting plan usually done by the horticulturist in conjunction with the original planner, or by means of special specifications. It will indicate the depth and the kind of soil to be used in each case, what areas are to be seeded or sodded, what kind of playground apparatus will be installed and where. In total the plans and specifications will describe in detail exactly how the park is to be constructed. The plan should give sufficient detail for any contractor to be able to state a price for which he is willing to construct the job.

Although the county, state, and federal parks are not as compactly developed as are the local parks, correspondingly detailed plans and specifications are necessary to permit intelligent bidding by contractors. Because of the magnitude and variety of facilities, separate working drawings may be necessary for water supply and distribution, sewerage facilities, electrical supply and distribution, roads, buildings, horticultural ornamentation, and so forth.

OPERATION AFTER CONSTRUCTION

The finest plan and the best of construction can be nullified to a small or large extent by operation which misinterprets the plan. Also a similar effect results if the planner has not taken full account of how the park is to be operated. Consequently, a complete planning package should include a manual of operation which outlines the main functions of the park, the activities for which it is designed, maximum capacities of areas, what to do in case future expansion is necessary, how each area is to be maintained, and special manufacturers' instructions for use and maintenance of products. In short, the operations manual should contain the results of all conferences which went into decisions for planning, together with such special instructions as may be necessary to convey administrative policies.

PLANNING PROCEDURE SUMMARIZED

1. The making of the investigative report.
2. Inspection of the site with the report and topographic map at hand.
3. Making of several diagrammatic sketches and the final selection of one as the basis for preliminary plan.
4. The preliminary design.
5. Working drawings and specifications for construction.
6. Manual of operation.

CHAPTER SUMMARY

The main purpose of this chapter has been to discourage the making of a park plan by an amateur. A rather detailed description of the process has been made to indicate that the job is not a simple one and that it is a job for professionals, actually more than one professional. Small departments having but one administrative head may have to forego the luxury of professional guidance but they should avoid that necessity as much as possible. If they are pushed into the corner of necessity, the foregoing may provide some clues for the making of a plan, but it certainly is a long way from constituting a course in planning. The criteria given, however, may aid the administrator in constructively criticizing plans which are made by professionals. The administrator who has both planning experience and park theory is in an admirable position to have his department produce excellent plans, but this is an exceptional case. Good planning is always possible when talent is available and is thoughtfully guided.

Instead of developing a complete planning division of its own, park and recreation departments often rely upon professional planners and consultants to perform the planning functions. This is especially true if the chief administrator has little or no background experience in such matters. But the hope of introducing alternative ideas from the outside may also dictate the use of private professionals. To place *all* responsibility for the success of the plans on a hired consultant is not recommended. There should be developed within the department enough planning expertise to counsel with the consultant and to complement his detached point of view. The local expert must share the consultant's responsibilities. The administrator should be able to say to his superiors "I and my staff have studied all phases of the consultant's proposals, believe them to be good, and are happy to join him in recommending their adoption." Therefore the defense of that proposal does not rest entirely on the consultant but upon him and the department together, which is as it should be.

Chapter Nine

Personnel
Organization

The operation of a park and recreation service at any and all levels of government is dependent on a systemized banding together of many talents and of people who possess those talents in such a way as to act as a unit. Briefly it is called personnel organization.*

Viewed comprehensively, the whole personnel will include elected officials and administrative appointees above the rank of the park and recreation administrator, as well as employees under the direction of the latter. In this chapter primary attention will be paid to the employees.

The political makeup of the governing body is a part of the general political organization of the level of government within which the park district operates. The relationship of the park authority to the whole organization is usually consistent with the political environment in which the operation takes place. Out of that political environment, statutes and city charters have been adopted which set forth the powers and duties of the park authority. It is the state of affairs in which the administrator finds himself and he has no influence on the form it takes—at least in the beginning. Years of experience may lend authority to his voice in altering those laws or in the enactment of new ones, but that process the author deems to be too advanced a function to be dealt with in this elemental work. Anyway, the form of park authority has much less effect on the basic principles of park administration than the caliber of people in office. So attention will be centered on the organization of personnel below the level of the legislative body. However, a brief listing of the principal types of governmental organization in which park departments may be found is not at all amiss.

ORGANIZATION OF PERSONNEL

TYPES OF GOVERNMENTAL ORGANIZATION

Without discussion on the merits of various types of organizations above the chief executive level, the student should at least know that the types have no relationship to population classes or to sections of the country. Some of the more prevalent types include the following:

1. The Mayor-Council type of city government, with either a strong mayor or weak mayor, in which there may be several governing boards for various city functions, one of them a park and recreation board. Such a board usually, but not always, has the power to select its own chief executive, known either as superintendent of parks and recreation, director of parks and recreation, manager, administrator, or some other suitable title. Where the board does not have authority to choose its own chief executive, such an executive is usually selected through a civil service system. Usually such a board has governing powers, but there are some with only advisory powers.

2. In the Strong Mayor type of government, some boards may be advisory only and in some cases there is no board at all, the chief executive of the park and recreation department reporting directly to the mayor.

3. The City Manager type of government has a chief executive for the entire city operation who is chosen by a city council. In the operation of parks and recreation there may be an advisory board or there may be no board at all, the chief executive reporting to the city manager.

4. City organizations of the foregoing type or modification thereof in which there are separate departments for parks and recreation with full governmental powers.

5. A Commission type of city government in which usually several commissioners and a mayor are elected; each commissioner given certain municipal assignments, one of which will be parks and recreation. Usually there is no park board; the superintendent is usually a civil service appointee.

6. Park districts organized under special legislative acts or pursuant to general state laws usually have complete governing authority and consequently select their own chief executive.

7. State park departments usually operate without a commission, are usually associated with divisions of state forests, game and fish, drainage and waters, and similar functionary divisions, often under one head known as the Conservation Department, the Department of Natural Resources, or some similar designation. The top authority may be either a commission or an individual known as a commissioner. In such a case, the State Park is a division of the Conservation or Natural Resources Department of the state government. In some states and in some counties, a park and recreation department may be a subdivision of the state or county highway department.

8. The National Park Service is a division of the Department of the Interior reporting to the Secretary of the Interior. Recreational functions are carried on by other agencies of the federal government. Each is a division reporting to its appropriate Cabinet Secretary. Planning (other than site planning), coordinating outdoor recreation services, and federal aid to states for outdoor recreation, are vested in the Bureau of Outdoor Recreation in the Department of the Interior.

The advantages and disadvantages from the point of view of the park activities involving each of the foregoing types of organizations are not matters of discussion here. It is assumed that the young park and recreation executive is going to have small influence upon the type of organization in which he finds himself. Consequently, the succeeding discussion will be on organization of the personnel, beginning with the chief executive.

THE ESSENTIAL FUNCTIONS OF THE WHOLE PERSONNEL

Whether in a one-man organization, in a small organization of only a few people, or in a large organization of hundreds of employees, the following are the functions that will have to be performed and for which some special knowledge and training is required. The list could be expanded by going into more detail but is reasonably complete.

Administrative functions

Legal matters

Real estate and land economics

Planning and research

Engineering, construction, traffic control, etc.

Maintenance of grounds, buildings, and equipment

Biological matters, including horticulture, floriculture, turf management, arboriculture and forestry, entomology

Interpretation of recreation resources, recreation leadership and promotion, public entertainment

Police and ranger service

Operation of special merchandising and marketing services (sometimes called revenue- producing operations)

Public relations

Liaison with other agencies

Budget control, accounting and clerical

In recent years some of the large departments have found it useful to include the following as division functions:

Personnel and labor relations

General service standards and performance appraisals

If present, such other services as zoos, aquariums, planetariums, observatories, museums, sports stadiums, outdoor theaters

None of these will be included in the following discussion but each may require a manager or director with supporting personnel.

ASSIGNMENT OF FUNCTION TO PERSONNEL

The assignment of functions to individuals depends to a great extent upon how many individuals there are, or in other words, how large the organization is:

1. In Small Cities. In towns under 25,000 population, the chances are strong that the chief executive will be working alone with probably one clerk. The chief executive in this case will be either the recreation or park specialist. Inasmuch as this individual will have to perform all of the functions outlined above or see that they are performed by somebody else (the street department or otherwise), he is apt to be selected on the basis of his proficiency in the functions the village needs most. Often this turns out to be the graduate of a school of Recreation, because the maintenance of grounds can be taken care of by some other department of the village government. However, in other instances it may be a graduate of a school of Park Management, because the function of playground director can be performed by a high school coach or similar individual. In this case, it will be noted that the graduates of either Park Management or Recreation are very apt to have a "blind spot," which is one of the difficulties of operation in a small organization.

In towns of 25,000 to 50,000 population, the chief will probably have an assistant, together with some clerical help. He is now beginning to require specialists in park maintenance, inasmuch as he will have under his direction neighborhood areas and possibly playfields or even large city parks. Even in the two lowest categories (those under 50,000 population), it is important for the park manager to understand the necessity of engaging qualified professional help to supplement the personnel of his own department.

As the size of the community grows, the intricacies of the personnel organization increases. For further study, an organization suitable for a city upwards of half million population, or for a metropolitan park system will be assumed. In the latter case, as with a state park system, there will be a greater emphasis on the interpretative programs (naturalists and so forth) and less emphasis on the recreation programs, police, etc. In the case of state and some regional parks, the practice of horticulture may lean heavily toward silviculture and toward ecology. Otherwise, the organizations will be similar.

2. General Types of Personnel Organization. Sometimes types of organizations are distinguished by the following: (a) the staff-line type in which orders that originate at the top are transmitted through assignments to subordinates, each of whom controls all the functions within an area of the total operation; (b) the functional type of organization in which the whole operation of the organization is divided up into functions with subordinates in charge of each function; and (c) a combination of the two types mentioned above in which the line type organization is modified by receiving services of a functional nature from other divisions.

Because of the many kinds of specialists involved in carrying out the total responsibility of the park and recreation organization, and because of the necessity of quickly getting orders from the top straight to the bottom, a combination of line and functional organization is commonly used. Smooth functioning depends upon close cooperation between division heads as well as careful allocation of duties and frequent interstaff visitations. Frequent communication between divisions in such an organization is essential to good operation of the whole department.

3. Organizing Into the Main Divisions of the Department. The functions enumerated on page 147 (The Essential Functions of the Whole Personnel) may be grouped and organized in many different ways. The student will have no trouble in assembling a number of park organization charts from different sources. They will be almost as varied as there are numbers of park and recreation departments. The park department in each case has analyzed its own requirements and its peculiarities of politics, civil service requirements, personnel resources, and the job to be carried out, and so they all differ. Rarely will one find an organization chart which will fit one's own needs. Charts do, however, provide suggestions. In this book the time will not be taken to indulge in chart exploration, but attention will be given to more generalities, logical possibilities, and a few specifics.

The initial process of personnel organization is to group the enumerated functions into a few major categories, each of which may be assigned to possible assistants. The actual number of major categories depends somewhat upon the magnitude of the job to be done, but generally three to five groupings will suffice. Some logical divisions, all under the chief executive, are as follows:

Type A. *Secretary* having charge of the records, general office, budgets, real estate, public relations, and possibly special services.

Engineer having charge of plans, construction, equipment, and related matters.

Division of Maintenance having charge of the maintenance of grounds and buildings and horticulture.

Recreation having charge of the recreation program, athletics, golf, permits for the use of grounds, music, and entertainment.

The foregoing excludes *police* and *law*. Police must be included if it is a function of the department and not a function of the general city, county, or state police. Legal matters are usually handled either by the city attorney, county attorney, attorney general, or by a private legal firm. Only in very large organizations is there enough legal work to justify the employment of full-time counsel.

Chief and *Assistant Chief* handle administration and liaison matters. This is also the case in Types B and C.

Type B. *Secretary* or *Comptroller*, having charge of records, the general office, budget control and accounting, real estate, and public relations.

Engineer or other having charge of planning, design, construction, maintenance, and horticulture.

Recreation director having charge of programs, sports, golf, entertainment, and special merchandising services.

Type C. *Secretary* or *Comptroller*, as above.

Engineer having charge of planning, design, and construction.

Maintenance having charge of grounds, buildings, and equipment.

Horticulturist having charge of the greenhouse and nursery, street trees, and turf management.

Recreation director having charge of playgrounds, sports, entertainment, permits, golf, and related matters.

Promoted and supervised recreation in the cities becomes less prominent in the counties, still less in the states, and almost nonexistent in federal agencies. On the other hand, interpretive programs in the cities consist only of minor nature appreciation activities, but increase in the counties, the states, and find their greatest development in the federal agencies. Hence the function of recreation, as discussed above, becomes the more appropriately named interpretation in the nonurban agencies.

The foregoing situation has been prevalent for many years, but the situation is no longer as definitive as here expressed. The ever-present change factors—population growth, ease of mobility, increase in leisure time, and a less constrained mass of users—have more closely unified the recreation services of local, regional, state, and federal agencies so that interpretive programs of national parks may closely resemble guided recreation programs, while municipalities may give greater emphasis to ecological matters which have been the almost exclusive province of state and federal agencies. Outdoor Recreation is losing its identity as Recreation in all its aspects becomes the "baby" of *all* public agencies.

The greater areas of jurisdiction of nonurban agencies make distances between parks greater than they are in the cities. In consequence of this, it becomes expedient in County, State, and National Park (and other) Services to divide their operations into regions and/or districts. In such cases a region will comprise a number of park holdings, each park having a park superintendent who has the maintenance and operation responsibilities for his park. These duties do not include such general functions as financing, planning, construction, or administration, all of which are carried on at headquarters. Regional directors are regional supervisors.

In large cities, a similar regional or district organization is in operation.

In the past decade, the trend away from separate city park and recreation departments has resulted in a combined department of parks and recreation with still two separate divisions, one park and one recreation. This is not complete integration and has these objectionable features:

√   Such a division of responsibilities perpetuates an undesirable professional rift in an otherwise unified park and recreation service.

√   There is no clear-cut division between the two functions. The division must be arbitrary and the assignments very much detailed out to be understood.

√   It does not take into account the many other functions which are performed for both these two divisions, e.g., legal services, real estate, accounting, etc.

√   Possibilities of conflict are greater where overlapping functions may occur, e.g., in public realtions work. This will be increasingly noticeable as the study of divisional organizations progresses.

Difficulty of efficient communication between divisions and otherwise increases as the size of the organization grows and is made especially difficult where complete integration of park and recreation functions has not been accomplished. Correction of this fault usually results in corrective patch upon corrective patch and an inefficient organizational structure.

4. Organization of the Staff. Sometimes an assistant chief or deputy chief is interposed between the chief executive and the division heads; at other times the division heads report directly to the superintendent or chief executive. Regardless of how that is handled, a line of succession should be established extending to at least three persons. If the chief is off the job for any reason, a previously designated person will act in his stead. If the second in command is off the job, a third predesignated individual assumes the top

spot. Illness, vacations, out-of-the-city business may easily cause two of the top individuals to be away at one time.

The executive staff usually consists of the chief, his assistants, and the division heads. For staff meetings, appointment should be made from the staff of someone to compile agenda, call meetings, take minutes, and distribute minutes, unless it is the policy to have only informal staff sessions without records being made. The actual functioning of the staff will be discussed in the succeeding sections.

With the aid of division heads, the details of the organization are completed, after which an organization chart is prepared and distributed. Such an organization chart is essential for a clear understanding of the responsibilities assigned to each individual or group of individuals and becomes a standing order with which everyone in the organization should be familiar.

Possible Divisional Organization

Secretary or Comptroller having charge of an office manager, chief accountant, real estate section, and the public relations section.

The office manager will have charge of the general office, its discipline, the assignments of clerks, stenographers, stenographic secretaries to division heads, machine operators, and secretary for board minutes. He may or may not have charge of auditors and bookkeepers, depending on the duties of the chief accountant.

The chief accountant or assistant comptroller will have charge of the accounting procedures, the compiling and controlling of the budget, and may or may not have under his direction auditors, bookkeepers, and bookkeeping clerks who otherwise might be under the direction of the office manager.

The real estate section will have charge of appraisals, real estate negotiations, and land records. A portion of the land record function might be carried on under the Engineering Department, but under the actual direction of this section.

Public relations includes the assembling and publishing of house organs, bulletins, and publicity releases. It maintains contacts with news agencies, and makes arrangements for speakers at public functions. In very large organizations the public relations section and its functions may be of enough significance to warrant the status of a division. In that case the public relations official becomes a division head and a part of the executive staff.

If the operation of special services and the merchandising of salable goods are a part of this division, a word of caution is in order.

Inasmuch as these functions require auditing to ensure that all monies taken in over the counter actually reach the city treasurer's office and to prevent or expose other fraudulent practices, it would be improper to have auditing a part of this same section.

Engineering Division, having charge of plans, construction, and equipment and including planning by the engineering staff and the construction done partly by the departmental crews and partly by contract.

Office crew, headed by a landscape architect or civil engineer and having charge of landscape architects, engineers, draftsmen, stenographers, clerks, specification specialists, estimators, and cost analysts. In some cases these specialists may be grouped into subsections of preliminary planning and analysis, clerical, working drawings, and cost estimating.

Field crew, headed by a civil engineer or land surveyor having charge of land surveying, construction supervision with various helpers such as rodmen, chainmen, and others all known as engineering aides.

Equipment crew, headed by a mechanical engineer or automotive mechanic having charge of all automotive and stationary equipment. The organization will consist of mechanics, helpers, janitors, dispatchers, and clerks.

The equipment crew may just as logically be under maintenance as under the engineer, depending upon the talent available. If the entire organization is large enough it is desirable to have this section headed by a professional mechanical engineer rather than an automotive mechanic. If this is the case, such a professional can handle other matters such as electrical installations, air conditioning, and so forth.

Sometimes the functions of planning are separated from construction on the theory that whoever plans and specifies (the architect or the engineers) should not construct (the contractor). One should prescribe and supervise and the other should execute. In such a case the planning division, headed by a professional architect or civil engineer versed in landscape and urban planning, is distinct from construction headed by a civil engineer not necessarily so specially trained. In that situation the planning section must prepare a master plan for the entire park and recreation system, including acquisition and improvement of each of the parcels, prepare preliminary plans for projects ready for execution, prepare working drawings and specifications of those projects, estimate the costs and supervise the letting of contracts, supervise construction, prepare long range plans and estimates of cost for capital expenditures, make models and other visual aids for public interpretation.

To the extent that private planners and similar consultants are engaged, the planning functions of this division are reduced, but only in the very smallest of operations should the planning functions be eliminated or reduced to the extent of not retaining enough expertise to judge the worth of outside planners or to interpret the long-range objectives of the department.

As mentioned previously, land records are frequently kept in the office of the engineer under whose direction the land surveying actually takes place. Even in those cases, however, the real estate man can still supervise the keeping of those records.

Because of the mechanical and engineering functions so frequently encountered (sewers, drainage, buildings, pavements, fencing, and layouts) it is not wholly out of order to assign the maintenance functions to the engineer. This, however, is seldom done. The arrangement is illogical because horticulture poses a problem unless horticulture is a separate division.

Maintenance Division, having charge of the maintenance of grounds and buildings, shops, and automotive equipment. The central shops will usually be the headquarters for the division chief, but otherwise the organization may be according to geographical districts or by separate functions.

The central shops will be headed by a shop foreman with janitors, storekeepers, and yard men.

There may be a separate organization for maintenance of buildings and structures which include electrical crews, painting crews, cement crews, plumbers, carpenters, etc.

If automotive equipment is in this division it will probably be headed by an automotive mechanic having with him other mechanics, including automotive mechanics, mechanics for the care of lawnmowers, sprayers, and miscellaneous equipment, and a dispatcher to schedule the equipment. Automotive equipment may otherwise be a responsibility of the engineer.

Maintenance foremen, having charge of miscellaneous crews for such things as pavements the maintenance of sewers, fences, playground, and other miscellaneous equipment.

Maintenance of grounds and buildings throughout the park system (that is, the general housekeeping functions), may be patterned in two ways, to wit: parkkeepers may be assigned to individual parks throughout the system or parkkeepers may be assigned to only the larger parks with traveling crews maintaining or performing the housekeeping functions in the many smaller parks. There are advantages in having parkkeepers at individual parks because of the greater service they can be to the public and the more information they acquire concerning the various neighborhoods. The disadvantage is one of cost, for seldom can the cost be justified except in large parks. These housekeeping functions include grass cutting, the clearing of walks, the opening and closing and cleaning of toilet buildings, and a minimum attention to plantings. Often there are district supervisors overseeing the housekeeping functions in the several geographic areas of the entire park district.

The care of trees and shrubs is a part of the horticultural functions which may be a section under maintenance or may be even a separate division. In either case horticulture will include the horticulturist, foremen and crews of tree trimmers, operators of spraying equipment for trees, weeds, mosquitoes, a turf specialist, a florist to handle the greenhouse and gardens, a nurseryman to handle the nursery, and possibly an entomologist.

Division of Recreation, having charge of recreation programs, sports, golf, use permits, and entertainment.

In the past, a usual form of organization included a chief or recreation director with two assistants, male and female. Under present circumstances this is seldom the practice.

The permanent staff usually consists of supervisors in the following categories: playgrounds, city-wide sports, community centers, golf course managers, sports stadium director. Community centers operating the year round will, of course, have their own permanent staff. Each center will be headed by a community center director.

Craft and activities specialists may be part-time or full-time, depending upon the volume of work. They will direct activities in music and entertainment, nature appreciation, arts and crafts, drama, dancing, and pageantry wherever these activities take place. In other words, they are in a position to travel from place to place. Included in this group will be a sports and feature writer separated from, but correlated with the public relations section; the principal duties here are to keep the news agencies acquainted with sports and playground activities and to report the results of competitive games.

Part-time help will include playleaders, lifeguards, attendants at bathhouses, golf courses, and elsewhere, playleaders at community centers, and sometimes sports officials such as umpires and referees.

The clerical force will be permanent and include stenographers, clerks for the purpose of issuing permits, handling schedules, sometimes keeping team records, and mimeographing. There should be included here one chief bookkeeper assigned from the Accounting Department to compile and control the recreation budget.

The recreation division usually engages in, sponsors, or organizes city-wide sports leagues and other sports not organized into leagues such as skiing and speed skating, for competitions all of which result in champions being declared. Custom has decreed that champions may be awarded something besides an emblematic trophy, e.g., a team trip to play other sectional winners or to sports meets in other cities. Expenses are involved which in many cases the municipality or park district is not empowered to pay for, even though team and individual entrance fees have been charged to pay for officials, incidental expenses, travel, meal, and hotel expenses for winning teams. Once these fees have reached the treasurer's office, the aforementioned expenses cannot be legally paid.

In order to obviate such difficulties it has been possible for some recreation divisions to establish a quasi-public organization frequently known as the Municipal Athletic Association with close ties, and perhaps veto powers resting in the recreation director but otherwise governed by a board of directors selected by participating leagues and teams. If such an organization exists, certain precautions are necessary. It should be established with the full knowledge and consent of the park and recreation authorities. Its financial operations should be audited by a private certified public accounting firm, and it should have an agreement with the Park and Recreation Department about use of facilities. Its legality should be assured by the Legal Department.

In the operation of community centers and other buildings the operation of soft drink machines, candy bar machines, and similar devices emerges to a surprising extent and with surprising informality as to arrangements. The local community center director often permits such an installation with the proceeds assigned to some of his club work. In each case authority for such installation and for the use of the net proceeds ought to be authorized by the governing body.

Police. The chief arguments for having a division of police within the Park and Recreation Department are: (1) police work within this department is a specialized branch of police work requiring special training which will not be given by a general Police Department, (2) a more complete control within the Park and

Recreation Department is possible so that police work can be integrated more readily with the rest of the park and recreation services.

The principal argument against this arrangement is that all police functions ought to be under the direction of one Police Department with assignments being made to the Park and Recreation Department where necessary. When this practice is followed, the Park and Recreation Department is inclined to believe that it gets the least competent men of the Police Department assigned to it. With proper coordination of the Park and Recreation Department and city or state Police Department, a very satisfactory separate park and recreation police division is completely feasible and in the writer's opinion more desirable.

Assuming that the Park Department has a separate police division, it must be kept in mind that the service is a 24-hour service seven days a week, accomplished with men working only 40 hours a week. The division is usually headed up by a captain or lieutenant with sergeants and patrolmen reporting to their superiors. In this case the captain would be acting as the chief, the lieutenant as the assistant chief, the sergeants would act as supervisors, and patrolmen as the actual workers.

Only in the larger parks will there usually be a foot patrolman assigned and then for only certain hours a day. The rest of the organization will be assigned to squad or patrol cars. Because of two-way radios, squad cars can patrol a great deal of territory and still respond to calls almost any place in a very short time. As a result, they can easily coordinate their work with the Police Departments of either the city, county, or state.

Whether patrol cars should carry one or two men is a matter of opinion. Certainly there are many circumstances in which two men are essential and one man is at a tremendous disadvantage, e.g., serious accidents, possible drownings, criminal assault. However, to use two men for relatively few emergencies when one man can do the business is a waste of manpower. A careful analysis will disclose situations in which a one-man patrol beat is adequate and others where two are more frequently necessary.

Some of the patrol cars will cover a definite beat, may have to interrupt their patrol to be present for a couple of hours at a special function, or they will be required to handle the crowds and perhaps do some temporary traffic work. All of the parks for all seasons of the year need not be patroled 24 hours a day. Experience will indicate the most feasible way of handling this situation.

Patrolmen may be assigned to special duties such as in the investigation of outbreaks of vandalism, a specific crime, the analysis of the character of special crowds, census counts, and otherwise.

In summary as to personnel organization, the manner of divisional assignments is not nearly so important as the qualifications and adaptability of the individuals involved. As can be seen from the above, there are certain groupings of functions into divisions which are logical, but in each case several variations are possible. While the makeup of the organization is flexible, once it is determined it can be considered to be fixed and the assignments definite and adherence to those assignments religiously kept.

Probably the most important and at the same time the most difficult to attain in personnel operations is adequate communication between divisions horizontally and from the boss to the workman in vertical line direction. Those should be two-way streets.

OPERATION OF STAFF AND PERSONNEL

All the preceding discussion, that is, the consideration of the nature of park and recreation management, and the makeup of the park and recreation system, and the organization of personnel leads up to the functioning of that personnel in carrying out the job of providing a park and recreation service to the people of the park district. How do we best use the tools at our disposal to accomplish our final purpose?

We might visualize our undertaking by imagining all of the assets in land, improvements, personnel, including the board or other superior authority, as being on board a ship headed for a port on a distant shore. That port is our goal: the best and most appropriate park and recreation service possible. If our established policies are in one direction we will be heading for Port A, if another direction, Port B, or even still another, Port C, and so on. But we will have a definite goal and a definite port to seek. On this voyage we will be buffeted about by various elements and we will have to steer our way through various obstacles. The lack of sufficient funds will blow us in one direction, public apathy may increase our drift, sudden prosperity may blow us in the other direction. Possible collision with other vessels of state, the presence of restrictive laws, and temporary court decisions all may veer us to one side or another. But always we try to get back on the course toward our goal.

The captain of that ship is the park and recreation administrator or chief executive, by whatever name known. He has on board his board of directors representing the owners to whom he is responsible, and who may influence orders or even prescribe that Port B rather than Port A is the final goal. Our purpose, however, is to see that the ship as a whole works in unison and seeks the most desirable port. The captain, being the professional, will do all in his power to keep the ship operating without friction, to keep it on course and, if possible, direct it toward the most favorable port.

THE CHIEF EXECUTIVE

As captain of the ship, the park and recreation administrator must possess a solid professional background. In addition, he should possess those qualities of leadership which will cause his associates to willingly accept his decisions, not because of a show of power, but because of good example, and recognition of his competence. He should possess practically every good quality there is in the book and at the same time have enough minor vices and frailties to be human and, consequently, to be tolerant to a degree and even occasionally quite humble. To some, the qualities of leadership come easily and to others it is more difficult. All can improve their potential by a constant broadening of their knowledge of subjects included in their basic university education. This requires constant study beyond the professional realm, not only through reading but through personal contact with people.

The development of leadership calls for well-prescribed specifics to any one individual; generalities are often misdirected. Besides, they may be slanted in directions which are favorites of the advisor. Taking such a risk the writer suggests a review of the following:

1. Contrary to the situation in past generations the present-day public administrator cannot afford to be an autocrat. He must be forceful, but he cannot habitually impose his will because of the authority he possesses. He must earn compliance through the good will of his associates. He must be decisive, but only after hearing all the evidence. His fairness must be apparent. His judgment must be based upon sound professional knowledge and appreciation of human values.

2. Helpfulness, courtesy, and kindness must be constantly practiced. No one in our society is self-sufficient. All depend upon others for some part of their existence. A lot of people on occasion depend upon us; we depend upon a lot of other people. In such an environment it seems only sensible to conclude that if we are to receive aid from others we must build up a credit of helpfulness toward others. Therefore, the chief executive should be one who is ever ready to be of help and assistance in all of his contacts—contacts in society, in business, in professional organizations, in church, and in civic affairs.

3. Because a park and recreation service permeates all through society, the manager of such a service organization, either personally or through other personnel with whom he is in daily contact, must be associated with a great many organizations. The manager should carry his share of the load in this respect and should attempt to carefully choose those organizations in which his kind of ability is most needed; for again he is not merely

a hanger-on, he is a helpful worker. He should beware of being only a name on a masthead—a "front."

4. There must be a genuineness in his desire to be helpful. A false front is soon recognized and the "help" takes on the character of a bribe. As the poet says, "The gift without the giver is bare."

5. Confidence is an essential element in leadership but over-confidence and snobbishness are definite liabilities. Because the chief executive possesses human frailties, it is occasionally desirable for him to back off and to appraise himself objectively. A wife can sometimes do this very well. Close friends can help. Accept criticism so as to be modest and tolerant; but criticism should not destroy solid confidence.

6. Most people are good citizens and most people are friendly and helpful, but they are all human and on occasion most anyone can participate in a sharp deal. The ignorant and the incompetent are the more likely transgressors. In spite of the desire to be always helpful, the park manager must be of sufficient keenness of mind to detect chicanery and unethical motives early in the game. Forewarned is forearmed and the good administrator will know what to do about it. An aggressive exposure of the sharp deal, however, is seldom the correct procedure.

7. In all actions and consideration, the eye of the park administrator must be kept on the final goal. Even though he may be momentarily off course, he should bide his time and get back on course as soon as conditions will permit.

This list could be extended but the foregoing suggests enough to permit its expansion by individual analysis.

At the risk of seeming naive, the writer is inclined to suggest thoughtful consideration of time worn attributes of leadership: (1) the incorporation of "copy-book" virtues into a sincere belief in the supremacy of noble goodness: idealism; (2) the emulation of a hero's attitude of courageous adventure—a willingness to step into the unknown with a confidence born of a solid knowledge of the known. In sum total, here is the suggestion of a childlike faith in the triumph of goodness over the forces of evil as manifested by a courageous and skillful white prince over the treachery of the prince of darkness. Unrealistic? No. Rather it is an inspirational and satisfying attitude as opposed to a "cynical" or even a so-called "realistic" viewpoint.

THE BOARD OR SUPERIOR AUTHORITY

Considerable thought and attention must be given by the park administrator to the board or other authority establishing the general policies under which he operates. It should be kept in mind that the men who are elected to such boards or even an individual acting in the capacity of supervisor are either lay persons or persons not especially versed in the operations of park and recreation departments. It can be assumed that they have the genuine interest of the operation of the department in mind; what they lack is a special knowledge of parks and recreation. Consequently, they need a great deal of help in acquiring that information. Generally, they have other business or professional interests occupying their time in making a living and can devote only spare time to park and recreation activities. Consequently, information given to them must not be in overwhelming doses. The information should be brief and concise and specifically informative.

Personal contact with superiors should be brief unless invitation to the contrary is received; but personal contact can be frequent, even if it is no more than a telephone call so long as such calls do not become a nuisance. Regardless of the relative social status of board members and the chief executive the latter should recognize his official place. He should not be forward, but should permit the board member to make the overtures in all social intercourse. The ideal relationship should be one of mutual respect, friendly helpfulness, and a happy relationship that comes from a mutual genuine interest in a common undertaking. The relationship between the chief executive and his superior authorities is a prime concern; a good relationship is of great value in unifying the commanding operation of this "ship" of ours.

STAFF OPERATIONS

In small organizations (50 to maybe 100 people), the chief executive may be capable of making all, or almost all, major decisions of administrative policy without more than superficial consultation with subordinates. The larger the organization, the more complex the department's relationships become, the more important it is for the chief executive to have the benefit of ample discussion of issues with subordinates on administrative policy matters and even on policy recommendations to the legislative body. Staff operation is also a means of keeping the entire supervisory team aware of departmental problems and objectives—a means of getting the entire organization to pull together as a unit.

A special emphasis on supervision and coordination through adequate communication is warranted by the observation that in the larger organizations adequate supervision and communication are difficult to attain. Because of this fact, it is not infrequent that a special division of performance appraisal is instituted which is a sort of efficiency division whose investigations may lead to the setting of such standards as the number of employees at each of the parks of a given size, or at each golf course; how often the grass is to be mowed, when and how often water is to be applied, fertilizer applied, minor repairs can be made, etc. The service of each recreation center is standardized so this is much like supervision from the top with no reference to daily variations of local conditions. The supervisor is here shorn of much of his discretion and the workman and playleader of nearly all of it. Uniformity of appreciation of manpower and supplies is achieved at the expense of localized public service. It is a "bookkeepers" kind of supervision instead of a professional kind of supervision. It is usually the result of inadequate staff work. The team has not learned to pull together as a unit.

THE EXECUTIVE STAFF

The executive staff consists of the chief executive and his assistant together with his division heads, making in all about half a dozen persons. On occasion others may be invited to sit in. The chief must decide early whether he will call his staff together at regularly stated times or whether the meetings should be periodic when matters of staff significance are ready for discussion.

1. Meetings. The frequency of meetings is a matter of individual choice. Regularly held staff meetings have the advantage of frequent contacts which is a desirable objective. No excuse is left for letting things go beyond appropriate times for decisions. On the other hand these meetings can be perfunctory because there is little time for full discussion; they become time consuming because of their frequency, and might militate against efficient operation.

Calling irregularly scheduled or periodic meetings when matters worthy of discussion have accumulated has the advantage of the meetings being purposeful, more interesting, and thought provoking; they clear the air more completely, create a closer bond of fellowship, and tend to do a better job. The disadvantages are that too long a time can elapse between staff meetings because they last longer, scheduling of time is more difficult, preparation must be more carefully done, records must usually be kept, and the day's routing for division heads is interrupted.

In the opinion of the writer the periodic staff meetings are preferred in spite of the disadvantages, provided that no 30-day period elapses without a staff meeting. In addition to the staff meetings, there should be opportunity daily for division heads to confer with each other and each with the chief executive. This can be accomplished by establishing an office hour at which all division heads are expected to be available. This may occasionally cramp a division head's style but infrequent exceptions can be condoned.

2. Mechanics of Staff Meetings. If staff meetings are held at frequently scheduled times it may not be necessary to take minutes and record decisions. Such meetings are usually brief and their frequency minimizes the necessity of note taking. However, if meetings are periodic the mechanics should be better organized. The assistant chief can usually be held responsible for making up the agenda under the direction of the chief, to

arrange for a time and place, and to see that the suitable notice to division heads is given. Some other staff member may be appointed to take the actual minutes of the meeting and to have them transcribed and delivered to each of the participants.

The chief will preside at the meeting but otherwise the discussion is democratic throughout. The consensus is noted by the chief, who usually accepts that as the final decision but, of course, he does have veto power and the final decision. The atmosphere of such a meeting should be entirely relaxed; the cue for such is usually given by the chief. If he is friendly and in good humor, that will be reflected in the discussion. Every opportunity should be given to be entirely frank about everything with chances for misunderstanding or the grating together of incompatible personalities minimized to the greatest extent possible. The stage for this may have been set by previous social contacts and an occasional good fellowship session.

It is at a staff meeting that the policies of the board or other superior authority are transmitted and aired and the chief may obtain suggestions on policy which he may transmit upward.

3. **Suitable Subjects.** The following list of appropriate subjects for consideration at staff meetings is presented as being suggestive rather than complete.

The budget. This will involve free discussion between division heads about the relative merits of divisional requests and since decisions are usually arrived at by consensus of opinion, the pros and cons of all division requests cause the subject matter to be viewed in a purely objective way. The main items of the budget will divide themselves into such things as the ordinary housekeeping items that recur year after year, recreation programs which may be expanded or contracted, depending upon various conditions, and nonrecurring items such as major repairs and lesser capital expenditures. The latter items can be varied from year to year but consistent neglect over a period of years becomes expensive. Although the same items do not occur annually, there are items of this nature in almost all annual budgets.

Somewhat in connection with the budget discussion is discussion pertaining to the expansion or contraction of service to be rendered. This is usually dependent upon available funds, but may depend upon a number of other factors.

The formulation of recommendations for staff attendance at professional conferences held out of the city or out of the district.

A review of operations in any one or all categories periodically during the season or at the close of the several seasons.

The plans for an in-service training program and the assignment of duties to carry out that program.

The discussion of current matters presently before the governing body, which discussions lead up to definite recommendations by the manager.

Discussions as to various methods which may be employed in unifying the operations of the entire department; in other words, getting the entire crew to pull together.

Long-range finance plans both as to capital expenditure and as to current operations. This may lead to suggestions for a change in laws by some legislative body.

Any modifications in the organization chart.

Matters which normally come under the heading of labor-management relations including matters which may involve the civil service.

In regional, state, and federal operations (even in some very large municipal operations) where there are long distances between either districts or individual holdings, each of these units has a manager and staff of its own. Periodic meetings of all local managers must be arranged to coordinate operations, absorb departmental policies, and unify the whole operation. Otherwise the staff organization is much the same in principle as that of the municipality.

PREFACE TO DEPARTMENTAL OPERATIONS

The following discussion on departmental matters is presented to introduce the student to some of the possible detailed operations and the selective way in which an administrator views these operations so that he may be aware of the policy and objectives of each without his having to know all the techniques involved. The chief executive cannot possibly be up-to-date on all the detailed operations of his department, but he should be aware of the efficiency of each, and that all divisions combine to supply a unified operation. In this discussion the student will also get a general idea of the ramification of the whole department without investigating each one. Every department involves many techniques that are largely acquired through experience and in-service training.

MAINTENANCE DIVISION

The work of the maintenance division consists mainly of routine, seasonal operations, and a few which involve special work which may not recur the following year. Some of the seasonal functions applying to park organizations in the temperate zones of our country include the following:

Spring operations usually begin in late March or early April.

However, if horticulture and greenhouse operations are included in this division, the growing of plants will have begun a month or more earlier. In the snow belts, the melting of the snow calls for the cleaning of roadways and lawn spaces of the debris accumulated over the winter, and the preparation of lawn areas for the coming growing season. Buildings will be inspected and clean-up paintings and repairs accomplished, all preparatory to the gradual use of these buildings—first the toilet buildings and proceeding through the various kinds of buildings to the bathhouses which probably come last. Athletic fields are put in shape for play; playground equipment, having been repaired during the wintertime, is now reinstalled and that which has not been removed is cleaned up and gotten ready for use. Grass cutting begins early and is continued throughout the season. The installation of beach equipment and marine facilities is included here. In summary, everything is done in the spring to prepare all facilities for summer's intensive use.

The summer season is the intensive use season and usually begins early in June, quite probably about the closing of the public schools for summer vacation. Bathhouses, pools, and beaches and boating facilities are already in use. The summer season is one of continual grass cutting, picking paper and debris from all areas—parking areas, picnic areas, neighborhood parks, playfields, everything. Painting and minor repair of buildings can continue through the summer season. Pavement and other road repair is done now. The peak of the season may be reached in July. From the middle of August on, the process of dismantling gradually begins.

By fall, athletic attention has switched from baseball and softball to football, soccer, and similar field games. The recreation program has been shifted from summer playgrounds to school buildings and playground activities after school hours. The community center recreation buildings gradually begin their indoor activities. As the weather gets colder, the removal of leaves, the taking in of moveable equipment, the preparation for snowfall with the installation of snow fences, the draining of pools, the cleaning up of roadways preparatory to winter, all become matters of prime importance. It is very possible that a lull in activities may take place at the end of the fall season or the beginning of the winter season.

Winter activities, usually beginning in December sometime, include the preparation of skating rinks or the making of ice on skating ponds, the clearing of them, and the maintaining of them throughout the winter season. These jobs use most of the manpower. Preparation of ski runs, sliding hills, and other winter sports facilities is also taken care of. The recreation program has now shifted definitely to indoor activities including the use of school buildings for basketball, probably some craft work, and social activities. These same activities take place in the Park Department's own recreation buildings. Snow removal becomes a problem. The overhaul of summer equipment and the manufacture of some items is a winter activity. Toward the end of the winter season there may be again a lull which may call for a reduction of manpower on a seasonal basis.

These routine chores are often carried on by regular seasonal assignments, but weather conditions and other factors may require temporary shifting of these assignments. In consequence, the superintendent of maintenance has a constant job of scheduling personnel for various days of the week and sometimes various hours of the day. Heavy rains or storms or other weather conditions may come any time of the day or night, requiring great flexibility in the operation of his manpower. It is very likely that the peak of the summer season will find him short of manpower so that nonrecurring jobs cannot be scheduled at this particular time. Inasmuch as this season is also one in which there is a constant public demand for little special jobs, the superintendent of maintenance is often hard put to satisfy these demands. It is not until the peak of the summer season is over that the maintenance division is in a position to undertake some of the major repair items which are on the list to accomplish. No doubt one or two special crews have been doing special work during the summertime. Now the maintenance superintendent is in a position to draw some of these off and add additional manpower to do major repair work.

The various building trades are part of the maintenance organization. There is much routine work for carpenters, plumbers, cement finishers, and electricians, involving minor repairs to equipment and to buildings occasioned by the breaking of windows, faulty doors, failure of lighting equipment, the breakage and plugging of plumbing equipment, etc. There are also some seasonal jobs such as the draining of toilet fixtures, golf course water lines, the reequipping and redirecting of athletic field lights, and beach lights. Then there is a gradual shift from outdoor to indoor work for carpenters and painters and cement finishers.

If the operation of automotive and other equipment is a part of this division, it will be occupied with the scheduling of equipment for its daily use. Major repairs will be done in the off-season periods and field repairs during the operating season. For example, all mowing equipment will receive an annual overhaul and reconditioning during the winter season, and only field repairs or major breakdowns will be taken care of during the operating season. The same is true of all automotive equipment.

If horticulture is a part of this division, it, too, has its seasonal aspects. Greenhouse operations include the growing of plants during the appropriate time preparatory to placing them out into the gardens for display purposes. Inasmuch as both annuals and perennials are involved, the starting of annuals is at appropriate times of the year while perennials may be propagated either during the growing season or in the off-season in the greenhouse, depending on the species. Propagation may take place through cuttings or from seed and the plants may be grown for display purposes indoors, either in the greenhouse or at park buildings. Greenhouse operations may include a display conservatory where exotic plants are grown, in which case there is a year-round maintenance job in this connection, as well as in the preparation for special seasonal displays.

The operation of the nursery involves the growing of plants of the woody type, shrubbery, trees, etc. While this operation has its seasonal aspects, it also requires long-range planning, for certain species may be in the nursery for a period of 10 years before they are actually used in the field. The techniques involved include budding, grafting, transplanting, propagation from cuttings, experimentation in the development of hardier species.

The planting and the care of all plants, trees, shrubs, and flowers are of concern to the horticulturist. The detection of diseases, insect infestations, is done by continuous inspection. Proper applications are made of insecticides as well as growth inhibitors, fertilizers, and other aids of plant life.

The maintenance of trees (those in parks as well as those on streets) is another responsibility of the horticulturist. A regular program of pruning, spraying, and surgery is usually carried out in almost all seasons of the year except perhaps just prior to and during the planting season.

The operation of the maintenance division exposes to view all of the varied operations of the department affecting its physical properties. The variety of crafts, skills, and duties makes this function of park operation susceptible to all sorts of confusing situations if the divisional organization is not carefully made and assignments carefully made and scheduled. It involves the greatest number of men of any division and, consequently, is the object of greater attention in the fields of communication and in-service training. It also is the source of most of the problems of labor-management relations. It deserves an unusual amount of attention by the park manager and his assistant. Indeed, the assistant may possibly be specifically charged with the responsibility of overseeing this division.

Some of the more important concerns of the administrator in the operation of the maintenance division include the following:

Make sure that the organization of the division is such that all functions are adequately provided for, including provision for emergency response.

See that there are sufficient cost records of individual operations to disclose any inefficient operations. Craftsmen in this division are prone to experiment and improvise where the purchase of ready-made goods would be more economical and to grow things which can be more readily and economically purchased.

Check on the operations of the stores to see that supplies

are adequate, that obsolete items are not stocked, and that odds and ends of materials and tools are not stored over long periods of time, eating up space and taking time in inventorying and record keeping.

See that matters of departmental policy filter through to the many workmen in this division that come in contact with the public.

See that the items which are budgeted to be performed in the current year are properly scheduled for completion so that everything does not pile up for the end of the season.

See that public complaints are promptly and courteously attended to.

RECREATION

Basically, this is the division for which all others are provided—the division that should express and demonstrate the objectives of the whole department. This statement applies to all tax-supported recreation agencies in all levels of government. Recreation is the common denominator of all efforts at providing those services to the people—local, state, and national.*

A division of recreation usually refers to a municipal operation because public recreation was born and reared in that kind of environment. Its purpose was incidental to living and not a fundamental requirement of life as it is today. Today recreation points the way to a constructive use of leisure time. Its "guidance" techniques are as applicable and necessary to the unorganized, free-time sort of recreation (hunting, fishing, touring, exploring) as it is to a well-organized, year around both-sexes-all-age-group type of operation that is encountered in the usual municipal operation. Imagination and innovation are required in the relatively new field of so-called outdoor recreation. (Witness the touring service of auto clubs, travel agencies; the guidance of sports reporters on fish and game; ski instruction; the reorientation of the interpretive programs of the National Park Service; camping and mountain climbing instruction.)

Recreation divisions of municipal departments are usually headed by university graduates with a B.S. degree in Recreation from a school of Health, Physical Education, and Recreation. They are competent in play leadership, programmed recreation, the techniques of arts and crafts, the fundamentals of the performing and visual arts, sports and athletics. They have some good recreation philosophy, sociology, and techniques of communication. Those with advanced degrees have much broader understanding of the great responsibilities and opportunities of recreation.

Hence, for the ordinary municipal operation, the administrator can

*Refer to discussion of recreation and leisure in Chapter 1.

assume that the usual programs which aim at providing fun, play, satisfying craft work, and some dancing and dramatics are well in hand. What the administrator needs to concern himself with is the appropriateness of the guidance programs being offered as they relate to the current needs of the several classes and age groups of people being served.

A well-rounded recreation program should include activities which are of general interest to, and participation by all age groups and both sexes at all times of the year. The thing to avoid is the adoption of programs catering to only a comparatively few people, unless it can be shown that such programs are the only programs which will appeal to the specialized group and then only if they can be given within reasonable cost. The park and recreation administrator and the recreation director should concern themselves with this average unit cost from which any great deviation ought to be avoided. This unit attendance cost might be in the neighborhood of 20 to 40 cents. Deviations might cause some items to be three or four times this figure, while other mass activities might be very little. The higher cost may be justified by programs involving experimentations, with the expectation that additional and increased attendance will reduce the unit cost. There are often other good and sufficient reasons for higher unit costs in some instances. User fees sometimes bring high unit cost activities down to average unit costs.

The late L. H. Weir attempted to determine the fundamental instincts of people, which instincts he thought ought to be susceptible of satisfaction through recreation programs. He was inclined to judge the worth of a program by seeing how many of these instincts could be experienced by a given service. These are reproduced here for reference purposes.

1. Provision for physical activities.
2. Constructive, creative facilities for handcraft and handcraft art activities.
3. Opportunity for learning of the natural world.
4. Experiences in communication, such as conversation, discussion, debating, public speaking, story telling, writing, etc.
5. A chance to express feelings and mental concepts in beautiful ways, such as in music, graphic and plastic arts, dramatics, dancing, etc.
6. Opportunities for people to mingle together in social intercourse, picnics, celebrations, etc.
7. Without the state being mixed up in religion, there should be provided opportunities for communion with a higher power outside one's self.

Still more recently, the objective of these has been oriented toward social betterment of the neighborhood or community somewhat in coordination with the efforts of the voluntary social welfare agencies—especially in poverty areas. But by and large, municipal programs (sometimes conducted by school departments) are stereotype programs of organized play. Such programs fall short of involvement in the social and recreational needs of children, youth, and adults. Both here and in the areas of so-called outdoor recreation, a greater manifestation of imagination in relating the recreation process to the aspiration of constructive use of leisure time is needed.

Before leaving this discussion, it should be noted that there is little in the education of the play-leadership type of recreation that prepares one for business operations or the sensitive operations of government. Therefore, it is prudent to add to the staff of this division one versed in business affairs, budget preparation, and budget control, for there are many small business operations that often are handled very casually otherwise.

ENGINEERING DIVISION

This division is invariably headed by a professional engineer who is properly licensed. Those in his employ who exercise independent judgment in the making of plans, drawing of specifications, etc., likewise are professionals. These training and experience requirements ensure a high caliber of performance in the great majority of cases. In other words, the individual operations are executed according to good general professional practice.

Matters of concern to the park administrator, however, do include these:

See that there is proper coordination of the operation of the division with the other divisions of the department, particularly in regard to the service that can be rendered to other divisions. These include the drawing of specifications for equipment and machinery in consultation with the appropriate mechanics and division heads; the drawing of specifications for materials and supplies of a construction nature but used in, for example, the maintenance division; consultation with others in regard to the care of pavements, care of sewer and water lines, the repair of bridges and structures where engineering may be involved, etc. Occasionally, the Engineering Department will be charged with the special investigation or survey involving not only technical matters but some involving park managerial judgment and political acumen which will require attention by the park administrator. Having some general knowledge of the engineering functions, the park administrator should request justification for the engineer's judgment in such matters as estimating, the use of certain materials, and the propriety of engineer-contractor relationships.

PUBLIC RELATIONS

When the park department's operations are large and varied, the public relations function may be important enough to assume the status of a separate division and not be a section of some other division. Its broad function is to provide public information service and to present to the public a picture of the character of the entire department.

The functions ordinarily performed include the production of brochures describing the services the department renders, bulletins on various subject matters, publications circulated within the department in the form of departmental news; aid in preparing speeches and articles for publication; the taking of pictures and the preparation of slides, movies; the preparation of feature stories for news agencies such as magazines, newspapers; arranging for public appearances before audiences, on radio and TV; maintaining smooth communication between the department and the various news agencies—newspapers, radio, and TV; the making of an annual report of the department's operation from material collected from the various divisions under the direction of the park administrator.

All of these functions need to be performed within a well thought out program which has been the result of executive staff discussion, approved by the administrator, and adopted by the governing authority. Without such a definite program, none of the foregoing functions ought to be performed. Simply letting a public relations director loose on the general operations of the department is a poor investment in time and money. The program should be just as carefully drawn and budgeted as a program of dollars and cents expenditures.

Preparation of the annual report deserves more specific attention. Annual reports of park departments the country over vary in shape and size, degree of attractiveness, cost of production, extent of circulation, and variety of content. This disparity of uniformity probably stems from a desire to do too many things with one publication: (1) The recording of history requires a detailed description of the happenings of the year on virtually each piece of property. (2) Managerial observations certainly form a part, and, viewed over the long pull, will give greater appreciation of the objectives of the department than anything else. (3) Then there is the desire to describe the salient characteristics of the department together with considerable statistical matter. (4) Certainly, there will be included an annual report of the financial transactions of the previous year.

Taken separately and considering historical obligations first, a complete description of all transactions, philosophical observations, and financial affairs is a desirable document, but is one that is of more value in the archives of the department than it is for general distribution. The general public will be more interested in an attractive four-page affair than it will in a large document. Even such a brief annual report will find limited circulation.

The second type of general information can again be done attractively showing, in various degrees of detail, the facilities and the programs available to the public. These will require wide distribution.

The makeup of annual financial statements poses some interesting problems. Professional accountants will invariably begin by attempting to draw up a statement of assets and liabilities—a balance sheet. In this we encounter the first major difficulty: that of capitalizing the value of park properties. To be sure, we can keep track of the expenditures for land, place a valuation on donations, and add to these the cost of improving park lands, but that does not give us a true picture of the present worth. Improvements become obsolete and expenditures for new improvements added on to the old simply distort the picture. No accepted way of valuing park property in dollars and cents has yet been devised. The mere presence of a park enhances property in its vicinity and to compare private land values to obtain the values of adjacent park land is an erroneous procedure. We come down to the fact that the balance sheet will disclose the flow of cash but give a poor picture of the net worth of the organization.

Statements of income and expense, if drawn simply enough, provide the public with the essential financial information. Park departments frequently operate in a number of different funds. Attempts to consolidate all of these operations into one statement may be an interesting accounting exercise, but it can be very confusing to the taxpayer. A great deal of thought can profitably be given to the makeup of financial statements.

Annual reports are of considerable interest, not only to the home team but to park departments elsewhere and to public libraries where such information is used for reference purposes. A desire to fill this need can frequently complicate the issuance of annual reports. Those that are attractively produced and are of substantial size are the ones more apt to be chosen by reference libraries.

Just a word about statistical material. Without reference to the same material of the year before or five years before, or without reference to some other operation, or some other city, or park department, statistics can have relatively little meaning. Statistics should be given with some reference by which the statistical material can be valued or measured.

SUMMARY

In this chapter we have escaped much of the detail of a discussion of the form of political organization in which a park and recreation department may find itself on the grounds that a recent university graduate just entering into a civil service position will have no effect upon the type of organization he finds himself in and will have small influence on the form of that government for some years to come. He should, however, recognize that there is no ideal which can be pointed to as being far superior to any other. Some may be better than others, but only pro tem. For it happens in American political life, especially so far as municipalities are concerned, perhaps less so on the state level, that reform follows corruption and corruption ultimately follows reform. The full cycle may be anywhere from a few years to a few decades, but the cycle still is there. When reform takes place there is usually a change in the governmental structure. In the interim, persons, their person-alities and talents, are of more importance to good government than the political structure.

This may be as good a place as any to make some observations about the body politic through the eyes of one Charles Paul Keyser, a very old and esteemed compatriot. In doing so, let us be reminded that we are considering the opinions of only two men (Keyser and the author) whose claim to knowledge of the subject is based wholly on personal lifetime experiences, each in his own bailiwick and without reference to scholarly appraisal. They do not claim to be theorists, they are pragmatists.

Keyser, in an address before a professional group in 1951, said that democractic government is composed of self-promoted politicans backed up by a "majority or busy minority," and that they rule in the guise of "servants of the taxpaying public." Actually, they respond to pressure groups so long as they can make it look like something good for the public welfare. He pictures the mass of the people as passive, willing to be led (or fooled) by political leaders so long as a certain "tranquil compromise" of their individual and conflicting wants is not disturbed. The political leaders are careful not to disturb this "tranquility" and will sidestep decisions or conflicting demands until tranquility is once more achieved.

Reforms or new issues of any kind may unbalance the "tranquil compromise" but it takes real campaigning to revise that tranquility into a *new* state of tranquility. That campaigning is an essential part of the political process and politicians are expert at it. Even minority groups and minority issues can produce results, but hard campaigning is required to stir up the lethargy of the majority.

Reforms come about usually by the agitation of important citizen groups. Often within such groups a consensus has been reached that government ought to be more businesslike, and the reforms are made about this central theme. Economy and efficiency are something the taxpayer is always striving for. Whether one agrees with this standpoint or not, it is important to point out that from a practical standpoint, and without reference to any textbooks on the subject of municipal or state government, it is the author's opinion that there is a great difference, and an essential one, between business and government. The purpose of business is profit. Since competition is present, great efficiency of operation is all-important. Usually efficiency finds its capstone in a concentration of power at the top in one individual or in as small a group as possible so that policy decisions can be made promptly and orders carried out immediately. Efficiency in business fosters autocracy in management.

On the other hand, while efficiency in the operation of governmental processes is desirable, it is essential that government must continue to be the reflection of people and their wants and desires, their need for protection of their minority rights as well as the rights of the majority, the adherence to the fundamental principles on which this country is based, the constitutional rights of individual people (freedom from persecution, domination, the corruptive practices of boss rule), and indifference to the unjustified wants of individual and organized pressure groups. These are the primary objectives that citizens' groups ought to look for in a governmental organization. A concentration of power in management may produce greater efficiency of execution but it is a dangerous threat to the public welfare. Abuse of that power may be costly in money and in the loss of constitutional protection. Checks and balances in governmental structure cost money, but they are worth it.

The tendency toward autocratic management in department operation of government also needs attention. It is fundamental that every individual has possessive and domineering characteristics, be the individual male or female, rich or poor, educated or uneducated. Each one wants to be superior to, or to dominate either delicately or forcefully, his colleagues and associates in business and in the social world. Even man and wife have that difficulty. This tendency, left to itself and unhampered in the operation of public business, inevitably leads to abuses. What would appear to be a virtue in a private business operation (this tendency toward autocracy), must be offset in public business by a certain degree of checks and balances.

An administrator in the park and recreation field, for example, whose ideas dominate all action, who surrounds himself with so-called "yes" men, who does not have the benefit of objective reasoning or the reasoning of others, who does not have to justify his plans and his actions to a superior authority, commission, or other nonprofessional, is apt to run a very efficient department, but one which can easily ignore the rights of individuals and whole classes of citizens and, indeed, operate with bland unawareness of even the changing conditions brought about by chronological time changes. It must be kept in mind that no one man knows all, especially in this day of rapidly changing techniques, technical developments, modes of living, concentrations of population, the need for interchange of ideas with other disciplines, and a coordination of more disciplines into a more meaningful public service. In the face of these, the position of the lone operator is much more untenable than it ever was before.

Hence, the genius of the administrator is to lead his personnel into the habit of inquiry as to fundamental and changing objectives and to encourage free discussion among them and with him for the purpose of arriving at a balanced conclusion. For this purpose, he will need specialists in every direction and of every kind, demanding an ever higher standard of knowledge and performance. He must provide much of the correlative thinking required to mesh his operations with all other public services that deal with people.

The total function of park and recreation service can be broken down into a reasonable number of major divisional functions. The text has used a dozen or more which may or may not be all-inclusive. It assumes that this is the proper approach to personnel organization for permitting assignment of duties to the logical vocational and professional groupings. It is assumed that a combination of line and functional organization is inevitable and that staff operation is superior to individual management. The main objective or, more precisely, the main difficulty in this type of organization is the matter of communication—communication between divisions, between individuals on a horizontal level as well as communication of orders from the top to the bottom. The staff type organization permits this sort of communication between division heads at least, and also between subdivision heads. Other devices to cover the rest of the personnel cannot be ignored and must be especially provided for. But in sum total, communication, however it is obtained, is quite necessary to the smooth functioning of this type of organization.

Within each division the rank and file employees are grouped within vocational or professional classifications with subgroupings into grades, each with salary ranges attached. A personal observation here seems a propos. Unlike physical park properties, which were previously discussed, personnel consists of people that have motivation, animation, and mobility. Only a part of this talent is hired and paid for by the park and recreation service. These people have talents of various kinds and have varying degrees of proficiency, all or part of which may be utilized in the eight hours' daily work for which they are being paid. The personality and adaptability of the individuals involved are as varied as individuals may be. Although the talents of any one class of individuals may be similar, the impact of the individuality of each is reflected to a more or less extent in the overall proficiency of the job they are paid to do.

These characteristics, peculiar in each individual, are usually ignored in personnel classifications, but every manager of personnel knows they exist and that they influence the character and the quality of the work produced by each individual. Probably because of this situation as much as any other, the fitting in of individuals into classifications of personnel carries with it the urge to make special cases of the more proficient or the more adaptable. The seed of reclassification is thereby sown. History shows that when exceptions to the classification schedule become numerous, the painful process of a new classification study is made and reforms instituted.

This latter characteristic of individuality and personality adaptability should be taken into account by the administrator when devising his staff of division heads. A formal organization chart is one thing, but if it needs to be modified to get the right man, both from the standpoint of professional proficiency and personality adaptability, then changes should be made. After all, the effective life of an administrator is too short for him to wait for development to produce for him an efficient organization. He should try to bring that about himself.

Chapter Ten

Budgets

Budget is such a common term that presumably everyone under-stands its meaning; and yet a discussion of budgets is an ever-popular subject, particularly at meetings of young park administrators. These young people have been in the business just long enough to know that the term budget can mean different things to different people, and there arises a degree of confusion. The discussion of this chapter seeks to clarify the subject matter without getting into a complete dissertation of budget compilation, analysis, control, and integration with accounting procedure. Each topic is enough involved to warrant special study. Enough will be discussed so that an administrator will know how budgets are compiled, how they can be used in the management of his department, and in what ways and to what degree the adoption of the budget may constitute operating authority.

According to the dictionary, a budget is (1) an estimate, often itemized, of expected income and expense, or operating results for a given period in the future; (2) a plan of operations based on such an estimate; (3) an itemized allotment of funds for a given period. The compilation and adoption of such a budget, consequently, may contain all three of the above ingredients, or only one of them, or parts of two or more. This accounts for the confusion in the significance of the term, budget, as used in ordinary conversation.

When the legislative body adopts a budget, it, in effect, is saying to its chief executive, or administrator, "Here is how much money we expect to take in; here is how we expect to spend that money; and when we adopt this plan of income and expense (budget) for the coming year, that adoption is your authority to do one of these things:

1. Expend the funds as nearly in conformity to this plan as your judgment dictates, so long as you do not exceed actual income. Of course, you will be expected to submit any great deviation from the budget or any actual deviation from the implied *intent* of the budget to your superiors and to receive confirmation of your proposed course of action—or,

2. Expend funds in the various categories up to, but not in excess of, the detailed estimates unless further authority is obtained—or,

3. Expend funds as provided for in paragraph two, but for only a three-months' period, or until a review is made of operations up to the end of that quarter and revisions made for subsequent quarters."

Trouble usually results when the intent of budget adoption, as provided for in the three foregoing plans, is not clearly set forth—when there has been no clear-cut understanding between the legislative body and the chief executive as to exactly what is intended by the adoption of the budget. The first step in budget matters, then, is to determine just exactly how much authority the adoption of the budget extends to the administrator.

The first plan provides the greatest leeway for the chief executive. It implies a great deal of confidence on the part of the legislative body in the chief executive; and it gives the chief executive great latitude in operation. At the same time, it places the responsibility of suitable fiscal control squarely upon him.

In the second plan, the authority to expend is greatly curtailed; and in this case, the legislative body has actually made an itemized allotment of funds for the given period. No opportunity for transfer of funds between categories or for exceeding the total amount is within the discretion of the chief executive; he must go back to the legislative body for further authority. In this case the legislative body is attempting to hold a greater control over the acts of the chief executive and in so doing, of course, limits to some extent the dispatch with which the functions of the department can be carried out.

In the third case, a still further restriction is placed on expeditious operation through budget adoption by providing for the expenditure of funds for only a limited period of time. In the example given we have used a quarterly period of time; this might easily be semiannual, or otherwise. This is the most stringent kind of restriction of the authority granted by the adoption of the budget and greatly hampers the operation of the department.

In case one, the budget is an estimate of income and expense, a plan of operation, and an allotment of funds. Cases two and three are modifications and restrictions on the above. In all cases, the actual plan of operation is not complete until the actual budget of income and expense is supplemented with a budget of actual things to be done in terms of units of accomplishment, or man-hours of work, or units of materials and supplies to be purchased. To provide this, some further discussion about the makeup of the budget is desirable.

Insofar as the budget is a plan of expenditure, as well as a plan for anticipated revenue, the items in that budget correspond to accounts carried in the accounting procedure. Usually such procedures require accounts for (1) the expenditure of personal service (payrolls) in the various categories and (2) the expenditure for the various classes of materials, supplies, manufactured goods, contracts, and such other things as are classified as "other than personal" expenditures. This sort of "personal" and "other than personal" compilation may or may not coincide with the needs of the executive for the management of his operations. He may be more interested, actually, in how much is expended for certain operating functions, such as the maintenance of roads and park areas of various kinds, preparation for celebrations, the costs of constructing various items of improvement, the moving of facilities from one place to another, the delivering of supplies, and various other functions which utilize combinations of personal service, supplies, and materials. Hence, from his standpoint, a compilation of the budget by functions, rather than by "personal" and "other than personal" items, may be more advantageous.*

Not infrequently, even a third compilation is desirable for a large system in which the amount of money expended for each of the various parks becomes a desirable bit of information.

In reasonably large systems, a budget is not only an itemization of income and expense and an allotment of funds, but also a plan of operation. The complete compilation is an intricate correlation of "personal" service and "other than personal" service, hooked up to functional procedures or operations, as well as to the costs allotted to individual locations, all of which must tie into the accounting procedure for accurate control. Fifty to a hundred pages of typewritten and tabulated matter may easily be necessary to support a budget of income and expense covering only one or two pages of typewritten material. An examination of some of this material may be of particular interest.

At this point it should be noted that public park departments frequently carry on operations financed by several different funds; for

*See tabulations on pp. 183-86

example, general tax funds for ordinary operating purposes; one or several capital expenditure funds financed by the sale of bonds; separate funds for the operation of revenue-producing activities, such as refreshment stands, refectories, restaurants, golf courses, and so forth. The question immediately arises whether there should be one overall budget for all of these funds; separate budgets for each; or separate funds for some, and combinations of others. Funds financed by the sale of bonds, which have been authorized for a specific purpose, must be accounted for separately and, consequently, must have separate budgets. The operation of revenue-producing activities might be combined with functions of the operating budget which are financed out of general taxation unless special commitments have been made for disposition of the revenue of one or more of these revenue-producing activities. In the latter case, the budget and accounting must again be separate from other funds. Generally speaking, from the operational and managerial standpoint, it is better to have a separate budget for revenue-producing activities, using only the net results—profit or loss— as part of the general operational budget. Inasmuch as both methods are used, any comparison of operation budgets between cities ought to note whether the gross income from revenue-producing activities, or only the net income, is used to augment tax receipts, and also whether the total expenditure includes the gross expenditure of revenue-producing activities, or none at all. Comparison of statistics between cities without this correction being made is, of course, misleading.

For the sake of simplicity, in this discussion we will assume that the general operating fund does not include the gross expense of the operation of revenue-producing activities and that the income is largely from taxation, augmented only by the net result of the operation of revenue-producing activities; also that the expenditures, in consequence of the foregoing, do not include expenditures involved in the operation of the same revenue-producing activities. We can therefore concentrate our attention upon the compilation of budget for the general operating functions of the department.

Referring now to the first form of compilation into two general categories, "personal service" and "other than the personal service," the personal service section will probably account for two-thirds of the total expenditure of the department. It is divided into the various kinds of personal service which the department employs, all the way from administrative and supervisory help through clerical, labor, various crafts (carpenters, painters, mechanics, plumbers, etc.), recreational leaders, etc., etc.* Such a listing does not indicate where or how this personal service is used; and from a strictly managerial standpoint, the list is insufficient.

A similar situation exists in this same compilation, wherein the

*See p. 183.

"other than personal" service category is itemized. The subdivisions in this category include such things as outside consultant service; the communications services of postage, telephone, telegraph, etc.; travel and transportation service, including auto allowance; binding and reproduction services; rental service (buildings, grounds, equipment); cleaning and waste removal; utilities; repairs; departmental supplies of many kinds; building materials; road materials; agricultural and gardening materials; awards and indemnity; insurance; and perhaps some minor capital outlay. As in the case of personal service, the amount spent for each of these items is not allocated to functions of performance; and, again from a managerial standpoint, they are insufficient.

We come now to the second compilation in which budget expenditures are broken down into functional operations, each of which is a combination of both personal service and other than personal service. Such a breakdown, combined with the compilation above mentioned, improves the control considerably. The subdivisions contained in this compilation are maintenance of parks, parkways, and playgrounds (if this is itemized according to parks, it provides the third compilation spoken of in the first part of the chapter); rehabilitation of grounds and installation of recreational facilities; walk and curb repairs; special road repairs; special building repairs; special park and parkway lighting repairs; special repairs to storm drains and water lines (in each of the foregoing special accounts, each of the items is nonrecurring year after year, but the total item is recurring; this group of items is subject to variation from year to year); winter sports; greenhouse and nursery operations; operation of bathhouses and boatdocks; recreation promotion and supervision; operation of playgrounds and neighborhood community centers; general administration of the department; engineering; planning; police; stores; care of tools and equipment; and other items applicable to the specific park system in question.

These two compilations should be supported and supplemented by an enumeration of the units of work* expected to be performed in each of the foregoing categories of Compilation No. 2, together with the location at which such work is to take place. For instance, in the category of special repairs to buildings, this should be accompanied by a complete list of the buildings which are to receive this service, together with an estimate of time and material required to do each individual job. This, then, becomes the program that is the plan of operation for that department, or that division. The budget recites that Building "A" is to receive painting in such and such areas, outside or inside, or both; and certain alterations, and possibly a new roof, are to be provided. Each item is estimated in terms of man-hours for the

*See pp. 185-86.

various crafts to be used, together with costs of materials. In the case of the painters, for example, the summation of such items all the way through the budget constitutes the plan of operation and the allocation of funds for the painters for the entire year. The same would be true of the plumbers, the carpenters, and all other crafts.

Another example: In the case of road repairs, the budgetary item is supported and accompanied by a list of roads which are to be repaired, together with an estimate of man-hours of various types of personal service required, as well as an estimate of the amount and cost of materials required to do each job. Here again, the summation of these items, so far as general labor is concerned, will constitute the man-hours of general labor required for the entire year and will support that particular item in the budget Compilation No. 1.

Still another example: The items of recreation supervisory service, playground operation, and the operation of community center buildings, will indicate which buildings and which playgrounds are to be operated for the year and what the season of each will be—that is, when they open and when they close—if there is a season. Again, the summation of the man-hours of work in each of the personnel categories will correspond to the amount of money set aside in the two compilations above referred to. Materials and supplies costs will also add up to the total set out in the compilations.

In summary, then, the budget is a listing of income and expense, compiled in more than one way, for both operational and accounting control and will also have the statements of the amount of work to be performed in each of the categories, together with schedules, in certain cases, for the seasonal operation. The adoption of a budget of this sort constitutes an estimate of income, a plan of expenditure, and an actual plan of operation for the entire year. Such a budget facilitates the entire park operation and, if properly managed, permits various division heads and supervisory help under those division heads to be responsible for a certain section, or subdivision, of each of the categories involved in the entire budget, all of this, of course, within the limitations established by the legislative body.

The rigidity with which budget allocations for individual items are adhered to depends upon how much leeway has been given by the legislative body and how much leeway the chief executive has delegated to his subordinates. It also depends upon unforeseen and unpredictable incidents within the operating year. In any event, when the adoption of the budget has taken place and anyone in the entire organization encounters something which ought to be done and was not provided for, he approaches his superior for authority to digress. If the superior has that authority, it will be limited to minor variations within his own budget, but certainly not to the extent of increasing it. He may be able to forego doing one thing for the sake of doing some other thing, or he may not. There should be some limited leeway in each case, the degree depending upon how much leeway the chief executive himself has. The significant point remains, however, that the adoption of a budget is the adoption of a plan of expenditure and a plan of operation with flexibility limited to whatever degree the legislative body sees fit.

The following tabulations illustrate the various ways compilations of expenditures are made, as was discussed in previous pages. This is condensed from the budget of the Minneapolis Park Board.

Compilation No. 1

ESTIMATED EXPENDITURES
By Accounting Codes

PERSONAL SERVICE	$2,283,100
Divided into 27 categories, such as Administrative, Clerical, Engineering, various building trades, Maintenance Labor and Supervision, Horticulture (Labor and Supervision), Recreation (Supervision, Play Leaders, Attendants), Mobile Equipment Operators, and others. Each item can be supported by number of employees, hours of work, exact length of season, thereby constituting a plan of employment.	
CONTRACTUAL SERVICE	556,735
Expert and Consultant, Communications and Travel, Printing and Binding, Rent, Cleaning, Utilities, Repairs.	
MATERIALS AND PARTS	188,230
Office, Chemical, Household, Recreation, Building, Maintenance, Agriculture.	
OTHER CURRENT CHARGES	8,340
Insurance, Indemnities, Membership Fees, etc.	
MINOR CAPITAL OUTLAY	28,595
Building and Plant Equipment, Construction, Equipment, Furniture and Fixtures.	$3,064,050

Compilation No. 2

ESTIMATED EXPENDITURES
By Operating Function

MAINTENANCE OF PARKS, PARKWAYS A third compilation (No. 3) breaks this figure into expenditures for each individual park.	$ 957,000
SPECIAL MAINTENANCE AND IMPROVEMENT ACCOUNTS These are items that do not occur each year, although others may take their place. They include Grounds, Recreation Facilities, Shoreline Repairs, Walks, Roads, Buidings, Drains and Sewers, Park Equipment, etc.	235,650
WINTER SPORTS Skating, Hockey, Ski Slides, etc.	332,850
HORTICULTURAL Nursery, Greenhouse, Gardens, Forestry.	178,100
BOAT DOCKS, BATHS, BEACHES Individually itemized.	121,750
OTHER OPERATING ACCOUNTS Tennis Center, City Wide Sports Fields.	16,850
RECREATION PROMOTION AND SUPERVISION Administrative and City Wide, Community Centers, Playgrounds, Concerts, Central Stores.	503,850
GENERAL ACCOUNTS Administration, General Engineering, Park De- sign and Research, Police, Care of Tools and Equipment, Purchase of Tools and Equipment.	700,000
	$3,064,050

Note: Each item of this compilation is supported by estimates of cost and units of work to be done (See Compilation No. 4).

Example of Compilation No. 4
This supports the item of Special Building Repairs ($65,000) which is part of SPECIAL MAINTENANCE AND IMPROVEMENT ACCOUNTS in Compilation No. 2 and which has a total for all such accounts of $235,650. Other items in this category have similar supporting estimates, the total of all of which is $235,650.

SPECIAL BUILDING REPAIRS

PERSONAL SERVICE

111	Maintenance Labor (465 hrs)	$ 1,545
114	Plumbing Labor (15 hrs)	65
141	Carpenters (1,220 hrs)	4,940
142	Cement Finisher (450 hrs)	1,850
143	Electricians (290 hrs)	1,300
144	Mechanics (13 hrs)	50
145	Painters (7,000 hrs)	27,300
146	Plumbers (25 hrs)	125

TOTAL PERSONAL SERVICE . . . . $ 37,175

OTHER THAN PERSONAL SERVICE

541	Advertising	10
552	Rental of Park Equipment	540
582	Contract Building Repairs	16,700
599	Misc. Contract Service	200
602	Small Tools	65
603	Shop Supplies	25
609	Misc. Operating Supplies	25
653	Plumbers Materials	160
654	Painters Materials	6,320
655	Electricians Materials	1,000
656	Carpenters Materials	2,720
658	Cement and Concrete	60

TOTAL OTHER THAN
PERSONAL SERVICE . . . . $ 27,825

TOTAL ESTIMATE $ 65,000

The program will follow the attached schedule as closely as possible, although the listing does not necessarily indicate the priority of the projects. See next page for program.

Note: The hourly costs used here include general items such as cost of vacations, sick leave, etc.

The said listing is in the following form:

PROPOSED PROGRAM OF SPECIAL
BUILDING REPAIRS AND IMPROVEMENTS

LOCATION	CARPENTER $	PAINT $	PLUMB. $	ELEC. $	CONTRACT $	MASON $	TOTAL
AUDUBON PARK							
R Paint wading pool		200					$200 R
BRYANT SQUARE							
I Tile floor in office & craft room	190						190 I
R Elec. outlets in office				100			100 R
I Cabinets in craft room	200	59					259 I
R Rewire lights				350			350 R
							$899
CALHOUN LAKE							
I New roof for boathouse	630						630 I
R Paint mast		250					250 R
FOLWELL PARK							
I Cupboards, kitchen	150	60					210 I
R Touch-up painting		190					190 R
R Paint flag pole		100					100 R
							$500
FRANKLIN STEELE SQUARE							
R Paint wading pool		200					$200 R
HOLMES SCHOOL							
R Paint wading pool		200					$200 R
JACKSON SQUARE							
R Paint wading pool		200					$200 R
KEEWAYDIN FIELD							
I Kitchen cupboards	120	35					$155 I
I Storage cabinets in craft room	150	60					$210 I
R Paint window and door frames		200					$200 R
I Soundproof ceiling	600						$600 I
I Gas convert, stand-by heat (School Board)					5,000		
TOTALS (6 pages later)	$9,450	$32,918	$350	$2,660	$16,917	$2,705	$65,000

Note: R = Repair, I—New improvement—other items of the "Special Maintenance and Improvement" accounts have similar programs.

Note: In separate memos, each of the above items is divided into personal and other than personal components, each coded so they can be woven into the compilation by codes on p.

In the realm of government operations the path of budget requests from presentation to final approval is long, tortuous, and seemingly continual. This may be one of several reasons why the subject of budgets is both fearsome and mysterious to many young executives.

This text attempts to take some of the mystery out of budget preparation, but probably has not stressed sufficiently certain practical aspects, e.g., is budget "padding" of estimates a desirable procedure? How does one avoid the "awful" possibility of arbitrary reductions of budget requests? What methods of justification of requests are most effective at hearings before boards of nonprofessionals? And so on,

The fact is that, in summary, budget preparation, its justification through a maze of governmental procedures and budget control during actual departmental operations, is technical, time consuming, and often aggravating. Moreover, during the whole process, at one time or another, the administrator is called upon to exercise the highest degree of talent he possesses. And all simply to get the wherewithal to do the principal task of providing a suitable park and recreation service. If there is a thrill to obtaining land and buildings, in improving them for public service, and in providing the actual service, then one may consider the drudgery part of the job to be that of budget attention.

Let us follow the budget process in a typical municipal situation.

The fiscal year is assumed to be the same as the calendar year and so begins on the first of January. Adjustments in final budget figures are probably still being made at this stage so that a final printed operating budget may be issued by, say, February first. During January and all succeeding months, money is expended presumably within the budget figures of the current year. Charges and distribution of costs are the concern of the Budget Director. He has worked out the correlation of budget with accounting procedures, so each month financial experiences are compared with budget allotments. During these months the Director is collecting information preparatory to the making of the request for funds for the next year.

The budget request for the next year usually is due July first of the current year. Hence preliminary budgeting begins soon after the final current year's budget is issued or roughly six months before operations begin. Do we "pad" this budget? The answer depends on departmental policy. The author's opinion is that the budget request should be solidly prepared to cover the costs of those operations which can be defended as suitable for the department. There is no overestimating, no underestimating. It is a true estimate. The request does not assume there is no use requesting funds for some things that are almost sure to meet with disfavor. Here is an opportunity to show what is desirable in the operation of a good department. On the other hand, overestimating is like a falsehood: it is harder to defend than the truth and once discovered destroys confidence in any and all budgets that may be submitted and questions the validity of all statements made in defense of even an honest request.

Lesson number one is that the budget request is an honest request reflecting the kind of department the administrator can justify as desirable. The items in it are carefully estimated, its compilation made understandable, and the detail readily available. Being sure of the estimates, and with confidence of the worth of the administrative operations implied in the figures, the executive can approach a budget hearing with reasonable assurance.

The first test of the worth of the budget request comes in getting approval of the board or superior departmental authority to submit the request to a formal legislative hearing. The latter hearing usually occurs about September first when all other departmental budget requests have been turned in and some sort of comprehensive compilation made of them. The departmental requests may be heard over a period of a month or more, but probably by October 15, decisions will have been made.

Legislative hearings are often dreaded by young executives; they are quite different in the techniques used than the hearing before the departmental board. In the latter case the main justification has to do with what is good for the department. In the legislative hearing, the park and recreation department is in competition with every other department of the municipality. The point of view to consider is not only what is good for the PR department, but what is good for the city, county, or state as a whole. It is not enough to beat the drum for the PR department. The request of the PR department should be woven into the desirable requirements for the kind of city operation that will enhance its worth for business enterprises and for enjoyable living. It is at this stage of the procedure that the young executive feels frustrated, principally because he has not prepared himself with a knowledge of what is required for his particular city to best serve the interests of the whole municipal entity.

Lesson number two—broaden your knowledge of what constitutes a good city in your section of the country. Learn the hopes and ambitions of other departments of the municipal government. Join with them in coordinating services. Work for a joint approach at budget hearings. If the objectives are sound there will be popular support for the individual requests. Don't compete. Join hands for cooperated effort.

The final legislative decisions very likely will affect little more than the total appropriation for the department. Sometimes other limitations are imposed, but almost always the department is left with the task of adjusting the budget figures to fit an operation which must now be at variance with the original request. This procedure is initially done by the administrator and his budget director and then it is once more presented to the PR departmental authority for final approval—hopefully before December 31. A year has now passed. Only during brief intervals has the spotlight of administrative attention veered away from some phase of budget procedure.

For the usual municipal situation the foregoing procedure applies only to budgets for current operations. Requests for capital funds financed by the sale of some form of municipal bond usually follow another path. That path may involve a referendum, or it is possible that the chief governing body has authority to issue bonds within certain legal limits. In the latter case, hearings on long-range and immediate capital outlays follow some abbreviated procedure similar to that of current expense budgets. Referendum procedures need not be discussed here.

Budget procedures in state and national situations have similar considerations to those of a municipality but with appropriate differences. Budgets for current operations and capital expenditures are usually combined into one, are presented and justified at the same time. The fiscal year often extends from July 1 to June 30. The budget may be for two years rather than one. The estimates must often be made a year and a half in advance, but the budget may be presented only once in two years instead of annually.

Much of the distasteful aspects of budget procedure can be eliminated by having complete confidence in the figures presented and solid reasons for the operational functions which are the bases of the budget figures. To obtain this sort of confidence certain suggestions seem appropriate.

1. The accounting procedure should be so designed that functional costs are readily available.

2. Functional costs, being accurately tied in to the departmental financial accounts, can then form the basis for sound functional estimates.

3. The compilation of the budget can then be made in accordance with the processes outlined in the text.

4. A true tie-in with the regular financial accounts makes possible proper budget control during the year's operations.

5. A thorough knowledge of the goals of operation and service that the department hopes to achieve influences the decision as to the items to be included in the budget.

6. A continuing study of municipal affairs in general, the hopes and aspirations of other municipal colleagues, the attitude of business and the general public, help to formulate justifications for the budget before formal legislative bodies.

Private businesses prepare annual budgets involving forecasts of expected sales and corresponding costs based upon the volume of expected sales. Government agencies engaged in the sale of merchandise and services as adjuncts to the main recreation purpose of the department are likewise expected to prepare operating budgets for these functions. The first such budget may not be nearly as close to performance as subsequent budgets based upon past experience. Budgeting of revenue-producing functions coupled with cost analyses provides the basis of efficient operation of those activities.

The preparation of budgets of capital expenditures is a continuous operation principally for the planning and engineering staffs. The figures are estimates of cost of acquisition of land and of construction of facilities. Usually such plans envision the accomplishment to extend many years into the future. Cost estimates are, therefore, expected to undergo revision from year to year and are considered final only for the year in which the actual request for funds is made.

In some cases development of the organizational structure of governments at all levels has complicated the simple patterns discussed in Chapters 8, 9, and 10. Generally these complications have tended to separate from the PR administrator some of the functions which this text has treated as integral parts of PR administration: part or all of the planning may be done by a central planning agency; personnel matters may be handled by a civil service department or a department of systems and analysis; budget control and accounting may be done in whole or in part by a control auditing department, and there are others.

Where such separation of PR functions exist, it is obvious that the PR administrator is no longer a full-fledged department head responsible for a complete park and recreation service. That service has become fractionalized and is no longer completely responsive to the public.

In such cases the administrator should take steps to gain sufficient control of those wayward functions to enable him to once again unify and consolidate his department. Altering the govermental structure may not be possible, but supplementing the centralized external control operations with a minimum of similar operation within the department is often possible. In fact with cooperation of the external agencies a much improved service can result.

The important point here is that the situation must first be recognized by the PR administrator. He must make the first move at improvement. Then diplomacy and persistence should produce satisfactory results.

Chapter Eleven

Policies —
In General and
on Relationships

POLICIES IN GENERAL

In making decisions, it is very difficult to weigh the pros and cons of a subject without having some idea of the historical background of previous decisions made under similar circumstances or what the current local and nationwide practice is in regard to similar matters. A knowledge of these decisions and current practices would help a great deal because these decisions no doubt were made only after many discussions on similar subjects everywhere. If these decisions could be shown on a graph, they no doubt would fall in a band somewhat above and somewhat below a median line which might be called policy. The lines above and below the median could be likened to habits which have not yet become a part of the median policy. Policy is really a station in a progression which begins with habit and ends in law as here described.

First there is *habit* which the dictionary describes this way: "An aptitude or inclination for some action, acquired by frequent repetition, and showing itself in increased facility of performance or in decreased power of resistance." "Habit is a cable; we weave a thread of it each day, until at last it becomes so strong we cannot break it," as the old saying is.

The dictionary has a number of definitions for *policy* but the one most applicable here is "a settled or definite course or method adopted and followed by a government, institution, body or individual." Presumably a policy results from pursuing a habit for some period of time.

The next step is a *rule*, which is "a prescribed guide for conduct or action; an authoritative enactment; a regulation; a prescription; a precept." The habit has here been pursued long enough for it to have acquired some authority.

Finally, there is the *law*, which is "the binding custom or practice of a community; rules or modes of conduct made obligatory by some sanction which is imposed and enforced for their violation by a controlling authority." The "cable" is now complete.

Habit, Policy, Rule, Law—in that order do we increase the rigidity of the statement and hence decrease the flexibility of choice in adhering to it. Policies emanate from the best habits applicable to the business at hand. The more inflexible policies result in the adoption of rules of conduct; and the most inflexible rules become law. Choice in the decisions that can be made is greatest as to habit; there still is some latitude in reference to policy. Rules require adherence to avoid some possible unfortunate consequence, and that consequence is most severe when the law is broken.

Policies are not immutable laws or rigid rules. In toto they indicate a settled course—a course which can change with the times. Decisions made contrary to a policy should be considered deviations from the "settled course," probably marking a turn in the road. Deviations are, therefore, important enough to ponder carefully as being just what they are; a turning away from the old way of doing things and not just a momentary exception to a general rule. Deviations from the general policy should be made only with a full determination that the new way is distinctly better than the old—that the policy itself ought to be changed. To make a step away from a set course with the expectation that the next step can be made back onto the old course is a pretty optimistic viewpoint to assume. One deviation leads to another. Hence, it is of prime importance that, in some way or other, the first point of deviation from the settled course may be promptly detected. Before a decision at that point is made, a review of the possible consequences should take place.

However, if deviations from policy were *never* made, little progress in the evolution of administrative practices would be made. When to condone minor deviations or when to completely discourage them is often a real dilemma for the administrator. His official, tongue in cheek, position must be to encourage rather strict adherence to policy in order to minimize deviate practices.

Much of the success of the administration of the particular function momentarily at hand depends on how well judgment and finesse are exercised in resolving this dilemma. Being fallible human beings, all of us are sinners to some degree; our good reputation rests upon the small degree and the little extent of our sinning, as well as upon the acceptable standard in which we are operating and the extent to which these shortcomings may be offset by exceptionally good performances.

Deviating from the established policy, like sinning and lawbreaking, is fraught with danger. Policies, therefore, may be closer to rules of conduct than simply broad guides of behavior and bases for decision. Policies should be made within a framework that is humanly feasible of attainment and socially and politically acceptable. Periodic review and revision are necessary to keep policies current and meaningful. The time of first deviation from the settled course of procedure should be the automatic signal for "stop, look, and listen"—a time for review and possible revision of the established policy. The first deviation should not be ignored.

Inasmuch as the making of decisions in the absence of reference material is difficult and very often inconsistent, the enunciation of policies is of prime importance. But policies are often distilled from many small decisions made over a long period of time, may have evolved imperceptibly by habit, and may or may not be in written form. A new employee, or an old employee in a new position, finds out such things by making unfortunate errors of judgment. The whole operation of the department would be much better if there existed in each department a "book" of general policies.

It is helpful for the purposes of this text to consider policies to be of two general classes: (1) Legislative Policies which are formulated by legislative bodies or by individuals above the rank of PR administrator, and (2) Administrative Policies which govern methods of procedure within the Legislative Policy framework, and the formulation of rules and regulations to ensure compliance with established policy.

Legislative Policies emanate from the laws which create the Park and Recreation Department and enable it to function. Within this legal framework the legislative authority adopts rules governing its own legislative procedure, ordinances governing the use of park property, and general policies governing the operation of the department.

Although the administrator may take part in advising the legislative body about the formulation of Legislative Policies, his special province lies in establishing Administrative Policies, rules and regulations for daily operations of his department, all within the policy guidelines laid down by the legislative body.

The two general classes of policies facilitate the compilation of policy manuals. Rather than having one unwieldy, large book of Policies and Manual of Operation, separation of subject matter into two classes makes the whole more understandable.

The discussions on relationships which follow may be considered to have been derived from both Legislative and Administrative Policies, being the net result of decisions of both the commission and the chief executive. It is also from the suggestions contained in the following discussions that policies may be formulated—some legislative and some administrative, as may be appropriate to any department under consideration.

POLICIES IN RELATIONSHIPS

A park and recreation department in any of the levels of government will have many relationships with other governmental agencies as well as private agencies in allied fields. There also will occur relationships of importance between divisions or division heads within the same department. If the department has a legislative and policy-making board, important relationships will exist between the legislative body and the chief executive and his staff.

Established and well-recognized policies in governing these relationships are important aids in the efficient and friendly operation of the department. Both the relationships and the policies which might occur in connection therewith are too numerous to compile in one volume which presumes to cover all levels of government and all geographical areas. Enough is included in the following discussion to enable the student to get some concept of how these relationships may be treated and to recognize policies when he sees them stated. The student should recognize, however, that as regards the former, there frequently exists opportunity for differences of opinion for any given set of circumstances and that there may be alternative and more applicable statements in various special circumstances.

THE CHIEF EXECUTIVE AND HIS LEGISLATIVE BODY, WITH SOME COMMENTS AS TO PROCEDURE

Every Park and Recreation Department is established by some law, state statute, park district law, municipal charter, or, in the case of the federal services, the Congress. If the powers and duties in connection therewith have been assigned to a legislative body such as a Board, that Board will probably have adopted rules and regulations for its own conduct and in doing so has prescribed duties and powers for the chief executive, all as part of legislative policy.

Within the limitations stated in the "Rules of the Board,"* the administrator is expected to operate the department. However, the statement of duties and authority in the Rules is probably so broad that further

*See p. 232.

clarification is desirable. This clarification comes about by either an elaboration of the original statement (an extension of the Legislative Policy Statement) or by a period of experience in dealing with matters of administration during which time the administrator is testing the limits of his authority in dealing with departmental affairs without specific legislative guidance. In other words, the administrator seeks to exercise as much authority as he can within the general legislative policy without incurring the displeasure of the Board itself. The legislative body is just as apt to invade the province of the administrator as the reverse situation.

Obviously, there is going to be some difference of opinion on some issues as to the appropriateness of the administrator's action, which, in time, may cause modification of the original policy statement. It is well, therefore, to anticipate as many of these possible conflicts when the policy is first adopted rather than to wait for emotions to becloud sound judgment as differences arise. There are PR departments that never do draw the line between legislative and administrative prerogatives, letting the matter work itself out during changes in personnel—not a really happy solution.

MATTERS PROPERLY BEFORE THE BOARD

Matters requiring action of the Board probably originate in three ways: petitions and communications from the general public, reports of its officers, and by members of the Board speaking from the floor under the heading of new business. A typical functioning may be as follows:

Citizens wishing the Board to act on certain matters which cannot be disposed of by the chief executive and his staff because of lack of authority are informed that they can lay the matter before the Board in the form of a petition or communication. Sometimes they will appear before the Board in person, but generally speaking, this is discouraged (unless a public hearing on the subject is called for later by the Board) because such impromptu appearances interfere with the orderly procedure of the Board and the scheduling of matters to be brought before it. Also, the subject matter is usually prematurely discussed because no investigation has been made, making it difficult for the pertinent points involved to be brought out and logically discussed. Ordinarily no citizen should be entitled to speak before the Board without the consent of the Board. Occasionally, the Board may give its consent as a matter of courtesy to visiting V.I.P.s or to anyone for some brief and noncontroversial matter.

The chief executive and his staff are always acting under Board direction, deriving all of their powers and authority from the Board. Much of this is in general terms as provided in the rules of the Board, the adoption of the annual budget, the approval of plans for new construction, and similar matters. Nevertheless, these and many specific items require Board approval.

Consequently, the chief executive or other officers of the Board sometimes present matters for Board action through official reports.

Under the heading of new business, any board member is entitled to present any matter to the Board for its consideration. For the sake of both harmony in Board procedure, and good public relations, board members should show discrimination in the subject matter brought to the Board's attention in this manner. Details of administration which could be taken up privately with the administrator or his staff ought to be avoided. For example, "Why wasn't the skating rink cleared on a certain day?" "One of my constituents has complained about how the tree in front of his house was trimmed, that he 'saw loafing on the job,'" and hosts of similar questions and complaints. These can be readily handled by the superintendent and his staff. However, if board members do not get satisfaction from the administrator on repeated occasions, the subject matter can be brought before the Board and investigation made. It is well to keep in mind that if open criticism between board members or between board members and staff members occurs in open Board sessions at which the public's eyes are focused and their ears attuned by the presence of newspaper reporters, the effectiveness of the Board's influence on public matters suffers. Every effort should be made toward frank, private discussion which may eliminate misunderstandings in open meetings, thereby permitting complete harmony and decorum to prevail.

Matters which are appropriate for board members to bring to the attention of the Board include: items pertaining to new projects which ought to receive special attention, subject matters which require special investigation, and in general, matters pertaining to policy and legislation which is the broad function of the Board. Even on these matters prior consultation with other Board members and sometimes even with the executive officers may point out the most orderly and expeditious way to resolve the subject matter.*

Usually in carrying out the intent and purposes of the law under which they are operating, the Board has assigned all administrative matters to its chief executive officer, and his staff and has retained for itself all legislative matters and matters of general policy. It is important that these areas of activity be carefully followed. While frequent conversations take place between individual members of the Board and the administrator and his executive staff, it should be fully recognized that the actual orders to the administrator come from the Board as a whole and not from its individual members. It is equally important, on the other hand, that the administrator and his staff recognize that action on policy and on legislative matters, or on any other matters, are paramount to the individual opinions of members of

*See Appendix, pp. 308-310.

the executive staff and should become wholeheartedly the attitude of the entire department. The administrator should have ample opportunity to make recommendations to the Board involving all matters, even including suggestions as to future policy, but once the Board has acted, that action, be it in accordance with or contrary to the recommendations, must be accepted wholeheartedly as the conclusion of the entire department.

While the rules of the Board may establish certain procedures for the operation of committees and for the conduct of Board business generally, the time available to individual members of the Board to attend meetings necessarily requires certain deviations not only as to meeting dates but as to the orderly presentation of some matters. When that becomes necessary, however, it should be the policy of the executive staff to keep the board members individually informed so that the spirit of the orderly procedure outlined in the rules of the Board can be carried out.

In his relationship with the Board and with his executive staff, the administrator ought to have an understanding with both the Board and his staff members as to how frequently and on what subjects direct contact between board members and staff members may occur. Generally speaking, there should be easy communication between them. However, it should be thoroughly understood, especially by the staff members, that no conversation of significance should be withheld from the chief executive. Occasions do arise when board members like to pry, or shall we say spy, to see if some rift cannot be nurtured between the chief executive and his staff for the purpose of discrediting the chief. The staff member, on the other hand, feeling that a ready line of communication has been opened with an influential individual, thinks he can further his own prestige by aiding in the discrediting of his superior. This is a good way for a board member to "divide and conquer." However, with suitable staff organization and staff operation, such situations can be avoided. In any event, it should be noted that the circumstances above described are more the exception than the rule. Generally, the entire relationship involving the chief executive and his executive staff with the Board as a whole is a friendly one.

In summary, policies in regard to the relationship between the Park and Recreation administrator and his governing body may be expressed as below; the spirit thereof might apply to any authority superior to the chief executive.

1. Although the general duties of the governing board are to adopt legislation and broad policies and the chief executive is to operate the department within the law and the general policies, it is desirable that the lines of authority and responsibility between the two be carefully drawn.

2. Even though the responsibility for adopting broad policies rests with the governing board, the chief executive, being a professional in his field,

should be permitted to make recommendations as to policy as well as to matters of operation.

3. Once the governing board has acted and has established policies, those policies must be wholeheartedly accepted by the administrator and by his executive staff.

4. In transmitting orders from the governing board to the chief executive, it should be understood that those orders come from the Board acting as a whole and not from individual members.

5. Attempting to place himself in the position of the individual board member, the administrator will do all in his power to keep individual board members informed of significant operations so that they will be able to supply responses to questions from their constituents.

6. In regard to social contacts, the administrator should take cognizance of his relative position and allow the individual commissioners to take the initiative regardless of the relative social and financial status of the individual member. The administrator should do all in his power to keep the friendly associations between himself and individual board members the same for all members.

7. In general, the administrator should recognize that while he is presumed to know more about the field of park and recreation operations inasmuch as he is a professional, he should also recognize that the individual board members are interested and very likely enthusiastic supporters of public parks and recreation even though they are without professional training in that respect. Therefore, the professional should do all in his power to improve the specialized knowledge of the board members, but at the same time accept decisions of the governing body as coming from the electorate which in the final analysis is that body of citizens for which the entire service is being provided.

RELATIONSHIP OF ADMINISTRATOR
TO HIS EXECUTIVE STAFF

The following succinct description of the role of the manager by Robert S. McNamara, Secretary of Defense (1962) appeared in the May, 1962 issue of the magazine *U.S.A.*:

> The role of the public manager is very similar to the role of a private manager; in each case he has the option of two major alternative courses of action. He can either act as a judge or a leader. In the former case, he sits and waits until subordinates bring to him problems for solutions, or alternatives for choice. In the latter case, he immerses himself in the operations of the business or governmental activity, examines the problems, the objectives, and alternate courses of action, chooses among them, and leads the organization to their accomplish-

ment. In the one case it's a passive role; in the other case, an active role. . . . I've always believed in and endeavored to follow the active leadership role as opposed to the passive judicial role.

In the case of park commissions it is more appropriate for the board members to assume the judicial role; the administrator the active leadership role.

1. The general attitude of the manager should be such as to create within his executive staff a spirit of unity and mutual cooperation, a relaxed but businesslike atmosphere, and an esprit de corps aimed at operating the staff as a unit. That unity of purpose should permeate the entire park and recreation department.

2. The manager should recognize the need for continual professional self-improvement of his staff members and should encourage them to participate in the affairs of professional organizations applicable to each and to see that they get opportunity for carrying their share of the responsibilities in such organizations.

3. The manager should see that staff meetings are held with reasonable frequency and with definite purposes but not so often as to nullify their effect. He should see that an organization is perfected for the smooth functioning of such meetings, the making up of agenda, the calling of meetings, the recording of them. In such meetings, the relaxed and informal manner should encourage full, free, and frank discussion, and if at all possible, the manager ought to accept as his, the position which represents the consensus of opinion of the staff.

4. Having confidence in the professional ability and integrity of each of the staff members, the manager should be willing to support his staff members in matters of controversy until proof to the contrary is produced.

PARK DEPARTMENT WITH THE PLANNING COMMISSION

The relationship here is one between the general practitioner and the specialist. The Planning Commission is responsible for the planning of the entire city, county, or state, the coordination of all services, the zoning of properties according to suitable land use, and in general the responsibility that the parts fit together into a sensible whole.* The Park and Recreation Department is responsible for the planning of a park and recreation system together with the designs of individual properties. When each recognizes its respective responsibilities, the two departments can work out their own problems in a well-coordinated fashion; without such a relationship, the results and the processes both are most unfortunate.

It should be added that the rapid shifting of population segments

---

*In federal matters, the Bureau of Outdoor Recreation closely approximates this function.

(and other factors) is becoming most confusing to the best of planners and the nice division of respective responsibilities suggested above can be obscured, especially in the metropolitan complexes now developing. All planners, lay and professional and the new breed of specialists known as urbanologists, are in need of help in determining causes and anticipating effects. In consequence, park and recreation departments must necessarily broaden their role in planning far beyond the confines and general purposes of recreation areas alone, even to the extent of including in their staffs planners of general outlook rather than special interest in recreation services.

RELATIONSHIP OF PARKS AND SCHOOL DEPARTMENTS

The objective here is to get both park departments and school boards to agree that both parties have a responsibility in community recreation as a public service because both have facilities which are useful in the performance of that service. The basic understanding should be that the school department is primarily, if not exclusively, responsible for education and that the responsibility of the park and recreation department is to provide a park and recreation service to the people as a primary if not an exclusive function.

This understanding takes on special importance in situations which have arisen more frequently in recent years with the rapid expansion of urban growth out into rural areas. The general acceptance of the necessity of adequate public support for education has enabled school districts (whose boundaries do not necessarily coincide with village corporate boundaries) to acquire generous school acreage far in advance of actual village land occupancy. Children are transported to schools and hence school location may be almost independent of the presence of local built-up areas, and also independent of local village planning. Schools may assume initial responsibility for some community recreation in connection with their physical education program. As the villages become better organized and more built up, more complete and comprehensive recreation service becomes necessary. At that point schools may have some properties in excess of purely education needs, while park and recreation departments are competing with housing and industry for adequate park and recreation land. Recreation and education are thrown together; both must discharge their respective responsibilities, but now with greater emphasis on public economy.

Both departments have physical assets which are of value in performing the primary service which is the responsibility of the other. When these responsibilities are understood and accepted mutually by the parties, then the basis has been laid for some specific policies:

1. The requirements for site location in the case of elementary schools and neighborhood parks being substantially identical, there will be

cooperative planning for the selection of sites for both of these purposes. If possible, the identical sites should be acquired.

2. In the acquisition of properties, each department will understand that it will acquire for itself the area necessary to carry out its full function without overlapping onto the properties of the other.

3. When elementary or junior high school or senior high school properties are located adjacent to or in connection with park properties, the two properties shall be jointly planned to provide one coordinated, single, community asset with the best possible arrangement of facilities regardless of property lines. In case of park facilities overlapping onto school property or vice versa, permits for the use of such property should be exchanged.

4. Suitable agreements shall be entered into for the interchangeable use of the facilities so that each may carry out its primary function with the privilege of using the assets of the other.

These provisions may be followed by numerous rules and regulations and even some statements of policy to further clarify the functioning of the two departments.

RELATIONSHIP OF PARK DEPARTMENT TO SO-CALLED RED FEATHER AGENCIES OR AGENCIES OF THE COMMUNITY CHEST, PRIVATELY SUPPORTED.

1. The spirit of mutual understanding and cooperation should be fostered and friendly operational relationships established.
2. Conferences should be held for the planning of facilities and operational programs for the purpose of avoiding duplication and overlapping of services.
3. Aid should be given the private agencies in the organization of athletic leagues and permits for the use of properties in connection therewith on an equal basis with but not preferential to any of the department's own activities.
4. The park department should stand ready to aid in the training of leaders in specialized fields when such training is difficult to obtain elsewhere.

RELATIONSHIPS WITH OTHER LOCAL GOVERNMENTAL AGENCIES

In this category there are large numbers of agencies with which the park and recreation department has business and with which it has numerous contacts. Such agencies include civil service commissions, legal departments, the treasurer's office, register of deeds, county and state highway departments, state conservation departments, health departments, and others.

In each case, the park and recreation department should endeavor to develop a friendly and cooperative relationship but without sacrificing by default its own powers and prerogatives. Suggestions as to policy methods include the following:

1. Keep the paths of communication open by an occasional call, even if there is no definite business to transact.
2. Keep in mind the responsibilities of the other agencies and confer with each of them whenever matters in the park and recreation department arise which would be of interest to the other agencies.
3. Keep in close enough touch with other agencies' planning and work to anticipate possible future contacts. Often conferences in the early stages of planning will avoid serious conflict which might occur after the plans have been developed.

RELATIONSHIPS INVOLVING STATE AND FEDERAL AGENCIES

Recognizing the increasing evidence of the inability of local governments to solve their most aggravating physical and social problems, the federal government has within recent years assumed a major responsibility to help—by partial financing, and because of financing, also by establishing policy for solving local problems. The federal government also has aided states and prodded the states to further aid local governments. Sometimes federal aid to metropolises is direct and at other times it is funneled through the states. A myriad of such programs exist.

It therefore becomes an essential and a new function of local governments (as well as state governments) to be aware of these programs, the requirements by which each becomes available, the bureaucratic rules and regulations that must be followed, and the devious ways by which action may be stimulated.

If aid is genuinely needed and expected to be forthcoming, whole-hearted cooperation with federal bureaus must be given. There will be irritating situations, rules to be complied with, some delays and frustrations, even criticism of results, but these are the price to be paid for the aid.

Time may reveal that local problems cannot be successfully and efficiently solved in Washington; that the financial aid is actually money collected at the local level by federal agents; that the inability of local governments to cope with local problems arises from at least two causes: (1) the inability to see the whole forest of situations rather than only the single trees of local ideas, and (2) the lack of sufficient sources of tax revenue. The exchange of philosophy and techniques between federal and local agencies presents possibilities of more efficient and equitable operation.

Should such hypotheses or others of similar nature prove to be logical, the PR administrators should equip themselves with the proper knowledge to enter into discussions which may lead to improved methods. In the meantime, it seems sensible to recognize that the purposes of the present programs are worthy ones, and that their inauguration has been an incentive to advance and an eye-opener into greater possibilities of recreation objectives. The word, then, is to cooperate.

PARK AND RECREATION DEPARTMENT
WITH THE PRESS AND THE PUBLIC

1. No official meetings of the board shall take place at which the press is excluded.
2. All matters which have been officially acted upon become a part of the public record and are accessible to the press and to the public.
3. The press and the public have a right to know what the policies of operation are when those policies are fixed by official board proceedings or established by executive order.
4. Executive policies, especially if not written, are not necessarily subject to public examination. They may not be official records.

Chapter Twelve

Acquisition and Development Policies

ACQUISITION IN GENERAL

Parks like factory sites, retail stores, hotels, and shopping centers are acquired with a definite purpose in mind. One does not simply look at a vacant lot and say to oneself, "That would make a dandy playground; let's buy it," or a wooded vale with a babbling brook running through it and say, "What a spot for a nice park! Let's add it to our system." In the chapters on the makeup of park systems, and again in the chapter on the design of a park, certain general criteria for site selection were mentioned. The most important one is that the site must be of such a size, of such a nature, and of such a location as to fit into an overall plan of the whole park system of which it is to become a part. If the proposed site does not nicely fit into the scheme of the overall park system, whether it be too small (or too large) or too flat, or too rugged, too barren, too wooded, or in the wrong location, it is not right for the purpose and should be acquired only under extenuating circumstances.

This applies to property that is about to be donated as well as to property that is to be paid for with taxpayers' money.

The supposition is that there does exist a master plan for the park system in question. That plan is not an unrelated entity all by itself, but a part of a plan of greater extent involving the physical development of a city, county, region, state, or the nation of which this particular park system is a part. If federal and state participation in financing is anticipated, then approval of the park plan as a part of a plan for a larger geographical entity is a prerequisite. Furthermore, the impact on the environment of this park project must be investigated and a report of it properly made. Since the environment includes people as well as the flora, fauna, topographical characteristics, historical and archeological features, the demography of the affected population and its structural habitats must be included in such an investigation. All this is a prerequisite to the establishment of any proposed park and recreation system or to any significant part thereof.

   If such a park and recreation plan exists and all prerequisites are fulfilled, acquisition of properties can proceed with sensible confidence. Without such a plan the acquisition process is doomed to failure.

   As to actual departmental policy of acquisition within the system of prerequisites above stated, some guidelines are herein proposed to facilitate the acquisition process. The guidelines or policy statements pertain to the ideal situation for each classification of parks as described in Chapter 8 and must be modified for situations which vary from that ideal. Hence, to begin with, we have these policy statements: *A definite plan for the entire system of parks is essential. Acquisition of properties should be in the location and of the proper character consistent with that plan.*

SITE SELECTION NOTES

   The plan of the park system denotes the location and size of the lands to be acquired, but there is usually some small flexibility in location (very little for neighborhood parks, more for larger parks, and perhaps considerable for state parks), a little flexibility as to size, and some as to character. Here are some points to keep in mind.

   1. Since neighborhood parks are supposed to be in the center of a neighborhood the general dimensions of which are 3/4 mile to 1 mile square any location away from the center reduces the full effectiveness of the proposed park. Moving off the center as much as 300 feet may be permissible if the difference in land costs is great. Hence, *acquire property away from the center of the neighborhood only with great reluctance.*

   Access to neighborhood parks should be complete on all four sides, either from streets, alleys (less advantageous than streets), or other public ways. Avoid the situation where public and private properties have a common boundary; this leads to conflicts, the public being a nuisance to the private property owner and vice versa. Playlots and large parks, even state parks can also suffer from this situation.

Otherwise poor land can be used for parks, but in the case of neighborhood parks, the location is paramount to all else. The reclamation of a poor piece of property (e.g., a swamp) to a good park is not justified if the location is not right or the access inadequate or faulty. New and small towns are prone to utilize poor properties regardless of location or access because the land developers have donated such land with little or no value for building lots. Location and access must be right or else leave such properties alone.

One or two existing buildings in one corner of a 10-acre plot may tempt the park department to omit its acquisition. The omission will be regretted when the park is fully developed.

The size and shape of a proposed neighborhood park should be as prescribed in the table of standards on page 72 and in conformity with departmental policies as to the inclusion or exclusion of such facilities as athletic fields, swimming or wading pools, buildings, etc., some of which may be provided by other departments such as the school board or by quasi-public or private agencies included in the United Way organization. This suggests that *some schematic plan of development ought to be prepared before acquisition becomes final.* A neighborhood park of a size sufficient to provide some horticultural embellishment is a distinct asset to a neighborhood whereas one of cramped design can be a nuisance to adjacent property.

2. In acquiring land for community playfields, and regional athletic fields, there is a little more flexibility in site location for two principal reasons: (1) the area being served is probably two miles or more across instead of one mile or less as in the case of neighborhood parks and (2) instead of walking to the playfield most patrons use a bicycle or an automobile. Even so, *a location very close to the center of the area to be served should be selected.*

In both cases—neighborhood parks and community playfields—*the usable ground is the flat ground.* Undulating or rugged topography, ground cover (e.g., woods and brush land) as well as water areas are of no value; indeed they may be a detriment unless the total area is large enough to accommodate all the active recreation facilities without the rough ground and water area, in which case the interesting topography becomes a real asset.

Access and shape of site are just as important for playfields as they are for neighborhood parks. The possibility of acquiring neighborhood park and playfield sites jointly with school sites should not be overlooked.

3. Site selection for large parks, parkways, and special use parks (golf courses, zoos, etc.) present problems of their own. Geographic location may be important in some cases, but *size, coupled with topographic and scenic values, will be paramount in almost all situations.* Hills and valleys, woods and clearings, lakes and streams, upland and swampland, beautiful and unusual scenery are all sought in establishing large city parks—and county and state

parks as well. Variety of scenery lends enchantment; and yet there must be present enough reasonably level and open areas for active use, e.g., picnicking. *Stream valleys and lake shores should be acquired as completely as is possible.* Only an abundance of such natural advantages can justify private ownership to a limited extent. The reasons are more readily set forth than the accomplishments can be achieved. Private ownership of shorelands limits the real enjoyable benefits and hence real estate enhancement to shore owners alone, whereas public ownership with suitable (i.e., roadway) access spreads the benefit to all the public and especially not only to those fronting the access road, but to those properties reaching some distance away—as much as a half mile or more. Real estate developers (or city fathers) can rarely see that selling a few shore properties at high prices is not as advantageous as selling many more properties (some just across the access road and many more a block or two away from the lake or stream) at an overall higher average price. An owner of a 40-acre tract having stream frontage could actually afford to donate a reasonable stream right-of-way for park or parkway purposes because of the benefit it brings to his remaining real estate. This situation is advantageous to the city because of the improvement of the tax base. The alternative to public ownership is usually spotted development and an administrative problem of water control, cleanup, and possible pollution. Conclusion—*make public ownership of lake shores and stream valleys as extensive as possible.*

The extent in depth of shorelands to be acquired depends upon the possible use and possible extent of the flood plain. If the scenic aspect of a stream from a bordering roadway (possible parkway) is all that is required and if the flood plain is narrow or even nonexistent, the public right-of-way may be quite narrow—one to a few hundred feet. However, if picnic grounds or other concentrated uses are contemplated, or if the flood plain is broad, acquisition lines must be drawn accordingly. Lake shore public properties must be quite extensive, for water draws people and people require space. It does not pay to underestimate required size.

About 150 acres are required for an eighteen-hole golf course. It may be crowded into less, but this is not advisable. If accessories such as driving ranges, and pitch-and-putt courses are added (and it may be well to anticipate these), additional acreage is, of course, necessary. Availability of suitable acreage is more important than geographical location although the latter cannot be entirely ignored. Gently rolling (not rugged) topography is desirable. Some open woodland and water areas (lakes, ponds, streams) are distinct assets. Because of the large grass areas to be maintained, soil conditions are very important. Adequate water supply and possibility of sewage disposal must be present or possible of attainment.

From 75 to 200 acres are required for an adequate zoological garden. (Avoid the mere gradual accumulation of a group of animals confined to a small space resulting in something in the nature of a menagerie.) Actual site selection is a matter for the specialists in zoological garden operation and planning.

The employment of specialists or teams of specialists is advisable in the selection of sites for many of the special use areas: golf courses, zoos, arboretums, aquariums, marinas, outdoor theaters, great municipal stadiums, sites for museums, planetariums, observatories, and a number of other items.

In an earlier time, parkways and boulevards were essential elements in the park system of the city. Times have changed. The unifying effect on the whole city, the element of grandeur and imposing appearance, the locale for the exhibition of fine horses and carriages, have been supplanted by other elements in the city plan. Parkways have not entirely been done away with even in cities. Counties and even the National Park Service have built parkways in relatively recent years and are planning for still more. But today's parkways must be planned on a much larger scale. Too often, however, the acquired right-of-way widths have not kept pace with the need for greater scale. When horse-drawn carriages were traveling 5 to 10 miles an hour, or when automobiles did not exceed 20 miles an hour, a new viewing experience was just around the bend a few hundred feet ahead. In the interim, there was time to look closely at the verdure on the roadside or the attractive homes 50 to 100 feet away. Today's 30 to 50 mile an hour pace permits no close view of small plants or fine homes close to the roadway, and if the "bend" in the road is not a half mile to several miles ahead, the road is dangerous. Our views are farther away and on a much larger scale. These viewing areas must be protected if the parkway is to preserve its intrinsic value.   Hence, *the rights-of-way to be acquired (or controlled) should be generous enough to protect and maintain for all time those attributes which first made the site appealing enough to locate a parkway thereon.*

In state and federal acquisitions, special attention must be given to the classification systems of BOR, National Park Service, Forest Service, and others. Acquisitions should be made according to the criteria established in each of these services, keeping in mind that, for example, scenic parks of the NPS carry with them a preservation obligation which is not necessarily a provision of National Recreation Areas. Hence the native aspect, while important in all categories, is more binding for scenic parks.

FINANCING CAPITAL OUTLAYS—ACQUISITION AND DEVELOPMENT

Groceries cannot be bought on the installment plan, but almost everything else can. Radios must be fully paid for in a shorter period of time than automobiles, which, in turn, must be fully paid for in less time than homes. Anything that is not immediately consumed or has a life during which some value exists can be "mortgaged," thereby extending full payment up to somewhat less time than the life of the article.

In government business, consumable goods or items of current expense must be paid for out of current income. Short-term borrowing may be permitted to tide over the agency pending the receipt of current income (an easy procedure especially when the forthcoming income is from taxes which have already been levied), but there is no chance of long-term borrowing to pay for current expense items. (Exceptions are the U.S. government and some states as hereinafter noted.) In almost all cases, the use of the proceeds from long-term borrowing to pay current expenses is illegal; violations carry stiff penalties. Generally speaking, *governmental corporations pay "cash" for consumable or current items* of the departments' budget.

Tangible items having an economically usable life span measured in years are generally known as capital goods and the payment for them is called a capital expenditure. Governments have an option as to methods of making capital expenditures: they may pay cash (i.e., out of current income) or they may buy on the installment plan (i.e., issue bonds or other securities). The choice rests upon consideration of a number of factors, but the basic one seems to be; "Will the political constituents stand for a high enough tax rate today to pay the whole cost of something that will be used for many years to come, even extending into the next generation?" Usually they say, "Let our children pay part of the cost," or "We cannot afford it today, but give us time to pay for it as we use it."

Seldom may a government engage in a complete "pay-as-you-go" procedure in spite of the presence of much argument as to the value thereof.

The net result then, is that *the usual practice is for government to pay for current expenses out of current income and to go in debt for capital expenditures.*

*The borrowing of money for capital expenditures usually takes the form of selling bonds for cash.** A government bond is evidence of indebtedness—a promise to pay the face value of the bond on a certain date and to pay interest at specified intervals upon the surrender of interest "coupons" attached to the bond. Bonds are classified as to type of security, time of maturity, interest rate, purpose of issue, and otherwise.

In private installment buying, the written agreement usually provides that if certain payments are not made at the times prescribed, the seller may

---

*Note: For the purpose of quick and general understanding of the subject, the discussion of bonds in this section has been oversimplified. Do not use it as a guide to the issuance of bonds in any specific situation. Consult the applicable laws and seek legal counsel.

retrieve the capital goods sold and the purchaser forfeits all equity in them. A government bond of similar nature would be a mortgage bond which provides that if the bond holders do not receive the payments called for in the bonds, the capital goods (usually land) can become the property of the bondholders after certain legal steps (foreclosure proceedings) have been taken. Usually, bondholders are not interested in foreclosing on public park improvements and in some instances, foreclosure or the enforcement of liens for the recapture of public real estate by private parties is not possible. Municipal corporations may, however, mortgage real estate in the usual way, if the law specifically permits it.

The usual government bond is secured by the "full faith and credit" of the government and its pledge to levy and collect taxes to pay the full interest and principal of the bond. When issued in compliance with the law pertaining to the issuing agency, the provisions of the bond are legally enforceable and the collection of interest and principal is secured so long as the particular government is solvent. These bonds can be sold for cash. Whether the amount of cash that bond buyers (wholesalers who in turn sell bonds to retail buyers) are willing to pay is the face value of the bonds at the interest rate called for, or more or less than this, depends on the market for bonds at the time of sale as well as upon the credit of the issuing agency which, in turn, is dependent on the agency's history of financial responsibility.

Special assessment bonds are secured by the collection of special assessments on "specially benefited" real estate. The situation arises as follows: The establishment of a park (in each of the stages of acquisition and development) imparts a special benefit to real estate in some zone of influence. This benefit is measurable in the actual rise of real estate values. Special assessments are levied against the benefited real estate in the form of taxes which are over and above the ad valoreum tax on real estate. Receipts from these special assessment taxes are pledged to pay for the interest and principal of bonds which have been issued to raise money to pay for the original capital expenditure, i.e., the acquisition and/or the development of the park. Since delinquencies in tax collection do occur, there could develop a shortage in funds to pay bond interest and principal. Hence, to add to the security it is advisable for the issuing agency to pledge itself to make good any collection deficiency out of general taxes. Special assessment bonds backed up by the full taxing power of the issuing governmental agency are as sound as any other of the bonds of that agency.

The other extreme of soundness of this sort of security is encountered when public works are financed, not by bond issues, but by the issuance of special assessment "certificates." These may be given to contractors for work performed, or to real estate sellers for real estate, instead of cash payments. Because of possible delinquencies in collection of special assessments (assuming such collections to be the only monies promised to pay these "certificates") the certificates are often not worth their face value, and are susceptible to heavy discounts.

There is great merit in the special assessment process and it has been used for many public works. A few cities and some counties have used it to finance all manner of parks from neighborhood parks to large parks and parkways. But, in the majority of localities, especially in suburban towns, the public has not been used to this method of financing park acquisition and development and so *the special assessment plan has not been widely used.*

If the proposed capital expenditure is for *some project which is to be operated at a "profit,"* revenue bonds may be issued to finance the undertaking. The security may be limited to the net receipts from the operation, in which case the marketability of the issue is dependent upon the probable financial success of the project. Hence, if the success of the project is a "cinch" this type of revenue bond can be successfully sold. When the project is financially more hazardous, but not entirely so, the issuing governmental agency may further secure the bonds by pledging to make good any deficiency in net income by levying the necessary taxes. Municipal stadium financing quite frequently requires the added security of the tax levying pledge of the municipality. The establishment of municipal golf courses in many instances may be financially sound enough to dispense with the added security of tax levies. Revenue bonds are a useful financial tool and are resorted to in a number of special cases, but are not extensively used to finance park and recreation facilities in general. In some cases, as a sort of substitute, the municipality may issue general city bonds to finance the project and then require the park and recreation department to deposit all net receipts from the operation of the enterprise into the "sinking fund" until the project is paid for or for a specified number of years.

All the foregoing discussion on bonds applies principally to levels of government lower than the state governments. The fiscal policy of the federal government and some state governments calls for a different kind of operation. Capital expenditures of the federal government and items in the annual budget are not financed by specific bond issues. United States bonds are secured by the "full faith and credit" of the U.S. government and are issued in various categories and under various names to supply cash as needed to finance any and all governmental operations pending the receipt of budgetary income items, whereas a municipal bond is issued to finance capital investment projects. The U.S. bonded debt is an accumulation of budgetary deficits over the years, and, of course, some part of that budgetary deficit might conceivably be caused by capital expenditures. In that sense there is a similarity between municipal and U.S. bonds but not enough to make the foregoing bond discussion applicable to the U.S. government or to the states that operate similarly.

The student should be familiar with other characteristics of bonds. They are issued in more than one form, at various rates of interest, and for various numbers of years.

One form may prescribe that bonds will be issued in denominations of $1000 (or other amounts) with interest coupons attached calling for the payment of an amount equal to interest at a specified rate (say 4%) for six months or three months or twelve months, as the case may be. Payment of interest is made by the surrender of these coupons, usually at the office of the treasurer of the issuing agency. Upon a specified date of X years from the date of issue, the principal sum of the bond becomes payable. Such bonds are known by the number of years between date of issue and date of maturity, e.g., straight ten-year bonds, or straight twenty-year bonds, etc. During the life of the bond, the only annual payments required are the interest payments, but at maturity the whole whopping principal becomes due. Usually provision for this lump sum payment has been taken care of by accumulating funds from each year's taxes in a so-called "sinking fund" out of which both interest and principal are paid. The "nonworking" capital in the sinking fund may sometimes be reinvested pending its actual need. Sometimes such "idle" funds may even be used to temporarily finance other capital projects. In practice, the financing of capital improvements and the manipulation of the sinking fund can become quite involved; many legal safeguards have been provided to insure the integrity of bond issues and to avoid slipshod operations.

General bonds may be retired piecemeal over a period of years, say one-tenth or one-twentieth each year for the ten- or twenty-year life of the bond issue. These are known as serial bonds. Each individual bond is for a specified life, but the maturity dates of the various bonds are selected to make one-tenth or one-twentieth of the total number fall due in successive years. Obviously, the sinking fund for serial bonds retains money for periods of only months (the time intervening between tax collections and payment dates for principal and interest on bonds), instead of for years as in the case of straight bonds. For most counties and municipalities, *the issuance of serial bonds has an advantage over the issuance of straight bonds.*

The length of life of a bond issue usually hinges on two factors: (1) How close to pay-as-you-go financing is the issuing agency willing to consider? The closer to that plan of operation, the shorter will be the life of the bonds. (2) The economically useful life of the capital purpose for which the bonds are issued, e.g., "radios," "automobiles," or "houses" as first mentioned in our installment buying analogy. Because of rapidity of technological advancements, this useful life of things is shortened as much or more by obsolescence as by physically wearing out. The trend, therefore, is to avoid long-term bonds. Taxpayers don't like to pay for dead horses.

Pause for a moment now to succinctly summarize the foregoing suggested policies having to do with financing capital expenditures with money that ultimately comes from the pocket of the taxpayer.

√   A pay-as-you-go plan may be a fine idea but very few governmental agencies will find it possible to adopt it. Paying for capital expenditures out of current funds, except in small amounts, is not feasible and should not be relied upon.

√   The issuance of bonds is the most reliable method of financing capital needs. Of the various kinds of bonds, general serial bonds of relatively short term—say ten to twenty years—will fit most situations better than any other form. However, other types of bond issues may be investigated for special cases.

√   Special assessment procedures are very much worth looking into. Bonds issued in these situations ought to be backed up by the full faith and credit of the issuing agency.

√   Projects susceptible of turning an operating profit sufficient to amortize any capital indebtedness might be financed by the issuance of revenue bonds. These again, should be backed up by the full faith and credit of the issuing agency.

√   In extreme cases, mortgages (rarely mortgage bonds) may be feasible.

√   Many things are sometimes possible with the use of idle cash in the treasurer's office. Sinking funds may even have a surplus over and above outstanding requirements. Investigate possibilities, but move with caution and then only upon legal advice.

√   Direct appropriation in the annual budget is the normal method of financing capital needs in the case of the federal government and for some state governments.

FINANCING BY SALE OF USE RIGHTS, TAX FORFEITURE, PRIVATE GIFTS AND BEQUESTS, AND MISCELLANEOUS SOURCES

Capital needs are frequently acquired with funds from sources other than by bond issue or direct taxation. Rights to use public property may produce cash; private lands may be forfeited to the state for nonpayment of taxes; lands and items of land improvement may be given or bequeathed by private parties, or money to buy land or to make improvements may be donated. These are examples of a number of ways that capital needs are met.

Land being the basic ingredient of park holdings in all levels of government, and land inherently containing, as it does, things of negotiable worth, money may be obtained by selling, leasing, or otherwise granting the use of portions of it. Excess lands, or seemingly excess lands, may be sold or leased for long periods of time. Mineral or oil drilling rights may be sold. The right to graze cattle, to farm, to cut timber, to dam streams for water power or other purposes, to use as public parking lots, to construct airstrips thereon, innumerable rights for innumerable purposes—all these are worth money. Sometimes they are valuable enough to cause prospective buyers to arouse public sentiment in favor of such sales and to lobby for them in our legislative halls. What to do?

Perhaps fortunately, in the past a segment of the park and recreation fraternity has considered all park lands to be park lands for all time to come, held only in trust by the present administrations, not to be changed in outline or to be exploited by private interests or to be "mutilated" in any way whatsoever. Such an attitude is the natural heritage of a park and recreation administrator, who recalls the firm stand taken against the many efforts to invade New York's Central Park with all sorts of "gimmicks"; how the Congress directed the National Park Service to "conserve" for posterity the wonders of our national parks and how nobly the NPS has fought off timber barons, ranchers, power and mining interests, even sportsmen in order to preserve inviolate the nation's parks; how in our own day we band together and sympathize with each other over the havoc being wrought by the terribly heavy hand of the highway engineer and the urban redeveloper. These noble and courageous acts of resistance deserve emulation today, so the safe and supportable attitude seems to be to assume that parks of all kinds are entirely inviolate and that they are everlasting fixtures of an unchanging civilization, or nearly so.

Laudible as this attitude may seem to the fundamentalist, it seems to the author* to be both unrealistic and in the nature of a crutch on which to rest our more normal analytical ability to make present-day evaluations and decisions. It is unrealistic because if parks and their functions are everlasting, they constitute one of the rare things in this universe that does not change. Also some things have happened to parks over the years that seemed questionable at the time, or they have gradually evolved over the years, that now are taken for granted with scarcely the raising of an eyebrow—the famed Ellipse in front of the White House has become an athletic field; Central Park has its cocktail lounge and dance hall; an amusement park has been added to the park system of Westchester County, New York, but some of its parkways

*The student is warned that there are many administrators who hold fast to the idea that once a property is dedicated as a park it remains so, unless the park department is forced to relinquish by forces beyond its control.

are part of the State Highway System; the Outer Drive in Chicago is labelled highway; Mt. Rushmore has been carved into forms representing some of our Presidents; a parking garage was built under, first, Union Square in San Francisco, and then later, under several other of our city parks. How about the development of power of Niagara Falls and its effect on parks on both sides of the river? Somehow these and other innovations have been accepted without much damaging effect on the basic usefulness of parks. Realistically, changes have already taken place, and may be expected to take place in the future.*

It is unprogressive to rely so heavily on tradition and the judgment of our forebears as to believe that judgment to be infallible. It is equally unwise to assume that park properties may be nonchalantly disposed of, or that their commercial possibilities may be exploited willy-nilly, or that entrance for all sorts of enterprises may be gained with impunity. Not at all. What is suggested is serious reappraisal of a past policy in the light of possible new evidence, even though at first a traditionally park-partisan viewpoint is taken.

The following principles then are suggested in the consideration of possible sales or leases of park lands, or the granting of use permits for a monetary or other consideration:

1. The decision to grant or not to grant is a decision of today—not of yesterday. History, heritage, tradition, and past policy all are part and parcel of that decision, but unless the pending matter is minor, routine, or trivial a reevaluation of past policy is in order with a full recognition of the fact that a new or revised policy may be the result. Warning must be here given that when the crutch of tradition is discarded, the administrator must have the ability to analyze, to wisely decide, and to effectively defend the new position.

2. The proposed sale, lease, use permit, or whatnot must be advantageous to the park authority over the long pull. It must leave the park system as a whole in better shape to perform its function than it was before the transaction.

3. This transaction must not set a precedent which, if followed in the future, will be embarrassing, damaging, or frustrating. If repeated in future cases the result should be just as advantageous as this one.

4. This proposal, if carried out, should be for the overall public good. This asks the park administrator to judge the proposal objectively, especially if in some aspects, the acceptance of the proposal is damaging to the best park interests. Here, the administrator can defend the park interests to a reasonable extent, acquiescing only when the overall good is adequately proven.

*See Appendix, pp. 322-324.

In the matter of leases there is one overriding policy to guide the decision in all cases. It is this! The PR department, be it city, county, state, or federal, as an agency of the general public, should always have complete control of all of its properties and everything on them.

If any private interest has temporary possession of any park property, the government agency ought to be in a position to repossess such property promptly at a prearranged price and under prearranged conditions agreed upon at the time of the private interest's original entry. There should be no opportunity for the private party to negotiate conditions in a situation which finds the public agency in a position of duress because of the need for prompt repossession.

An example may help to illustrate this point. A ten-year lease is given a private party to build a facility on park property, the facility being for the purpose of rendering a service to park patrons. All terms as to price, etc., have been agreed to. One other provision is needed. The terms and conditions under which the lease may be terminated and full possession of the property returned to the public agency must be negotiated and not left to future settlement. If this is not done, the public agency, when it wishes possession after five years may find itself in the position of "paying through the nose" not only for the value of the facility, but for the value of a leasehold still having five years to run which cost the lessee nothing in the beginning. The facility could be a cheap refreshment stand or a multimillion dollar hotel or motel. The policy is the same.

If possession of the public property is for a long time (in excess of fifty years) or is to be permanent, the subject matter is one of sale and not permit. Here the merit of the sale is the issue and not the policy concerning permits and leases. The flooding of public land may be an illustration of the situation.

Capital assets, both acquisition and improvement items, may come about as a result of gifts, bequests, trust funds, endowments, and other miscellaneous ways. This applies especially to land.

Coming from private sources, the forms these acquisition possibilities take are many and varied: outright gifts of land, the establishment of trust funds from which acquisitions can be made, provisions in wills for the donations of money for lands, securities, or real estate which can be sold and the proceeds used for the purchase of park lands, and any similar device which the ingenuity of donors can think up.

Because these are donations, the donors may attach conditions to the acceptance of the gifts and conditions which must be met after the park is acquired, sometimes with reversionary provisions in case the conditions are not met. Here are some:

√   Donation of a piece of property with the condition that the house on it may be occupied by the owner until his death or the death of himself and his wife.

√   Donation of a piece of property for public park purposes which, if not used for that purpose, reverts to the owner or his successors and assigns; or that the property must be used for a certain park purpose in perpetuity, otherwise it reverts to the heirs or successors.

√   A man deeds a portion of his property to the park district for park and parkway purposes on the condition that the remainder of his property shall be exempt from all future special park assessments. (In one state, this was held to be illegal and of no effect because the government agency had no power to contract away its taxing power. However, if the deed of gift had provided that the owner should be exempt from special assessments up to a certain definite amount, that was held to be a legal contract.) Or that the owner may continue to water his stock in the creek or erect a windmill or have a dock for his private use.

√   A piece of property is donated with the understanding and deed provision that it shall not be added on to.

√   The property has been donated for a municipal zoo, but it is not sufficient for a zoo and additional properties to add on to it are not available for any acquisition.

√   A trust fund has been established, the proceeds of which may be used for the acquisition of properties, but the trust may be limited to such securities as to render the interest from these years later almost too small to be practical.

Such a list might be continued almost indefinitely. It behooves each park department to look these gift horses squarely in the mouths, determine whether the conditions imposed are going to prove embarrassing or impossible of compliance years hence, and attempt to get the provisions altered before acceptance of the gift.

In general, it can be suggested that where conditions are definitely limited in time (a stated number of years, or when some event happens which is sure to happen, like the death of an occupant), the gift may be acceptable; but if the condition operates in perpetuity there is present an element of future embarrassment and even frustration in carrying out in the future the full purpose of the law; and consequently, such a condition should be avoided.

Embarrassing conditions of gifts can sometimes be limited or eliminated years hence through the process of condemnation and sometimes other legal procedures may be effective where the conditions are wholly out of harmony with the times.

In spite of sometime difficulties attendant to gifts of land, a great deal of public property has been acquired that way and the process is important enough for every park department to take special steps to encourage further private donations.

Except in the case of donations, properties which are acquired must somehow be paid for if fee title is conveyed, but in the process a number of methods may be resorted to for one reason or another. Here are a few: In the filing of a plat of land for subdivision into lots, one or more parcels may be dedicated to the public for park purposes—sometimes the mere filing of the plat conveys a provisional title and at other times some action on the part of the park department is necessary to complete the transaction. In either case, this is not conveying the property in fee simple. It is a use right which is obtained, and whenever that use ceases, the fee title stays with the platter of the property or his successors and heirs and only the use of the property reverts back to the original conveyors. *The park department is not in a position, in this case, to convey title to the property for it does not have it.*

Property on which taxes are not paid regularly reverts to state ownership after the reversionary provisions of the law have been complied with. Sometimes, the state may transfer title to some other governmental agency including park districts. Almost invariably, the states, in doing so, retain mineral rights to the property and usually there is a provision that if the property is not used for the public purpose for which it was conveyed, the title reverts to the state. *This sort of title does not give the park district freedom of action to do whatever it will with the property, including its sale.* Incidentally, federal participation in the financing of lands for park and recreation purposes (through BOR and HUD) may also carry conditions affecting the fee title to not only the lands thereby financed, but to the lands already owned to which the new acquisition is to be an addition. Read the fine print carefully.

Reservoir properties under the jurisdiction of the Army Engineers, and also some under other governmental agencies, are sometimes leased out (or use permits are given) to villages, cities, counties, and states to operate them as public park and recreation grounds. *The length of time of such leases and use permits ought to be long enough to justify the permittee to make respectable type improvements thereon. The lease or permit should also grant the right to govern the leased property* so long as there is no interference with the basic purpose for which the reservoir was constructed.

Property on which a museum, stadium, or other facility is placed may be conveyed to the park district with the provision that the donors may have exclusive use of the facility which is placed thereon and in case that use ever ceases, the property remains the property of the park district. Variations of this arrangement are many. One is that the city is the owner of the facility including the land and has leased the land from the previous owner with the understanding that after twenty years or some other suitable time, the fee title to the entire facility will pass to the park district.

One park district confronted with certain limitations, legal and otherwise, which prevented it from entering into a contract for deed payable over a period of time, resorted to this device. It acquired only a portion of the property during the current year, say one-tenth of it, and paid an additional sum which would have equaled 6 percent of the deferred payments under a contract, this additional amount being the price of an option on all the remaining property of the owner, the option to be exercised at the discretion of the park department piecemeal over a period of years. The option price carried with it restrictions on the use of the owner's property pending the exercise of the option.

The number of variations on this sort of transaction is limited only by the ingenuity of the parties to the agreements—all of course by the law.

PROCESSES OF ACQUISITION

There are two procedures which may be followed in the acquisition of lands for park purposes: acquisition by direct negotiation with the owner and by eminent domain going through condemnation proceedings. There are also two main purposes to be accomplished: to acquire the desired property at a fair market price and to leave a record which will substantiate the fact that it is a fair market price.

1. By Direct Negotiation. In direct negotiations with the owner, there are certain advantages: process is usually quicker, face-to-face conversations usually result in a better understanding between purchaser and seller, minor variations in the sale can be effectuated, and greater flexibility is always present. The great disadvantage is that direct negotiation is open to public criticism as to motive, as to price, and as to the possiblity of so-called graft. In order to obviate this situation, park districts frequently resort to appraisal by disinterested and competent realtors before a negotiating price is arrived at. If that negotiated price shows any substantial variation from the appraised figure, full explanation ought to be left in the record.

2. Condemnation Proceedings. Governmental agencies usually have the power of eminent domain and may take any property by going through the proper legal procedure and paying the market price, or in this case the appraised price, for the property. The advantage of this method is that it is one in which the process is usually minutely provided for in the law, that it provides suitable protection for the property owner through appeals from the first appraised figure, that good and sufficient title can be obtained from owners unwilling to transfer title by deed. The acquisition is positive as to

time and property described. The main advantage is that such a proceeding leaves very little or no opportunity for so-called graft or undercover negotiations.

The disadvantage of this process of acquisition is in its inexorable characteristics; no flexibility to meet an owner's peculiar situations is present, there is no variation in time element, the process is long, possibilities of delay through technicalities are numerous, and the proceeding is frequently irritating to both parties. Often it is not conducive to the establishment of good will.

A fixed policy to fit all conditions is seldom practical over an extended period of time. Direct negotiations are usually more practical in smaller parcels of land and where price determination is easy. When protected by a sufficient number of reliable appraisals, large tracts of land and large numbers of parcels may be also practical. However, when there are large numbers of parcels covering a great variety of properties, and time is not an element, condemnation proceedings usually produce the best result. Over a period of time, both methods will be used.*

LAND RECORDS

A record of all lands owned or controlled by an operating park and recreation agency ought to be on file in every such agency. This is so self-evident that it should not be necessary to call attention to it. However, there are enough instances of laxity that have come to the attention of the writer that he feels the need of mentioning it.

Land records should consist of the attorney's opinion of the title, and the deeds or other evidences of ownership together with documents that satisfy the requirements of the opinion. These are of such primary importance that they are usually kept in a very safe place. Copies of the significant portions of them are kept separate for ready daily reference. Such records include: (1) legal descriptions of the land, (2) conditions of ownership, (3) where the deeds are filed in the official files of the government, (4) official actions affecting the title such as street vacations, etc., (5) other miscellaneous information bearing on the title or the dimensions of the property.

Land plats showing outside dimensions, as well as dimensions of parcels of the total, the official land subdivisions, and original government surveys are necessary. These plats should correlate land titles with land surveys and this correlation should be shown on the plats.

---

*In the cases of acquisitions using grants-in-aid money, the granting agency, either federal or state, may prescribe the process of acquisition to be used.

SITUATIONS PARTICULARLY APPLICABLE TO DEVELOPMENT

A. AS TO PLANS AND BASIC DATA

The process of the development of a park plan preceding the construction of the project has been dealt with in Chapter 8. The complete planning package includes: Investigative Report, Topographic Survey and Map, Diagrammatic Sketch, Preliminary Plan, Working Drawings and Specifications, and finally a Manual of Operation. Who is to prepare each of these?

Basic data are usually assembled by staff employees if the material is of a purely statistical or informational character. However, in the preparation of topographic maps, preliminary plans, and working drawings, choices are possible depending upon the policy laid down by the authorities. Topographic mapping as well as property surveys may be made by employees of the engineering division or the work may be contracted out. Some topographical mapping may be accomplished through means of aerial photography and that usually is contracted for or else the maps purchased if they are already on the market.

Preliminary planning may be done by members of the planning section or the work can be contracted to be done by private planners. Working drawings and specifications may be made by the engineering division, or again, the work may be contracted for.

It is not impractical for smaller organizations to contract with a park specialist to compile original surveys as to requirements, prepare preliminary plans as well as working drawings, specifications, and to supervise the construction. This is true also of buildings, only in this case an architect will be engaged.

A department may resort to a combination of these situations depending upon the particular project at hand. For example, the engineering department may be so organized as to be able to take care of surveys, both topographic and property surveys, to supervise construction projects, but not be organized for park planning either in the preliminary stage or as to final working drawings and specifications, in which case the missing links must necessarily be done by outside contractors.

If the park district is of sufficient magnitude, it is desirable to have as many of these planning and survey processes done within the department itself. This permits a more continual process, a greater insight into the peculiarities of this particular park district, a better conception of long-range plans, and usually these plans will get the benefit of more internal criticism than otherwise. On the other hand, an occasional intrusion of outside talent will prevent the sameness of plan and developments from producing monotonous effects. In some cases, some of the engineering and planning will be done by agencies allied with the park district. These include separate planning departments, the use of public works departments, and sometimes even other governmental agencies.

While any one of these situations will produce satisfactory results depending upon the quality of personnel available, *it is generally more desirable to have as many of these functions performed by employees of the park district as local conditions will permit.*

B. CONSTRUCTION

Here again, choices may be made. The park district may organize itself with sufficient talent and machinery for carrying on sizeable construction works or it may choose to minimize this part of the organization and carry out all of its construction by contract with private parties. A third possibility is the combination of these two in which the department may do some of its own constructing and contract out the balance. Variations of these would include having the construction done by other agencies of the government such as the public works department or the state highway department, but these would be in the same category as letting the jobs out to private contractors.

The choice here depends very much on the same factors as the choice in the case of the preparation of plans. Considering the magnitude of some of the park improvement projects and the large investment in heavy earth-moving equipment, the park district would have to be of considerable magnitude to undertake all of its construction in all its various forms as well as its various magnitudes. On the other hand, the department must be very small if it is not prepared to carry on any of its own construction. Consequently, *most park districts will do part of the construction by force account and part by contract.* A fairly good sized park organization ought to be prepared to do a fair amount of construction itself in order to ensure the completion of jobs at scheduled times or to escape from contractors who are too busy to undertake their contracts at the proper time. Not infrequently, a department having a pretty good construction force and suitable equipment can command competitive prices when otherwise competition may not be present. This is not quite so applicable in complete projects, but in portions of the projects this advantage is not unusual. The disadvantage of having too much of a force for construction is that such a force must be kept busy all of the time for the operation to be efficient. Equipment and manpower cannot be subject to frequent layoffs without the organization losing efficiency. When equipment is idle, depreciation continues. The highest quality in manpower can command jobs where layoffs occur.

C. THE LETTING OF CONTRACTS

Somewhere in this discussion of relationships between park department officials and private business interests, there must be presented two topics of great importance to the park administrator, namely, conflict of interest and gifts. The seriousness of these subjects hinges upon not only the legality but the propriety of certain acts which if handled in the wrong way can lead to serious impairment of the good will of the park department and the possible ruination of the reputation and career of individuals involved. These subjects are very delicate ones and must be handled with tact, understanding, diplomacy, and above all, absolute honesty. Because of the possible appearance of these offending situations in construction work, they are dealt with here.

1. Conflict of Interest. The law, including our local city charters, usually prohibits elected public officials from doing business with the governmental agency of which they are a member. In other words, a member of a park commission cannot sell or buy or otherwise do business with that particular commission. If he is a member of a firm or connected with a firm doing business with the park department, he must either relinquish his business association or his membership on the park board. Sometimes it becomes the delicate job of the park administrator to inform a board member who has innocently in ignorance of the law gotten himself into such a position. Delicate as this task is, it must be done for the sake of the reputation of the department as well as the individual commissioner. The park administrator cannot afford to simply close his eyes to something of this sort of which he is aware.

Elected park commissioners cannot hold any other elected office which the courts have decreed or common sense will indicate is incompatible. *Incompatibility arises out of any situation in which the individual may find himself acting on both sides of a bargaining table or by being both an appellant and a judge at the same time.* For example, a member of a park board which on occasion must appear before the state legislatures for modifications of the law cannot very well be a member of the legislature also. In such a case he is appealing for a decision and he is also in a position of making the decision.

Park managers or members of the executive staff cannot be in the position of being associated in any way with a firm that is doing business or might do business with their own department or any other branch of their level of government. Some occasions may arise where this situation is unavoidable as in the case of a public employee holding property which may be acquired by his own board, in this case, he must disassociate himself entirely from the transaction, in other words, disqualify himself in that particular case. It is not unusual for men of high ethical standards to disqualify themselves from such transactions even though they may have been disassociated from the firm or from the public agency for some time.

Favoritism is akin to conflict of interests. The public always presumes that favoritism is going to be shown to relatives, close friends, and close business associates of the recent past. It is not always possible to avoid doing business with these classes of individuals, but such associations should be avoided as much as possible. Where circumstances prevent such avoidance, every precaution should be taken to ensure the fact, and the *appearance* of the fact, that the association is entirely on a business basis and that no favoritism develops.

2. Gifts. Gifts range all the way from an occasional complimentary luncheon to items of considerable value as everyone knows who reads the newspapers, particularly in regard to involvement in these matters of high government officials of the federal government. All of this is separate and apart from a money bribe, which is punishable by fines and imprisonment. In this discussion, gifts refer to matters of propriety where bribery cannot be proven. The whole question before us here is where do good will and friendly gifts end and influential bribery begin?

Private companies as well as governmental agencies have struggled manfully to devise codes of ethics to cover these matters. Except for a complete prohibition of the giving or acceptance of any business gifts, no general standard has been devised which will fit all circumstances and all conditions. Even complete prohibition proves to be too inhuman to be realistic. Where human kindness and human appreciation for a happy association are too prevalent to happily accept complete prohibition, guides to action become difficult to even suggest because they are easily misunderstood as justification for excesses not intended. Assuming the reader to be completely honest (not being of the grasping and parsimonious type), to being responsive to high ethical standards, to being somewhat gregarious but having what is normally accepted as uncommonly good common sense, the following guides are timidly suggested.

First, make sure of the motive of the giver. If a business representative suggests that you take lunch with him, decline by making some polite excuse unless you know him well enough to know his motive: that it is entirely upon a friendly basis, that he knows that there is no possiblity of influencing you. Even in such cases, it is well for you to make the point that you intend to reciprocate this friendly gesture. Motives are not so easily hidden that they cannot be detected by anyone who is forewarned and who hesitates enough to examine the situation in his own mind. Therefore, unless the motive is positively understood by the park manager (or members of his staff), no gratuities or business courtesies of any kind are ever to be accepted.

Secondly, not only must the motive be devoid of the expectation of a business favor, but even the appearance of a questionable motive must be absent. For example, the business manager cannot be seen frequently in social association with contractors who are doing business with his department. This has the appearance of unholy intimacy, and suspicion will immediately rise in the minds of some people. Any association with business people must be on a general plane where others in like situations are present. The appearance should always be on such a level as to produce the impression that business associates and public officials are mingling upon the basis of mutual reciprocity where the entertainment might be at the expense of one as well as the other, where the social standing of one is in the same circle as that of the other.

Thirdly, if the motive and the appearance of motive pass muster, the acceptance of small favors can be justified. It can be recognized that pleasant business associations can induce the participants to express their gratitude in modest ways. However, there is just as much excuse for the public official to appreciate that association as there is for the man in business. Hence, *this is not a one-sided transaction by any means.*

Fourth, just how small does this favor have to be, to be acceptable? Some have said that it ought to be small enough to be used up in a day or consumed in one sitting, probably in the amount of $5 or $10 or something which you would be willing and are ready to give your business associate in return for the pleasure he has given you in past associations.

In the course of his business, the park administrator will, on occasion, be called upon to solicit funds for the benefit of some project which his department is undertaking—a convention, a campaign of some sort (nonpolitical), or a particular public project. One of the sources of prospects of solicitation will be companies with which he has done business. Many departments try to avoid this sort of solicitation. If it is permitted, solicitation ought to be very discreetly and carefully made and complete freedom of decision must be left with the business. No pressure of any kind, no threat of business retaliation, no dictation as to the amount or any implication by word or tone of voice must be given in the request for support. The businessman must understand that his contribution, if any, is of his own free will and is not associated with his business dealings with the department.

3. **Personal Conduct.** Candidates for elective public office quite glibly put forth the trite expression, "A public office is a public trust." The politician can often say this without considering its significance, but the administrator must try to keep this thought in mind always. If he does not, his animal instincts will lead him to treat public property and his own position as personal appendages. Birds and animals stake out and defend their territories extralegally. The household dog will keep away all comers from his

habitual haunts. A PR administrator gets so familiar with public property and so used to having his word have the force of law that unconsciously he thinks he owns the whole business. He needs to remind himself that he is only working here—that he is only the agent of the general public.

This attitude manifests itself when the "chief" expects preferential treatment at public events even if it inconveniences the public; when he habitually ignores rules and ordinances that the general public is expected to observe. Usually he does not mean to be officious, but familiarity with his domain has unconsciously made him feel that all this is for him about the same way the house dog treats the new mailman.

Familiarity breeds the "usual" and the "habitual" which become the acceptable, the policy. Why not favor a friend? Why not accept a "gift" from him? Why not have a business of my own on the side and why not throw a little business that way? Why not give members of my family a little preference in hiring? If these motivate the decisions of the administrator the so-called public trust becomes more like a private fief. Continued a bit further, involvement in the law takes place and the law for public business is much harsher than in private business. Careers can be easily ruined that way. Too much stress cannot be given to the practice of objective honesty and the "public trust" phase of public business.

A reminder: Habit is a cable. We weave a thread of it each day until it becomes so strong we cannot break it.

4. Purchasing Agent. Purchasing agents are usually interposed between the manager of a park department and the actual letting of contracts or the purchasing of goods. This does take some of the "heat" off the manager in regard to some of the relationships mentioned above, but purchasing agents are not provided for that purpose. Their job is a specialist's job requiring special training in the art of purchasing. The establishment of a purchasing division enables the park department or even larger groups of governmental agencies to pool their purchasing power and to make uniform the method by which goods and services of a contractual nature are procured.

Quite often, a separate purchasing department may be established for all of the agencies of the state, or a municipality or a county, or the federal government for that matter. Purchasing departments establish their own rules of procedure with which other agencies must comply, including the park and recreation department. Some discretionary matters, however, are left with the park and recreation department. These may include a limitation on the monetary limit of any item permitted to be purchased without advertising for bids, the actual specifications of material and services to be contracted for, whether or not the furnishing of material is to be covered by a contract or a purchase order, whether the purchasing agent is to join in the recommendations as to the acceptance of bids or the rejection thereof.

Assuming the park department has something to say about the matter, when will a purchase order suffice and when is a written contract needed? Contracts will be needed for the construction of all of a particular project. They will be required for the purchase of goods, the delivery of which is extended over a long period of time or in which the amount is considerable, or where the quotation is on a unit basis which in turn is based upon estimated quantities (for example, the furnishing of bituminous material for a season's operation in the repair and construction of roadways, the construction of sidewalk in a geographical section of the city), but with quantities unknown until the job is finished.

Contracts will be required wherever it is necessary to ensure fulfillment of an agreement which is sufficiently complex to warrant all the conditions being specified in writing.

The simple purchase orders which in effect are contracts may be sufficient in the supplying of most of the goods purchased and even of the rental of equipment where the equipment can be made easily identifiable.

5. Bids and Letting of Construction Contracts. Specifications accompanying plans for the construction of a project are usually given out to contractors about two weeks before the date set for the receipt of their bids. These bids are usually accompanied by a certified check of a certain percentage of the estimated cost of the job, and some deposit for the use of plans and specifications is usually required to ensure the return of these documents.

As contractors study over the plans and specifications, some questions will arise, and an occasional error will actually be noticed which will require the park department to issue memorandums of alterations to all of the contractors who have plans and specifications in their possession. These alterations become a part of the original plans and specifications.

Bids are received by the purchasing agent and opened at the specified time in the presence of contractors who wish to be present and representatives of the park department. Bids handed in after the specified time are disqualified and returned unopened to the bidder. The bids are tabulated and examined sufficiently to eliminate discrepancies, evaluate alternatives, and later to investigate the reputation and financial responsibility of at least the two or three lowest bidders. These bids are retained by the purchasing agent pending the authorization of a contract. A tabulation of all bids is transmitted then to the governing agency with the recommendation of the purchasing agent and the manager of parks and recreation.

This recommendation will be to accept the lowest responsible bid or the rejection of all bids. The latter situation may occur if the bid price is beyond the financial limitations of the department or the appropriations established for this job, or for any other reason—all because the right to reject all bids has been written into the specifications prior thereto. The best bid is usually recommended to be accepted. If some other bid is recommended, then the full reason therefore must be thoroughly explained, and the reason must be based upon conclusive proof that the low bidder is irresponsible in one way or another, or that his bid is improper and did not comply with the plans and specifications.

At this point, a public park and recreation department is not in the position of bargaining with any of the contractor bidders for a preferred situation. The department is not in the position of suggesting to the bidder that if he alters this, that, or the other thing in order to reduce the amount to come within the appropriation, his bid would be accepted. This is entirely an unethical procedure and certainly is open to serious public criticism. Either all of the bids must be rejected, plans and specifications altered and readvertised, or one of the bids must be accepted.

Specifications for the purchase of equipment or even certain supplies must be drawn by the park department to permit the receipt of competitive prices. In other words, the specifications cannot be drawn to limit competition to one specific piece of equipment when there are other similar items on the market. Not infrequently, the specifications may call for a specific make of machine of a specified character and then add "or equal."

In this case, after bids are received and the favored machine is of higher cost and the manager wants that machine in preference to the machine which has bid the lowest, the manager must be in a position to prove that the wanted machine is superior either in composition by comparing specifications, or that it is of distinct monetary saving to him in the operation of his department. When this matter arises, the park manager must be very sure that his technical specialists are sound and thorough in all their arguments.

6. Supervision of Construction. Once again we are confronted with a choice as to who actually supervises construction—a choice which depends upon the policy we are following in connection with the construction function. If the construction is being done under contract according to plans and specifications prepared by the department engineer, the engineer is the logical one to supervise construction. If the construction work is being done on a building for which an architect has been retained, the architect is the logical supervisor. If the park is being constructed according to plans and specifications prepared by a landscape architect or park specialist outside of the department, the arrangement with that specialist may or may not include services for supervision. If it includes supervision, of course, he accomplishes that task, but if the supervision is not contracted for, then the engineer will very likely assume that responsibility. If the work is being done by departmental crews under force account system, whichever division or section

drew the plans and specifications ought to supervise construction and see that compliance with the plans and specifications takes place.

If the work is being done under contract, the contractor usually is entitled to part-time payment every 30 days. Whoever is supervising the work in behalf of the owner certifies the percentage accomplished and, by various means, determines the amount of money that is due the contractor for the work accomplished. Usually there is a percentage (about 10 per cent), withheld pending final inspection of the completed job.

Regardless of who has supervised the construction on behalf of the owner, before the completed job is accepted, it is inspected not only by the supervisor but by others in the park and recreation department. These usually include the park manager and may, on some occasions, include a representative of the board if there is a board. This final inspection is a rigid one, because at that time, full compliance with the plans and specifications is determined and every minute detail is checked. When a certificate of inspection has been properly placed before the board or final authority and adopted by them and payment ordered, there is no further recourse except any guarantee provision which may have been included in the specifications.

Because of the importance of the final inspection, the governing authority of the park department will usually have a set policy as to who is to be responsible for making the inspection and making the final certificate of acceptance. Usually that is left with the park manager, but it sometimes is left with the park manager and a representative of the board. If the park manager is inclined to delegate his responsibility to the engineer, for example, the manager still is responsible in the final analysis. It is possible that the policy laid down for the process of final inspection and acceptance routine may vary with the size and importance of the contract or construction work being carried out. In other words, there may be certain classes of construction which are left to the park manager and others in which the board expects to have a representative present. The presence of some definite policy is very desirable.

7. Shifting from Construction to Maintenance. Offhand, it would appear that as soon as the construction job has been accepted, the jurisdiction and responsibility should shift from the construction or engineering division to the maintenance division. This is the intent. However, in the construction of parks, we are dealing with growing things such as grass, trees, shrubs, etc., that do not mature promptly, and consequently, there is a period of time in which either division could logically assume responsibility for overseeing the work. Therefore, a policy should be determined as to the routine which must be followed to place the responsibility on a completed job or partially completed job from one division head to another.

Normally, a report of the status of the job should come from the construction division to the park manager who decides the right moment for placing the responsibility on the maintenance division. Incidentally, it is not at all unusual to include a year's maintenance cost in the appropriation for construction. Also, if it is expected that possible ground settlement or other alterations in the project may take place in a year or two from the time of completion of the job, it is logical to reserve an amount from the appropriation to take care of restoring the job to its original completion form.

Chapter Thirteen

Policies of Operation

In the operation of park and recreation systems, the possible circumstances requiring determination of policy are so frequently encountered and so varied in character that the entire field could not be covered in a generalized study such as this. Some of the more common situations will be discussed. Sometimes a right and a wrong policy may be apparent, but in most of the situations there is no clear-cut right and wrong; success, in these cases, depends upon the evaluation of local conditions and the ingenuity of the park manager and his staff. An attempt will be made to cite the usual pros and cons in these cases as guides to future decisions.

POLICIES ALREADY ESTABLISHED BY BASIC "GROUND RULES"

There is a basic law, charter provision, or executive mandate that is the authority for the existence of every governmental park and recreation agency. That "authority" will give the purpose, the responsibility, and the powers of the park and recreation agency. It frequently will establish certain policies. These policies are usually found in the description of the purpose, and sometimes in some sort of preamble. It is essential that these laws and edicts be examined for the basic policies which they contain.

The park and recreation administrator is always subject to some higher authority—a commission or board, a single commissioner, a cabinet officer (state or federal) or a department head. In other words, the superior authority may be an organized body or a single individual.

In cases where the superior authority is an individual, the park and recreation administrator should find out what policies of administration his superior has. This should be determined early in the game before differences arise through subsequent administrative experiences.

Boards and commissions may have established policies either formally in written form or informally by habitually following a settled course and without recording the practices. In the latter case, each new commissioner and each new administrator is left to learn these policies over a period of "wait-and-see" experiences. When policies are in written form, even though not formally adopted, and therefore constituting only a record of practices, a great deal of time is saved and misunderstanding avoided by referring to that record. A wise administrator will see that during *his* administration such a record is made and kept current.

Most boards have adopted rules governing board procedures, and these contain matters of policy. If an administrator finds that no such rules exist, he should propose a set of rules for the board's consideration and subsequent adoption. The subjects usually covered by board rules are as follows.

1. Meetings—Time and place of regular meetings, who presides, how many members make a quorum, how special meetings may be called, order of business, rules of conduct, process of adopting ordinances, a statement as to whether or not all meetings are public.

2. Officers—What officers are provided for, how they are elected, and what are the duties of each. There may be a paragraph or so about the chief administrator: how he is selected, the general scope of his responsibilities, how much authority is conferred by the adoption of the budget, the submission of monthly reports, and similar matters.

3. Naming standing committees, prescribing duties, limiting authority to investigations for report to the whole board, relationship to administrator, the appointment of special committees.

4. Other provisions—The agenda and its significance, the conduct of public hearings, clarifying the authority and prescribing relationship of individual members to the board as a whole and to the administrator.

5. Amendments to the rules, their repeal and the suspension of the rules. Robert's Rules of Order usually govern when not in conflict with the law or the specific rules of the board as herein provided.

The law, the written policies (or those implied by repeated practice), the rules of the board, all constitute existing policy "ground rules." One other document might be added, namely, the ordinances of the park and recreation department; but that subject will be touched upon later. Quite obviously, these "ground rules" constitute the foundation on which is constructed the superstructure of departmental policy.

MATTERS REQUIRING BOARD ACTION— EFFECT ON FORMATION OF POLICY

The skeleton of the policy superstructure to which reference has just been made emerges from formal acts of the governing body or the decisions of a superior officer before whom subject matters have been placed. In the succeeding discussion, reference will usually be made to a board or commission as the governing authority, but more or less parallel circumstances are present in cases where the authority which is superior to the park and recreation administrator is an individual.

In the original understanding between the park administrator and his superiors a general area of responsibility for the respective parties has been laid out. If there is a board of commissioners, the board is expected to do the legislative work and to outline broad policies for the guidance of the park administrator, and the park administrator is expected to have complete jurisdiction over the operating affairs of the department. As in most generalized situations, there is an area of gray between the black and the white—an area which logically could become the responsibility of either party, or partly of one and partly of the other. The succeeding discussion will help to clarify some of the more common situations.

THE PURPOSE OF THE BOARD RECORD

The minutes of the board meetings should show authority for all the actions which the board and its employees take. Often this is accomplished by actions delegating broad responsibility to the administrator and his staff and by the declaration of policies.

The board may adopt rules governing its own conduct and may also fix the duties and responsibilities and powers of its officers, including its park and recreation administrator, as previously referred to.

It may have authority to adopt ordinances for the proper use of its properties and the conduct of people using them. Subjects covered by laws and ordinances include: the proper use of the several park areas; the permitted hours of use; the defacement of buildings and other structures; littering and vandalism; use of beer and alcoholic beverages; improper personal conduct; the building of fires; use of firearms; hunting, fishing, and trapping; public speaking and religious services; commercial enterprises on park property; a whole series of sections dealing with traffic; another group on bathing, boating, use of water areas, and water pollution; the protection of flora and fauna. The specific provisions are by no means the same in all park systems; they will reveal some general policies consistent with the local social environment of the particular park system rather than policies calling for general debate on the national level. Some exceptions may be discussed later.

The *law* will prescribe certain actions which the board *must* take. These usually involve procedures for the acquisition of property through condemnation proceedings and sometimes otherwise, or the procedure for the taxing of property for park purposes or for requesting funds, both current and capital, preparatory to direct appropriation by other departments of the government, or for the issuance of bonds.

It must approve all contracts.

It must approve the payment of all bills, although this may be modified by granting to the park manager and his staff authority to pay bills as they come due, especially those where discounts are permitted for prompt payment, and then reviewing a listing of bills and confirming the park manager's actions. This review does not alter the actual payment of any properly-contracted-for indebtedness, but it does permit a review of the park manager's judgment which, if differing from the board's desires, can be altered in future cases.

Aside from the foregoing more or less standard board responsibilities, there are other actions which carry varying degrees of authority with them.

THE ADMINISTRATOR AND HIS STAFF ORGANIZATION

Usually, but not always, the administrator is expected to obtain approval of his board or his superior for the makeup of his staff and the type of personnel organization with which he expects to function. This is desirable even though not required in order that there may be a unity of understanding as to the method of operation. Also, it indicates, at least in general terms, the numbers of classifications of employees graded as to rank. In some cases, the board or superior authority may fix the number in each classification and require specific authorization to increase that number. This is a matter, however, that must be considered in connection with the authority accompanying the adoption of the financial budget.

SALARIES AND WAGES

Unless salaries and wages are fixed by some other agency such as a civil service commission (and not infrequently when such commissions exist), authority to pay specific salaries and wages to either individuals or classes of individuals must be obtained from or confirmed by the governing authority. It is usually expected that the administrator will submit specific recommendations on salaries and wages.

THE OPERATING BUDGET (REFER TO CHAPTER 10)

The adoption of the annual budget by the board may carry with it broad authority for the administrator to undergo all expenditures authorized or enumerated in that budget, to hire all help necessary to carry out that budget, and to order all materials involved therein, subject to the normal process of the approval of all bills to be paid, the fixing of wages and salaries, and sometimes limitations as to number of employees in each classification.

Various limitations in connection with operation within the budget may be established either by policy, custom, or specific board action in specific instances. Sometimes the administrator is restricted from exceeding expenditure in one category of the budget even though savings in another are made. If there is confidence in the administrator, this restriction is decidedly impractical. There must be some flexibility left to the administrator.

Sometimes there is not just one annual budget, but four quarterly budgets or two semiannual budgets. In other words, the total annual budget is released for authority to operate every three or six months. This again is a restriction which hampers efficient operation.

PLANS FOR NEW PROJECTS

Plans for new projects are normally submitted to the board for approval, first in their preliminary form and later in the form of working drawings and specifications. Authority to request bids is requested at the same time. There are times when the approval of working drawings and specifications is left to the discretion of the administrator after the preliminary plans have been approved.

MATTERS NOT COVERED

The park and recreation manager (administrator, director, or superintendent, by whatever name known) is confronted with all sorts of situations which require daily decisions. He must feel confident that in making these decisions he has the authority to make them and that authority has been granted to him by the board either because of custom, the adoption of definite policies, or because of his knowledge of the usual reaction of board members. If there is serious doubt as to his authority, the administrator is wise to refer the matter to the board for guidance. A new manager in a new situation involving new board members finds himself in more doubt than an old hand in the matter. An experienced manager can rely upon past custom for his usual action, explaining such to the board at the proper time. However, a new man in an established department will find it politic to get more frequent guidance in these matters. The student will recognize, in this situation, a comparison with the President and Congress of the United States. A strong President and a weak Congress will find a greater responsibility being borne by the President and on other occasions the opposite is true. So it is with administrators and their boards and commissions, and sometimes with an individual who is the administrator's immediate superior.

The authors' suggestion is that the able manager assume as great a responsibility as his board will permit him to assume—up to a point. When the manager has succeeded in making practically *all* the important decisions with the board willing to approve without much discussion, he is on his way to becoming an autocrat, and this is not good. An autocratic manager loses his ability to think objectively and his decisions tend to become personal whims. His board is not questioning him enough or in the manner that their constituents might question him, and the manager loses his ability to defend his plans, not infrequently because they have become indefensible.

On the other hand, a weak manager afraid to assume responsibility and take independent action is of small account. Associate him with a weak board and the park and recreation service is apt to become deplorable.

A board whose members seem to be so strong-willed as to want to assume all administrative responsibility and are continually nagging at the manager and his staff members, in time will find themselves without a competent professional and the job which lay board members can do will again be inferior.

This entire relationship is a test of the executive ability, tact, and diplomacy of the manager.

DISCUSSION OF SOME OPERATING POLICIES COMMON TO MANY SITUATIONS

NEIGHBORLINESS AND COOPERATION

Neighborliness and cooperation are intangibles woven into the spirit of the department in such a way as to constitute a policy of attitude. The larger, the stronger, the better equipped, the more technical know-how it has, the more should a park organization help those in less fortunate circumstances. Something has happened in recent years to remove some of the luster from that glowing thought. Competition for space, for money, and the fierce pride in local autonomy cause friction between the central city and its suburbs and between neighboring suburbs. Sometimes a neighbor may not use another suburb's properties without paying more for this use than local citizens—a sort of tariff barrier has arisen between communities. The central city and its suburban towns expect the metropolitan or county park systems to provide those things which urban areas have difficulty providing for themselves; and all of these, towns and county alike, look further upward to the state to supplement local effort; and in turn, all expect the federal government to do more than it is doing. Much energy is being lost squabbling with each other and the practice ought to be stopped. Greater cooperation coupled with a greater sense of self-reliance brings about a more uniform and satisfying service throughout the several governmental levels. Help from above is, indeed, present, but every park administrator ought to recognize that this sort of "incentive help" will not wholly satisfy the needs of his district. Each district must still rely upon its own sound plans and must possess the aggressiveness to execute those plans. Nevertheless, helping one's neighbor helps all.

ATTENDANCE AT PROFESSIONAL MEETINGS

When the board authorizes any of its members or executive staff to attend conventions in a distant city, there is always a segment of the public that believes public officials are going to a gay party at public expense. Sometimes, unfortunately, this can be true. The proper policy on this matter should ensure public benefit equal to or more than the expense involved.

Improved methods of organization, operation of equipment, and processes are emerging constantly from hundreds of manufacturers all over this country and foreign countries as well. Many professional meetings are held annually at which men attempt to explore and evaluate possible improvements to their operation and to see what is going on someplace else. All of this is of real value to the professional and the work he is attempting to perform in his own bailiwick. These meetings are likewise of inspiration and a source of greater knowledge of park and recreation services to nonprofessional board members. Much good emerges from these meetings and that good ought to be taken back home, reported in written form, and the report distributed to appropriate staff members and board members.

Not all of these meetings and conventions are of national scope and national importance. There are many sectional and local meetings of similar nature where the expense of attendance is much reduced. This might make possible the attendance of those whose expense to attend national conventions would not be justified. Sometimes the board is willing to grant the manager discretion within limits in permitting attendance of employees at such meetings.

There should not exist the spirit that authority to attend meetings is granted simply as a reward either for past performance or simply for membership on a board. The policy should be to authorize attendance in cases which will yield specific valuable results; i.e., (1) either those attending the conventions ought to bring back information and material of real value, or (2) men possessing special leadership qualities and technical know-how that is of value and inspiration to the entire profession should be sent to the conventions to contribute to the general welfare and, incidentally, to add to the prestige of the local community.

FEES AND CHARGES

For what services, if any, does a park and recreation department make a charge? There have been more discussions locally and nationally on this subject than on almost any other policy matter confronting park and recreation departments.

It will be recalled that the justification for the various levels of government providing park and recreation services is founded on the responsibility of government to promote the general welfare. Specifically in the case of parks and recreation, it has been well accepted that this function is so broad in its application and so general in its distribution of benefits that it comes well within the general welfare provisions. Having that thought in mind, a large number, if not the majority, of municipal park departments established a no-charge or no-fee basis for their services unless that service was a special one provided for a special class of people who found government more capable of rendering their specialized service than private enterprise. Here are some examples:

Golf courses were established and the golfers were expected to pay the costs of that service. There was confusion at first because some departments concluded that golf was a logical form of recreation and ought to be subsidized by the government and the fees charged were either very little or nothing at all. Most park and recreation departments considered this to be a specialized service and made appropriate charges from the beginning. Others justified a lower fee because golf courses, as beautiful open space, contributed to the general welfare even if golfers were not present, hence, to some extent, golf ought to be subsidized. Presently, if public golf is subsidized at all, it most likely escapes the usual amortization charges devolving upon self-supporting and self-liquidating enterprises.

There has never seemed to be any question about making a charge for refreshments and other saleable merchandise. However, there is a difference of opinion as to providing firewood, charcoal, and similar picnic accessories. Charging for attendance at swimming pools has been quite general except for younger children. Parking the family car is generally free, but parking on a pay basis is gradually increasing, especially where the parking fee becomes the means of collecting a fee for use of beaches and picnic areas.

Making a charge for general revenue purposes has come into being in recent years particularly in state park operation. State legislatures, harassed on all sides by mounting expenses and increased requests for funds, have been rather niggardly in appropriating funds for the expansion and operation of state park systems. Managers, confronted with almost impossible operating conditions, have advocated that nominal charge be made for each person or automobile that visits the state park. These fees are sometimes used for capital expenditures, and sometimes for general operating purposes. The practice of charging has apparently been accepted by the residents of the states in which it has been tried. If success continues, the practice may be extended to many more states.

However, this practice raises the fundamental question of propriety in the minds of the fundamental theorists. Indiana long ago resorted to fees and charges probably on the grounds that state parks in themselves constitute a special service. The general demand for, and accessibility to state parks now raises the question as to whether or not that service is general enough to promote the general welfare of all people and therefore to justify the service on a free basis. This theory is that all people should be taxed because of the general good that arises from the mere presence of the park, regardless of any special benefit that might accrue to the user.

All in all, there seems to be no set of basic principles on which decisions concerning the making of fees and charges can be based. There are, however, some pertinent facts that should be kept in mind in rationalizing the appropriateness of any proposal for imposing a fee or making a specific charge:

1. It has been firmly established that park and recreation services may justifiably be supported by general taxation but that when charges are made for that service, under some circumstances the operating governmental agency may be operating in a proprietary, and not a governmental capacity, and in so doing, sacrifices liability immunity granted to governments when acting in their governmental capacities.

2. The mere presence of a park may impart a benefit even without being entered upon. In some instances parks may enhance the value of nearby property and thereby justify the levying of a special tax on that property. The *use* that is made of some parks may, on occasion, be detrimental to adjacent private properties.

3. The public does not obtain all its recreation from public parks and recreation services. Some recreation services available to the public are attractive enough to command sufficient price to be profitable to the entrepreneur. The propriety of tax-supported recreation entering into this sort of business is a debatable issue.

4. Some recreation services offered by privately supported welfare agencies sometimes demonstrate such a wide general appeal and offer so much general benefit that government may be justified in enlarging its repertoire of services to include those services that have enjoyed such wide public voluntary financial support. That has happened in the past with the

result that the "floor" of tax-supported service has been raised. This is one of the forces that is continually at work to raise standards. Minority pressure groups constitute another force. Activities which are the subject of these moves to raise standards are susceptible to the application of special fees prior to their inclusion in the tax-supported category. Where tax support ends and special fees begin remains the debatable issue.

5. The amount and variety of park and recreation service that warrants tax support is not fixed in any one situation except temporarily. It is but the momentary result of a continuous conflict between taxpayer groups and user groups.

Some further insight as to when to make a charge for services may be found in examining the matter in the separate spheres of city, state, and nation. The underlying problem is the same in all cases but the degree and frequency of making charges may vary. Historically, municipal services were originally considered to be wholly tax supported; there was practically no tax support for national parks; there always was a difference of opinion as to state parks. Time has wrought changes but tradition is still discernible: National and state parks now have tax support but fees and charges are more frequently encountered here than in municipal systems. There may be more logic to these current practices than mere tradition would indicate and for that possible additional logic we need to examine the degree of use that the several classes of parks get.

It has been previously noted that the equivalent of the whole population uses municipal parks once every week or two.* Such general participation in a park and recreation service suggests a justification for broad tax support. To be sure, some modifying factors are present but the eligibility for tax support remains very prominent. The use of state parks by the equivalent of the whole population is once in three to four months, or roughly one-tenth as much as municipal parks. Visits to national parks by the equivalent of the whole population are only once every two or three years, or about one-eightieth the frequency of municipal parks.

Does this imply that the justification for tax support for state and national parks is only one-tenth and one-eightieth respectively of the justification for tax support on the municipal level? Hardly.

There is at least one other important factor to consider—long ago the Congress and the states concluded that the preservation of their unique and historic areas warranted tax support at least to the degree of securing title to them. Where *use,* as distinguished from *preservation,* is the dominant service offered (e.g., in recreation areas) the foregoing reasoning has some appeal—

---

*These estimates of frequency of visits vary from year to year with the mobility and affluence of people, i.e., the greater the mobility the more frequent the visits.

not conclusive enough for general acceptance, but intriguing enough to someday pursue further.

Some very general conclusions as to when, and for what, fees and charges are justified, now may be timidly suggested. (1) Seldom make charges on the local government level. (2) Be very careful about making charges for state and national parks where *preservation* is the dominant purpose. (3) Be frequent in making charges at state and national parks where *use* is the dominant function. (4) In all cases, be sure that *some* benefit accrues to the taxpayer for the payment of his tax. (5) Aside from the foregoing, the specific services to be charged for and the fee should be matters of local choice, experimentation, and finally public acceptance.*

AMOUNT OF TAX SUPPORT

It has been previously stated that the extent and variety of services that warrant tax support are by no means standardized. Also it has been suggested that the administrator might do well to examine costs per attendant unit in deciding the eligibility for tax support of that particular activity. Are similar correlations valid in arriving at the *amount* of tax support park and recreation services should enjoy? Even though no such standard measurement of tax support can be justified, an examination of current practices may prove at least interesting.

On the municipal level, the 1961 Yearbook of the National Recreation Association will be the reference.** At the outset, it should be realized that although the reference is the best available, the statistics are not always comparable as between cities, and the actual figures are not always precise. We start out from an imperfect reference point, so the results are indicative but not exact. The cost of tax support that cities give to park and recreation operation and maintenance ranges from $1 per capita to $10 per capita. In cities having populations in excess of 100,000 the per capita appropriations run from $2 to $3 in the South with a very few important exceptions. Comparable figures rise to $4 to $6 as we go north into the Middle States and New England; from $5 to $8 on the West Coast. The largest cities of the country also run from $5 to $8 per capita, regardless of geographical location.

There are no statistics reliable enough to yield municipal appropriations in terms of attendance. On the other hand, the most significant statistics on state parks are those based upon attendance.

"State Park Statistics—1961," a publication of the National Park

---

*Both the federal and state governments now impose entrance fees for parks. The practice is not so all-inclusive for entrance to forests, reservoir lakes, or wildlife refuges,
**The 1966 Yearbook of NRPA contains a greater variety of information but because of the greater complications of metropolitan political subdivisions, the amount of tax support for each is not so easily available as in the 1961 edition.

Service, is also the best in its field, but is plagued by faults similar to those of the National Recreation Association publication. It shows that the cost per visitor for operation and maintenance is 22¢ which may be offset by revenue which reduces the cost to 14¢ net. The corresponding per capita costs would be 33¢ and 21¢. If frequency of use were a logical way of measuring tax support, the appropriation for state parks should approximate say one-tenth of about $5 or 50¢ instead of 33¢ or possibly 21¢.

This sort of investigation might be carried on with the National Parks, National Forests, Army Reservoirs, etc., but aside from being an intriguing mathematical exercise, it will aid little in our search for a base on which to formulate policies for tax appropriation. Oh, a city *could* declare that it will limit appropriations for park and recreation services to, say, $5 per capita. (Indeed, that approach has already been taken.)* A state could approximate its appropriation for state parks by multiplying anticipated attendance by, say, 13¢. In both cases, additional income and added service could be realized from fees and charges. ORRRC suggested a system of fees and charges for outdoor recreation to supplement tax appropriations. Did ORRRC anticipate this sort of approach? Techniques are as yet not sophisticated enough to permit general acceptance of this idea. Maybe some day more precise statistical data, some method of evaluating the ever-changing factors involving standards of services, and the determination of a few other elusive factors, will produce some meaningful mathematical formulae. But not now. Cut and try, hee and haw, pressure against resistance, propaganda and fact, all work on the present scene to produce temporary results good only from day to day.

WHO OPERATES REVENUE-PRODUCING BUSINESSES?

The activities included here are those that are ancillary to the primary function of parks. They are services that make the recreational experience of the park visit more enjoyable and more complete and a charge is made for them. The sale of refreshments, meals, souvenirs, and other merchandise, the rental or use of equipment, the furnishing of overnight lodging are examples of an almost endless array of special services. Who shall make the capital investment and who shall operate these businesses—the park and recreation agency or private individuals or companies?

The simplest of these businesses involves the sale of refreshments, souvenirs, and incidental merchandise. Advocates of self-operation by government usually cite these advantages:

1. The department has complete control of the service at all times.

---

*Hennepin County, Minnesota once was permitted a levy of only 18¢ per capita for park operation.

It can rectify promptly any complaints. It can provide service during hours when profit is questionable. It has complete control of personnel, of quantities and quality.

2. If a private operator can make a profit in this operation it stands to reason that the public agency can make that profit plus the license fee the private operator pays to the public agency. In other words, the public makes more money.

3. Self-operation by the department eliminates any chance of the establishment of private vested interests on public property.

Those advocating private concessionaires make these points:

1. Believing that private operation can be more efficiently done than public operation, they charge that the public makes more money by private operation.

2. The department is relieved of many bothersome details in the matter of hiring personnel (no civil service requirements), purchasing regulations, and similar irritations.

3. Where initial investment is required, private operation enables private investment without public appropriation.

4. As rebuttal to departmental operation, the private concessionaire believes that quality and hours of service can be adequately provided for in a well-drafted contract.

Examples of successful operations are numerous for each of the systems. The authors are inclined to favor departmental operation unless local restrictions are too severe. If concessions are let out to private operators on bid, there are some minimum precautions which ought to be made:

1. The private operator ought not to have the opportunity of establishing any vested right on park property. Admitting that this can be provided for in contract, the wailing that private concessionaires can do when this matter is enforced all too frequently makes the public agency appear to be persecuting them. However, instances can be cited where contracts have been extended time and again beyond the agreed-upon termination date as the concessionaires request until for all practical purposes he has acquired vested rights. If he is permitted to make an investment on public property, rigid contractural provisions ought to be made as to its depreciation and valuations at stated times in case the public agency wishes to buy that interest. This whole situation is fraught with so many unfavorable possibilities that too great a caution cannot be taken to avoid any possibility of private rights being established on public property.

2. Contracts designed to ensure the park department's control of hours and seasons of service, quality of service, deportment of attendants, correction of complaints, methods of supervision, payment of money, and various other matters of operation require pages and pages of provisions. As

years of this sort of operation continue, the contracts will probably be lengthened in an attempt to cover all possible loopholes. It is well for the beginner to obtain contracts of this sort from other operators, or from other cities and other park departments as guides to his own contract draftings.

3. Specifications accompanying the request for bids should contain provisions permitting the park department to make investigations of the financial responsibility and business reliability of the concessionaire permitting the park department to use discretion in the exercise of judgment as to which of the bids received is the most favorable one to the park department. The reason for this is that the high bidder may not be capable of performing satisfactorily under the terms of the contract, this fact being positively demonstrable by reason of the experiences in past operations. This is a ticklish sort of business, but the park department should not be bound to accept the high bidder when it is convinced that the concessionaire cannot perform except very unsatisfactorily. After all, the primary purpose of this service is not profit but service to make the park experience more enjoyable. Profit is a motive, but not the primary one.

The biggest businesses in the park and recreation field involve the National Park Service and some of the state park operations, especially in providing hotel and summer-resort type of accommodations. The National Park Service has always contracted with private operating companies to build and operate hotels and tourist cabins. In order to permit the private investment to be amortized out of earnings the length of the term of lease has been extended over the years to as much as thirty years. The operation has had its vicissitudes as is well described by Professor John Ise in his "National Park Policy"* previously referred to. That discussion illustrates the problems arising from private investment on public property as well as some of the usual ones inherent in private operation of this sort of service. To obviate some of these problems the NPS has sometimes resorted to operation by a government-controlled nonprofit corporation acting in a monopolistic fashion. In a sense, this approaches self-operation.

State parks often followed the example of the National Park Service in providing lodges for overnight guests but usually made the investment themselves. In more recent years, the standard of this type of service has risen and in the case of Oklahoma, the state has virtually gone into the tourist business with convention type accommodations at the central hotel supplemented by a system of separate lodges. In this case, the capital investment is made by the state; the operation may be leased out in whole or in part. In other instances, proposals for elaborate tourist hotels on state park property have been submitted by private companies.

*See particularly page 606, etc.

At reservoirs of the Army Engineers, the rules of operation may not permit the investment of any government capital for any revenue-producing facilities. This often results in a crass temporary exploitation of public property and poor service to the public, especially in such operations as marinas, fishing docks, refreshment stands, etc.

Between the big businesses of national, state, and some of the larger municipal operations, and the very simple refreshment stand operation at the small local park, there is an array of enterprises that are useful to park and recreation service and that are susceptible of either government or private operation. In all situations there are at least two very basic precautions that the park administrator must look out for. (a) He must at all times be able to control all phases of the operation in order to provide to the park user those services which will make the user's visit a happy experience—the real reason for the enterprise in the first place. (b) He must prevent private control, either real or implied, of any public property. The government must always be in unencumbered control and possession of its physical properties. Private investment on public property does not permit that unencumbered public control. There ought to be provisions for ultimate government ownership of any private capital investments that for one reason or another have been made on park lands or on any in-holdings of real estate within park boundaries.

What might appear to be exceptions to the foregoing, but really are not, may be those quasi-public services which are provided by a "partnership" of government and private enterprise—museums, outdoor theaters, some zoological gardens, arboretums, sports stadiums, cultural and art centers. Many of these facilities are financed partly by government and partly by private capital. Often the most satisfying arrangement is for government to hold title to the physical property (buildings and real estate) and private nonprofit organizations to maintain and operate.

PERMITS AND LEASES

Requests for the use of park property for various purposes (private, commercial, recreation) from individuals and organizations constitute a considerable volume of the official business of a park and recreation agency. Many of the permits are of a routine nature—picnic permits, permits for use of ball diamonds, etc. In these cases, rules and regulations have been established in accordance with general policies aimed at conveniencing the park user while at the same time ensuring safe and socially acceptable use of the facilities without undue damage to park property. Requests for other park uses are special cases requiring special consideration—religious services, political meetings, public speaking generally, commercial ventures, and demonstrations, money-raising schemes for "good causes," celebrations, etc.

Public Speaking—Indiscriminate public speaking (religious, political, current issues) can be a distinct nuisance to crowds assembled for purely recreational purposes. Many park and recreation departments have enacted ordinances forbidding the practice except by special permit. The denial of permits in some cases resulted in appeals to the courts which, generally speaking, have upheld the rights of citizens to freely assemble in public places and to speak their minds. This has put quite a dent in enforcement of ordinances prohibiting public speaking. A sort of hopeful compromise has been adopted in some instances, namely, designating certain locations at which public speaking on any subject will be permitted. Permits may still be required, but the purpose is only to serve as notice to the issuing agency so that if police protection seems advisable, it can be provided for. These locations are chosen so that the speaker will not find an already assembled audience to harangue; he will have to supply his own audience. However, to be a reasonable defense against the probable legal restriction, the location should not be so remote as to be entirely frustrating. In brief, the purpose is to permit public speaking without inconveniencing or annoying those seeking recreation in public parks.*

Religious Services—Public park and recreation services are provided without religious impetus or motivation, and hence, church services are to be accorded the same treatment as general public speaking. Where the granting of permits does not interfere with recreation enjoyment, approval is in order. However, religious activities can take many subtle forms and the administrator is warned to look out for the possible establishing of precedents in other directions.

Political Meetings—These are to be treated like religious meetings. Here it must be kept in mind that when an elected official appears on the platform he is going to talk politics, and usually partisan politics. But you cannot completely stop them. Stern warnings may soften the most blatant aspects.

Commercial Ventures—These include the short-time permit to sell Christmas trees, mobile refreshment carts at special functions, the testing out of a new piece of equipment, and a variety of other services. These situations should be scrutinized in some such way as this: Does the proposal do any damage to park property and, if so, is it readily repaired and will the permittee be willing to stand the cost? Is a fair rental charge possible? Will it inconvenience nearby private property owners? Will it unfairly compete with private business? Is it of such a character as will be consistent with the dignity of the department and consistent with the attractiveness of the area? Is it a

---

*In the 1960s, public assembly and public speaking as civil rights have been so rigorously and often violently asserted by organized groups as to constitute special problems for law-enforcing agencies.

legitimate service to the public? If the project passes these tests it may be approved. However, it is generally desirable to keep the number of these permits to a minimum.

Houseboats, Launching Ramps, Marinas, Water-Skiiing, Boat Clubs— Park departments owning property on navigable streams, particularly rivers, may find themselves harassed by the presence of houseboats docked on the river bank. Like squatters, houseboat owners often are used to circumventing the law and bluffing authorities into believing that they know their rights better than park departments. They will claim they have a right to dock because their boat is on the river, only the gangplank going over to the shore. They insist upon having access to the land not only for themselves but for the delivery of goods and supplies which they need, that they are not in the nature of transients and can stay as long as they please. An appeal to suitable police authorities discloses the fact that generally speaking, police are not too well versed in the park department's rights to evict the houseboat owners from use of the adjacent land. Fact of the matter is that while houseboat owners or any other boaters can use the river to their heart's content without molestation and can tie up to any shore in an emergency, the owner of the adjacent land, even if the land itself lies between the established harbor line and the edge of the water, has control of who docks there and who uses the adjacent property. Consequently, the adjacent owner has the right to establish docking rules and regulations and establish fees for the use of such docks and the privilege of access to the adjacent land.

Marinas for boats of various purposes and of various sizes have been provided by many agencies of government in all its levels. The establishment of fees for the privilege of using the facilities is a legitimate operation. Like entering any other enterprise having to do with the sale of goods and services on public property, all the necessary precautions must be taken to see that the park department received the money that is actually taken in over the counter and that it is otherwise protected by insurance against the usual hazards of doing business. It must be remembered that when a governmental agency gets into a business enterprise such as this, it loses certain immunities from liability it has when it is acting in a governmental capacity. In this case it is not acting in its governmental capacity, but in its proprietary capacity. Therefore, it is subject to all of the hazards of a private individual in the conduct of his business.

Inasmuch as lightweight boats of various sizes are now on the market, many owners find it convenient to store their boats on their own property some distance from the water and to transport the boat by trailer or otherwise to the scene of the launching. Numerous launching ramps have been provided by various governmental agencies for the convenient launching of these craft. Generally speaking, no charge is made for the privilege of launching, but inasmuch as cars are parked in adjacent parking lots, it is not unusual to invoke an automobile or trailer parking fee.

Water-skiing being the popular sport that it is, certain precautions ought to be taken in governing the use of the waters on which this sport is carried on. The purpose of regulations is to segregate the activity of water-skiing from the enjoyment of fishing and from the danger which water-skiing might have to swimmers. It is not unusual to encounter a situation where the government of the waters does not rest with the owners of only a portion of the abutting land. While this produces complications, either the regulations or the opportunities of getting onto the water from the land can be manipulated so as to secure the necessary safety for the enjoyment of all the sports.

The park department may fully realize that the construction of private buildings on public land, even though the buildings may be used for recreation purposes, is a practice which leads to many difficulties. In this connection, boat clubs may present a special problem. The situation can arise in which all the possible practical access points to public waters are in the hands of the park department. In some forms of boating, which for proper enjoyment require club facilities, it is difficult to deny the construction of such facilities on public property. While it may be true that the necessity for these facilities is decreasing as the mobility of people increases, still a park department may find itself in the position of being unreasonable if construction privileges are not granted. However, it should be recognized that public property is being used for private purposes and, therefore, a legitimate lease arrangement ought to be entered into providing for the payment of an annual fee for the use of the land, the land to be occupied only at the discretion of the park department. The lease may be in force for a number of years and if the privilege is revoked within that period then definite liquidation costs ought to be established for each of the years, these costs being based upon the gradually depreciating value of the building which may be placed on park property. Sometimes in the past it has been argued that inasmuch as yacht clubs, privately owned but still to some extent open to the public, constitute a legitimate recreation use they therefore should not be subjected to an annual lease payment but ought to have the privilege of using the property for a nominal payment of a dollar a year. The fact remains that this is a special privilege given to a special few people which ought to pay a special price for that privilege.

Privately Owned Buildings on Public Property—Metropolitan and state parks and on some occasions city parks have been considered ideal sites for special use buildings by privately supported groups engaged in recreation work, either as a means to some other end or even as an end in itself. Such organizations include Boy Scouts, Campfire Girls, YMCAs, the projects of service clubs such as Optimists, Kiwanis, and others.

Influential people representing these worthy causes may successfully argue to the park department that they are engaged in recreation and ought to have the privilege of placing a small center of some sort on the public property. Various reasons will be given why it is unobtrusive and good causes such as theirs should be properly supported by the public agencies. They may even suggest that the building will be open to others under their guidance.

No matter in what honeyed phrases these thoughts are expressed, the cold fact remains that a special, privately endowed group catering to a special class is seeking a special favor from a governmental agency pledged to serve all people on an equal basis and deriving its support broadly from all people within the district. If these requests are granted they should be on a monetary basis. Leases should be drawn requiring payment of a sum which is equal to that which would be charged by any private owner of similar property and also with provisions for removal under equitable circumstances. If these buildings are of general service to the public, another possible solution is for the park department to construct such buildings itself and if used generally by all people in sufficient amount the service could be properly tax supported. If used only by a special few, a fee could be charged to cover the cost of operation.

The point is made here that there should be no privately owned buildings on public property and that if any such exists the owner should pay a fair value for the privilege that is conferred and the department should take all necessary precautionary steps to save itself from any liability whatsoever and to be free to recapture complete possession at any time under equitable circumstances.

Access to Boulevards and Parkways—Parkways are a part of many of the park systems of the country. One of the characteristics of parkways is that access to them is limited. This is not necessarily so of boulevards. Adjacent private property owners often request driveway access to their private property from the parkway. In almost all cases this is an objectionable situation, sometimes very mildly and sometimes quite aggravated so. The rights of the department in denying such requests must be investigated in each case for the laws and the situations to which the law may apply are not uniform. Very early in the history of Minneapolis parks one such request was denied which resulted in a lawsuit. The court decided that if the adjacent property owner had no other access to his property than from the parkway the private property owner was entitled to access. If, however, he had some other access possible to his property, the park department was within its rights in denying him access to the parkway. Where access is granted without the department being forced to do so because of the limit of the legal situation, the park department might find it desirable to grant such a permit for only a period of years so that the matter can be reviewed from time to time in the light of new circumstances. Also, it may be possible to have the private property owner relinquish some inherent rights he may have, such as absolving the park department from damage in case of change of boulevard grade or parkway grade in front of his house.

High Tension Line Permits—High tension power transmission lines need rights-of-way to ensure adequate maintenance of the line and maintenance of the structures necessary to carry that line. Rights-of-way entering the city from quite a distance away, and sought after the city is pretty well built up, are difficult to find. Sometimes it is necessary to request a right-of-way of the park department over some of its properties. When this request appears it ought to be carefully examined to see if there is any other alternative route, or if none, the route across park property should be screened and the screening blended into the plan of the park. A lease fee or right-of-way price should be exacted and that price should be commensurate with prices paid to private property owners. Incidentally, if strenuous objection is often enough raised, the power companies through research might find some alternative method of power transmission and reduce the frequency of this objectionable feature, especially in urban areas.

Social Welfare and Charitable Organization Requests—As a preliminary word of caution it should be noted that a public park and recreation agency is devoid of sentimental or emotional feeling in dealing with charitable and religious organizations. The promotion of these causes, however worthy they may be in the ordinary sense, or the promotion of anything other than public recreation by the governmental agency sets the precedent of promoting some causes of questionable worth. Therefore, when requests for the use of park and recreation facilities are made by any of the agencies referred to, be it in a preferential capacity or to raise money for a good cause, or to assist in promotion of their objectives—these requests must be accorded the same consideration as similar requests from other segments of the population. Some of these agencies will be providing recreation services as a means to their primary social welfare end. While close coordination of these services with the public service must be recognized and provided for, the use of public facilities should be on the same basis as for other organized groups and individuals.

One final word of caution in regard to permits for the use of or entrance upon park property: Have the permit in writing and the conditions therein imposed agreed to, as evidenced by the signature of the permittee; ensure compliance by obtaining a cash deposit or a performance bond; ensure relief from any and all liability arising from the issuance of the permit by requiring the permittee to secure and pay for insurance protecting the grantor of the permit against such eventuality.

Chapter Fourteen

Law Enforcement
and Public Safety
in Parks

The root of an understanding of law enforcement and public safety in parks lies in an understanding of why parks are created in the first place and how well that purpose is reflected in the design and operation of the park in the second place.

If we go back to basics it is axiomatic that there has to be a reason—a purpose—before the natural resource, whatever it may be, can be developed. In the case of developing parks out of raw land the reason for the development is invariably recreation. But recreation has many facets and numerous short-range as well as long-range objectives.

It is the administering agency that determines what kind of recreation is best suited to the needs of the prospective users. This decision is based on an informed intuition or, more often in recent years, by a sampling of the prospective users. The park is then built and subsequently managed to reflect the purpose.

There may have been a time when providing the public with a park was all that was needed. People were assumed to use the park in the way that was consistent with its purpose and design. That naive notion was early shattered. People had to be guided, instructed, coerced, and somehow made to understand that a specific park was designed for a specific purpose as set forth by the administration and for no other purposes.

Policy determination, purposeful design, and restricted public use have characterized parks in all urban, state, and national situations in all American history. The conflicts which came out of the confrontations of park users and administrative decisions are the law enforcement problems of today. The real causes of conflict may lie in the original determination of purpose, a faulty design, the guidance mechanism of police and recreation leaders, changing social attitudes, or a combination of any of these. Certainly it is not always faulty law enforcement.

Central Park in New York was created (circa 1858) to provide a vehicle for a certain kind of recreation uppermost in the minds of many people: to provide the healing and pleasurable comfort of the countryside to a city population burdened by congestion and long hours at hard work in unattractive surroundings. The design by Olmsted and Vaux reflected that purpose.

Although the vast majority of users were satisfied with the park, and its virtues were extensively extolled, a minority abused the landscape, engaged in muggings and criminal assaults, vandalized the property often enough to mar the unhampered recreation of the people. Guidance and restraint became necessary. Uniformed "parkkeepers" were employed to "prevent misuse of the park"—the first commandment to the new force of parkkeepers. Olmsted wrote ". . . every tree, bush, as well as every arch roadway and walk has been fixed where it is with a *purpose* and upon its being so used that it may continue to serve that purpose to the best advantage, and upon its not *being otherwise used,* depend its value."

Olmsted assumed that the original conceptual purpose was correct and that the design reflected that purpose perfectly. It was the public that needed stricter guidance when abuse and misbehavior took place. To a degree he was probably right but as time went on it became evident that the original purpose and the original design did not satisfy the user needs. But the administration was all too slow to alter its course, to the great detriment of the park's appearance, its usefulness, and the public safety. Examples of this sort abound in almost all of the systems of the Olmstedian era and adjustments are still being made.

Problems of law enforcement and public safety are not restricted to large city parks. The problems may differ in kind and degree according to the type of park, community, uses, location, and administration. The problems occur in park and recreation facilities located in ghettos and suburbs, indoor as well as outdoor, and include national, state, and local parks and reservations and reservoir properties.

Within fifteen years of the development of Central Park, Yellowstone Park was established as the first national park. It was to be preserved for all time (it encompassed a fabulous array of unique natural phenomena) and at the same time it was to be enjoyed by all. The public was expected to comply.

There are comparatively few people, outside of those employed by the National Park Service, who are aware that the law enforcement problems at Yellowstone National Park were at one time so great, and available finances and law enforcement powers so limited that it became necessary for the U.S. Army to first protect the park and then assume complete control for its operations. This arrangement was not a short, stop-gap measure either; it started in 1886 and lasted 30 years and then terminated only as World War I. approached and the troops were needed elsewhere. Congress shortly thereafter created the National Park Service. The Yellowstone staff could not handle the many problems of encroachment by timber and grazing interests and hunters because of their extensive holdings and small field force. There was also the problem of bringing a suspected poacher before a federal commissioner 150 rugged miles away. While the Army helped to keep Yellowstone from wholesale despoliation, there were other unique areas without national park designation undergoing the ravages of vandals and over-enthusiastic collectors. There were scientists as well as tourists who found collecting artifacts irresistible. Fortunately, before our Indian heritage and the petrified wood disappeared into the insatiable commercial outlets and museums, the Antiquities Act of 1906 was passed. This Act provided for the establishment of national monuments which, unlike national parks, could be quickly designated by the President without the usual lengthy, time-consuming discussions required for congressional approval. Therefore, protection of unique natural areas was assured from the federal government as it was needed.[1]

On the other hand, many of the large city park and recreation systems during the early 1900s established special park police forces to control vandalism. Many were developed because it was believed that park police required a different background than the crime detection attitude prevalent in the regular city force. Moreover, park superintendents harbored the feeling that city police departments were prone to assign their least efficient men to the parks. It also became a matter of professional pride for some superintendents of parks and recreation systems in the larger cities to establish a park police force. Some grew to include horse-mounted police. There are few remaining forces of this kind, such as the mounted police of the Fairmount Park Commission in Philadelphia and they are mostly used as walking patrols in the large parks and for ceremonial parades. The National Park Service, of course, maintains a horse-mounted force in the National

---

[1] For a comprehensive historical review of U.S. National Parks Policy see John Ise, *Our National Park Policy* (Baltimore: John Hopkins Press, 1961).

Capitol Parks and is now considering an expansion of a horse-mounted ranger force in other parks.

The practice of developing and training a special force of walking or motorized park police diminished as the number and quality of regular local police increased to the point that it seemed a useless duplication of effort. During the past 30 years the responsibility for law enforcement in city parks was generally assumed by the regular community police agency.

When the Army left the national parks, the ranger force was initiated to serve and protect the park visitor. The park ranger in his distinctive uniform became known for his interpretation of the environment and his courtesies to visitors and few considered him as a law enforcement officer, that is, until the high visitation concentrations began to threaten the natural environment and created situations conducive to antisocial behavior. Now the National Park Service is increasing its law enforcement capabilities to accommodate large crowds of visitors and attendant law enforcement problems of crowding.

Similarly, there is a resurgence of interest in creating special park police forces by urban governments to protect visitors to local parks.

But these limited examples are merely a resurrection of a stereotype—the park policemen in uniform patroling large open areas. The pressing need today is to guarantee the public safe recreation opportunities not only in large parks but also in the thousands of indoor places of recreation—the small park and indoor recreation centers of all types in every community in the country. It is in these recreation areas and facilities where the vast majority of recreation experiences take place, manyfold more than in large parks, and conventional wisdom, lacking anything better, suggests that this is where rules, regulations, and laws are most often broken or ignored. This is where the job of law enforcement is most difficult because it is in the indoor recreation areas where the density of use and emotional involvement of the participants are greatest.

It also seems that it is the recreation director of these facilities that does the better job of law enforcement because this is the professional in parks and recreation who is dependent on his leadership abilities and little else. His primary concern for people has been his professional hallmark, with physical resources being a secondary consideration.

The nation's general preoccupation with "crime in the streets" starting in the late 1960s also reflects on their attitude about safety in public parks and recreation areas. In a study relating public safety to incidence of crime in parks, H. L. Malt Associates[2] found that the major concern of the

[2] Harold Lewis Malt Associates, "An Analysis of Public Safety as Related to the Incidence of Crime in Parks and Recreation Areas in Central Cities," U.S. Dept of Housing and Urban Development, Washington D.C., 1971.

police and park and recreation officials interviewed was vandalism. Very little data was available on crime in city parks or on park usage; however, all public officials interviewed in the 10 major central cities involved in the study referred to people's fear of crime in parks.

Based on a review of studies on Chicago, Cincinnati, and Seattle, the Malt study concluded that crime in parks is low. Further study of reported crime and census tract data of the various areas around parks suggested that park crime was lower than originally predicted. Their study concluded that the incidence of crime of all types was lower in parks than in surrounding neighborhoods, but that there was a high degree of fear associated with using public parks.

The 1967 Commission on Law Enforcement and Administration of Justice found that the fear of crime is very prevalent throughout the nation and that approximately one out of three persons surveyed in a major urban area reported that they were afraid to walk alone at night in both the streets and public parks.[3] It also reported that fear of being physically attacked was the major fear of those who were afraid to walk alone.

In a large sense, whether the incidence of crimes in parks is low or high is academic to the public's perception of parks as safe places of play and fun. If they have been taught to consider parks, especially at night, as places to be avoided because they are the strongholds of society's depraved, then it requires only a few years for a generation of children who were ordered to shun public parks to similarly counsel their children.

Unless this perception of the fear syndrome can be countered, it quite logically will grow to reality because a fearful public will abandon its parks and public places and when a park no longer attracts people, it ceases to be a park and become a place to be feared and avoided.

It therefore seems that from both an historical and contemporary perspective the new dimension for education and training for law enforcement in park and recreation is really a need for new leadership capabilities for all professional recreation and park personnel as well as for law enforcement personnel.

Coupled with changing social attitudes about public service and protection the need to develop a set of professional principles on the role of the park and recreation agency in matters of law enforcement and public safety seems obvious. These principles should be highlighted with the premise that the primary responsibility for search, seizure, and arrest resides with regular police or special park and recreation law enforcement personnel. All park and recreation personnel should have law enforcement training but their

[3] The President's Commission on Law Enforcement and Administration of Justice, *The Challenge of Crime in a Free Society*. Washington, D.C: U.S. Government Printing Office, p. 26.

primary responsibility is to exercise the kinds of leadership that preclude and prevent antisocial behavior in their areas of responsibility.

All professional park and recreation personnel should, however, also be knowledgeable in preparing and calling for emergency plans when required by uncontrollable circumstances or events. This means that when large groups or gangs begin to congregate in the larger regional, state, and national parks, the interpreter ranger should begin to meet with them in the evenings as well as during the day to help them understand the purpose of the park and the environment. On the other hand, if word is received of organized violence coming their way, the park and recreation personnel should be able to initiate an appropriate emergency plan with special law enforcement personnel of the park and recreation department in cooperation with other available police agencies.

Time and distance are critical factors in determining the role of law enforcement personnel in outlying or remote areas as opposed to the city situation close to regularly established law enforcement agencies. It is because of time and distance that the large resource-oriented park and recreation agencies should develop a core of specially trained law enforcement officers. In the event of violence within a park or forest or reservoir area, the public is without protection when a uniformed person walks away from the situation because he does not have the necessary police powers or training. This kind of power is generally not as necessary in cities and communities where regular law enforcement agency personnel are quickly available and special park and recreation enforcement personnel should not be necessary.

In the local systems, it also means that if uniformed park and recreation rangers are to have law enforcement responsibilities, they should continue to be primarily responsible for helping and advising park visitors, and to be most effective in this they should receive part of their training in a humanistic approach to leadership by working with personnel from the recreation centers and with the recreation activity leaders—in-house sensitivity training.

This is not to say that law enforcement problems will go away if administrators merely piously pontificate their views on not being policemen. But it does suggest that new ways should be developed to head off situations that might galvanize into hard case law enforcement problems. When such an unexpected problem arises, then park and recreation personnel should be prepared to protect their clientele and the areas under their control by instituting emergency plans.

This then is the first major point: law enforcement as it embraces search, seizure, and arrest is antithetical to the nature of recreation as a personal experience as well as to the professional who is charged with developing and administering a delivery system to assure the public a quality environment.

There is a deep-seated problem that seems fundamental to all large public agencies: the bureaucracy is not easily responsive to change. As a sociology-of-organization kind of observation, that comment is becoming trite in its obviousness. Nevertheless, unless it is recognized that employees who have hitherto been shielded by their long-standing civil service status do not or cannot always change their emotional commitments on being assigned to a new position or area of responsibility, the entire business of retraining personnel as enlightened enforcers of the law could be a disfunctional exercise; the individual that becomes upset over the necessity to change his basic views about "the kind of crud who won't stand up for the American flag" may become a very unhappy person incapable of fulfilling his assignment. Individuals with strong attitudes and beliefs often resist retraining that includes a reevaluation of those attitudes and should, therefore, not be forced into such a situation. If the bureaucracy is large enough, possibly they can be shifted into less emotional kinds of responsibilities.

It is also important to note the differences between law enforcement responsibilities of field personnel. On the one hand, there are thousands of professional recreation personnel who have daily face-to-face program contact with recreation users. They are assigned to a great variety of places and locations ranging from playgrounds, recreation centers, swimming pools, and marinas to nature centers and theaters. They are responsible for providing the public with recreation opportunities in these settings that are not only specialized for the particular area or facility but also for an ability to be innovative in developing programs and activities which they feel will interest the people they serve. They are the cutting edge of the park and recreation profession. They are the prime delivery part of the delivery system.

On the other hand, there are other professionals responsible for providing recreation experiences which do not require face-to-face contact with the recreation user. In fact, it is the lack of such close contact with professional leadership that is often considered a desired hallmark of the outdoor recreation experience. Users of a city park or a wilderness area generally do not want continual face-to-face programming experience. Therefore, leadership in an outdoor recreation situation is generally of an interpretive type, either interpreting the natural phenomena of the area or interpreting and advising on rules, regulations, and providing directions.

There is another component of this mix of field personnel, and that is the maintenance and concessionaire force. They are generally para or nonprofessional personnel who nevertheless are often important interpreters of the agency and the area. They are often the most visible representatives of the agency. When in need of information or in a state of distress, the public will expect a standard of performance from the paraprofessional to be equal to that of the professional.

These categorizations of field personnel are generally accepted as being standard in all park and recreation agencies, most appropriately, of course, at the local level. But they are also applicable for state and federal level agencies that have recreation responsibilities with the possible exception of face-to-face program leaders. These characterizations were obviously developed over time and are based on the experience of personnel in the various agencies. But today park and recreation departments are experiencing a different set of problems which present standards do not generally accommodate. Personnel performance standards and training seldom address the problems of antisocial and deviant behavior of park users—not that they are all new, but most importantly the scale of these problems is different, thereby suggesting a need for new dimensions and change in the training of park and recreation personnel—professional as well as paraprofessional.

In developing training methods to address those problems, the following principles are recommended:

1. *All personnel should thoroughly understand the nature of the recreation experience.* The recreation user of public facilities is not the stereotyped hard-working, hard-driving American citizen. Instead he is attempting to be the fulfilled American. He is young or old, male or female, rich or poor, employed, unemployed, or retired and a variety of colors. He no longer apologizes for aspiring to this kind of fulfillment, especially if the area he intends to use was developed with public funds.

2. *The primary responsibility of all park and recreation personnel is to assist him in achieving this fulfillment.* If, in his activity, he deviates from the regularly prescribed rules and regulations in his attempt for fulfillment then it is the responsibility of park and recreation personnel to guide him back to acceptable patterns of behavior, or control the deviant user, or else change the rules and regulations.

3. *It must be assumed that every person entering a park or engaging in a program has equal rights and opportunities for this fulfillment.* Under no conditions is the representative of the agency to make judgments to the contrary based on personal beliefs unless the rights or safety of the participants or others are threatened. In other words, if the park and recreation professional permits his personal preferences as to how people should talk, look, or act interfere with the discharge of his duties, he should work elsewhere than in a recreation agency.

4. *A sincere, humanistic interest in people should be a prerequisite for all professional and paraprofessional personnel in both field and administrative levels of park and recreation agencies.* It is now clear that despite the overwhelming numbers of users ranging from children to senior citizens recreation leaders on playgrounds or in community centers service work with (and usually in confined spaces), they nevertheless have a better track record

of accommodating the fulfilled American than the park and recreation leaders who have an outdoor recreation responsibility. Street gangs are an assumed clientele by recreation program leaders in many communities and have been for many years. It seems quite reasonable, then, to suggest that those who are recruited to work in an outdoor recreation setting should, like program leaders, also have an interest in people, along with the education and training in leadership that will help minimize the antisocial and deviant behavior now found in many parks and recreation areas. Techniques in the use of Mace, or how to make an arrest, are after-the-fact training efforts. In a large sense, they are reminders of failure on the part of the park and recreation agency.

5. *Field personnel who work in outdoor recreation situations should be either environmental interpreters or heavily educated and trained in this field.* While recognizing that somebody has to direct traffic and administer first-aid, it would be much more in keeping to add these skills to a person who already has basic training in interpretation, a large part of which is communication.

By recognizing that an interpreter should have a humanistic approach to his work if he is to successfully communicate with the recreation user, it is suggested that a field force consisting largely of personnel with this kind of training be developed. It is hoped then that the park ranger will develop a relationship with the recreation user similar to what the program leader has so successfully developed with the recreation user in many communities. Paraprofessionals, similarly, have to be trained to recognize their responsibility to assist the fulfilled American in his quest for recreation experience. While any departmental training program should, of necessity, reflect the particular needs of the community it serves, the department and its personnel, the following general components may be adopted and included in most departmental in-service training programs in law enforcement and public safety.

IN-SERVICE TRAINING AND EDUCATION OUTLINE FOR PARK AND RECREATION LAW ENFORCEMENT

SECTION I: RECREATION AND THE COMMUNITY

I.   Introduction
- A.   Need for a law enforcement program in parks and recreation.
  - 1.   Socioeconomic characteristics of the community.
  - 2.   Historical perspectives, growth of areas and facilities, appropriations, and relationship to present need of the department.
- B.   Need and basis for trained and qualified personnel.

260 ELEMENTS OF PARK AND RECREATION ADMINISTRATION

      1.   Law enforcement's negative image in the past, and what is generally being done to improve this image.

      2.   Types of problems that result from accepting the law enforcement role.

Administrative staff in conjunction with outside lecturers from urban planning and police departments could provide instruction for this section.

II. The Nature of Recreation

   A.   Recreation as a service, profession; activities, areas, and facilities.

   B.   Economics of recreation.

   C.   Social and individual benefits of recreation.

   D.   Recreation policy of the department.

III. Changes

   A.   Changing population, leisure pursuits, and distribution of population.

   B.   Changing life styles—the young, new morality, leisure time, and mobility.

   C.   Changes in neighborhoods and transportation.

   D.   Changes in job opportunities.

   E.   Changes in public services.

IV. Antisocial and Deviant Problems in the Community

   A.   Problems in regard to demographic data of the community.

   B.   Major problem areas identified.

   C.   Identification of problems occurring in, on, or near park and recreation areas and facilities.

   D.   Develop correlation between antisocial behavior and recreation areas, places, and programs. If negative correlation is found, publicize it through mass media in order to reverse trend in public belief that park and recreation areas are the most unsafe places in the community.

   E.   Identify relationships which exist between the changes taking place in the community and the antisocial problems in the community. Develop hypotheses as to why these relationships exist.

V. Seminar on Resolving the Problems

   A.   New or intensified leadership techniques.

   B.   Changes in operational procedures to assure credibility of communications response and accessibility to decision makers.

   C.   Understanding individual problems and needs.

   D.   Employment practices.

      1.   Hiring, testing, and interviewing practices involving the disadvantaged.

2.   Training of new personnel.

E.   Design and planning for new and renovated areas and facilities—environmental design in preventing crime.

F.   New reporting procedures and development of accurate data—new technological advances in data collection and analysis and impact of such systems.

G.   Need for preventative methods, rather than control or correctional techniques.

VI. Development of Emergency Plans

A.   What constitutes an emergency.

B.   Types and availability of assistance from police and other agencies—cooperative assistance pacts.

C.   Emergency operational plan.

VII. Criminal Justice System

A.   Flow system of criminal justice—police, prosecution, court or trial, correctional and rehabilitation functions.

B.   Responsibility of park and recreation employee in testifying.

VIII. Criminal Investigation

A.   Responsibility of park and recreation employee in reporting.

B.   Elementary crime scene protection and criminal investigation techniques.

C.   Observation techniques and report writing.

IX. Civil Rights and Criminal Rights

A.   Civil rights of the public and of the professional serving the public.

B.   Effect of law on society and society's effect on law.

C.   Basic criminal law and criminal procedure—basic rights of criminals and discussion on arrest, search, seizure, and admissibility of confessions.

X.   Community and Human Relations

A.   Community relations—stressing the importance of the employee as a representative of the park and recreation department and as a public servant.

B.   Stress on the importance of public image.

C.   Human relations—importance of respect for clientele, integrity, honesty in dealing with public.

XI. Law Enforcement Operational Techniques and Equipment

A.   Basic operational techniques should be given all personnel, with specialized training in law enforcement and handling of various equipment given specifically to the law enforcement personnel of the department.

XII. Professional and Civil Liability

    A.   Cases and comments on tort liability.

    B.   Information should be stressed on prevention of negligence and nuisance removal.

XIII. Departmental Rules, Ordinances, Regulations, and Standards

    A.   Stress the importance of following these and stress importance of inputs of employees in making suggestions for improvements or new standards.

SECTION 2: SEMINARS ON INTROSPECTION

I. What Changes are Needed and How

    A.   Departmental rules, regulations and policies.

    B.   Community image of department.

    C.   Departmental organization.

    D.   Relationship with community.

    E.   Intergovernmental relationships.

SECTION 3: EVALUATION

I. Mandatory Participant Written Evaluation

    A.   Relevancy of subjects—recommendation on additional material to be covered.

    B.   Instructors' adequacy.

    C.   Physical aspects of the session adequate? Recommendations for improvement.

II. Verbal Discussion or Evaluation of the Session Prior to Conclusion of Training Session

It should be recognized that this is a basic outline which can and should be changed to fit the individual departmental needs. Any training session should be flexible and diverse. Hopefully, such training sessions will provide the participants with basic knowledge to better handle prevention and control over the crime problem of parks and recreation areas.

Appendices

Essays and Comments

A Digest of
Policy Statements*

by Charles E. Doell

A digest of three regional park and recreation systems is presented as a guide to authors of other proposed policy statements be they local, state, or national in character. A majority of departments depend upon their legal charter, adopted laws and ordinances, and a review of official departmental actions to reflect their policies. Some may even first drift along without making any formal statement. A declared policy statement is much to be preferred.

COOK COUNTY FOREST PRESERVE DISTRICT

LAND POLICY STATEMENT

FOREWORD

The work of governmental bodies is given a sense of direction by the making and keeping of policies.

Policies, well made and well kept, are the foundation and guide to the administration of the Forest Preserve District. Through our policies we maintain the sense of direction from a literal interpretation of the basic statute or charter. We insure that our land acquisition program is well planned and properly executed; that our lands are held and not dissipated by allocation to various and sundry other purposes than for which acquired; that our development program is simple and confined to the purposes announced in the charter; that special privilege to individuals and organizations is denied and that all our citizens are treated equally; that popular opportunism is disregarded; that all possible effort is made to improve the quality and diversity of use by Cook County citizens through a broad educational program of notable success; that through policies well made and well kept we insure economy of operation and development; that the forest with its cultural, sociological and spiritual values is paramount.

To the work of acquisition of lands, the development, maintenance and operation in the Forest Preserve District must be added the very difficult and constant effort required in holding the lands of the District for the purpose for which they were purchased. The basic

*Cook County Forest Preserve District (Chicago); Genessee County, Michigan (Lansing); Hennepin County, Minnesota (Minneapolis).

265

statute under which forest preserve districts are organized provides that boards of forest preserve commissioners have the power "to acquire— and hold lands containing one or more natural forests—or lands connecting such forests—for the purpose of protecting and preserving the flora, fauna and scenic beauties—and to restore, restock, protect and preserve the natural forests—along with their flora and fauna, as nearly as may be, in their natural state and condition, for the purpose of education, pleasure, and recreation of the public."

For its adherence to this policy over a period of many years the organization has been widely acclaimed. It has consistently followed a written policy of acquiring property at a ratio of 10 acres per 1000 population even as the population of Cook County rapidly increased.

Its policy statement is in the form of resolutions dealing principally with land acquisition and protection of its holdings.

As early as 1926 there was appointed an Advisory Committee of distinguished citizens which took an active part in working with the Board in its early acquisition and operating problems. It continued to function as special problems were referred to it from time to time. On April 6, 1946 the President of the Board referred to it a matter in the following language:

Mr. Edward Eagle Brown, Chairman,
Advisory Committee to the Board of
Forest Preserve Commissioners,
38 S. Dearborn St., Chicago, Ill.

Dear Mr. Brown:

With the end of the war we are confronted with a tremendous expansion of suburban areas of the county, with proposed developments of school districts, sanitary districts, highway departments, and various and sundry municipal governments. Many of the problems involved require additional lands. The Forest Preserve District, as the largest public landholder in the county, is looked upon as a possible source of space. At the present time we have four informal proposals involving important acreage of the District.

This letter is a request to our Advisory Committee to review again the policies in the original report to the Board, and to give the Board its beliefs in the matter. As the requests for lands come before the Board of Forest Preserve Commissioners, I shall request my fellow-members of the Board to refer such matters to the Advisory Committee for review.

I trust we may have the benefit of your time and advice.

Sincerely,
CLAYTON F. SMITH,
President

This elicited a lengthy reply calling attention to the original authorization of the District and its purposes as well as recalling certain encroachments which had been permitted under unusual and rare circumstances. The Committee urged the Board to remain steadfast to its original purpose, as a result of which the Board's committee on real estate submitted the following policy statement which was adopted:

To the Honorable, the President, and Members
of the Board of Forest Preserve Commissioners.

Ladies and Gentlemen:

Your Committee on Real Estate, to whom were referred sundry matters, having had the same under advisement, begs leave to report and recommend as follows:

SECTION 1

Your Committee has considered Communication No. 5236 from the Advisory Committee, containing a review of the policy regarding disposal of Forest Preserve lands for other purposes, which is published in its entirety, in the regular proceedings of the Board of Forest Preserve Commissioners, as of June 11, 1946. As a part of this report, the following Draft of Resolution appears. This resolution which follows herein, has been adopted by the Committee on Real Estate:

"Whereas in 1913, the Illinois General Assembly authorized the creation of County Forest Preserve Districts, and granted the Commissioners thereof, the specific power:

"To acquire and hold lands containing natural forests, or lands connecting such forests for the purpose of protecting and preserving the flora, fauna and scenic beauties, and to restore, restock, protect and preserve the natural forests and said lands, together with their flora and fauna, as nearly as may be, in their natural state and condition, for the purpose of the education, pleasure and recreation of the public," and

Whereas, the Forest Preserve Commissioners of Cook County, have acquired to date, a system of forested lands and lands connecting them, totalling 36,000 acres, in accordance with a comprehensive plan for the acquisition of a total of 39,000 acres; and

Whereas, the rapidly increasing growth of population in the outlying portions of Cook County, has resulted in the occupation of large areas by residential, industrial and business uses closely surrounding the Forest Preserve holdings, which as a consequence are of constantly increasing value and importance serving the purposes for which they were acquired; and

Whereas, this same population growth has caused municipal, school, park and other officials to attempt to obtain Forest Preserve lands for their public purposes inasmuch as their plans have been inadequate, and in the belief that the Forest Preserve properties are available for their purposes;

Now Therefore Be It Resolved, that the Forest Preserve Commissioners in the discharge of their statutory duty, reaffirm and strengthen their long standing policy to the effect that Forest Preserve lands were acquired for one purpose only, that under the law no power is granted the District to divest itself of title to such lands, that the said properties are increasing constantly in value, for the purpose for which they were acquired, and that the continuous acquisition of the additional lands in the Comprehensive Plan will be jeopardized by any severance from the present holdings; and

Be It Further Resolved, that no severance of such lands shall be made for other municipal, school, park and similar public uses for which such public bodies have power to finance and acquire needed lands, and

Be It Further Resolved, that where the rare exception may arise under which a public agency persists in condemnation of Forest Preserve property, the Board of Forest Preserve Commissioners may ask for an exhaustive analysis and report on the matter by the Advisory Committee. In general, the Forest Preserve District shall resist rather than accede to such action, in Court, and shall place in evidence such exhaustive survey and report, together with the current appraised value of the full, fair market value of the land, the forest and of any improvements; and

Be It Further Resolved, that for essential highway needs, for essential sewer, water, or other public utility, underground, surface or overhead improvements required in the interest of all the public, the District may accede to such grants, in court, or otherwise, on the basis of the full, fair market value of the property required.

Respectfully submitted,
JOHN F. TRAEGER,
Real Estate Committee

GENESEE COUNTY PARKS AND RECREATION COMMISSION—POLICY STATEMENT

RESOLUTION

In accordance with the legislative acts of the State of Michigan, the following policy statement is adopted as an official document of the Genesee County Parks and Recreation Commission in order that said Commission may more efficiently, effectively and equitably fulfill the obligations and responsibilities entrusted to it by the people of Genesee County

WHEREAS,

a program of parks and recreation should be provided in every community—rural and urban, for all people—children, youth and adults . . . and

WHEREAS,

opportunities and programs for recreation should be available twelve months of the year, . . . and

WHEREAS,

the program of parks and recreation should be planned to meet the interests and needs of individuals, families, and groups . . . and

WHEREAS,
education for the "worthy use of leisure" in homes, schools and other community institutions is essential . . . and

WHEREAS,
community planning for leisure requires cooperative action of public and voluntary agencies including civic, patriotic, religious, social and other groups which have park and recreation interests and resources . . . and

WHEREAS,
schools should serve, as adequately as possible, the education-recreation needs of pupils and be planned so that they will be efficient centers for community use . . . and

WHEREAS,
a fundamental and continuing obligation of all responsible agencies is to develop a public awareness of the social significance of recreation by interpreting its needs, services and opportunities . . . and

WHEREAS,
park and recreation services, actual and potential, should be evaluated periodically in terms of their contributions toward enriching individual and community life . . . and

WHEREAS,
each agency, organization or group which has park and/or recreation functions and facilities should employ an adequate staff of qualified personnel to meet its share of the community needs . . . and

WHEREAS,
a parks and recreation plan for the community should result in the fullest use of all resources and be integrated with long-range planning for all other community services . . . and

WHEREAS,
wherever possible, Federal, State and Local agencies should correlate their plans for the planning, acquisition and use of park and recreation facilities . . . and

WHEREAS,
park and recreation facilities, public and private, should be planned on a neighborhood, district and regional basis to provide the maximum opportunities and services for all age groups . . . and

WHEREAS,
local planning boards, parks and recreation commissions and boards of education should cooperate in long-range planning for the acquisition, development and use of park and recreation facilities . . . and

WHEREAS,
pursuant to the permissive provisions of Public Act 261, Public Acts of Michigan, 1965, the Genesee County Parks and Recreation Commission (hereinafter referred to as the Commission) was created by resolution of the Genesee County Board of Supervisors on the 28th day of February, 1966, and was vested with the general administration, management, and responsibility to acquire and take title to lands, and develop, maintain and operate such lands for County Parks, preserves, parkway and recreation and other conservation purposes in cooperation with the Genesee County Metropolitan Planning Commission and with

other duly constituted authorities of the County and its constituent incorporated and unincorporated areas within said County, as best serve the present and future recreation needs of the inhabitants of the County of Genesee.

NOW THEREFORE, the said Commission does hereby adopt the following as a statement of policy in order to assist and enhance the provision of Park, Recreation, Conservation and related lands, waters, facilities, and programs to better serve the populace of Genesee County.

Effective Date January 1, 1968
Date Adopted December 14, 1967

POLICY STATEMENT

OBJECTIVES AND GOALS

I.

COMPREHENSIVE PARK, RECREATION AND
OPEN SPACE LAND USE PLAN

It is a primary objective of the Commission, as provided for in Act Number 261, Public Acts of Michigan, 1965 to have prepared by and in cooperation with the Genesee County Metropolitan Planning Commission, a comprehensive land use plan of parkway, recreation, scenic, scientific, archaeological, historic, wildlife, and conservation areas, and preserves, playgrounds, open space, trails, and other lands, waters and facilities which are deemed necessary to preserve and enhance the quality of the environment and to provide adequate leisure time opportunities for the present and future residents, visitors and tourists within Genesee County.

GOALS:

1. To define within said plan, in cooperation with municipal, township, village, school district and other intra-county governmental bodies; and agencies of Genesee County, State of Michigan, and United States of America, the current and projected responsibilities of the said governmental bodies and agencies.

2. To formally adopt said plan, upon its completion, to serve as a guide in the planning, acquisition, development, maintenance and operation of park, recreation, conservation and related lands, waters, facilities, and programs for the benefit of the agencies of Genesee County and the other public bodies and agencies enumerated above.

3. To provide for the continuous evaluation of the plan by establishing a systematic and continuous procedure to ascertain preferences and suggestions by the citizenry and to establish a formal procedure whereby additions, deletions, and other changes in the plan may be made when and as deemed necessary.

4. To provide financial and other types of assistance to the Genesee County Metropolitan Planning Commission and other agencies involved in the preparation of the comprehensive land use plan.

5. To insure that the Parks, Recreation and open space elements are an

integral part of all county comprehensive land use planning and zoning.

6. To make certain that every effort is made to obtain proper zoning of lands and waters adjacent to property owned by the Commission or in any area where future acquisition has been planned.

II.
DEFINITION OF THE COUNTY REGIONAL
RECREATION AREA AND PARK SYSTEM

It is a primary objective of the Commission to provide a comprehensive Regional Recreation Area and Park System which may include parkways, recreation, scenic, scientific, archaeological, historic, wildlife, and conservation areas, preserves, open space, trails and related lands, waters and facilities, to service the residents, visitors and tourists within Genesee County. For the purpose of definition:

A county regional park is defined as a land and/or water site, scenic in character and large enough to serve at the inter-city, county, or inter-county level. The regional park conserves a large natural open space for the use and enjoyment of people. Developments are concentrated so as not to destroy the character of the land. The park is used by persons residing or working in a radius of 30 to 40 miles or by those who reach it in an hour's automobile drive from or within a metropolitan center. Users may come from several regions, an entire county, or from several counties.

A county regional recreation area is defined as a large land and/or water site reserved for special recreation activities. It may be located within the boundaries of a county regional park or as a separate site. It supplements special recreation purpose facilities available in urban centers or supplies space for outdoor recreation activities unsuited to urban centers. It is primarily used by persons residing or working in a radius of 30 to 40 miles or by those who can reach it within an hour's automobile drive from or within a metropolitan center. Users may come from several regions, an entire county, or from several counties.

In keeping with the above stated objective, the Commission does, within its statutory authority and financial limitations, hereby pledge—

GOALS:

1. To establish and maintain an equitable method of financing the planning, acquisition, development, maintenance and operation of Regional Recreation and Park Areas.

2. To provide continuous evaluation of Regional Recreation Area and Park needs and implement standards through amendments to the comprehensive land use plan.

3. To develop and maintain regional facilities designed to meet the specialized needs of the citizenry consistent with functional criteria and service standards established by the comprehensive land use plan.

4. To eliminate existing pollution of all waters crossing or located within the Commission properties and in all other recreation and conservation areas by cooperating with the Michigan Water Resource

Commission, the Genesee County Health Department, the Genesee County Drain Commissioner, and other appropriate agencies.

5. To encourage proper landscaping of private property adjacent to areas and facilities administered by the Commission.

6. To sponsor a continuous program to enhance the natural beauty through the restoration of the native landscape and for the elimination of unnecessary roads, fences and buildings on land and/or waters acquired for regional park and/or recreation purposes.

7. To encourage citizens and civic, service, social and other groups and organizations both public and private, to participate in the planning, acquisition, development, maintenance, operation and financing of county administered regional park, Recreation, Conservation, and related lands, waters, facilities and programs.

8. To maintain high standards of planning, design, acquisition, development, maintenance and operational services consistent with specialized obligations.

9. To develop and maintain a continuous program of education with the public and profession emphasizing the social, economic and ecological values of comprehensive regional park and recreation area developments.

10. To develop and maintain a comprehensive Park and Recreation Research Program and to share derived information with other governmental bodies and agencies.

III.

PARKS AND RECREATION RESPONSIBILITIES
OF INTRA-COUNTY GOVERNMENTAL UNITS
AS RELATED TO COMMISSION RESPONSIBILITIES

It is a primary objective of the Commission to encourage municipalities, townships, villages, school districts and other intra-county governmental bodies to plan, acquire, develop, maintain and operate neighborhood, community, and other urban Park and Recreation lands, waters, facilities, and programs required to serve their respective populations, both existing and projected.

GOALS:

1. To stimulate these intra-county governments to step up their efforts to secure open space, park, and recreation areas and facilities, in and around urban centers.

2. To provide such technical and advisory services as may be available within Commission resources to townships, municipalities, villages, school districts and other intra-county governmental units for the planning, acquisition, development, maintenance, and operation of parks and recreation lands, waters, facilities and programs.

3. To assist municipalities, townships, villages, school districts and other intra-county governmental units by providing park and recreation services under contract at cost to such bodies when these services are available within Commission resources.

4. To provide specialized assistance in training and education to professional, volunteer, and lay groups in park and recreation techniques, as necessary to increase the level of service available to all people in the County of Genesee.

5. To serve as an information center for local Parks and Recreation Commissions, and to aid in the coordination and establishment of programs of countywide interest.

6. To actively participate in the formation of public policy and programs at the local, state and federal level as pertains to park and recreation planning, natural resource protection and methods of financing affecting the leisure time opportunities of all residents, visitors and tourists within Genesee County.

7. To actively participate in professional societies and organizations dedicated to the improvement of all phases of the park and recreation field.

In order to protect, preserve and enhance in perpetuity, recreation areas and parks administered by the Commission for the present and future residents, visitors, and tourists within Genesee County, the following statements are recorded as attitudes and policies which the Commission will enfore in the exercise of its authority and responsibility.

IV.
PREPARATION AND ADOPTION OF
PARK MASTER PLANS

Each park, (recreation area, conservation area or other site) shall have a professionally prepared master plan of development.

The views of citizens, civic and service clubs, governmental agencies and other groups, organizations and community interests shall be solicited prior to the preparation of the plan.

The master plan for each Park, upon completion, shall be presented to the Commission, which shall set a time and place for a public hearing on said plan.

The members of the Commission shall within thirty (30) days after said hearing date approve or disapprove said plan as is or with modifications. Eight (8) votes (at least three-fourths of the total Commission membership) of approval shall be required for formal adoption of a plan. The master plan, once adopted, shall be the guide for development of the Park, unless and until it is formally changed as hereinafter provided.

V.
CHANGING OF ADOPTED PLANS

Any suggested major change of an adopted master plan, shall be directed to the Commission by letter. The Chairman shall, if the letter is received within a reasonable time before the next regular meeting of the Commission, read the letter at said meeting of the Commission and shall request the petitioner to be present to answer questions regarding his comments on said plan. After consideration of the comments, suggestions or recommendations outlined in such letter and as expressed by the petitioner, the Chairman shall, if a majority of the Commission approves, set a public hearing of the Commission for those persons or organizations who are interested in said changes in not less than thirty (30) nor more than sixty (60) days at a time and place determined by the Commission.

A notice of such hearing shall be published in a newspaper of general circulation within Genesee County not less than five (5) nor more than ten (10) days before said hearing.

Within the thirty (30) days following said hearing, the Commission shall publicly vote on the request for the major change of the master plan. Eight (8) votes (at least three-fourths of the total Commission membership) of approval shall be required before the master plan may be formally changed.

VI.

**STANDARDS FOR REGIONAL PARKS
AND REGIONAL RECREATION AREAS**

Outdoor recreation space standards represent goals which have proved to be desirable and practical. Therefore, the Commission adopts a minimum standard for regional recreation purposes of 20 acres per each 1,000 residents living within Genesee County or using facilities administered by said county. Such standards shall be updated as conditions may dictate.

VII.

**RESTRICTIONS OF FACILITIES IN
REGIONAL PARKS AND RECREATION AREAS**

Recreation facilities designed primarily for neighborhood and community purposes are not compatible with the purpose or concept of regional parks and recreation areas. The inclusion of these facilities would constitute encroachment on regional areas as surely as if the acreage were taken for a completely foreign use. Therefore, such facilities are prohibited on regional parks and regional recreation areas.

Lodges, motels and related facilities which can be more effectively provided by private enterprise shall not be included in the regional parks or recreation areas since these facilities would change the purpose of such parks and recreation areas from a day or week-end use facility to a longer period use facility.

VIII.

ACQUISITION OF PARK LANDS

Lands and waters for park, recreation, conservation, scenic, historic, archaeological, scientific and related purposes shall be acquired by direct negotiation whenever possible. Appraisals by competent appraisers shall be the basis for negotiations; where federal aid is involved, the federal procedures shall be followed. Title or rights to all lands shall be in the name of Genesee County.

IX,
CONDEMNATION OF PROPERTY
THROUGH EMINENT DOMAIN PROCEEDINGS

Condemnation of private property required for public park, recreation and conservation purposes will be exercised with control and restraint and only if other methods of acquiring such property prove unsuccessful.

X
ACCEPTANCE OF GIFTS OF
REAL PROPERTY, BEQUESTS,
CONTRIBUTIONS AND APPROPRIATIONS

The Commission welcomes gifts of lands, waters, buildings and other real property in the name of the county, provided that such donations meet location, size, access, topographical, and other requirements consistent with the comprehensive Park and Recreation land use plan for Genesee County, and only if such gifts are devoid of unnecessary limiting conditions. Gifts, bequests, contributions and appropriations for park, recreation and conservation purposes may likewise be accepted by the Commission. The Commission, at its discretion, may extend formal recognition to the party or parties giving said gifts, bequests, contributions, appropriations or real property.

XI,
NAMING OF PARKS, RECREATION
AREAS AND FACILITIES

The naming of all parks, recreation areas and facilities shall be a function of the Commission only.

Designation of such names shall be based upon geographical, historical, or ecological relationships indigenous to the region.

In cases where individuals have made exceptional contributions for a specific purpose or project, the Commission may, at its discretion, officially name a park, recreation area or facility after such individual. All maps, plats and other official records and instrumentalities of the Commission shall reflect the Commission's action.

XII,
TAKING OF PARK, RECREATION AND
CONSERVATION LANDS AND
WATERS FOR OTHER USES

The Commission shall zealously protect existing park, recreation and conservation areas against both public and private encroachment and shall yield such lands or waters for non-park and recreational purposes only if the adopted park master plan is amended by the Commission in accordance with prescribed procedures to permit such use; if lands or waters lost are fully compensated for or replaced by others of comparable value which serve the same population and if utilization of such land and/or waters for such purpose is proven to be in the best interests of the citizenry of Genesee County.

The remaining statements are not unusual and the following list of their titles should suffice:

XIII   Road and Utility Easements
XIV   Construction
XV   Proposals for Park Facilities by Groups
XVI   Acceptance of Federal, State, and Private Assistance
XVII   Revenue Producing Facilities
XVIII   User Fees
XIX   Relationship with County Boards and Departments
XX   Relationships with other Governmental and Agencies
XXI   Appointment of Advisory Committees
XXII   Promulgation and Enforcement of Rules and Regulations
XXIII   Recreation Activities, Code of Behavior
    ... Must be of a wholesome character, conventional and not offensive to accepted mores, and concepts of moral decency prevalent in Genessee County at any given period of time.
XXIV   Employment Standards
XXV   Employees and Political Involvement
XXVI   Corporate Seal
XXVII   Annual Reports
XXVIII   Public Relations

HENNEPIN COUNTY PARK RESERVE DISTRICT (Minneapolis)

POLICY STATEMENT—JANUARY 5, 1967

This policy statement, adopted as a whole, is made up of explanatory statements (omitted from this digest) followed by the policy statement itself. For the most part only the actual policy statements are reproduced here.

FORM OF ORGANIZATION FOR PARKS AND RECREATION

Therefore, let it be the policy of this Commission that it advocate the continuance of, and continuous strengthening of, the form of governing structure which permits autonomous action in the affairs of providing park and recreation service and the governing of the properties necessary to provide that service.

THE GENERAL ROLE IN COUNTY AND METROPOLITAN AFFAIRS

Therefore, let it be declared as a policy of this Commission that it assume responsibility for the adequacy of the park and recreation service of the entire Hennepin County by urging and aiding each of the political subdivisions to fulfill its obligations in regard thereto, and by supplying all other services needed to completely provide the people of the county with the kind and amount of service intermediate between that of the large city and the state; also that this Commission work for the ultimate establishment of a Twin City area metropolitan park and recreation system.

LAND POLICIES

A. How Much Land for Parks

Up to the present the Commission has used a generally accepted rule-of-thumb goal for County Park acreage of 10 acres per 1000 population. For Hennepin County this would require 15,000 acres as of 1985. County-wide evidence can be documented to show that this ratio is too low. But each county situation is an individual one, each requiring a much more precise estimate, the intricate methods of measuring which have only recently been tried.

The Commission has now either wholly acquired or has under consideration, and available finances for, a total of almost 15,000 acres, all (except less than 100 acres) in large tracts of 1000 to 4000 acres. This is sufficient to fulfill the rule-of-thumb requirements. Yet it is apparent that other and similar tracts, principally closer to the urban fringe, (and in the higher valued zones) will be needed to supply the full range of future service. The acquisition of these additional tracts may be postponed so far as is practical until an investigation of the precise nature aforementioned can be made. Such a survey will also facilitate the planning for development of the tracts. More will be said hereinafter under the heading of Development.

As a policy, this Commission considers present holdings as being less than a well balanced system, especially inadequate in smaller holdings in or near the urban fringe and consequently advocates further investigations and subsequent acquisitions to round out a well balanced system.

B. Classification of County Parks

Therefore, this Commission adopts as a policy a classification of county parks as follows:

1.*County Park Reserves*—Containing 1000 or more acres of predominately native attractiveness devoted to daytime and overnight use only partially, and to nature appreciation principally.

2.*County Recreation Parks*—Containing approximately fifty to several hundred acres of naturally attractive land suitable for development of a wide variety of daytime uses and located so the majority of county citizens will live within five miles of a county park or a large municipal park.

3.*County Historic Parks and Monuments*—Areas of indefinite size marking historic sites of county significance.

4.*County Parks of Special Use*—Parks of various sizes for special public or quasi-public recreation purposes of a county-wide or metropolitan character established as the result of special surveys and investigation to determine extent of demand, feasibility of capital and operating financing, legality and public support.

C. Restoration of Lands

To speed up this restoration it shall be a Commission policy to direct the immediate handling of park reserve lands, upon their acquisition and control, towards the ultimate goal of restoration of the native landscape and elimination of unnecessary buildings, fences, and roads.

D. Development of Parks

It shall be the policy of the Commission that park lands shall be developed in accordance with master plans of the system as a whole as well as for each individual park after said plans have been approved by the Commission. Opportunity for public review shall be part of the planning process.

· · · · · · · · ·.· · · · · · · ·

To coordinate the development of parks with the recreational needs of people the Commission resolves to have a comprehensive, socio-economic and ecological survey made and adopts as a policy that surveys of this nature be made from time to time in the future to keep pace with changing conditions.

E. Future Acquisition of Land

Lands shall be acquired by direct negotiation except in extreme cases to clear title or where negotiations have reached an impasse when eminent domain proceedings may be resorted to.

Appraisals by competent appraisers shall form the basis of negotiations; where federal aid is involved the federal procedures shall be followed. The Commission endorses federal and state aid and that aid shall be enlisted wherever the Commission can qualify for it.

Any land offered as gift, devise or otherwise shall be accepted only if it fits into the overall park reserve system and if it is devoid of all limiting conditions of ownership save those that terminate at a fixed date or an event takes place that is sure to happen (e.g., the death of the occupant or donor).

POLICIES OF GENERAL USE

Recreation uses must be of a wholesome character, conventional and not offensive to accepted mores and concepts of moral decency prevalent in the county at any given period of time.

The activities conducted on park property should be conducive to rejuvenation of mind and body in preparation of succeeding periods of productive activity, or of such inspirational nature as to enrich the hours of leisure in such ways as to promote the advancement of our culture which depends so much on the results of leisure time use.

More specifically, but still in general, the recreation service offered by the Commission is what has become currently known as "outdoor recreation" as distinguished from the organized and directed recreation programs usual with municipalities. Non-organized or low organized activities predominate: sightseeing, picnicking, swimming, boating, other water-based activities, nature appreciation, hiking, horseback riding, to name some of the principal examples. Entertainments and exhibitions consistent with the stated overall objectives have a place in the Commission's services, especially if special locations and facilities are provided and if there is county-wide support for them. The native setting is an essential accent in all service—more greatly emphasized in the park reserve than in parks of other classifications but none-the-less present in all. Beauty in pattern and design of all elements complement the general purpose of the total service and must be conscientiously woven into all man-made construction.

The Commission relies upon taxation for its financial support. Some of its services are subject to user fees and charges but are not fully self-supporting. Nevertheless, in each park there must be some element of service free of special fee, e.g. trails, roadways for sightseeing.

CONCESSIONS

It is the policy of this Commission that no encouragement be accorded to any attempt to conduct business enterprises of any nature on park property; the public shall not be exploited while enjoying such recreation as is provided in county parks. No private entrepreneur shall be permitted to make any investment on park property or to conduct a business thereon.

POLICY ON ENLARGEMENT OF DISTRICT

It is the policy of this Commission to cooperate in every way with forces seeking to enlarge the boundaries of the present district.

FOUNDATION FOR COUNTY PARKS

The park and recreation movement in past years has received many valuable gifts of land, endowments and other financial aids from generous civic minded benefactors. To encourage this practice and to aid possible grantors in converting assets which they may be inclined to donate to the public welfare but which may not be in a form usable by the District, the Commission looks with favor on the establishment of a nonprofit, tax-exempt foundation for the furtherance of the County Park Service.

The Commission adopts as a policy the practice of promoting private donations to the work of the Commission and, to facilitate the practice, the establishment of a nonprofit, tax-exempt foundation to act as a recipient agency for the Commisssion.

Elements of
Park Value

by Charles E. Doell

INTRODUCTION

To place a value on a park in economic terms was, for a long time, a purely academic exercise. Parks were not sold at the marketplace; they were not to be changed in outline except to be enlarged, for they were the one class of public holdings that symbolized the city's character, that imparted dignity and charm to the city's appearance, that permitted a city to breathe, that was to last forever. There was no practical need for establishing a price.

But like all else in this world, parks lost their "eternal permanence" and began to suffer changes. The importance of parks in characterizing a city's image diminished in favor of more imposing features. Justification for their very existence in many situations had to be proven; they were intruded and run over with apparent impunity for lack of valuations in economic terms. Today, it is a practical necessity to find ways of evaluating parks if the virtues which have always made them desirable are to endure. This is as true of county, state, and federal parks as it is of municipal holdings.

The value of a park can be examined from several view points: as a social amenity including therapeutic values; as an influence in raising property values of nearby real estate; as something to be bought and sold; as an attribute of civic or regional consciousness, something to be proud of, an inducement to attract people and business enterprises. There may be still other aspects of value, subtle, but nonetheless compelling, to round out total value. Some of the more apparent of these value aspects have facets numerous and intricate enough to command detailed inspection.

SOCIAL AND THERAPEUTIC VALUES

Parks are of ancient origin. New inventions as to shape, size, content, and expanding purpose over history's long and mottled past have only slightly modified their essential values. Those values are intrinsic to man's nature, health, happiness, and recreation; in a word, man's well-being.

That we may hold fast to this essential feeling for parks, let us review the definition of parks that Olmsted suggested in the late nineteenth century:

Whatever the various meanings of the word, park,—to the cottager of Chaucer's time watching the deer over the paling of the manor

280

woods, to the courtier of Louis XIV philandering through the broad allees at Versailles, to Mr. Humphrey Repton and Prince von Puckler-Muskau, to the East side urchin of today grasping his chance for play in Seward Park,—it always suggests to us some kind of green open space with turf and trees.

The common people's right to open space, natural landscape, and common ground for social intercourse is centuries old and, in principle, recognized by royalty and later by republican governments.

King Phillip, in his Royal Ordinances of 1573, concerning the laying out of new towns in the New World, decreed, "a common shall be assigned to each new town." A similar mandate governed the English colonies: Philadelphia, Penna.; Savannah, Georgia; many New England towns had commons and squares, some in quite generous numbers and acreages.

The early nineteenth century saw the royal parks of London opened to the public which appeared to them more as a right than as a generous act of kings and queens. Government committees decried the loss of open space in towns caused by urban growth and population density and one such committee declared it a duty of government to make adequate provision for "public walks and open spaces" to "conduce to the comfort, health and content" of the working class in particular.

In advocating a central park for New York, William Cullen Bryant wrote during a visit to London . . . "your sultry summers and the corrupt atmosphere generated in hot crowded streets makes it cause of regret that . . . no preparation was made . . . for a range of parks and public gardens . . . for the refreshment and recreation of the city during the torrid heat of the warm season."

In 1851 A. J. Downing was advocating at least 500 acres for "broad reaches of parks and beauty of green fields, the perfume and freshness of nature . . . lovely lakes and limpid water heightening the charm of the sylvan accessories by the finest natural contrast . . . forget the rattle of pavements and glare of brick walls . . . quiet and secluded walks . . . hold converse with whispering trees . . ." etc., etc.

Mayor Kingsland, in the same year, reported, "Establishment of such a park would prove a lasting monument to the wisdom, sagacity, and forethought of its founders and would secure the gratitude of thousands yet unborn, for the blessings of pure air, and the opportunity of innocent healthful enjoyment."

New York's struggle to get Central Park established was but the beginning of a contagious movement that affected many American cities in the last half of the nineteenth century. In the *Minneapolis Tribune* of May 23, 1880 (the Minneapolis Park Board was established in 1883), an editorial by John P. Rea speaks of ". . . pleasure ground. An open, ample breathing space for people . . . people can congregate on festal occasions . . . open air assemblies ... music, orators, fireworks ... with green turf under foot, with arching branches overhead, and Heaven's high dome for all to come together in a free communion of cheerfulness and good humor essential to the health as well as the happiness of thickly settled communities," and so on.

What was said and written, effusive as it was, in New York and Minneapolis were not isolated examples. These effusive expressions were typical of park demand in American cities in general, the bubbling over of a countrywide, if not worldwide public concern for a better and more tolerable human environment for city people. As Olmsted put it, "The park movement was not the result of any new invention, fad or fashion, nor did it originate in any one country ... but a common spontaneous movement of that sort which are conveniently referred to as the 'genius of Civilization' "; the expression of a human need ever inherent in man himself.

In all the literature concerning the so-called park movement of the last century, no reference was made to the placing of a monetary value on parks. True, some references were made to certain use-values, and to benefits to property values of nearby real estate, but economic values were not suggested. The reason for parks was social—social amenities as inherent rights in the welfare of man. Today this is still the most basic, the most potent reason for park establishment.

In the late twentieth century, a hundred years after the great park movement, a materialistic society does not respond to the evangelistic rhetoric of an all but forgotten era (perhaps we lack the inspired evangelists, too), and demands economic measurement of all things that are to be paid from taxes. Others tend to weigh the value of national park or forest land against the value of, for example, river development for power development, flood control, navigation, water supply; the latter can be measured in dollars and cents, the former cannot. Priorities, competition for space and quality of environment, coupled with questions of natural resource development, seem to make the valuation of parks in economic terms all but imperative.

Such being the case, public officials and scholars alike have explored the possibility that if social values in total cannot be monetarilly measured, some aspects might yield useful clues to continued research. Efforts in that direction include approaches such as these:

Can emotional response to a view be perceived? Yes.

Can the degree of response be measured? Not in a manner susceptible of calibration.

Why not? For one thing, fatigue, caused by seeing one view for a long time, sets in and response lags—something like "familiarity breeds contempt."

Can response to various attributes of a landscape be detected? Yes, but again the response cannot be quantified.

Such attempts seem to get no farther along the road to solution than appeared to be the case a number of years ago when it was reported the National Park Service inquired of a dozen or fifteen prominent economists if the social value of national parks could be evaluated. The answer was a unanimous, NO!

Although there remain a few economists who believe social values may yet be approximated, I for one, have given up all hope. As complicated, nebulous, and emotional as the social values of parks are, they are the ones that characterize parks and upon them must rest the justification of parks of all description.

However, other facets of park value come into play in varied situations and at such times are of very practical importance.

PARK VALUES THAT ENHANCE VALUES OF NEARBY REAL ESTATE

Five years after New York's Central Park was first acquired, it was found desirable to enlarge the park by the addition of 65 acres to the north. The appraised value of this addition at the time of the original park acquisition was $183,850, but in 1859 the Commission had to pay the then appraised value of $1,179,590—a more than sixfold increase in less than five years due to a number of factors, one of the most important of which was the success of the original park.

Many decades later (in the early 1920s), Westchester County (New York) established its famous parkway system, much of which was along the rivers running through the county southward to Long Island Sound. The Parkway Commissioners reported the spectacular rise in county real estate values each year during acquisition and construction periods and took credit for much of that land value increment. Many other park departments have had similar experiences over the years.

Two fundamental questions arise as to financing park projects in view of such special benefits: (1) excess condemnation and (2) special assessment against specially benefited property.

The theory of excess condemnation is that the increased value of surrounding land created by a public improvement, such as a park or parkway, should belong to the public and not to the adjacent private property owner. Therefore, it is proper to acquire more land than is currently needed so that in the subsequent sale of the excess land, the public may retain the added values due to the rise in price caused by the public improvement.

The principle may be sound but the machinery to implement the theory has not yet been perfected. Well-financed private development companies can apply the theory in the establishment of a variety of enterprises—golf courses, marinas, shopping districts, whole communities, and new cities. The excess property in these cases of private enterprise is not acquired by a public agency by excess condemnation, but by a private entrepreneur in direct negotiation. Nevertheless the excess land is bought for prices lower than would be the case if purchased after the development has taken place. The development and sale of the excess land are under the complete control of the entrepreneur and the profits are his.

But a public body, particularly a city, and even more specifically, a park department, is subject to the powers granted by the state legislature and state legislatures are not often willing to grant powers of general real estate operation to municipalities. Even if they were willing to do so (and it has been done) it is doubtful that eminent domain proceedings for the taking of land for other than governmental purposes would be legal. Aside from the questionable legality of excess condemnation, the process is bound to endow public bodies and public officials with undue power of manipulation not countenanced by a skeptical and often conventionally minded public. The theory may be logical but not good for public bodies and hence not used.

Financing by special assessment against specially benefited property is an altogether different and wholly legal matter. Within the meaning of the law, property is specially benefited when the proposed improvement would increase the value of the land, relieve it of some financial burden, or make it adaptable to some purpose which increases its value.

The use of special assessment laws for the financing of park acquisition and improvement are of long standing. New York City evidently had that right when Central Park was acquired; a portion of the cost was assessed against benefited property. Minneapolis had that right written into the original park enabling act of 1883 and a special law locally known as the Elwell Law passed in 1911 was the principal tool used in the acquisition and improvement of the numerous neighborhood parks established since then. Both Minneapolis and Milwaukee County used special assessment laws to finance part of their parkway systems. Considering the almost universal practice of financing, in whole or in part, many other public works—sewers, storm drains, street openings and paving, street lighting etc.—it is very likely that careful investigation would disclose that at one time or another many other cities financed parks and parkways by special assessments against benefited property.

Valid as special assessments for special benefits appear to be, the practice of financing parks by that method has declined to almost nil in the 1970s. The reason is that the circumstances and timing are seldom relevant, as the following will illustrate.

A rise in real estate values can readily take place when a park acquisition or development occurs just before nearby private property is extensively built upon, that is, before the character of the neighborhood is fixed by the construction of most of the homes. In such cases the new park has a marked influence in improving the general character of the neighborhood, justifying a higher type of development and higher values. A proposed mile square neighborhood development by a single developer can justify the establishing of a 10 acre park fully developed as his gift to the public and he can make money by doing so.

However, if the park is not acquired and developed before the neighborhood is built up and its character determined for the current generation, any new park will have very little influence in raising real estate values except in a slow, long-range process of retarding the aging process of the neighborhood. Special assessment in this case is not justified.

If one neighborhood has been assessed for its park, the park commission is inclined to treat all other neighborhoods the same way regardless of whether real benefits can be realized or not. The special assessment procedure if applied improperly, even though uniformly, becomes inequitable and causes the public to reject all special assessment procedures. Proper timing is essential to success and equity.

Most cities have now passed their development stages except in the suburbs, and so the application of special assessment procedures in the central cities finds very few present-day advocates.

The creation of whole new cities is quite another matter. Here, a single entrepreneur builds or controls the building of the whole city. Any special benefit arising out of the placement or development of any park land, or other public utility, is part of the income and expense statement of the whole undertaking. Private citizen involvement is absent and its effect may be considered as being reflected in the salability of the individual properties.

One would imagine that in new undeveloped areas, say in cases of county park acquisition, the special assessment idea would be applicable. Here, a different factor looms up: the loss of relatively large areas from the real estate tax rolls has a bad effect on the local real estate tax base. How much private property is left to pay for the upkeep of county roads after land has been taken for parks? Parks may not be wanted at all, so to mention special assessments against so-called benefited property is to add insult to injury. To make the park establishment more palatable, the acquiring body may make some payment to the local government in lieu of taxes for a period of three or five years.

Here, again, the question of benefits is a matter of timing. When parks are acquired long before nearby real estate is developed, they create a benefit, but it is a long-range benefit. The park may help bring the adjacent property into the market and then create a marked benefit, but its immediate benefit may be nil. If special assessments could be delayed until the propitious moment, and owners could understand the apparent "delayed action," special assessments might find favor. But not otherwise.

So, in concluding this section on park values it can be stated that parks do tend to raise real estate values of nearby property as has been proven in recent research projects, but the capturing of some of that real estate enhancement of specially benefited property by the public agencies is a matter of nice timing and favorable land ownership. Research at Texas Tech University indicates that over the "long pull," there seems to be a universal rise in property values due to the effect of parks even after many years have elapsed since the particular park was established.

ECONOMIC VALUES GENERATED BY USE

Economists frequently measure the value of a park to a park-user by equating the user's cost of visit with something which the user has given up to visit a park, say, going to the park for a game of tennis rather than spending a like amount of time earning a known amount of money plus the cost to him of sports accessories and cost of transportation. Such a resulting value is then equated to the public's cost in providing and maintaining the tennis court. The difference (public cost less user benefit), equals net value of the park facility. The summation of all such cost-benefit items for all varieties of users over a period of a year minus costs to the public equals annual value of park facilities.

The resulting figure might be a public cost or a public benefit, depending upon frequency of use and value to user. If a park is used a great deal by people whose time is worth a great deal the park may be quite valuable, and vice-versa. All depends on use, i.e., actually setting foot on park property. The greater the use, the more valuable the park.

By this measurement, a heavily used play area, such as a neighborhood park, would be much more valuable, acre for acre, than a large city park which is much more scenic. To take the analogy further, a county, state, or national park might fare successively worse. Quite evidently something is missing, and that something is the so-called social values including those elusive values represented by satisfactions to citizens who seldom visit parks but appreciate the fact that parks are available. Those values have not been successfully measured.

Clawson and Knetsch in their *Economics of Outdoor Recreation* (Johns Hopkins Press, 1966) take exception to the notion that "social values" cannot be included in total park values: and they present an ingenious way of doing this.

As a result of inquiries to users they determine how many are willing to pay $5.00 per visit to a state park, how many will pay only $4.00, how many will part with only $3.00 per visit, how many $2.00, and how many will not pay more than $1.00. By plotting numbers of visitors against dollars per visit, a curve results which is likely to be zero at maximum cost and quite large at minimum cost.

Illustrating this method on a hypothetical case for which illustrations were given, the authors are quoted on page 218: "The first 100 visits were valued by those who made them at from $5 to $4, giving a value for these visits of 100 times $4.50 or $450. Another 100 were valued at between $4 and $3 for $350; 500 at between $3 and $2 for $1,250; 500 at between $2 and $1 for $750; and the remaining 1,500 were valued at less than $1 for $750. The sum of these values is $3,550, which is taken to be the appropriate measure of the economic value of the recreation opportunities provided in this hypothetical situation.

Of course, certain adjustments of this gross theoretical income should be made (cost of providing the facility, attributes of management etc.) which for the moment are beside the point, which here is to acknowledge that presumably users in their valuation of a visit to the facility have taken into consideration social as well as other values. Our question is, have they really taken all social values into consideration in their valuations per visit? If use is the only measure of value, what do we do about such vast unique areas which are rarely or almost never stepped on or even seen by man—uniquely beautiful scenery, remote mountain vastnesses, wild rivers etc.—sort of stand-by recreation resources?

Other than user values are discussed by Clawson and Knetch, such as the economic impact on local economy in the vicinity of county, state, and federal park holdings. The method has been often used; roughly it consists of placing values on moneys spent by park users for supplies and services purchased locally as a result of the visit. In a remote way, this is analogous to measuring the impact on real estate in the vicinity of a park.

Various public agencies such as Army Engineers and Reclamation Service have placed values on visits of, for example, fishermen, boaters and others to obtain recreation values to add to economic values for justification of a given project. It has often been an accepted procedure, but only in the absence of more exact evaluations. Regardless of the method used, all measures of economic value fall short of true value because they are based upon use—a use that involves physical contact with the ground. The value of just seeing a park, partaking of the attributes of smell of horticultural plantings and their worth as sound barriers, windbreaks, air purifiers, the comforting feeling of merely knowing parks are available even if seldom visited and the effect of parks on civic pride and prestige—these are matters which are outside the scope of economic evaluation. Seldom, therefore, do economic values help much in the settlement of priorities between parks, and highways, river development, power plants, airports and such other economic-measurable installations.

VALUES THAT ARE THE RESULT OF BUYING AND SELLING

Perhaps the closest thing to real value of a piece of park land emanates from the process of buying and selling—the marketplace. It, too, has its inconclusive aspects as to price as was discussed in an article by the author published in the January 1968 issue of *Parks and Recreation*, and here reviewed.

The determination of price, sooner, or later, enlists the aid of real estate appraisals. In direct negotiation it is the basis for the actual beginning of the negotiation; in condemnation proceedings it is the evidence of value given by an expert. Considering its importance, it is proper to examine appraisals for their real meaning—their strengths, their weaknesses, and why they do not actually settle the matter of price.

Definitions can be brief or lengthy, depending on which authority is quoted, but, in effect, all mean that a real estate appraisal is the appraiser's estimate of a price that would be agreed to by a willing seller and a willing buyer, each thoroughly familiar with all pertinent attributes of the land in question and allowing a reasonable time for buyer and seller to locate each other. Methods usually considered in making the appraisal include: (1) a capitalization of the income from rental or use of the property, and (2) comparision with recent actual sales of similar property in the general vicinity of the property being appraised. Other methods may be used in some cases but the foregoing are the most usual. In all cases the highest and best use of the property in question is considered regardless of its present use.

Terms of values often encountered include: replacement value, speculative value, sentimental value, and separation value.

Owners of property being acquired often feel they should be paid enough to permit them to relocate in as good a situation as they presently enjoy regardless of the appraisal. Such a claim is made only if the appraisal is below the owner's expectation. Juries in condemnation proceedings are often inclined to consider this a legitimate claim; and cities often argue the same way when parks are invaded by highways.

In theory, speculation value is not to be given any credence in either appraisals or as evidence of value in condemnation proceedings, but frequently, if not as a general practice, some value of this sort creeps into most appraisals.

Sentimental value is often rewarded in condemnation cases by sympathetic commissioners and appeal juries.

Acquisitions which divide an owner's property into two or more units or which reduce the acreage in such a way as to limit or eliminate the remainder from being used as an operating unit are always considered in the valuation.

In some states (e.g., Minnesota) the highest and best use of the property includes the use for which the land is being acquired by the public agency. As far as the author has been able to learn, no real estate appraisal takes this value into consideration, but a knowledgeable lawyer will usually bring this out in condemnation cases. If land is being taken for a park, its value for that purpose can well be far above its otherwise highest and best use (farm, residential development, industrial or commercial site) and this value will not have been appraised. Land valued as a park (or other recreation resource) is worth what a park authority thinks it is and is willing to pay. (More about this later.)

Note that the appraisal assumes a willing buyer and a willing seller. In park acquisition cases the seller is more often unwilling than willing. If his unwillingness is not frivolous, but is justified because of his peculiar circumstances, his claim to a higher price to compensate for his hardship may be justified, even as compared to a seller of similar property who, because of his peculiar circumstances, is happy to sell. Although the validity of the appraisal is upset by the presence of an unwilling seller, too often it is assumed that it does not apply because the unwillingness is unjustified. It may not be so.

In direct negotiations between a park district and private owners, one or more appraisals may be obtained as a basis for the beginning of negotiations. Offers and counter offers may result in a price agreement considerably above the appraisal but still below what the park district considers the property to be worth for park purposes. Purchases made at prices above the appraisal may attribute questionable motives to the district commissioners because of the general belief that the appraised value is a true indication of what the maximum price should be. This administrative dilemma requires some finesse on the part of the Park District if it is to escape without adverse publicity.

Another problem occurs when federal aid through BOR, HUD, or another agency is involved. It is very probable that the federal agency will not participate in the financing of any part of a negotiated price higher than the highest of several appraisals. In other words, the federal agency either does not recognize that social values are a part of actual value when the purpose of the acquisition is for recreation, or it refuses to help to pay for that value. On the other hand, HUD, which has had long experience with urban redevelopment, recognizes costs of displacement of property owners, over and above the appraised values.

The only alternative that local park authorities have to modify or escape the above limitations is to use their power of eminent domain. This alternative obviates public criticism but eliminates much of the flexibility of dealing with individual situations. Retaining public goodwill during the condemnation proceedings is far more difficult than it is in direct negotiations where adjustments can be made for time of occupation, life tenure, extending time of payment over years for tax advantage to sellers, and numerous other possible settlements. Moreover, condemnation does not result in escaping the effect of the social value factor because, in one guise or another, evidence of this value will be introduced and will usually be given consideration.

Condemnation has some very useful purposes besides being a positive, inexorable way of obtaining title. It is useful in clearing an otherwise cloudy title to the land, in bringing together heirs and claimants who could not voluntarily agree on price, in obtaining clear title from a recalcitrant, stubborn landowner, and it is a very useful tool to bring owners to a reasonable price conclusion in direct negotiation cases. Condemnation proceedings are slow and expensive to both parties. Threat of proceedings facilitates price negotiations.

Inasmuch as condemnation often results in strained relationships and is resented by owners whose property is being taken, the power of eminent domain may be denied the acquiring agency because of the political power of the landowners.

Land acquisition for park and recreation purposes is not free from the effect of the law of supply and demand. Once land is designated to be acquired for park and recreation purposes, a new and additional value (other than its otherwise highest and best use) has been placed upon every parcel within the future park's boundaries. A new class of buyer, a new use, has come to the marketplace. Every landowner instinctively knows that the new buyer is prepared to pay more for the land than its present or otherwise potential use warrants. Call this new element demand, or social value behind the demand, or call this situation a hopeful sign of the presence of a "sucker" buyer, or an intelligent realization of a higher and better use, the hard fact remains that the demand price has risen. The gap between what a real estate appraisal is, and what the park district considers the land to be worth as a park, has widened.

Experience has shown that the acquiring agency can settle for a lower negotiated price for the first parcel of a large number, than for the last parcel. Why not? The first is one of many; the last is one of only one. Scarcity has increased the relative value of the last. A smart property owner, holding out to the last, is likely to get close to what the park district believes the land to be worth as a park—and this can be far above its appraised value as those appraisals are made today. Perhaps a nice question to raise is this: The Constitution says that no one shall be deprived of his property without due process of law and just compensation. If *just* compensation is the value of the highest and best use of his property, should not all owners be entitled to the value of their land valued as park land? Exactly what is that value?

THE TAXPAYER'S EVALUATION

The general public manifests its relative value of parks and recreation vis-à-vis other governmental services by the amount of its tax support. This turns out to be a difficult figure to obtain, not that such figures are not published, at least in part, but because the data on which such figures are based are not comparable, are not carefully determined, and often are misinterpreted.

For example, in the August 1971 issue of *Parks and Recreation* the National Recreation and Park Association reported these statistics:

1960–1970
PER CAPITA OPERATING
EXPENDITURES FOR PARKS AND
RECREATION IN 11 SELECTED CITIES

City	1960	1965	1968	1970
New York	$4.22	$ 6.48	$ 6.19	$ 6.92
Chicago	7.57	8.97	11.72	13.79
Los Angeles	4.78	5.67	4.77	8.72
San Antonio	1.72	2.56	2.83	4.98
St. Louis	4.82	5.57	5.85	8.44
Atlanta	3.67	4.76	9.11	9.85
Minneapolis	7.14	6.17	9.09	14.70
Nashville	5.09	4.50	4.52	5.95
Oakland	8.59	9.87	13.21	16.73
Dayton	5.70	7.15	8.90	12.73
Peoria	8.63	10.63	14.69	17.78
11 City Average	5.63	6.58	8.26	10.96

Questions unanswered include:
1. Does "Operating Expenditures" include capital expenditure as well as current operating and maintenance expenditure?
2. What parts of these expenditures result from taxes, and how much from net profit of revenue-producing activities?

3. Do expenditures include gross expenditures of goods resold at retail.

4. Are these figures truly comparable city for city?

5. How much state and federal subsidy should be added to arrive at full cost?

The above, of course, are not compared to what expenditures (or tax support) are made by other tax-supported departments.

If these missing facts were known and ambiguities clarified, some further research would be necessary to allocate values to individual parks.

In sum total any definite, significant, or useful valuation of a park seems unlikely from this source.

CONCLUSION

The elements of park values, each important alone or in combination, at various times and under varying circumstances, include social values, real estate value enhancement, market appraisals, taxpayer opinions and support, political environment, money resources, availability for consolidation in suitable acreages, and others.

In the final analysis, the value of a park is what the governing park agency thinks it is and is willing and able to pay for it. This is not much different than saying that a rare work of art is worth what a buyer thinks it is and is willing to pay for it. It's not a very precise method of pricing perhaps, but no more precise way has been found.

To purchase a park within the amount the park agency is willing and able to pay, or to raise money to come within the limitation set, all the elements of park value previously discussed may be resorted to. This has been the purpose of this discussion.

A Position Paper on Higher Education in Recreation

by Louis F. Twardzik*

I. INTRODUCTION

There are forces at work today creating new life styles, environments and taxonomies of people and their aspirations. The rate of change is in itself cause for concern but it is the substance of change that continues to be the primary condition to which man must still address himself and ultimately measure himself.

Within this context, the university, in preparing man and society for today and the future, continues to father and husband the knowledge that creates these forces. The extent to which the university succeeds in effectively channeling those forces into knowledge and the process of educating the young to utilize it, will largely determine the future quality of human life.

Much of this effort will need to be concentrated in exploring the elements that make up man's idea of a quality life beyond his subsistence level. Increasingly today, man calls this his recreation.

A NEW LIFE STYLE

Emerging from this mix of change is the realization that the better life for all men is at hand. It is not only possible now for all people to lead a life beyond subsistence and poverty levels, but because of the enlarged power of those who do not, it becomes a social imperative, economically as well as morally, for all men to have real opportunities to attain a fuller life. Man's search for the better life has been historically associated with leisure. The great value that men placed on leisure was not based exclusively on the availability of alternatives for the use of their time, but also because leisure represented a victory of man over man, his environment, or of man over other living things in which the vanquished was the exploited or the trained performed for the stronger, the avaricious, or the wiser. Leisure was never given, it was won. As man progressed in his organization of social and communal life, leisure became inheritable. In the twentieth century tech-

*Professor and Chairman, Department of Park and Recreation Resources, Michigan State University, East Lansing. Presented at the National Recreation and Park Congress, Chicago, September 13, 1969.

nological innovations created social conditions that made leisure (including enforced leisure) available without the need for muscle, wisdom, or lineage.

The beginnings of the twenty-first century reveal that man will be born with leisure, not as an inalienable right but because he will live his life in the relative absence of work. There is reason to believe that the term "work" will lose its historic meaning and that men will not be required to sacrifice themselves or to expend energy in productive activities that hold no satisfaction. This is not to say that men will not be required to produce in order to sustain themselves; rather the method of production, its environment, and the end product will be sources of satisfaction and enrichment. In the face of nations achieving economic self-sufficiency and in the absence of the need to engage in activities that are not self-satisfying, the use of the term "work" will either gradually fade out of use or its meaning will be transferred into a new term describing the activities of nonhumans. Machines will perform the tasks that do not provide satisfactions to man.

It would seem to follow, then, that the term "leisure" will also change. In its most popular quantitative usage it is a portion of time, discretionary time free of any requirements. Leisure for the masses is, therefore, largely dependent on work. It is often the result of exceptional or accumulated work. It seems reasonable, then, to predict that leisure will follow work as an outdated term.

The evolution of social performance is similar to that of animal life in that the new activities and their responses gradually emerge over time and the most effective and efficient survive. Although we might be hard pressed to follow this idea of a gradual rate of change in view of the rapidity with which modern technology develops, we are obviously in the midst of a unique social revolution. That being so, we should be able to identify, at least, what is evolving as a replacement of work and leisure.

Within the vast range of human activity that provides man a satisfying response, regardless of motivation or location or the time in which it takes place, during work or leisure, as long as the activity enriches the psyche, the spirit, or the body of man within an ethical and socially acceptable framework, that activity is recreation.

Undoubtedly, a hierarchy of recreation values will evolve in conjunction with the conceptual evolution.

It is suggested that recreation will ultimately supersede work and leisure as a way of life in this evolution. Because of the vast, complex forces of change now active, Re-created Man will evolve, quite naturally, from the same strain that developed the Industrial Man, and most recently, the Technological Man. The Re-created Man will concentrate his energies on achieving a quality life in a quality environment. It seems therefore, that we are approaching that state of human achievement promised by God and described by the ancient Greeks.

THE CHALLENGED UNIVERSITY*

The function of the university has been explored, to one degree or another, by many of the great minds and great men of Western civilization. As one of man's greatest achievements the university has for centuries withstood his ravages and rages, within and without. Today, the university is being asked to address itself to another challenge: an explosive demand for education in recreation. The challenge, quite typically, is in the subtleties; the leisure-work, natural beauty, lack-of-space syndrome is too simplistic, dealing as it does mainly with effects. To more accurately identify the challenge requires, instead, a thoughtful inquiry into the nature of recreation.

The much heralded explosion of recreation therefore is not limited to the present or projected demand for the use of resources or the environment. Rather, it includes whether the university will recognize the significance of recreation to the present and future course of man, provide the necessary theory, research, and knowledge and then the adequately educated professional practitioners, teachers, and scientists who themselves will be competent to accept the challenge.

The modern university labors between extreme positions. The one holds that it should provide a liberal education which is considered to be a way of looking at things, an education that frees the mind. The other calls for the studies of measurement to free man from physical labor. Cardinal Newman believed that a liberal education should be the process

> by which the intellect instead of being formed or sacrificed to some particular or accidental purpose, some specific trade or profession, or study of science, is disciplined for its own sake, for the perception of its own proper object, for its own highest culture. . . .[1]

While accepting the need for other interests to be represented at the university, Newman strongly maintained that the highest, and most worthy, object of the university is to be found in studying the classics.

Even though most thoughtful people today recognize the value of a liberal education, the challenge to a classical university education is most notable in the acceptance of technical works and vocational education as a

---

*Much of this section has been excerpted from the author's paper, "Education for the Outdoor Recreation Explosion," presented at the American Association for the Advancement of Science annual meeting, December 28, 1967, New York City.

[1] Newman, John Henry Cardinal, *On the Scope and Nature of a University Education* (New York, B. T. Dutton and Co., 1915).

university responsibility. President Horn of Rhode Island University notes that:

> Only a person oblivious of the facts of modern life would doubt the need of vocational education today. Specialization, which is just as much vocational education when it is designed to produce a nuclear physicist as it is when designed to produce a pharmacist or dietician, is the key not only to our material and technological progress, but also to our survival in a divided world.[2]

But as is often the case where divergent views are involved, a middle ground begins to emerge. Much of it is reflected in the views of Alfred North Whitehead. In *The Aims of Education*,[3] he states that

> There can be no adequate technical education which is not liberal, and no liberal education which is not technical; that is, there is no education which does not impart both technique and intellectual vision.

He classified the roads to culture as being literary, technical, and scientific. Whitehead believed that whichever of these three courses a student selects it should give him "a technique, a science, and an assortment of general ideas and aesthetic appreciation and each of these sides of his training should be illuminated by the others."

Some universities did pay attention to social needs and then developed curricula accordingly. This was recognized by Horn when he wrote,

> A liberal education today was unknown three hundred years ago when Harvard College was founded, let alone two thousand years ago. Each accretion to the liberal arts curricula has had to fight for acceptance against the bitterest opposition. The objection today to vocational courses—to business, journalism, education, for example—was parallel to yesterday by objection to the study of Greek, chemistry, and international relations.[4]

Passage of the Morrill Act of 1872 successfully challenged the idea of universities as being places of contemplation with no concern for the needs of society. The Land-Grant colleges established under this Act emphasize educational opportunity, as opposed to the many private academic institutions which catered to a limited clientele of aristocracy and intellectuals. This democratic concept of education so permeated the idea of a university that all educational institutions have been affected. Bonnen states it more explicitly:

---

[2] Horn, Francis H., "Liberal Education Re-examined," *Harvard Educational Review*, Fall, 1956.

[3] Whitehead, Alfred North, *The Aims of Education and Other Essays* (New York: Macmillan and Co., 1929).

[4] Horn, *op. cit.*

The overpowering fact of higher education today is that society had ceased to treat the university's output as a consumption good and now insists that much of its activities in teaching, research and service is a production good and *should be available to the whole of society*.[5]

If, then, a university education is one that imparts "both technique and intellectual vision," does the study of recreation constitute the basis of an acceptable profession? If recreation can fill this role and if the statement that in the future "man will concentrate his energies on achieving a quality of life in a quality environment" is accepted, clearly then the study of recreation is both technique and intellectual vision—a sound basis for a university education.

A profession is recognized as such if it contributes effectively to social needs. It exists, and is perpetuated in turn, if it is built on appropriate and systematic knowledge that permits a continuity of its effectiveness. The future of a profession of recreation will be determined by the ability of the university to provide appropriate and systematic knowledge. The present development of the profession has been achieved because those who are now employed as professionals in recreation career situations have contributed to efforts that are generally recognized and approved by society. The next question is not can the professional study of recreation continue to exist in the university but can it be established as a separate field of study and then create its own specializations, or will it be itself a specialization of the traditional fields of Forestry, Education, Fisheries and Wildlife, Physical Education, Public Administration, Sociology, or Landscape Architecture? Only the universities can provide the answer.

The criteria of establishing systematic knowledge, with its roots in research, can be easily satisfied because of the existing quantity and quality of research that continues to increase and improve. Except for the institutional problems of coordination, adequate research will continue to take place in a variety of univeristy settings. The institutional setting for research is therefore not a critical factor in determining the future status of the recreation profession because research in recreation will continue regardless of whether recreation exists as a profession or as a branch of a variety of professions. Instead, the critical decision is whether the university will gear itself within existing knowledge to begin the job of providing a philosophical and theoretical base for recreation. From this base, all professional education for future practitioners, teachers, and scientists within the various branches of study and professionalism in recreation may logically flow. It is in this way that the questions about education in recreation will be resolved.

[5] Bonnen, James T., "The Agricultural Economist's Role In The Changing Research and Educational Establishment," Western Farm Economics Association annual meeting, July 19, 1967, Las Cruces, New Mexico.

Outdoor recreation as part of an academic area of study has a rational relationship only when related to an acceptable philosophical and theoretical base. Outdoor recreation can no more contribute meaningfully to knowledge, and service, if based exclusively on natural resource fields, than can the economics of recreation if it fails to incorporate consideration of preferences. This comparison is equally applicable in a growing list of specialties in the profession of recreation.

Recreation as a major field of study, based on adequate theory and research, will naturally expand into a wide range of specialized areas. These now include outdoor recreation, environmental perception, park and recreation administration, recreation resource development, and therapeutic and geriatric recreation. Others will be added as social and professional needs are identified and then systematically built on a common foundation. Strong support will, however, be needed from the basic disciplines. There must be a close relationship between recreation and the basic disciplines if recreation is to justify its place in the university. The recreation explosion is too strong and fast moving to accommodate techniques as a field of study for very long, even if the university is temporarily misled into participating.

How to construct the institutional structure necessary to achieve those goals of higher education is another matter, deserving study in itself with only a few observations here. There seems to be a prevailing assumption that all interdisciplinary or decentralized arrangements naturally have good qualities. This is erroneous. The one inherent, good quality is in the resulting process of cooperation. Other than that, these arrangements may have negative qualities resulting from their use, or misuse, as a means of avoiding responsibility and decisions. Interdisciplinary arrangements may be used by individuals and groups as a way of isolating or scattering a threatening agent or force by assuring that it will not have the necessary opportunity to become visible or consequential. By keeping the agent scattered, the members of the interdisciplinary group grow themselves by draining energy from the agent, the agent being the field of recreation.

Interdisciplinary arrangements often serve best as short-term, temporary research and development efforts.

It would therefore seem that if recreation is to develop as a significant body of knowledge and become increasingly useful as a profession, the idea of spreading its component areas of study and research into a wide array of other field and academic disciplines wherein it loses its thrust and identity as a separate field of study should be reversed. In order for recreation to become a viable and identifiable field, an applied field, of study and research, it must draw upon the basic disciplines, biological, physical, and social sciences and the humanities, as the basis for its own unique set of philosophical precepts and theory.

THE PROFESSION OF RECREATION

The concept that there should be special efforts to supply the masses with recreation opportunities is new to the nineteenth century. Up until then recreation opportunities were found by the lower social and economic groups according to their ability to earn the time and pay the costs. The least costly often took place in the home and directly reflected on the quality of family life. At the other end of the socioeconomic continuum were those who paid others to amuse them.

Even though land ownership patterns shifted and changed and communal life developed more intensely, values based on religious beliefs, and buttressed by necessities of survival, held human aspirations for a joyful life in check with only periodic surcease provided during holidays.

Eventually, those who amassed large blocks of leisure and space and others who satiated their desires for conspicuous consumption of the amenities, began to share their fortune by making their estates available to the public for recreation purposes on certain days. This sharing of personal economic gains for public recreation use was followed by a variety of innovative arrangements including communal plazas, gardens, then public parks and then specialized places for children, who always had more time for recreation. Man's suppressed desire for the amenities of life began to surface and in absence of private means, public places were established in the form of national, state and local parks, recreation centers, swimming pools, ball fields, zoos, marinas and other specialized recreation areas and facilities.

It followed that the original caretakers of recreation places and the volunteers who supervised children at play, would be the nucleus for a public bureaucracy required to develop and maintain the places and programs for recreation. The largest such group consisted of those employed as recreation and park workers by local units of government. They are followed in number by state and federal agencies. A significant segment of the recreation bureaucracy can be considered quasi-public, those performing an important community function but under private charter or auspices. These agencies range from Scouts to the Y's. While much of the work of the voluntary agencies is related to youth, the public bureaucracy of recreation continues to divide itself into more specialized elements including therapeutic recreation, geriatric recreation, armed services recreation and others.

Since their inception, the professionals in recreation services were plagued with a singular inability to maximize their effectiveness through joint effort at a national level because of the variety of organizations representing them. In 1966, however, an amalgamation of five national organizations created the National Recreation and Park Association. The NRPA is headquartered in Arlington, Va., and staffs five regional offices throughout the country. Possibly the most unique and effective characteristic of this national organization is that it joins the resources of both lay people and professionals in a common cause. Although it apparently has the necessary organizational structure, NRPA has not yet developed a central theme cohesive enough to draw all specialists into a single professional consciousness, much less to envision recreation as the primary motivation in a search for a quality of life in a quality environment. In this respect, NRPA and the universities are much alike.

II. A POSITION FOR HIGHER EDUCATION IN RECREATION

The American universities and colleges have not full met their self-appointed obligations to society to discover and disseminate truth and knowledge. This failure is equally pronounced in their dualistic responsibilities as providers of liberal and technical education. It is most noticeable in recent campus reaction by both students and faculty and also by continued irrational and illogical social policy dominated by paradoxes: agricultural land banks and hungry people, air-conditioned automobiles and polluted environments.

To the end that the universities and colleges will recognize the importance of recreation as a basic human need and therefore a function and responsibility of society, in an effort to fulfill part of their obligations, the following position statements are submitted.

A. General Education

The fulfillment of an individual as an educated person, capable of contributing to society as well as to his professional interests, should be the major tenet of recreation education at the university and college levels.

B. Relationship to the Basic Disciplines and Applied Fields

It should be recognized that recreation is now, and will be in the foreseeable future, an applied field of study. As such its theories and concepts and research methodologies, to be of value, should be founded in the basic disciplines. The empiricism of the practitioner is no longer a proper basis for the study of recreation although necessary to its validity.

Professional education in recreation is often administered within another area of applied study, but its courses of study should not be limited to it.

C. Levels of Education

Professional education curricula are legitimate parts of the university only as they are constructed to provide a student with background in a field that has relevance to society and is grounded in the basic disciplines for application of concepts, principles, and theory.

Regardless of whether the programs are developed for undergraduate or graduate students, they should adhere to those principles of university education. Curricula with large inputs of technique courses are more properly offered in junior college terminal programs.

To follow this policy means that future recreation graduates of the university will be freed from the constraints of thinking exclusively about establishing and maintaining special places called parks or playgrounds or recreation centers and instead will begin to think, and lead society into creating and maintaining a recreation environment for individual enrichment and social good.

A program of study that addresses itself to the quality of life and the environment in which it is lived requires investigation into the contributions of all elements of society, including the private sector in recreation, especially its commercial elements. This concern should be reflected in course content and faculty involvement.

It is suggested that bachelor's and master's programs of study in recreation be developed to prepare students for careers at the administrative, policy, and decision making levels and that the junior colleges provide professional education for operational and recreation specialty levels. It is assumed that university graduates in related disciplines such as landscape architecture, physical education, horticulture, accounting, art, music, drama, geriatrics, forestry, and law would contribute their specialized talents in staff positions. The doctor's degree should be reserved for those interested in teaching and research and capable of undergoing the rigorous discipline and commitment to advanced study and research.

But regardless of the level of education, university and college programs in recreation should not be designed to equip the student mainly with those skills required at the entrance level of the profession at the expense of equipping him with a knowledge of theory and the understanding of principles upon which his future and the future of the profession will depend.

D. Internships

Professional internships or trainee programs should be based upon the concept that persons newly graduated from a university or junior college may benefit from a special program of on-the-job supervision and training.

Because of the various degrees of experience students bring to their first professional position, a mandatory period as an intern should not be expected of all new graduates. Instead, it should be the responsibility of the faculty adviser and the student to determine whether the need exists for additional training and for the length of time involved. Internships should not be for less than six months, nor more than twelve months' duration.

Faculty advisers are cautioned not to permit internships to degenerate into a cheap labor market for repetitious or routine tasks. Intern salaries should not be less than the amount recommended by the NRPA for beginning professionals.

It should be the responsibility of the Society of Park and Recreation Educators to administer a national program of professional intern training. The program should: (1) encourage agencies to provide intern training, (2) identify agency participants, and (3) recommend standards for such training.

E. Practicum

Practicum for credit during the school year should not be offered unless there are adequate supervisory faculty and meaningful professional work opportunities to assure useful experience. It is unrealistic to expect those agencies located near the institution to assure such experience for the students on a continuing basis. A point of nonchalance about the students is often reached in these agencies, quickly perceived by the students, and results in many of them leaving the field.

F. Summer Experience

A minimum of one summer of approved professional work experience should be required for graduation with a bachelor's or associate degree. Faculty should encourage agencies to provide a variety of professional work experience for the student during the summer.

If university policy requires that credit for summer professional work experience be limited to agencies within that particular state, then credit should not be required of the student. It is more important for the student to gain appropriate experience, if not available within the state, than it is to offer credit.

G. Criteria for Faculty

Qualifications of full-time departmental faculty should conform to those expected of teaching, research, and extension faculty required by other departments within the university and college.

As the intensity and complexity of knowledge related to recreation education increases, younger faculty with doctorates will replace teachers with extensive experience. To compensate for this lack of faculty on-the-job experience, qualified practitioners should be encouraged to teach appropriate professional courses and counsel students as visiting lecturers. There should be recognition that practitioners who serve as visiting lecturers contribute largely on the basis of acknowledged excellence in performance with advanced degrees being of secondary significance.

H. Faculty Exchange

While it is assumed that faculty preparing for sabbatical leave will individually arrange for teaching assignments in other institutions, there is now a pressing need for an arrangement whereby experienced faculty would be able to spend shorter periods of time lecturing at a number of universities and colleges. There is already a growing use of telephone and television for this purpose. These and other innovative arrangements to share faculty should be encouraged.

I. Student Involvement

Current unrest by students on campuses throughout the country is partially caused by their minimal involvement in departmental affairs and curriculum planning. Faculty are advised to seek students' evaluation at the end of each course by completing a university approved questionnaire. Results should be the personal property of the instructor, for his own information.

By appointing students to appropriate committees student views are more apt to be accurately represented.

Faculty have a responsibility to assist students in establishing and maintaining a student club and developing its programs. However, students should have responsibility for the affairs of the club.

J. Research Activities

Faculty teaching appointments should include provisions for continuing research. A graduate program of study has little meaning if it is not supported by qualified research faculty. Departments offering degree programs without research faculty should arrange for support in providing research oriented courses from other departments.

Graduate programs or specialties in recreation education should not be designed exclusively around the availability of research funds.

It is expected that the National Recreation and Park Association will fulfill its research mission by identifying problems and stimulating research by the universities and not by engaging in contract research itself.

When possible undergraduate students should be given the opportunity to participate in research projects.

K. Extension

The growing impact of Continuing Education and the Cooperative Extension Service's off-campus efforts attest to the need for the universities and colleges to systematically provide educational assistance throughout the states.

Departments are encouraged to provide the necessary extension specialists in recreation to make off-campus educational services more effective and when possible to establish close administrative relationships with teaching and research faculty. The appointment of extension specialists in recreation to departmental staff positions, with academic rank, is an effective way of creating such relationships.

L. Accreditation

It is assumed that relatively few of the more than 200 universities and colleges which currently offer curricula in recreation actually offer courses which could meet the systematic evaluation of an accreditation review.

Accreditation implies that recreation curricula have made their mark in the American university. There is no solid evidence to support this. Accreditation at this time would suggest a mold for standardization when courses of study and programs should instead be undergoing sweeping and continual review and evaluation and great change when necessary.

One notable phenomenon of emerging classes or institutions is a frenetic attempt to solidify new gains at the earliest possible time through legislative act or dictum. This does two things: announces to the world that the gains have been made (and by whom), and forces others to follow a similar route. Recreation education at the university level is not ready for either.

M. University and Junior College Relations

There is a continuing interest by junior colleges in establishing recreation and park curricula. It is in the mutual interest of both institutions and their students that a systematic exchange of information be established. It is strongly recommended that an annual meeting of representatives from all institutions of higher education offering recreation curricula be scheduled in each state for this purpose.

N. Admission Policies

There is a very real temptation on the part of emerging departments within universities to "over-stock" in enrollments at both undergraduate and graduate levels by extending themselves beyond faculty and physical resources. Enrollments should be limited to conform to a realistic view of available academic resources.

Faculty should exercise extra effort to assure that students represent a variety of cultures and origins, including a balance of out-of-state and foreign students.

University policy generally dictates admissions policies of under-graduates while the individual colleges and departments largely control graduate level admission policies. Because faculty in recreation are generally understaffed, and because graduate student counseling is time consuming, it is recommended that consideration be given to requiring a 3.0 (B) grade point average of a student's last two undergraduate years of course work, for admission to programs of graduate study.

O. Professional Attitudes

There are today more liberal views and policies about when and how a student may select or change his major area of study. While the student should be permitted to examine several possibilities before finally selecting a major field of study during his freshman and sophomore years, it should be noted that he does lose in the process by having limited exposure to the faculty of his major and fellow students. The rapport usually established between students and faculty and fellow students over a four year period adds much more to a student's professional perception than is possible in a two year period. There is also general recognition that in many majors throughout the university students take their degrees by merely fulfilling course requirements listed in the catalog. Faculty attitudes towards a student's professional career are generally responsible for this unfortunate situation.

There is also cause for concern over the development of professional attitudes in graduate students. As graduate programs of study become increasingly research oriented, there are fewer opportunities for students to become involved in professional affairs. Consideration should be given to developing graduate student involvement in state recreation and park societies on a continuing basis.

It is most difficult for students to develop proper professional attitudes unless individual faculty demonstrate an involvement in professional affairs outside of the university or college.

A program of student exposure to outstanding practitioners who can advise on developing professional attitudes and attributes would create a useful tie between academics and the profession.

P. The Quality of Teaching

The quality of teaching that a teacher brings to his students cannot be assured by either sanctions or administrative requirements, nor can its value be overstated. The commitment to quality teaching is entirely an individual commitment. The department however can reinforce the importance of good teaching by providing an adequate reward system.

The Administrative Process

by Charles E. Doell

For a general understanding of park and recreation administration it is helpful to consider the process as having two major functional parts. Function "A" consists of deciding which of several alternative directions should be taken in the service to be given and the priority of the steps necessary to achieve a satisfactory result—really a matter of selecting goals. It also includes marshalling the forces external to the organization needed to pursue the chosen direction to a successful conclusion.

Function "B" is the internal management of the organization's resources, designed to translate the policy goals into action. Function "A" has prescribed the course; Function "B" propels the machine. Actually, Function "A" has done a great deal in providing the means to obtain the machine and to fuel it.

The law or charter which authorized the founding of the organization and which defines its powers and limitations is usually couched in very general terms, e.g., ". . . shall have the power to devise, adopt and maintain a park and recreation system in and adjacent to . . ." some geographical area. The kind of recreation to be provided and the extent or character of the physical resources are seldom defined. The Congressional charge to the National Park Service to preserve, maintain, and make available for public enjoyment the many unique properties of the National Park system is an example on the federal level. Within the general purposes authorized by statutes and charters, many courses of action may be chosen. Here is where Function"A" becomes operative. It selects the appropriate direction.

The talents required for Function "A" are inherently personal rather than professional. Professionalism is highly desirable and enormously advantageous, but without native shrewdness, intuition, imagination and other nonprofessional attributes, professionalism loses its effectiveness in this aspect of administration. Attributes that *are* needed include, the ability to distinguish solid social trends from mere fads and fashions of the moment; the ability to *anticipate* future changes in habits and mores of the masses; the ability to cannily recognize the role that recreation as a whole will play in the lives of people and particularly what aspects thereof the public can be induced to foster by public taxation; a thorough knowledge of power and of the influence forces of the community—which includes the news media, the business community, the social organizations, the clergy, the tax-exempt foundations, the wealthy and influential individuals; an intimate knowledge of the political forces and their effect upon the government structure and operation. Such talents make possible community analysis which leads to a basis for goal selection.

At this point other talents must be available: those of the salesman and the evangelist to persuade the influential forces to act for community improvement. The stage is then set for Function "B"; but first a word about the personnel of Function "A."

The talents required for Function "A" are not often embodied in one individual. Municipal and metropolitan park and recreation systems are usually governed by some sort of commission. Even when that is not the case, the final authority is vested in the city council through one intermediary or another. State and federal departments are more often headed by a politically appointed bureaucrat who is limited in one way or another in his policy-making decisions. Professionals are involved in Function "A" usually in an advisory capacity; only occasionally do they have complete control of the entire Function. Fact is that only in some instances is the professional endowed with the personal attributes to qualify him to assume that responsibility—and the more readily he accepts the help of lay advisors the better off he is.

Function "A" should be, and usually is, a coalition of lay talent and professional talent. In what proportion the ingredients of this mix are desirable in a given situation cannot be predetermined—and therein lies the "art" rather than the "science" of administration. How well the professional works with his lay board, how well the combination chooses and maintains its goals, how well it achieves its objectives—of such is success of the administration constituted. Perhaps not entirely is this so because a breakdown in Function "B" can undermine all the good works of Function "A." This calls attention to the final chore of Function "A."

This last chore is not so visibly apparent as those that have already been described but it is one that may be likened to the frosting on the cake. It is the process of self-evaluation, an evaluation of the entire organizational operation. It is more or less a continuous operation. It requires a knowledge of the public reaction to its services which comes from the confrontation of the users with the personnel of Function "B" operations. It also comes independently from news media, public demonstrations, hearsay and gossip, all of which has to be analyzed for truth and credibility, and then interpreted for its value in establishing future policy and modifications of present operations.

Function "B" embodies all those functions that make up the day-by-day operations of a park and recreation organization. It is the visible part, the part that the public sees and whose services the public experiences. By its performance is the whole organization judged so far as the user is concerned.

The essential purpose of Function "B" is to carry out the decisions of Function "A" and to funnel back the results of that operation so as to keep the whole organization on target. This fact must not be lost sight of in the maze of internal problem-solving in the daily operations.

Function "B" is essentially a professional operation, headed by a park and recreation professional (hopefully, but other professionals may succeed if endowed with suitable executive ability), with other professionals such as those trained in recreation, engineering, maintenance of facilities, horticulture, business, law, and others usually as division heads or in supervisory positions. The remainder of the personnel are often para-professionals or craft and trade specialists. The assumption that the bottom layer consists only of the "strong back, weak mind" caliber is too general to square with the facts.

In the meetings of professionals, and in their publications, the subject matter covers the gamut of organizational structure: in-service training, how to build, maintain, and conduct, discipline, incentives, user preferences and reactions, research methods, budget control, even a smattering of goal selection. (After all, the chief administrator is an advisory element in Function "A.") So much has been aired about these subjects (and the subjects merit that attention) that this brief review of administration discussion will center on only a couple of salient points that are often difficult to achieve and sometimes hard to discern: (1) communication and (2) recognition that employees are not automatons to be governed by too restrictive a set of rules and regulations, but must have a reasonable latitude in exercising individual judgement.

The structure of park and recreation organizations is almost always a combination of the line type and the functional type. The nature of so many of the tasks includes the use of two or more professions, two or more craftsmen or other specialists. Few tasks can be performed by a single tradesman. An architect can provide the plan, a carpenter can construct, an electrician, plumber and painter can accomplish their assignments, and a horticulturist can embellish the setting, but it takes coordination to build the building in the proper sequence of tasks and to have it ready for use by the public and the management of the community center at a time when other facilities are prepared to take their place in a finished public service. Much the same kind of analogy applies to the everyday maintenance and operation of a city park anywhere, a state park or a federal park, forest, or reservoir recreation grounds.

Coordination of effort requires meaningful dialogue horizontally between functionaries as well as vertically between workers, supervisors and their superiors. It also requires communication between users and all workers who come in contact with the public and these user messages must find a path of communication upward. The path downward from Function "A" and chief administrator is an obvious one. Too often the path works only one way. To repeat—the job of the chief administrator is to mold all the resources of the organization into a single team to carry out policy. It cannot be done without a well-designed and developed communication system. Because this is such a tough and somewhat intangible assignment it is often not measured and hence is mediocre. A better effort is needed.

Efficient operation is essential for the best use of financial resources. It often is also a key to a more responsive operation. It is a difficult matter to train each employee to use his personal resources in such a way as to do the job best in the least time and with the most effective contribution to the overall objectives of the organization. To improve this situation cost analysis, supervisory instruction and in-service training programs have been introduced but they often lacked coordination between systems of separate divisions.

In recent years and in large organizations of hundreds of employees in which the opportunities for improvement seemed brightest, managers have installed a group specially trained in systems analysis. Operational systems are identified, examined for similarity, and procedures in common are put into practice. The systems usually detail the frequency with which certain functions are to be performed (e.g., number of grass mowing operations a week) and the time necessary to do the total task. Where feasible, automatic equipment is introduced to reduce manpower. Efficiency measured by amount of money spent (or saved) usually results. But, unless further investigation follows, unfortunate side effects appear.

Employees are human beings with human aspirations, as many assembly line operations in private business are discovering. They are not mere automatons responding to stereotyped instructions day in and day out without the experience having an adverse effect upon individual initiative, imagination, and job satisfaction. Innovation arising from an intimate experience with local situations becomes retarded. Frustration and even a cynical disrespect for administrative judgement can ensue. In fact, standardized instructions from a central office, without adjustment for field conditions by the man on the job, can result in some ridiculous situations—night operation of an automatic watering system during the rain is only one of numerous situations.

Systems analysis has its very excellent points but its credos must be subject to the judgement of those trained in doing a park and recreation service, however menial, as part of the organizations main goals.

Administration as a process is fraught with too many variables of expertise, personality, and native talent for anyone to presume that viewing it as two major functions will be the "open sesame" to a complete understanding of the subject. Such a viewpoint does, however, permit a clearer picture of the dual requirements of a chief administrator. His sensitive role in the selection of, adherence to, and vigorous pursuance of, the chosen goals of the organization becomes more apparent.

The professional management of the physical and personnel resources of an organization has received a great deal of attention from all angles and many sources. The role of the chief in respect to the policy-making apparatus has not been so widely discussed. It is often dismissed with the dictum, "The Board sets the policy; the executive carries it out." There is much more to it than that, but it is hard to explain.

The ideal lay and professional mix occurs when the lay commission or other lay hierarchy consists of intelligent people of wide interests, high degree of honesty and integrity, influential in business and public affairs with no personal ambition for gain (political or otherwise) because of their commission membership, and on the other hand, a professional administrator of similar personal talents except for his obvious employment as the chief professional administrator of the operating staff. He must have the restraint to act as an adviser rather than a full-fledged member of the lay group.

A less than ideal lay commission calls for a professional administrator capable of and willing to fill the deficiencies of a deteriorating commission. If the positions are reversed, the nonprofessionals on the commission begin to exercise executive authority. When the process reaches nearly a complete take-over in either case, the dominant side has lost contact with the supporting constituency; the resulting crisis calls for a new regime.

The fine line between lay leadership and professional advice is determined by experience. Schools, books, and expertise help but they are no substitutes for work on the job. Lack of practical experience is the real difference between the chief and his deputy. No matter how much professional proficiency the deputy may possess, his success as a top administrator is attained by performance in the top job.

Random Thoughts
on a Few Subjects

by Charles E. Doell

ON CHARLES PAUL KEYSER

C. P. Keyser is an old friend of mine albeit he is sixteen years older than I. His active life in the park and recreation field was at its zenith when, as a very young man, mine was just peeping above the horizon. We both were a part of the transition of the management of parks to the management of systems of parks and recreation—from a vocation that had no well-defined professional roots to a vocation that sought an identity of its own as a true profession. The generation I talk about was the first quarter of the present century—1900 to 1925. I awoke in the middle of that period at too young an age to know what it was all about at approximately the same time that Keyser did, but he was at least thirty years old. Keyser knew an awful lot more of life and the essential qualities needed for vocational survival in the public service than I did—and probably still does. At any rate, his analysis of the public, the public servants, and the social forces that both bind together and pull apart (the real sustaining fabric of a democratic society), I find intriguing, revealing, and a timeless assessment of American cities.

In his eightieth year, his fellow park executives of the Northwest Pacific area, including Canada, honored him at a dinner meeting. The following are excerpts from his written speech. It is in a colloquial language peculiar to Keyser, being a mixture of standard English, often of his own invention, laced with pioneer Western idiom. Read carefully to detect the sometimes hidden meaning.

In writing to his old friend, Will O. Doolittle, a product of his era (as the pioneer Executive Secretary of the American Institute of Park Executives Doolittle deserves a full-scale biography some day), Keyser identifies himself:

> First let us put the record straight, I was born on Friday the 13th of December 1878, and grew to manhood along with "Injuns," mustangs and other hardy denizens of the arid sagebrush country in Northwestern Nevada. Then I spent ten strenuous years rawhiding around in the vocation of a civil engineer. Who would have ever thought I would spend 40 years thereafter, to limn a career in this Green Country, engaged in the gentle arts of the field of Public Recreation?

He then makes the almost horrifying statement that . . . . "anybody with brains employed in public affairs would be an oddity." If a person had them he would "employ them in something more remunerative than in the administration of public recreation."

Times have changed as far as remuneration goes, but Keyser's reference to brains was not to the book-learning type but to something an administrator needed more—"what Solomon referred to as an understanding, together with initiative, vigilance, vision and imagination, plus a well-developed ... sense of humor, ... which are all highly developed in an administrator." Keyser continues:

Democratic government is necessarily politically selective, which means that it is a self-promoted organization primarily of and by politicians backed by a majority or a busy minority, ruling in the role of servants of the taxpaying public. In reality they manipulate for, or otherwise represent the active influences of the money-makers, the military, and the clergy, and withal contrive to engender a patriotism to provide cohesion and polity of, by and for the people.

Humanity is composed naturally of conflicting elements, fighting for peace and never satisfied. Down through the ages mankind has continued to dwell on earth, tribes to masses, surviving through a coordinating leadership in one form or another, with a control cast over the masses who either will neglect to think for themselves, or like to be beguiled by false prophets. This mass control, never complete, is the essence of government. In a democracy it resolves into more or less tranquil compromise, after so much shoving and dragging.

These individuals or groups, the politicians, who assume leadership ostensibly by consent of the governed, say what you will for them or against them, are the keepers of the national faith, the preservers of law and order, the getters of your public gifts. If they are an evil, they are a necessary evil and, as history shows in repeat, are not replaced for long by a more idealistic agency.

A politician to maintain his situation must go easy on both idealism and zeal to achieve. He is elected on a platform of issues and his main business must be issues. That would be all right if all issues to be met were clearly open or shut. A vocal minority will want its constitutional representative to take its partisan view. Another vocal minority will demand that a contrary stand be taken. Everybody will expect a piece of political pie, or a special improvement whether he plugged for it or not, and a reduction in his taxes. So the politician, who abhors counter-action, does nothing either way unless and until a more or less neutral or tranquil compromise may result. All of which is by way of leading up to the dictum that the preponderance of the body politic, that is, the rank and file of the citizenry, are passively progressive in their attitude toward civic betterment. We have mentioned the active interests. Mostly voters are normally passive. The politician knows that any measure can be successfully campaigned, and that nothing extraordinary will receive a favorable vote unless it is well campaigned.

Perhaps it would be well to spell out a few maxims pertaining to human living that might be called basic.

1. Man is a creature of the surface of the earth shepherded principally by Dame Nature.

2. While human life goes in cycles of tension and relaxation, variety will still be the flavor of living. That gives for fun and flowers.

3. God made man acquisitive and self-seeking for survival, yet everybody has a God-given natural urge to justify his existence above and beyond his baser acquisitive appetites.

4. We assume that the end or purpose of living is the true enjoyment of it, but we must recognize that the majority of the fickle public drift, and lack definite ideas of the sort of lives they may realize; and yet joy must have its own well-spring.

5. Because the pleasure of anticipation by and large exceeds the measure of gladness in the satisfaction of fulfillment, the majority of pleasure-seekers will gladly put at least as much into the pursuit of happiness as they expect to get out of it.

6. The people make the City or Community, and with a sense of proprietorship, like to take pride in belonging to it. They glory in its prosperity and enjoy its attractive or advantageous features.

7. The destiny of a City is cast in the works of its influential citizens.

8. There will ever be tides, and storms alternating with calms, and a general level of humanity that remains constant.

His own philosophy—

I take the world and my city and all that therein is and has come to pass, as I find it, and although it be a good city as cities go, I do my best to make it go better, as an abiding place for its people.

At this writing, 1973, Keyser has seen his 94th birthday. Come to think of it, John McLaren of San Francisco and Golden Gate Park fame was about that age when he made a trip to Philadelphia to a convention (can't remember the year) of the A.I.P.E. I was in the same bus as he as we toured Fairmont Parkway. He looked out the window and remarked, "Fifty years ago I recall seeing a statue of an Indian among those wooded hills. I wonder if it is still there." Two young ladies next to him remarked, "Fifty years ago!" "To me," he said "that's not such a long time ago." Then, with another look, "There's that Indian now."

Like McLaren's Indian statue, Keyser's "Indian," exemplified by the give and take of American life as he experienced it is as visible today as it was fifty years ago.

THIN THE HERD OR GET MORE PASTURE

Many times in the hundred-year history of cattle ranching, a manager has reported to his owners, or has said to himself, "When overgrazing is apparent, only two courses of action are present: thin the herd or get more pasture." He usually practiced what he preached. When thinning was reasonably profitable, he thinned; when thinning was impractical he roamed hundreds of miles from Texas to Canada for new pastures.

Park and recreation administrators are often up against the same problem of "overgrazing," except that it is called "overuse." The alternatives are the same as for the rancher; restrict the use or get more recreation land. The administrator must pursue his chosen alternative as vigorously as the rancher pursued his, for it is *the basic solution* to his problem.

Difficulty is compounded when the overuse is not discovered or recognized in its incipient stages, for after that the effectiveness of the chosen remedy reduces the chances for success. The soil has suffered from malnutrition, and erosion has progressed from rivulet size to gulch to canyon proportions; or available additional recreation land at reasonable prices has become mighty scarce. Even so, the "herd" remedy must be pursued for all it is worth even to its frustrating final impasse. At least partial success will usually be attained.

Referring back to the rancher, he was not infallible in his judgment either. He could not always tell when overgrazing was imminent until it was upon him. Then wind, rain, heat, and drought conspired to confound his judgment altogether, so that over the period of a hundred years, some ranches in the semiarid sections of the Southwest lost 80 per cent of their productivity. A similar lack of perception confronts the park and recreation administrator; but here it is more often the inability to observe the symptoms of overuse rather than the vagaries of nature that overtakes the administrator. He needs to observe more closely, to recognize what is happening, to know the principal of the herd, and to act.

For example, in that period of park history when recreation appeared on the scene as a government responsibility, it took too many cities too long a time to realize the need for more space. They tried to accommodate baseball diamonds, tennis courts, playground areas on parks designed for a less intensive use. Overuse resulted in destruction of a good park design. Those cities are still suffering from inadequate play space. The artistic and imposing design of Central Park and of the parks in Washington, D.C. and of those in many other cities is worn and tattered. The cities have waited too long to get more "pasture" and now must hope for a new era of reconstruction to remedy the situation.

The vast expanses of our great national parks and national forests have suffered overuse in only limited areas, but those areas are also the critical ones. Thinning the herd by restricting the use has been the principal solution to their problem. But that can be little more than a palliative, a sort of stalling for time, because it is difficult to lessen the population or to de-emphasize the appetite for pleasurable experiences of a people acquiring more leisure time, more mobility, and more affluence. NPS is attempting to change public habits. Time will reveal the success or failure of such experiments.

Influencing, even changing, habits of the user public is by no means a new idea. Modifying park design to more nearly conform to the habits of the user has been common practice for years. So have efforts to enforce laws and ordinances aimed at promoting constructive use of recreation property, efforts of play leaders, community center directors and, more recently, a new emphasis on guidance programs of the rangers and foresters of the NPS and Forest Service. If these efforts have appeared less than totally effective perhaps the application of these remedies needs to be stepped up commensurate with the ever-increasing density of use.

To sum up this "herd" theory:

1. Keep eyes alert for early signs of overuse and misuse.
2. At the first sign, "thin the herd or get more pasture."
3. If the situation still binds, try changing user habits by

a. investigating the design of the facility and adapting it to more closely fit the user habits.

b. more intensive education on the necessity of careful use of facilities.

c. more intensive and meaningful law enforcement programs.

If you are still stuck, you have either failed or you will raise Cain with the powers that be and stump for reform.

ON VESTED INTERESTS

Permit no private investment on public property and no use permit for exclusive use for a definite period of time, unless the original agreement specifies in detail the terms of reoccupation and possession of that investment or exclusive use at *any time* by the public agency. There should also be provisions specifying conditions of the property at the time of turnover at the expiration of the agreement. In brief, the public agency must always be in position to cancel and abrogate any permit or lease without penalty other than that provided for in the original agreement.

Such a dictum is a sound guide for a park and recreation agency in negotiating with private individuals and private and semiprivate institutions for the exclusive or even joint use of park or recreation property. As will be observed later on, some modification of this general rule may become mutually advantageous, but even in those unusual situations the rule should guide the process of negotiation. The general rule should not be neglected as apparently it has been in altogether too many situations of the past.

Some examples:

A permit was given to an individual to construct and operate a golf course on a public park with no provisions for public "take-over" except under such conditions as could be negotiated during operation, leaving the park department at such a disadvantage that the arrangement was continued for more than thirty years during which time the quality of operation was admittedly poor.

A metropolitan park agency permitted voluntary agencies of the United Way type to build and maintain buildings for its recreation uses. Only with subsequent difficulty and anguish was it possible to alter the policy and retrieve control of park property.

The National Park Service has operated its concession businesses in such a way as to be increasingly "in debt" to the lessees of hotels, camp buildings, motels, and businesses. This is now approaching a critical stage because of changing policies of administration of the parks.

The National Forest Service has previously granted long-term leases to individuals for summer homes and to various institutions for camp sites, outdoor education building sites, and private ski runs. A revision of policy is now attempting to undo the easy granting of permits in the process of attempting to recapture many of its properties. These are often close to centers of population and are needed for general public recreation purposes.

The Corps of Engineers has had some peculiar arrangements with private concessionaires as well as public agencies concerning the use of reservoir properties.

The Bureau of Land Management has its own peculiar dealings with ranchers, mining interests and others as to limitations for protection of the public interest.

In some cases of marina operations and permits to build and operate private yacht clubs, another class of peculiar arrangements becomes operative. The large marina operation of Los Angeles County involving 6,000 boat slips and hundreds of acres of land on which have been constructed apartment buildings, motels, restaurants, boat works, a "fisherman's village," shopping facilities, etc., grants 60 year leases at the termination of which everything reverts to the county. Sixty years is a long time, but the millions in private investments also represent an impressive figure. What happens in 25 or 30 years is not clear.

Strangely, public difficulties experienced over the years have occurred without one agency being aware of or learning anything from the experience of the other. Communication on this phase of operation was evidently inoperative between the city, the metropolitan districts or the different arms of the federal government. Each followed its own course and often to the disadvantage of the public.

Private enterprise and government may find situations in which public and private partnership may be of public benefit. Almost complete government ownership of potential winter sports areas (skiing in particular) attracts the winter resort entrepreneur (and the public as well) because there is no other such land available. Operation by the Forest Service somehow seems incongruous here, yet it is the only alternative to the private-public partnership if the best of skiing is to be made available.

The marina arrangement above alluded to seems a logical public-private arrangement except for a better safeguarding of the public interest as stated at the beginning of this article. Other projects of public-private participation are more and more being suggested by private developers—and more and more given the skeptical eye by environmentalists. Some projects, however, are bound to overcome objections and become feasible. In those cases attention is called to the guidelines cited at the beginning of this article.

A COMPREHENSIVE SERVICE AND AN IDENTIFIABLE PROFESSION

The vocational specialities of parks and recreation courted each other for fifty years before cohabitating in a single Park and Recreation agency. The marriage has still not been consummated. Although the two are usually consolidated in one department, the organizational structure is often such as to continue the two disciplines as two distinct divisions. Time and operational experience may modify such a structure, but operational emphasis and departmental priorities will favor one or the other depending on the training and experience of the top administration. True integration can take place only if top management is thoroughly familiar with the nature of parks (as represented by the development of natural resources to physical recreation resources and the maintenance thereof) and of recreation as being a way of life and the force motivating the creation of the physical recreation resource in the first place.

Cohabitation sans marriage is most prevalent in local park and recreation systems, but is also present in modified arrangements in state and federal departments including those involving forests, parks, game and fish, army reservoirs, and others in which physical recreation resources attract a recreation-seeking public regardless of the name of the managing agency. Except for the National Park Service and the Forest Service, and their counterparts in the states, most of the departments are so engrossed in the management of their physical recreation facilities that they are hardly aware of their cohabitors, certainly not of their attraction as marriage partners. Forest and Parks have learned of recreation as a real partner because of mass invasion of their sanctuaries, often causing considerable disruption to both properties and complacency. Courtship is intensifying; marriage is still just around the corner.

True integration in all situations is essential for top level recreation service. The public is suffering from the lack of it, practitioners are wandering about looking for an identifiable profession while universities concentrate more on fractional disciplines, vocations and professions than on the integration process much to the confusion of future administrators—the students. The young executive who may now be attempting integrated administration must rely upon native talent and keen observation for the key to professional performance. We all need to do better.

It should not be difficult to realize that the ability to prepare a plan for the physical development of an area even though based upon the most sophisticated demographic investigation and coupled with expert knowledge of engineering, horticulture, maintenance of land and structures is not sufficient to handle a public invasion of uninitiated users of heterogenous characteristics. An understanding of recreation as a way of life as well as a bundle of activities is needed to guide the original design and the subsequent operation of the finished product.

On the other side of the coin, an excellent grounding in the philosophy of recreation and the psychology of human behavior without a profound knowledge of and respect for the physical resources to be used in the recreation process is only part of the whole. Knowledge of the ecology of man in a world of humans is not the same as a knowledge of the ecology of nature (including man) and the effect of man's intrusion in a world of living organisms, both plant and animal. Much of the training for a career in recreation administration has to do with what recreation in its many forms does to and for people, and too little with what people bent on recreation pursuits do to physical recreation resources. Again, it must follow that what has been loosely termed recreation is only half the story of park and recreation administration.

I submit, as a matter of personal opinion, that integration, or true marriage of recreation philosophy with the creation and maintenance of places for recreation is the only way to run a park and recreation system of any kind. The integration concept is the basis for the development of an identifiable profession and it should be the ultimate objective of education for that profession.

Futuristic Leisure*

by Louis F. Twardzik

As early as the reign of Emperior Claudius in the first century A.D., Romans enjoyed 159 public holidays during the year. Ninety-three of these were devoted to games at public expense. Festivals were held to honor national heroes as well as military victories. By 354 A.D. the festivities had grown to 200 public holidays per year, including 175 days of games. To assure they would not suffer from overwork, the few remaining days of work usually lasted only until noon.

It is now generally conceded that the Romans' main problem was not having too many slaves, or an overextension in foreign affairs, or that the vestal virgins went wrong—important as all these were to the fall of the Roman Empire—but probably because they did not have a national recreation program. As a result, whoever served as their director of parks and recreation, probably known as the director of festivals and sports, did not have the benefit of a professional education to draw on in developing recreation programs of sufficient scope.

The director's Land and Water Conservation Funds, Open Space grants, State recreation bond funds, and local recreation tax were channeled into developing the monstrous Circus Maximus with a seating capacity of 385,000 and the Colosseum which accommodated 90,000 spectators. There were many other great arenas, forums and circuses and amphitheaters throughout the Empire. "Bread and circuses" became a means to appease the masses. It is generally agreed that the Romans had a highly structured and efficient government because an empire does not operate for centuries without workable systems. The degeneration of these people did not come about because they lacked the knowledge necessary to operate the various systems of government; instead, it is usually traced to their misuse of leisure.

Of course the Greeks had a better idea. They also had slaves and the attendant leisure. But their recreation was conceived in the aesthetics of art and culture and based more on developing a quality of life for all of their citizens. A philosophy of life evolved from their concept of leisure. The word work was not recognized at the time. The closest meaning in Greek was the

*This article appeared in the Winter 1972-73 issue of *Water Spectrum,* published by the Department of Army, Corps of Engineers.

term unleisure. Places for recreation were not limited nor centralized into community centers or parks. There were instead complexes of libraries, baths, and gymnasiums. There were few spatial limitations on where one engaged in recreation. Instead, the joy of discourse became part of a walk with friends. This life style nurtured the great Greek minds and subsequently the great ideas for a western culture.

Surely, there had to be some recreation park planners in that great society. Plato is probably the best known because of his plans for Utopia, the ideal state. Although his class-differentiated aristocracy, ruled by philosopher-kings, is not currently in vogue, it carried an early civilization a long way. Aristotle of course was the chief exponent of leisure. He held that "man worked in order to have leisure." And that "leisure is preferable to work; it is the aim of all work."

In America, now that we are beginning to accumulate large blocks of discretionary time called leisure, which course do we pursue? Will we continue to follow the Roman concept of designing standards for mass use—X numbers of playgrounds and parks and stadia located for easy and safe access—or will we follow the Greeks' concern for the quality of man's recreation experiences and emphasize the aesthetics of leisure and the place of individual man in the leisure age?

The Roman route is the easy one, of course; it is in easily understood and quantitative terms. If our stadia do not become larger than the Circus Maximus, at least we will have more of them and they will be air-conditioned. On the other hand, it's much more difficult to follow the Greeks by attempting to first find the right questions and then advancing suggestions about improving the quality of life for people as they live it—not merely as it is observed.

Government at all levels along with the vast array of entrepreneurs who make up the private sector are faced with a demand for recreation opportunities as never before—and all because of a new awareness that the distribution of leisure need not follow the traditional pattern of a five-day work week. One of the chief benefits of the book, *Four Days, Forty Hours,* edited by Reva Poor, is that it is timely and ready for public consumption.

No longer shackled with these limited concepts of time and production, the industrial community is now beginning to design work around both the optimization of production and marketing along with the leisure available to management and employees. Leisure patterns have become increasingly significant in the design of production patterns.

But this is only one part of it and we make grave errors if we feel that the increased leisure of the working force is the only leisure pool we must anticipate and accommodate in a viable society. To ignore the leisure patterns and recreation of other segments of society will set a Roman-type trap of focusing in on a limited segment of the public's recreation needs. The specific needs of youth, the retired, the elderly, the disadvantaged, and even the incarcerated have to be considered along with the work force.

RATIONALIZING SPECULATIONS

Projections of income and population can, along with other socio-economic data, with adequate qualifiers, be plugged into the planning process with a high degree of confidence that they will hold up. However, at this time, it is not possible to make valid long-range predictions of leisure use patterns. This is a period of not just social turmoil but changing social turmoil. There are just too many changing variables entering the leisure picture at one time to make predictions about it with total confidence. There are changing life styles, changes in the national philosophy about work and leisure, changing amounts of leisure and leisure markets, and of course changing technology. This means that planners are now being forced to make *short-range projections* while settling for questionable *long-range predictions* about the patterns, styles, and uses of leisure because even the short-range changes can be expected to continue in a radical fashion.

Even some model builders agree that although it is possible to develop a mathematical equation that will accommodate all of the variables involved in predicting the impact of leisure over long periods, and their complex relationships to society, the time and energy needed to continually "tend" the model with the facts and constantly changing inputs, make the value of the entire exercise questionable.

We are therefore at a point in time when we should recognize that the inherent social dynamics of leisure and the concomitant pressure to develop resources for recreation is so pressing and pervasive that long-range projections may be merely academic responses, and costly at that. It may mean that a more thorough short-range analysis of what we have, what we want, the costs, and what do we think will happen is the most useful approach to planning for the development of our free time and recreation resources.

This could mean that our present level of competency in planning, computerization notwithstanding, is limited to short-range assumptions and that their eventual accumulations will more logically develop the long-range projections. If nothing else, short-range planning will permit us the opportunity to continually evaluate the applicability of the questions we must ask about the future.

This then is how the following speculations on developing leisure and recreation are rationalized—they are intended to stimulate thought about the future implications of leisure and recreation resource development which would be required given these eventualities.

Perhaps the most dramatic changes will be incorporated in the life styles of people throughout the country. These often follow changes that first occur on the eastern and western coasts and ultimately impact all populations in between.

Chief among these will be the continued weakening of the family as the basic and authoritative social unit. We can speculate that this social disruption in tandem with increasing leisure, discretionary income and mobility will provide individuals, formerly tied to a family unit, with more separate recreation opportunities. In other words, the family that plays together may be the exception in the near future.

We can anticipate that:

1. High school and college students will drop out of school for a year at a time to acquaint themselves with the environment and the world. They will travel in mixed groups and move about the country and internationally until their wandering and wondering needs are satisfied. Most will return to school.

The demand created by this kind of unstructured, low-cost traveling (formerly known as bumming) by high school and college students may create a market for a system of low-cost hosteling facilities, in the European tradition. These will probably be developed in conjunction with the system of State and Federal trails. The sense of adventure that these young people now receive from traveling by automobile will be transferred to hiking and bicycling.

This particular life style will probably not be popular with the disadvantaged groups of inner-city areas. They may instead ultimately see special virtue and benefits in finishing high school and college in the traditional manner on the traditional schedule.

2. Second homes for middle and upper socio-economic classes may be located within the city where workers will spend their four work days per week living in apartments. The primary home on the other hand may be located outside the metropolitan area with distance dependent on improvements in mass transportation. The first flood of interest in this arrangement will probably result in the development of say 10-acre sites for the primary home. Within 15 years this should change to the point that the primary home in the rural areas will be an apartment or condominium or some other form of high density living serviced by vast common acreage.

For example, within 15 years all State and Federal forest lands in the northern part of the lower peninsula of Michigan will be ringed with this type of housing while within 20 years all such public and some private forests will be walled in with housing similar to the concrete walls around New York's Central Park. The current problems of obtaining adequate public access to oceans and lakes and rivers may be repeated in the near future, except it will mean purchase or condemnation of apartment houses to gain more equitable public access for the use of the State and Federal forests and parks, instead of seashores. The rate of similar change in high intensity development around many U.S. Army Corps of Engineers and TVA reservoirs will be dependent on the quality of their water.

3. Many of the small family farms of today will soon be changed into farm estates and ranches. Upper middle class families will take over from present farm families within five to 10 years and develop these marginal acres into hobby farms. Within 10 to 15 years, because of the increase in land values, they in turn, will be forced to sell to upper class families who will develop the farms into estates and ranches.

4. The vegetative life style, characterized by a constant climate, once found attractive by retirees in the Southeastern and Southwestern States will gradually lose its appeal, or at least be stabilized in the near future. By 1980, and probably earlier, retired people with better health prospects and longer life will either develop a preference for living a retired life in the Northern States with its changing seasons or spend portions of the year in the Northern States and the remainder in the Southern States. These retirees will settle for minimum and high density housing and in the absence of adequate zoning will create land use problems greater than those anticipated for "new towns."

5. An explosion in demand for winter recreation activities is imminent. Not only will there be more families with more leisure and money and mobility, but the pattern of leisure through the changing school year will permit more winter recreation. This change in seasonal demand will be further ballooned from the discovery by the elderly and retired that the new snowmobiles are not limited to youthful users. The smart set will abandon the down-hill skiing resorts and take to the woods, as some already have, via cross country skiing. In order not to follow the fate of the abandoned spas of the early part of the century, ski resorts will soon cater to the middle aged and elderly and provide a silent and easy-to-operate snowmobile. Ski tows will be used during the winter largely for viewing the scenery.

The northern, rural small towns that have retained a sound local government will be rediscovered by the early retirees and families seeking second homes. There is some evidence to suggest that not only are they attracted to the clean rural small town's natural environment with its slower pace and the anticipation of the beauty inherent in changing seasons, but also because of the feeling of security such a community imparts to its residents. It also often provides such security through old fashioned policemen constantly looking after "their" people, whom they know individually. On the other hand, a lack of law enforcement for the strung out lake and river front homes and cottages is beginning to take the bloom off the joys of such ownership. Vandalism, especially during the off-season months, will reach epidemic proportions among cottage owners shortly. Vandals have become increasingly mobile.

CENTRAL CITIES

Cost of demolishing large tracts of old housing, business, and industrial areas in central cities for the purpose of renewing the cities' aesthetics potential will not seem as high in the future. Within 15 years there should be recognition of the need for large scale changes needed to provide open spaces and other aesthetic amenities in order to remake central cities into living parks. The costs will seem a reasonable alternative to the present situation. The plight of inner cities will of course have to become a little more desperate than it is now before the aesthetic quality of the territorial imperative is recognized as being equal in importance to that of the separate and often dysfunctional components of roads, schools, jails, and welfare programs.

The concept of parks as isolated patches of greenery in communities will disappear from the inner city and other communities. In the future, park planners will take the place of community planners and the object will be to make the place where people live a park and recreation area. All community streets and alleys and streams and schools and shopping centers will be beautiful components of a beautiful community. The need for individual parks as isolated patches of space and beauty will therefore no longer exist. Housing will tend to cluster, freeing space to be held as common in order to make these manipulations for aesthetic and recreation uses on a community-wide basis possible.

CENTRAL CITY TOURISM

Tourist activity in central cities does not include a significant portion of the army of traveling campers. This is not because campers would not like to visit the cities to attend the various activities unique to them such as baseball and football games, cultural events, or even to shop and look, but rather because it is an environment alien to them.

The economic need to attract these millions of visitors to the central city should encourage the development of special, high-rise parking decks which would accommodate the camping rig. This would permit the camping family to live in their campers in the midst of the downtown area while enjoying the city's offerings. It is assumed that the parking decks will have water, electrical and sewage hookups and that the decks will be open, well lighted and patrolled and available at a fraction of the cost of a family staying at a nearby hotel.

RECREATION FARMING AND GARDENING

There should be a continuing awareness and sensitivity to the natural environment by the population in general. This will be manifested in the growing interest by people in the recreation activities of gardening and farming in which the micro-macro natural systems are discovered, understood, and enjoyed. The combination of awareness and recreation experiences could develop a counter culture for young families in which they may enjoy spending leisure together.

The heavy demand for family gardens, popular during World War II, as victory gardens, will require long-term leasing of land with the entrepreneur providing educational sessions on understanding the relationship of the natural systems existing in the land along with selling plants, seed, mulch, and water.

This extensive and intensive recreational use of land outside of metropolitical areas will become known as a classic foregone opportunity by the agricultural and extension departments. Not being made up of large scale production units, the new gardening movement will probably gain its impetus from ecology oriented associations with much of it based on organic methods of growing. The organic gardening interests will become secondary, however, as families strive, and even begin competing to grow more in limited spaces. The university agricultural community may then enter the picture by sponsoring shows to display the largest tomatoes and the county fair will be rediscovered.

FARMS AS SOCIAL AESTHETIC UNITS

As high quality agricultural lands are identified and zoned for agricultural purposes in some areas, the public will recognize that well managed farms add significantly to the aesthetics of the environment.

With farms providing this extra social benefit while the surrounding rural environment becomes increasingly junky, farmers will receive special subsidy to maintain and preserve and operate their farms as aesthetic units as well as for agricultural production purposes.

EDUCATION FOR LEISURE

It is quite possible that the kind of work that an increasing number of people will do will resemble the deadly boredom epitomized by the automobile worker who places wheel lugs eight hours a day. This means that the qualitative values originally associated with work will no longer be available to increasing numbers of people. With more people gaining less satisfaction from work and working fewer hours, the individual and social utility of leisure assumes greater significance.

Initial attempts to educate for leisure will continue to concentrate on skills in sports and social games. This superficial approach to education for leisure will be replaced with a battle between counter cultures in drugs, which stimulate people to various states of euphoria, and an intellectual attempt to resurrect the philosophic life of the ancient Greeks wherein discourse between people becomes the best use of leisure. The problem may be resolved by university programs of life long education.

CAMPING

The adventure mystique of family camping is disappearing as it becomes more of a second home on wheels during a vacation. Public agencies will gradually give up the responsibility for providing deluxe second-home camping facilities at a pace to be determined by the aggressiveness of the emerging private camping industry. They will also redesign parks to accommodate camping interests of a contemporary society.

Public agencies will limit camping experiences to the more primitive types. Those who prefer electricity and water and plumbing will automatically seek such accommodations in a private camping development.

Campers who opt for the commercial sites while traveling will be able to make reservations for their entire trip in advance.

SPECIAL POPULATIONS

The handicapped and disadvantaged including the aged and the poverty stricken will receive increasing attention by recreation planners. Unlike the general population that can usually make decisions about the kinds and amounts of recreation preferences, the special populations generally do not have options. Often they are immobile. Recreation opportunities, if there are to be any, have to be brought to them. Instead of recreation being a positive experience that brings satisfaction, it may in fact be a therapeutic recreation experience that instead brings relief or cure through treatment.

With the growth of special populations, it can be assured that recreation opportunities will be increasingly made available as a form of treatment to the institutionalized aged, mentally disturbed, physically handicapped, and the incarcerated.

It would seem a useful observation to note that these speculations are based on some real, if only unsystematic, observations. If there is any social utility in them it is in the thought that leisure and recreation resource development have grown full blown to the point that they successfully complicate the ultimate social process—the planning of life styles. And with the erosion of the old fundamental truths, the family, patriotism, sanctity of life and conservation—which in the past provided clear direction for social and natural resource development—planners may have to incorporate speculations into the planning processes, at least until replaced by a new set of social ethics. A last thought in defense of speculation as a tool in leisure and resource planning and development is in order: empirical futurists too often serve a limited use when run over by a speculative society.

Index